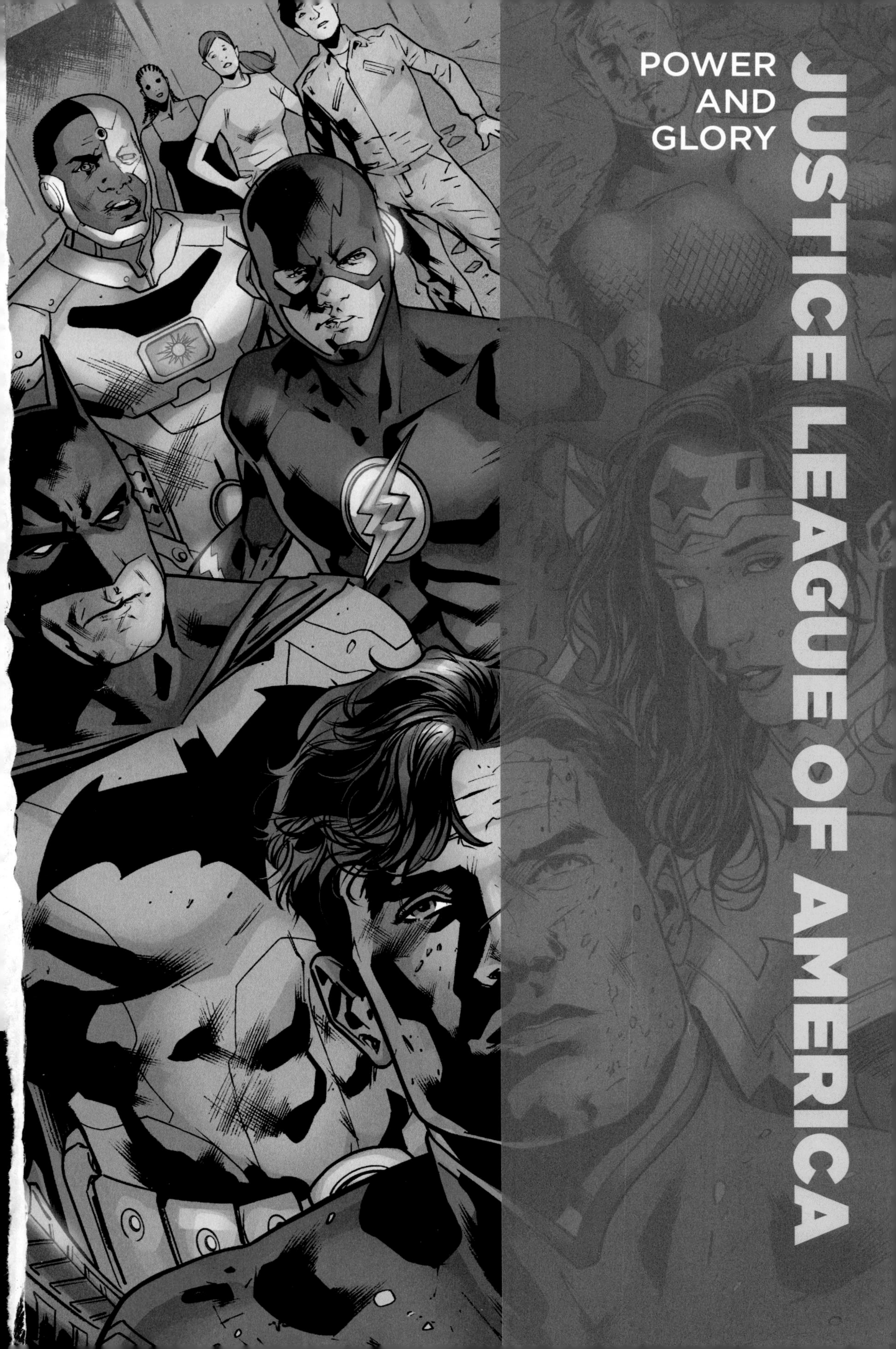
JUSTICE LEAGUE OF AMERICA
POWER AND GLORY

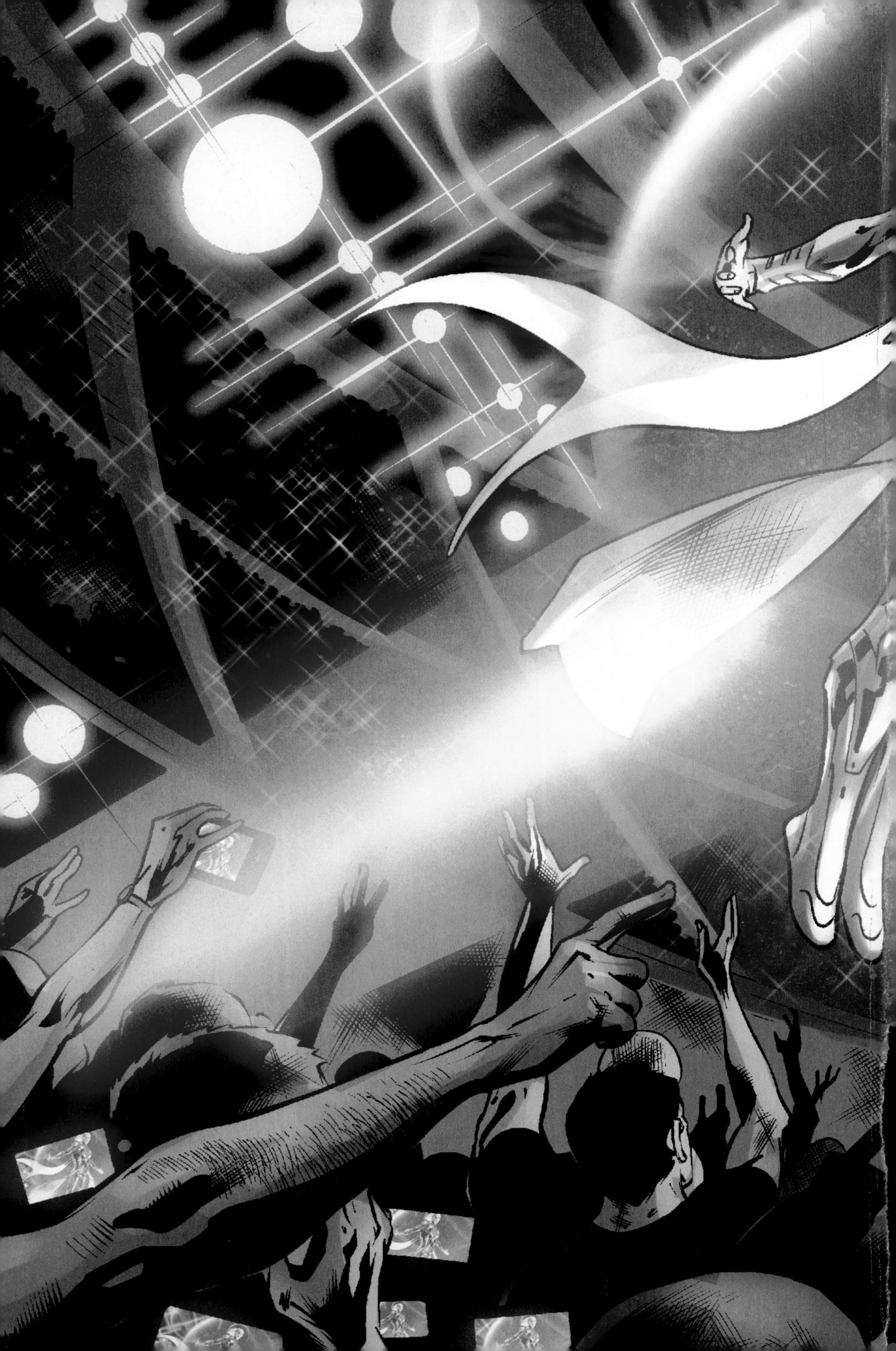

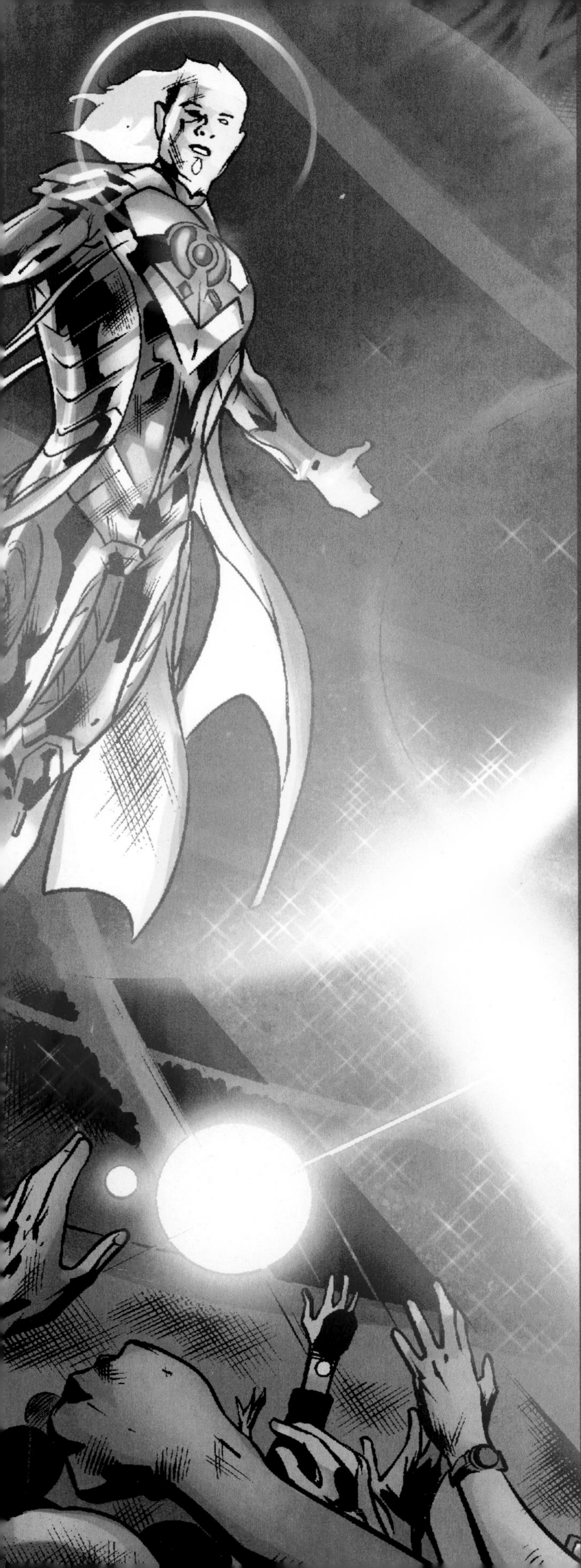

JUSTICE LEAGUE OF AMERICA

POWER AND GLORY

WRITTEN BY
BRYAN HITCH
TONY BEDARD

ART BY
BRYAN HITCH
DANIEL HENRIQUES
ANDREW CURRIE
WADE von GRAWBADGER
TOM DERENICK
SCOTT HANNA

COLOR BY
ALEX SINCLAIR
JEROMY COX
JEREMIAH SKIPPER

LETTERS BY
CHRIS ELIOPOULOS
CLAYTON COWLES

ORIGINAL SERIES &
COLLECTION COVER ART
BRYAN HITCH
& ALEX SINCLAIR

SUPERMAN CREATED BY
JERRY SIEGEL &
JOE SHUSTER
BY SPECIAL ARRANGEMENT
WITH THE JERRY SIEGEL FAMILY

BRIAN CUNNINGHAM Editor – Original Series
AMEDEO TURTURRO and DIEGO LOPEZ Assistant Editors – Original Series
JEB WOODARD Group Editor – Collected Editions
ERIKA ROTHBERG Editor – Collected Edition
STEVE COOK Design Director – Books
DAMIAN RYLAND Publication Design

BOB HARRAS Senior VP – Editor-in-Chief, DC Comics

DIANE NELSON President
DAN DiDIO Publisher
JIM LEE Publisher
GEOFF JOHNS President & Chief Creative Officer
AMIT DESAI Executive VP – Business & Marketing Strategy,
Direct to Consumer & Global Franchise Management
SAM ADES Senior VP – Direct to Consumer
BOBBIE CHASE VP – Talent Development
MARK CHIARELLO Senior VP – Art, Design & Collected Editions
JOHN CUNNINGHAM Senior VP – Sales & Trade Marketing
ANNE DePIES Senior VP – Business Strategy, Finance & Administration
DON FALLETTI VP – Manufacturing Operations
LAWRENCE GANEM VP – Editorial Administration & Talent Relations
ALISON GILL Senior VP – Manufacturing & Operations
HANK KANALZ Senior VP – Editorial Strategy & Administration
JAY KOGAN VP – Legal Affairs
THOMAS LOFTUS VP – Business Affairs
JACK MAHAN VP – Business Affairs
NICK J. NAPOLITANO VP – Manufacturing Administration
EDDIE SCANNELL VP – Consumer Marketing
COURTNEY SIMMONS Senior VP – Publicity & Communications
JIM (SKI) SOKOLOWSKI VP – Comic Book Specialty Sales & Trade Marketing
NANCY SPEARS VP – Mass, Book, Digital Sales & Trade Marketing

JUSTICE LEAGUE OF AMERICA: POWER AND GLORY

DC Comics, 2900 West Alameda Ave., Burbank, CA 91505
Printed by LSC Communications, Salem, VA, USA. 2/17/17. First Printing.
ISBN: 978-1-4012-5976-1

Library of Congress Cataloging-in-Publication Data is available.

PEFC Certified
Printed on paper from sustainably managed forests, controlled sources
PEFC/29-31-337
www.pefc.org

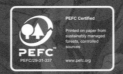

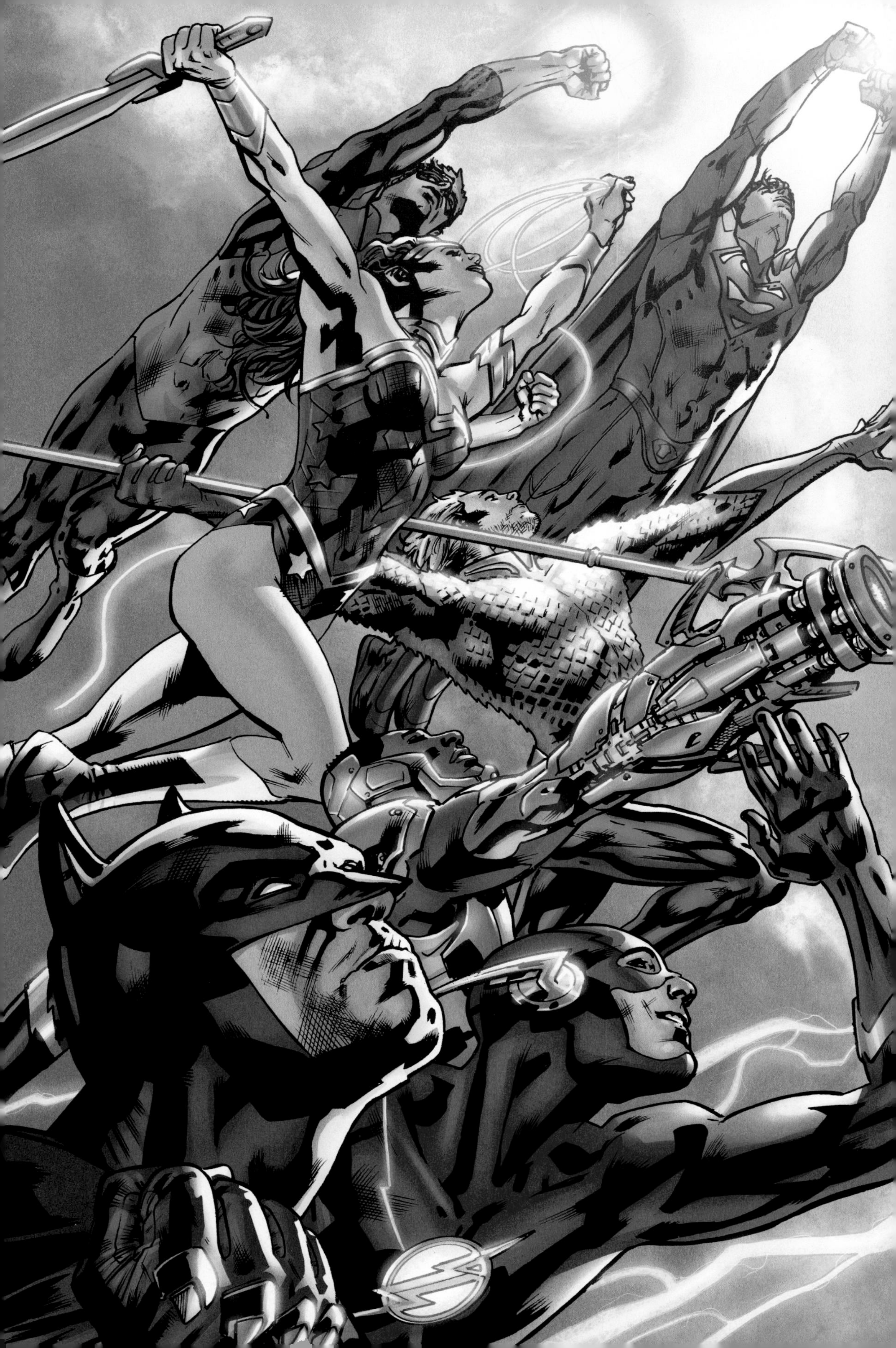

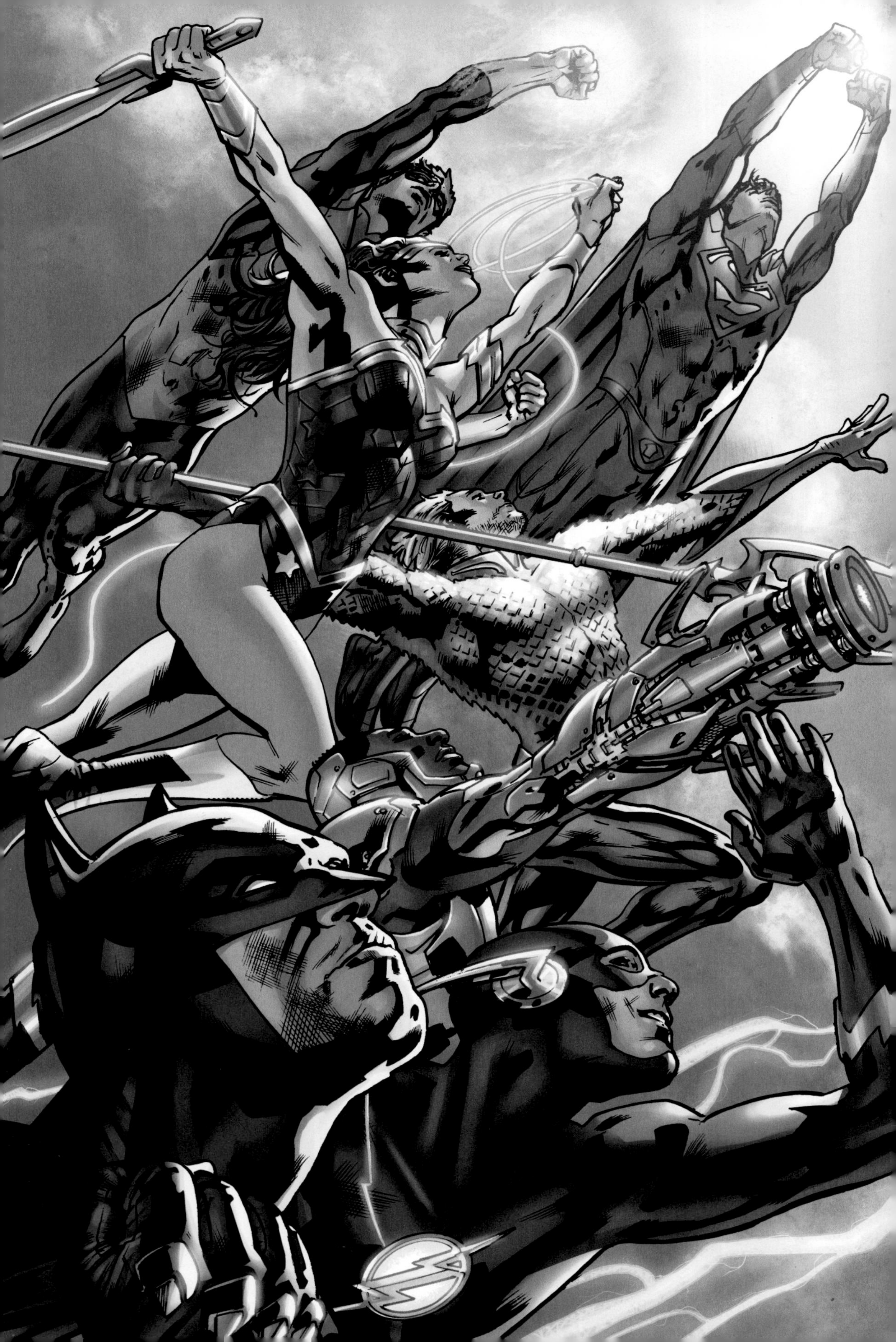

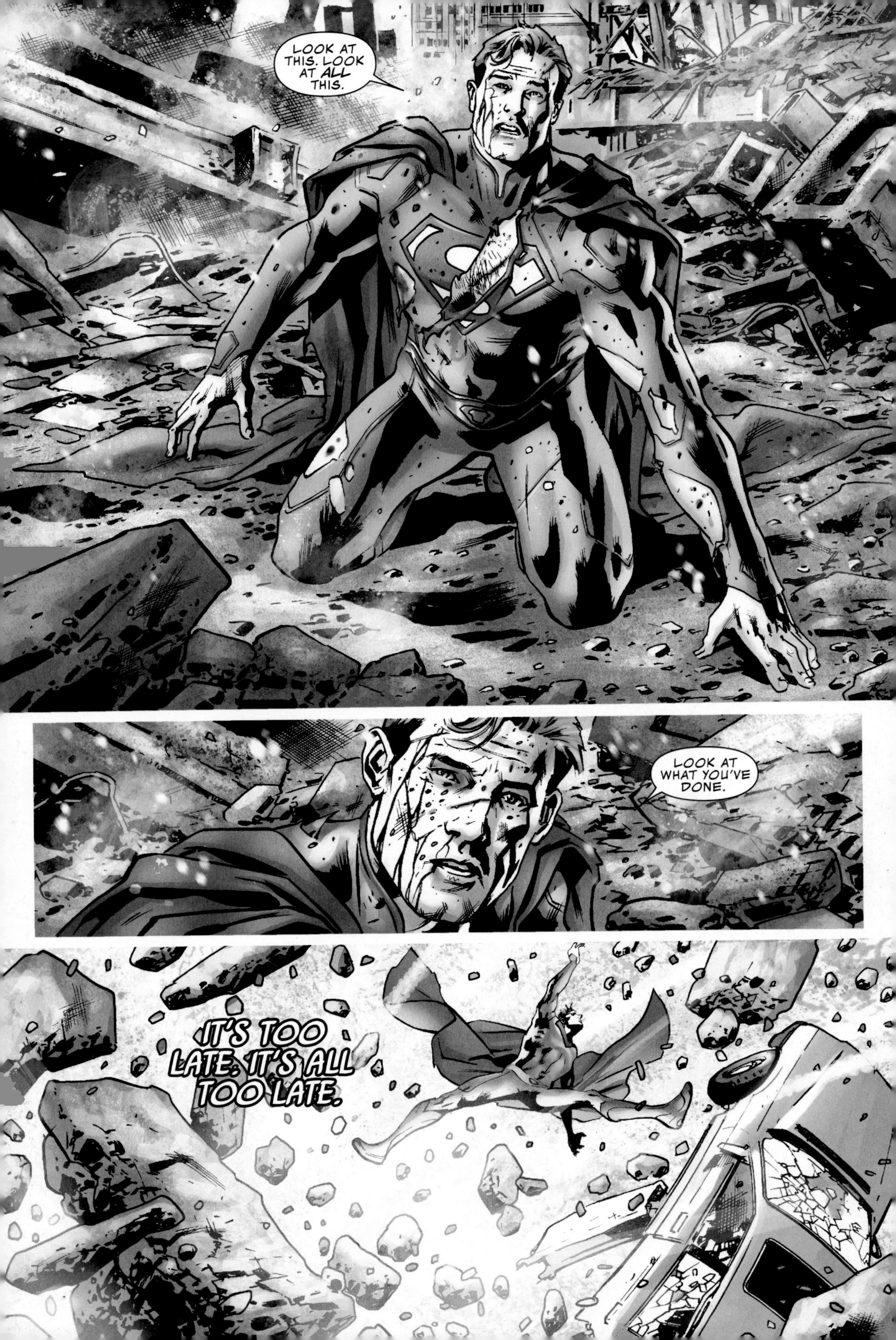
LOOK AT THIS. LOOK AT ALL THIS.
LOOK AT WHAT YOU'VE DONE.
IT'S TOO LATE. IT'S ALL TOO LATE.

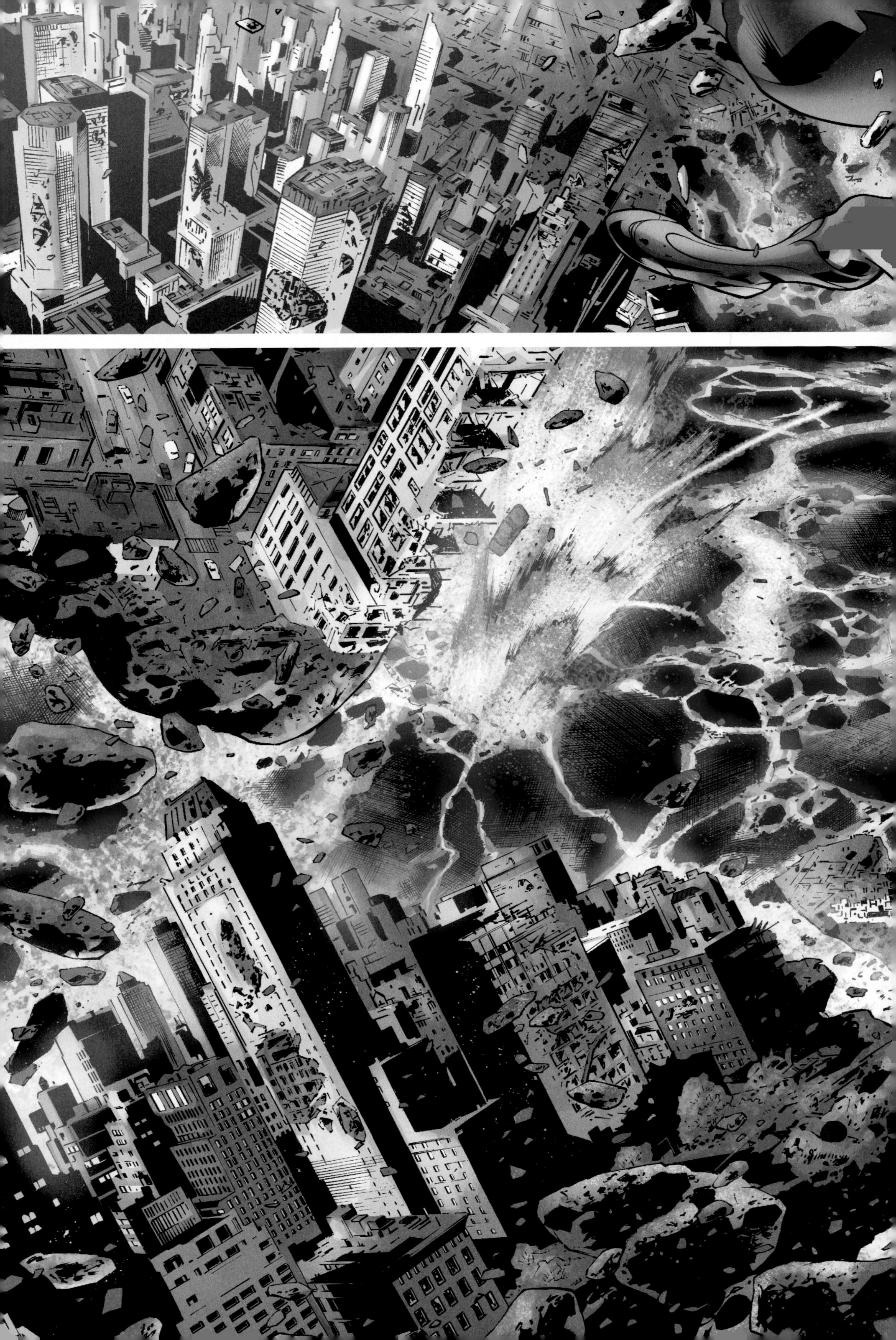

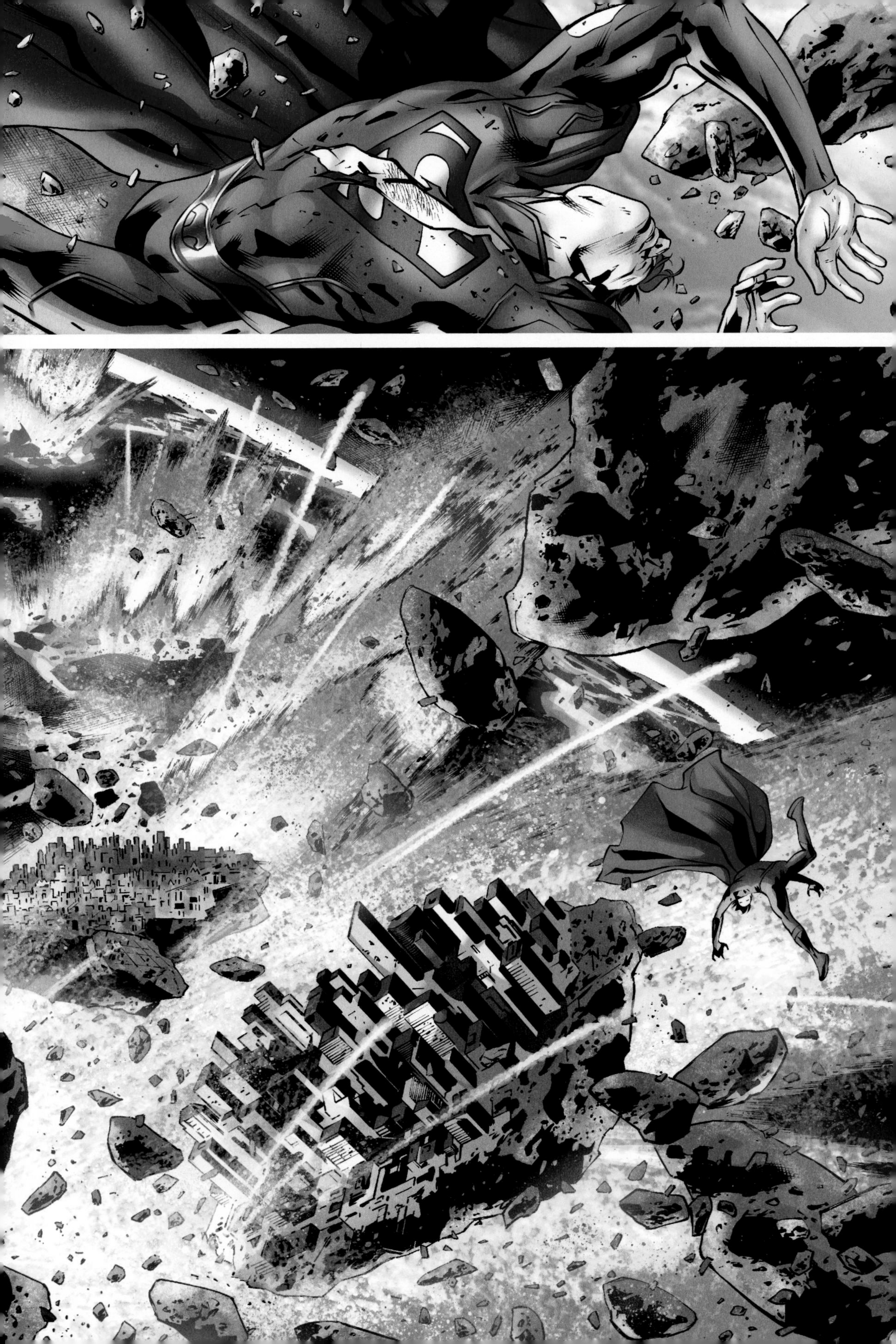

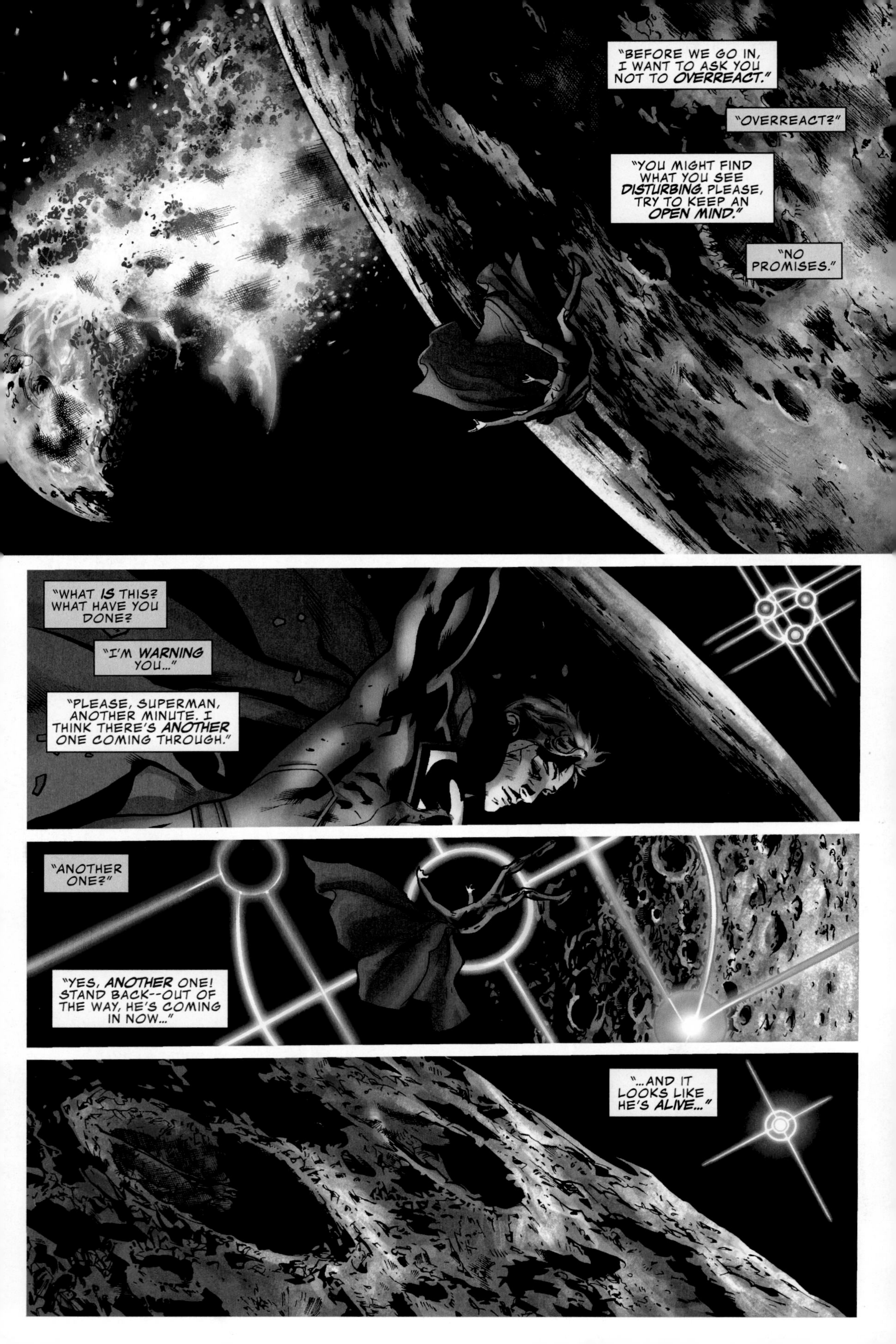
"BEFORE WE GO IN, I WANT TO ASK YOU NOT TO OVERREACT."
"OVERREACT?"
"YOU MIGHT FIND WHAT YOU SEE DISTURBING. PLEASE, TRY TO KEEP AN OPEN MIND."
"NO PROMISES."
"WHAT IS THIS? WHAT HAVE YOU DONE?
"I'M WARNING YOU..."
"PLEASE, SUPERMAN, ANOTHER MINUTE. I THINK THERE'S ANOTHER ONE COMING THROUGH."
"ANOTHER ONE?"
"YES, ANOTHER ONE! STAND BACK--OUT OF THE WAY, HE'S COMING IN NOW..."
"...AND IT LOOKS LIKE HE'S ALIVE..."

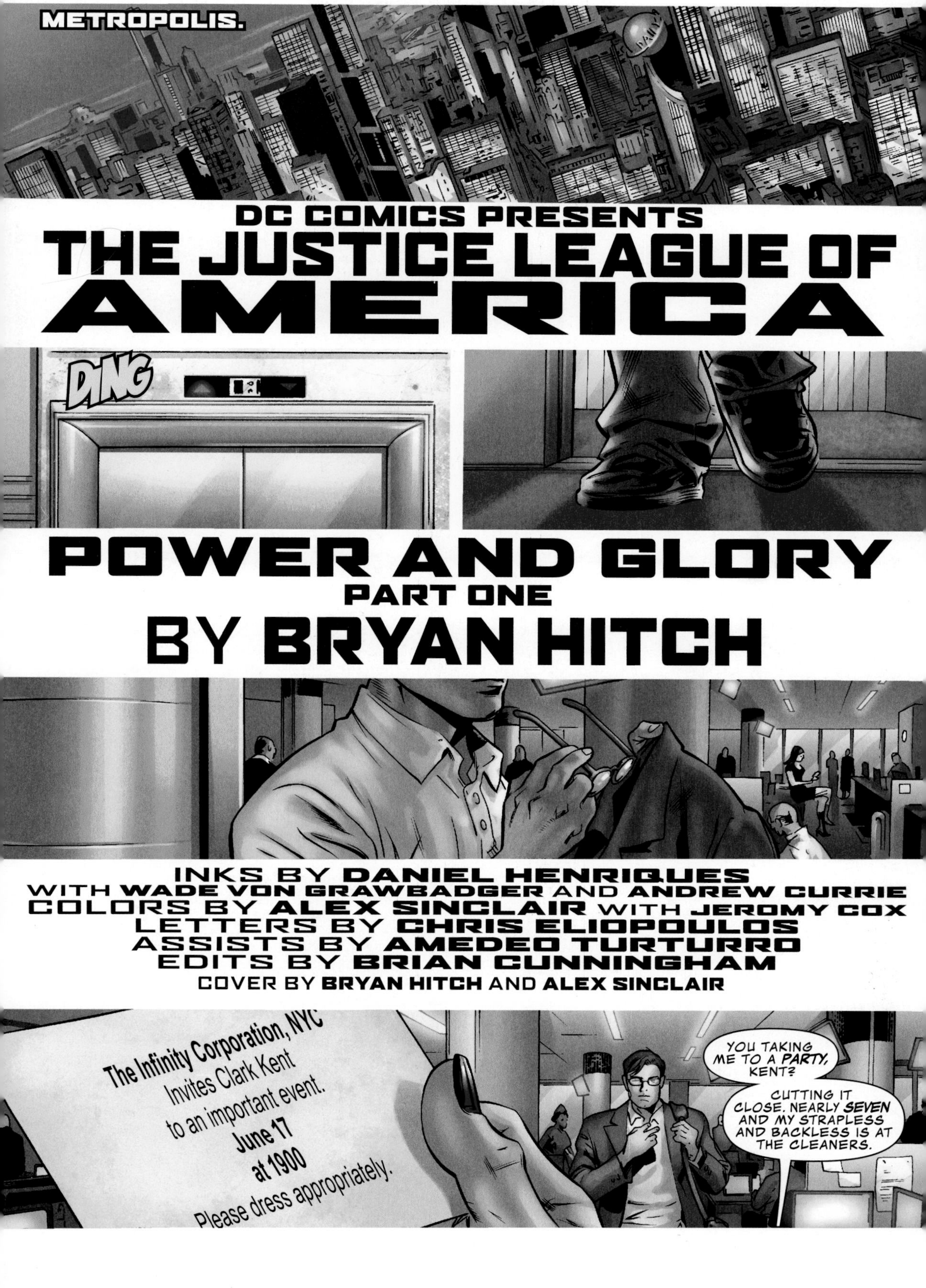
METROPOLIS.
DC COMICS PRESENTS
THE JUSTICE LEAGUE OF AMERICA
DING
POWER AND GLORY
PART ONE
BY BRYAN HITCH
INKS BY DANIEL HENRIQUES
WITH WADE VON GRAWBADGER AND ANDREW CURRIE
COLORS BY ALEX SINCLAIR WITH JEROMY COX
LETTERS BY CHRIS ELIOPOULOS
ASSISTS BY AMEDEO TURTURRO
EDITS BY BRIAN CUNNINGHAM
COVER BY BRYAN HITCH AND ALEX SINCLAIR
The Infinity Corporation, NYC
The Infinity Corporation Invites Clark Kent to an important event. June 17 at 1900 Please dress appropriately.
YOU TAKING ME TO A PARTY, KENT?
CUTTING IT CLOSE. NEARLY SEVEN AND MY STRAPLESS AND BACKLESS IS AT THE CLEANERS.

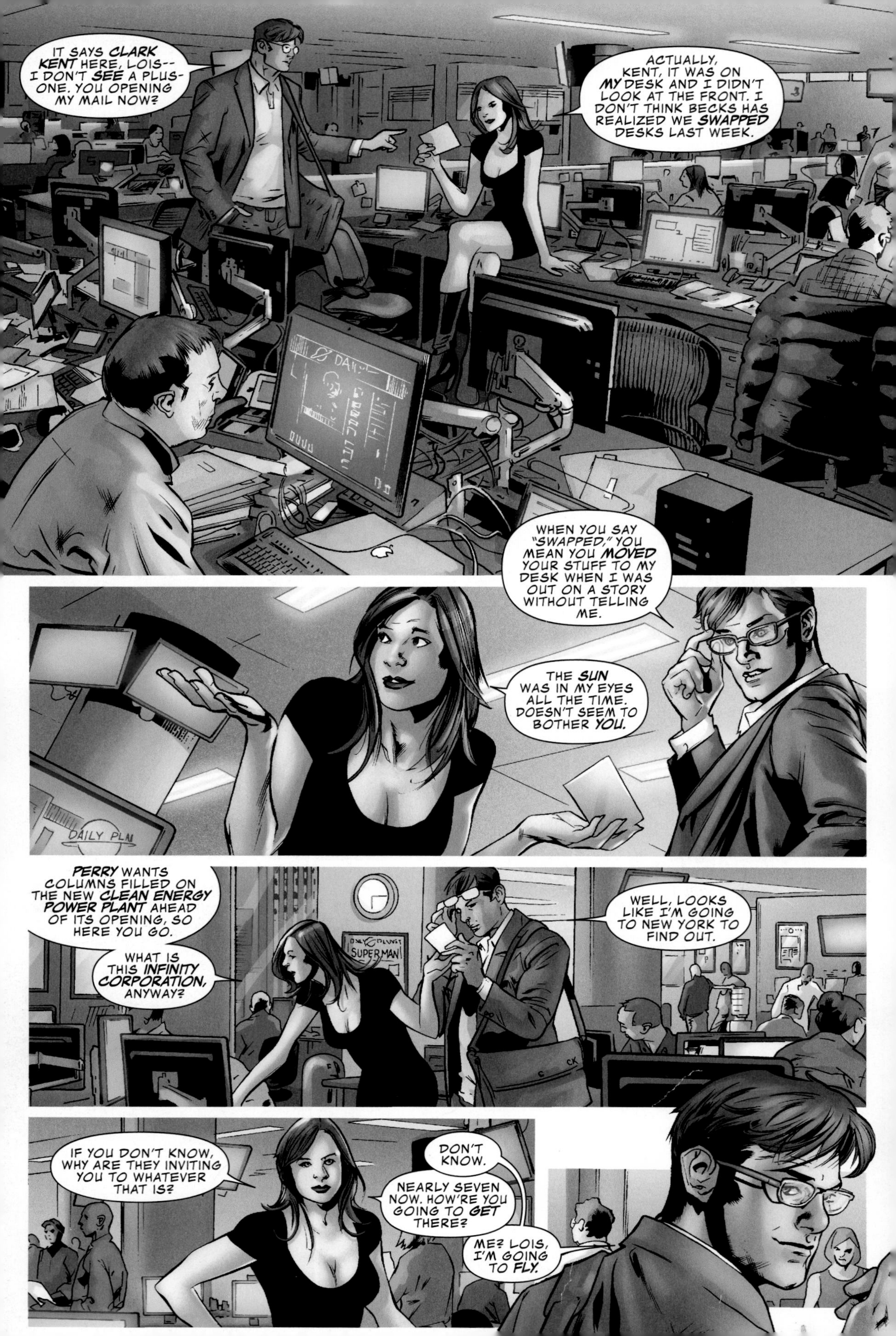

IT SAYS CLARK KENT HERE, LOIS-- I DON'T SEE A PLUS-ONE. YOU OPENING MY MAIL NOW?
ACTUALLY, KENT, IT WAS ON MY DESK AND I DIDN'T LOOK AT THE FRONT. I DON'T THINK BECKS HAS REALIZED WE SWAPPED DESKS LAST WEEK.
WHEN YOU SAY "SWAPPED," YOU MEAN YOU MOVED YOUR STUFF TO MY DESK WHEN I WAS OUT ON A STORY WITHOUT TELLING ME.
THE SUN WAS IN MY EYES ALL THE TIME. DOESN'T SEEM TO BOTHER YOU.
DAILY PLN
PERRY WANTS COLUMNS FILLED ON THE NEW CLEAN ENERGY POWER PLANT AHEAD OF ITS OPENING, SO HERE YOU GO.
WHAT IS THIS INFINITY CORPORATION, ANYWAY?
WELL, LOOKS LIKE I'M GOING TO NEW YORK TO FIND OUT.
SUPERMAN
CK
IF YOU DON'T KNOW, WHY ARE THEY INVITING YOU TO WHATEVER THAT IS?
DON'T KNOW.
NEARLY SEVEN NOW. HOW'RE YOU GOING TO GET THERE?
ME? LOIS, I'M GOING TO FLY.

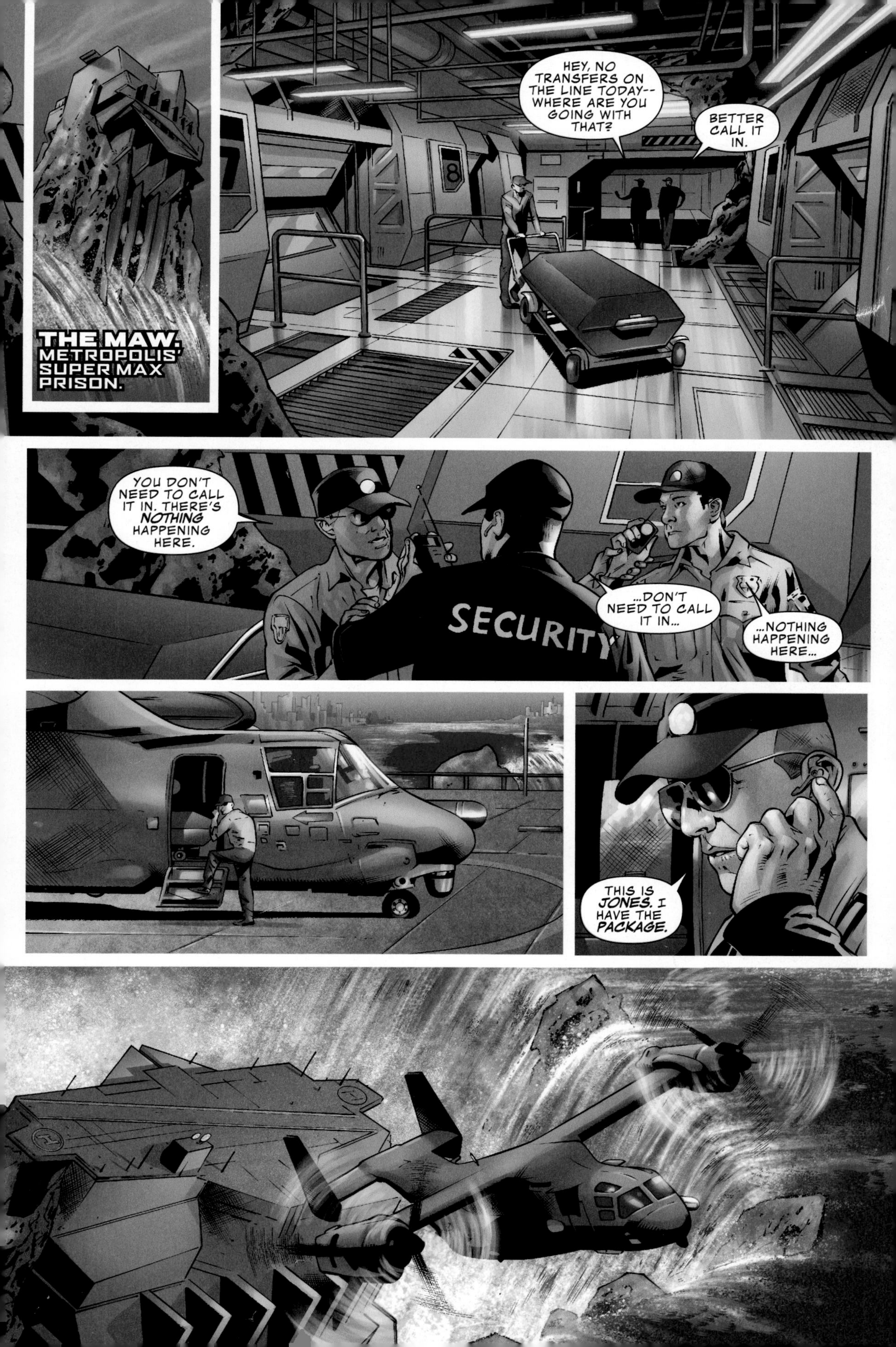
THE MAW. METROPOLIS' SUPER MAX PRISON.
HEY, NO TRANSFERS ON THE LINE TODAY-- WHERE ARE YOU GOING WITH THAT?
BETTER CALL IT IN.
YOU DON'T NEED TO CALL IT IN. THERE'S NOTHING HAPPENING HERE.
SECURITY
...DON'T NEED TO CALL IT IN...
...NOTHING HAPPENING HERE...
THIS IS JONES. I HAVE THE PACKAGE.

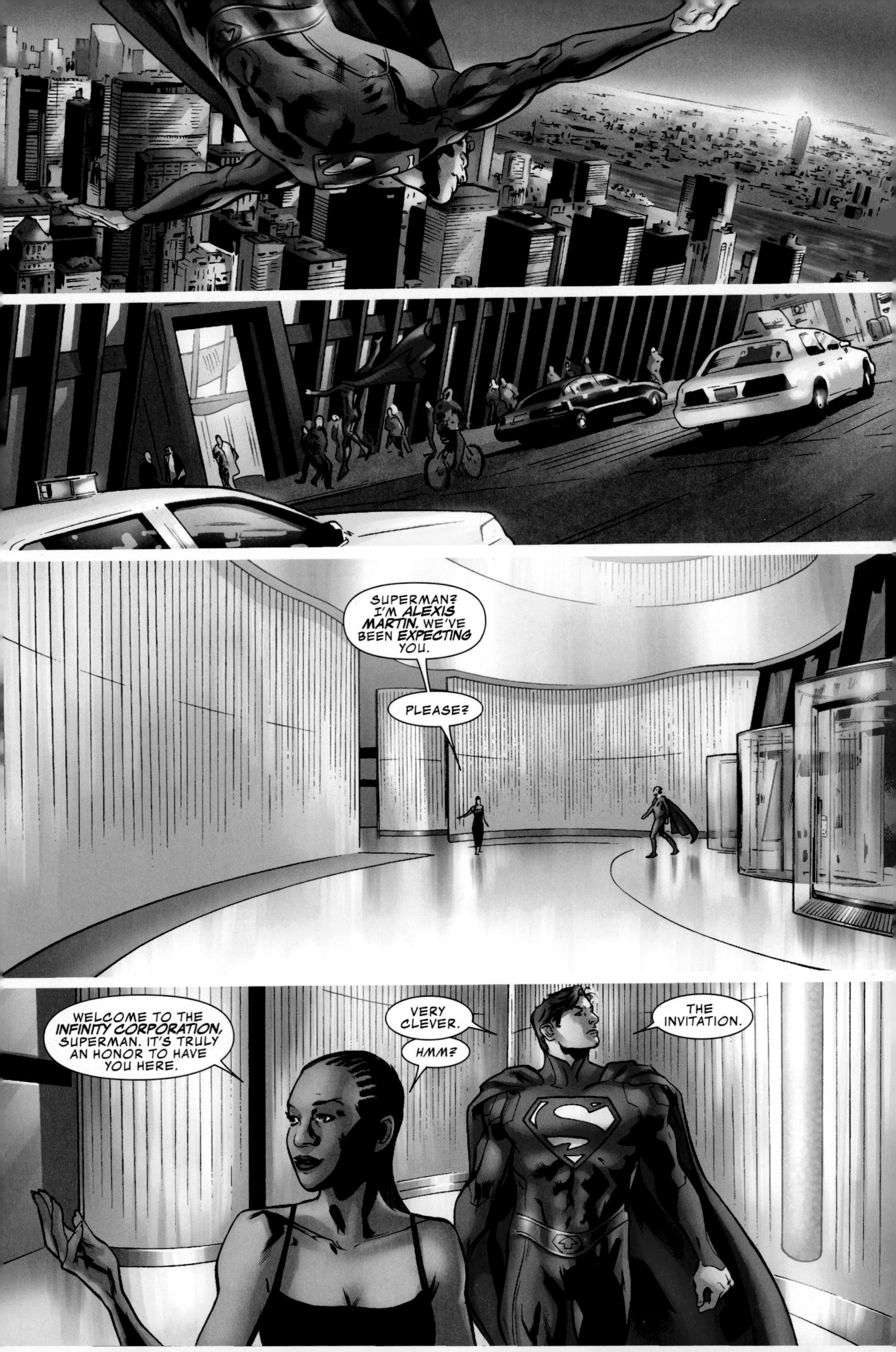

SUPERMAN? I'M ALEXIS MARTIN. WE'VE BEEN EXPECTING YOU.
PLEASE?
WELCOME TO THE INFINITY CORPORATION, SUPERMAN. IT'S TRULY AN HONOR TO HAVE YOU HERE.
VERY CLEVER.
HMM?
THE INVITATION.

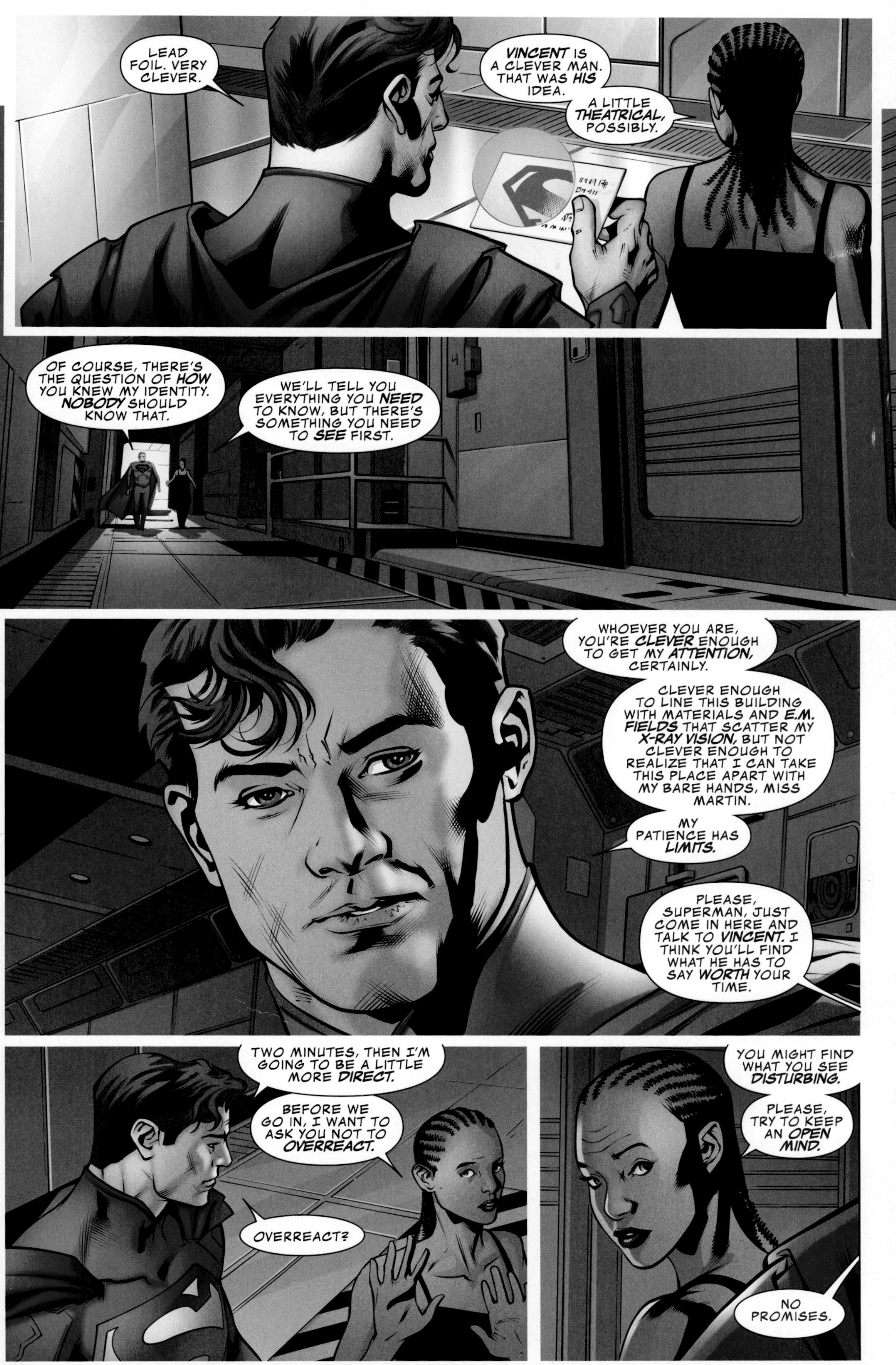
LEAD FOIL. VERY CLEVER.
VINCENT IS A CLEVER MAN. THAT WAS HIS IDEA.
A LITTLE THEATRICAL, POSSIBLY.
OF COURSE, THERE'S THE QUESTION OF HOW YOU KNEW MY IDENTITY. NOBODY SHOULD KNOW THAT.
WE'LL TELL YOU EVERYTHING YOU NEED TO KNOW, BUT THERE'S SOMETHING YOU NEED TO SEE FIRST.
WHOEVER YOU ARE, YOU'RE CLEVER ENOUGH TO GET MY ATTENTION, CERTAINLY.
CLEVER ENOUGH TO LINE THIS BUILDING WITH MATERIALS AND E.M. FIELDS THAT SCATTER MY X-RAY VISION, BUT NOT CLEVER ENOUGH TO REALIZE THAT I CAN TAKE THIS PLACE APART WITH MY BARE HANDS, MISS MARTIN.
MY PATIENCE HAS LIMITS.
PLEASE, SUPERMAN, JUST COME IN HERE AND TALK TO VINCENT. I THINK YOU'LL FIND WHAT HE HAS TO SAY WORTH YOUR TIME.
TWO MINUTES, THEN I'M GOING TO BE A LITTLE MORE DIRECT.
BEFORE WE GO IN, I WANT TO ASK YOU NOT TO OVERREACT.
OVERREACT?
YOU MIGHT FIND WHAT YOU SEE DISTURBING.
PLEASE, TRY TO KEEP AN OPEN MIND.
NO PROMISES.

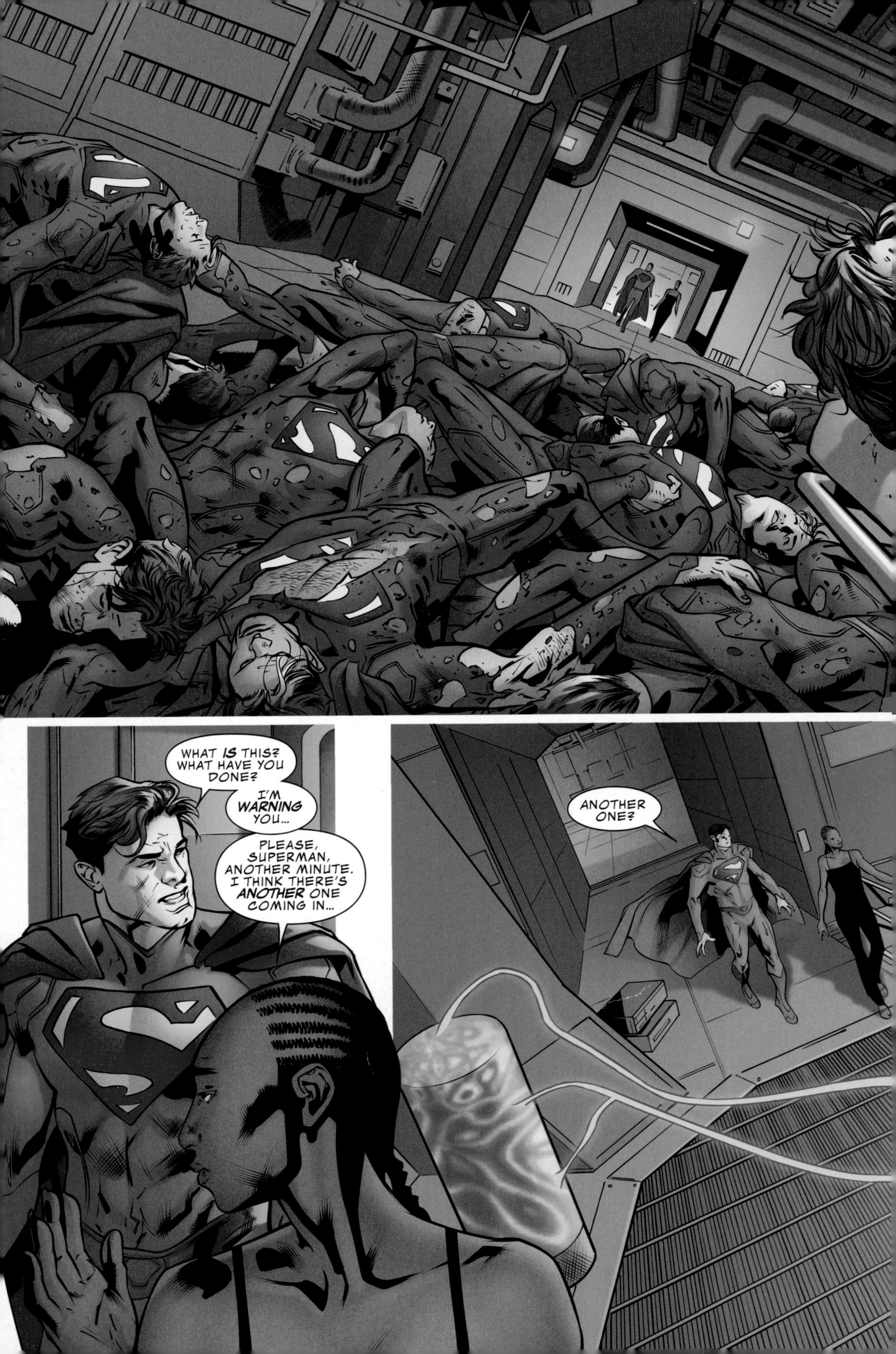
WHAT **IS** THIS? WHAT HAVE YOU DONE?
I'M **WARNING** YOU...
PLEASE, SUPERMAN, ANOTHER MINUTE. I THINK THERE'S **ANOTHER** ONE COMING IN...
ANOTHER ONE?

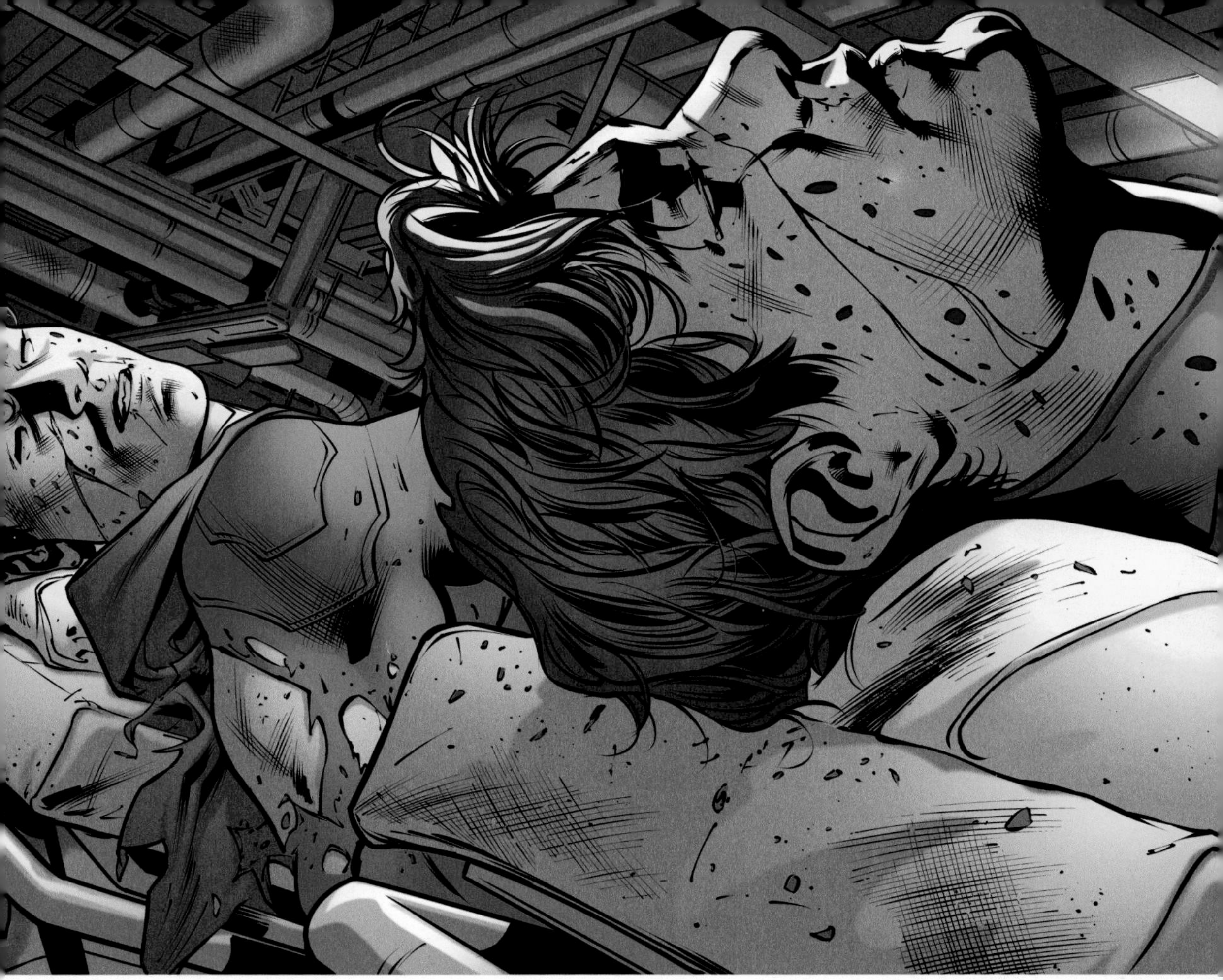
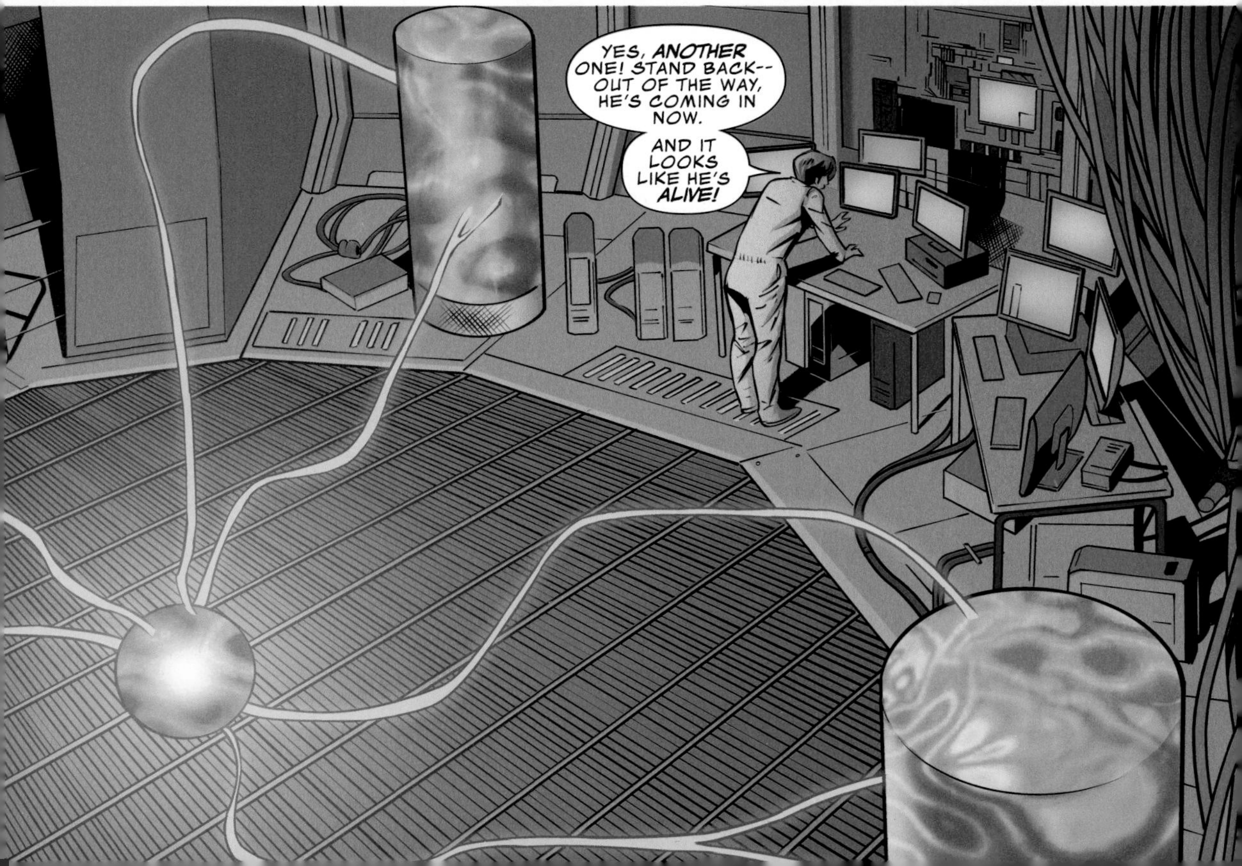
YES, ANOTHER ONE! STAND BACK-- OUT OF THE WAY, HE'S COMING IN NOW.
AND IT LOOKS LIKE HE'S ALIVE!

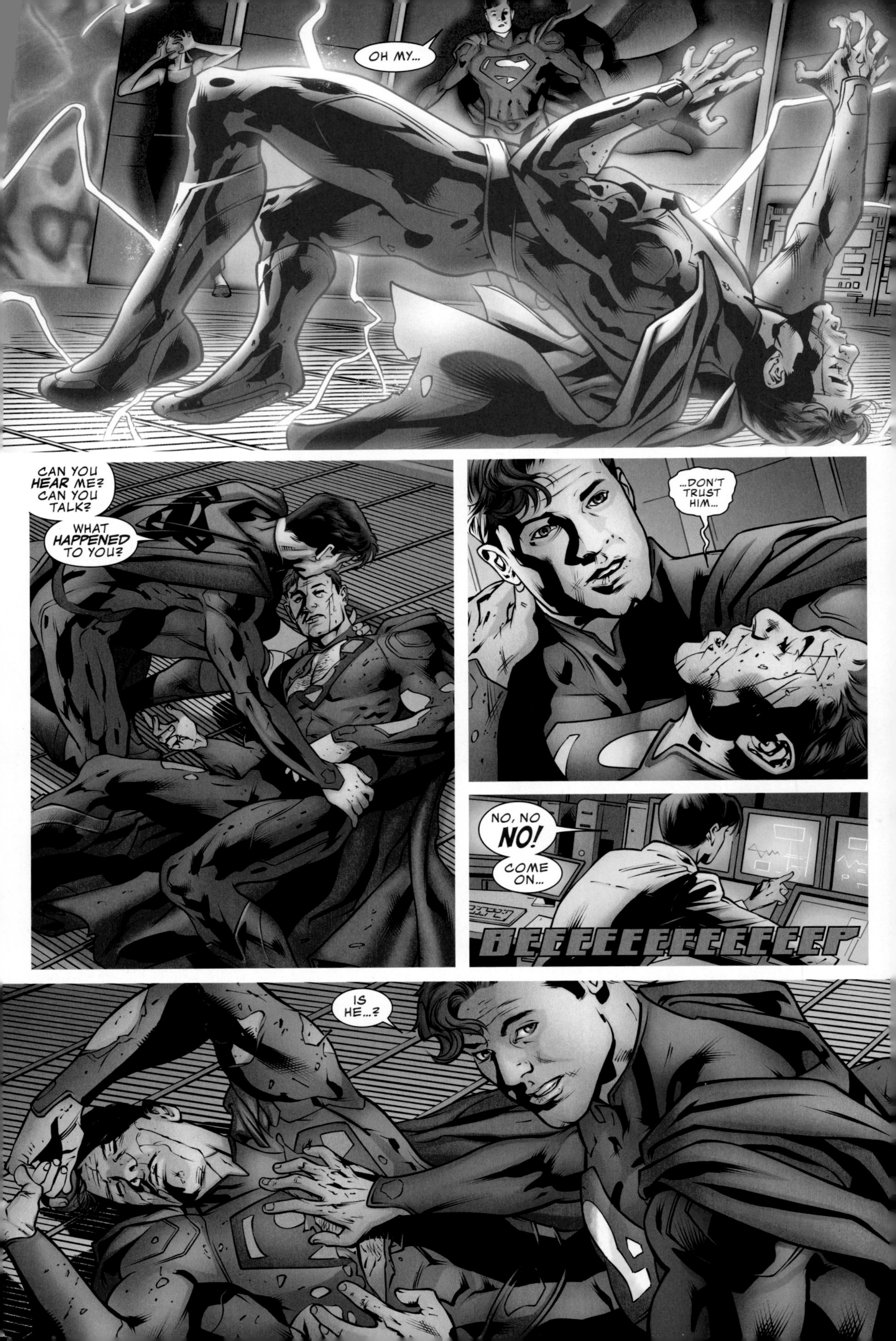
OH MY...
CAN YOU HEAR ME? CAN YOU TALK?
WHAT HAPPENED TO YOU?
...DON'T TRUST HIM...
NO, NO NO!
COME ON...
BEEEEEEEEEEEEP
IS HE...?

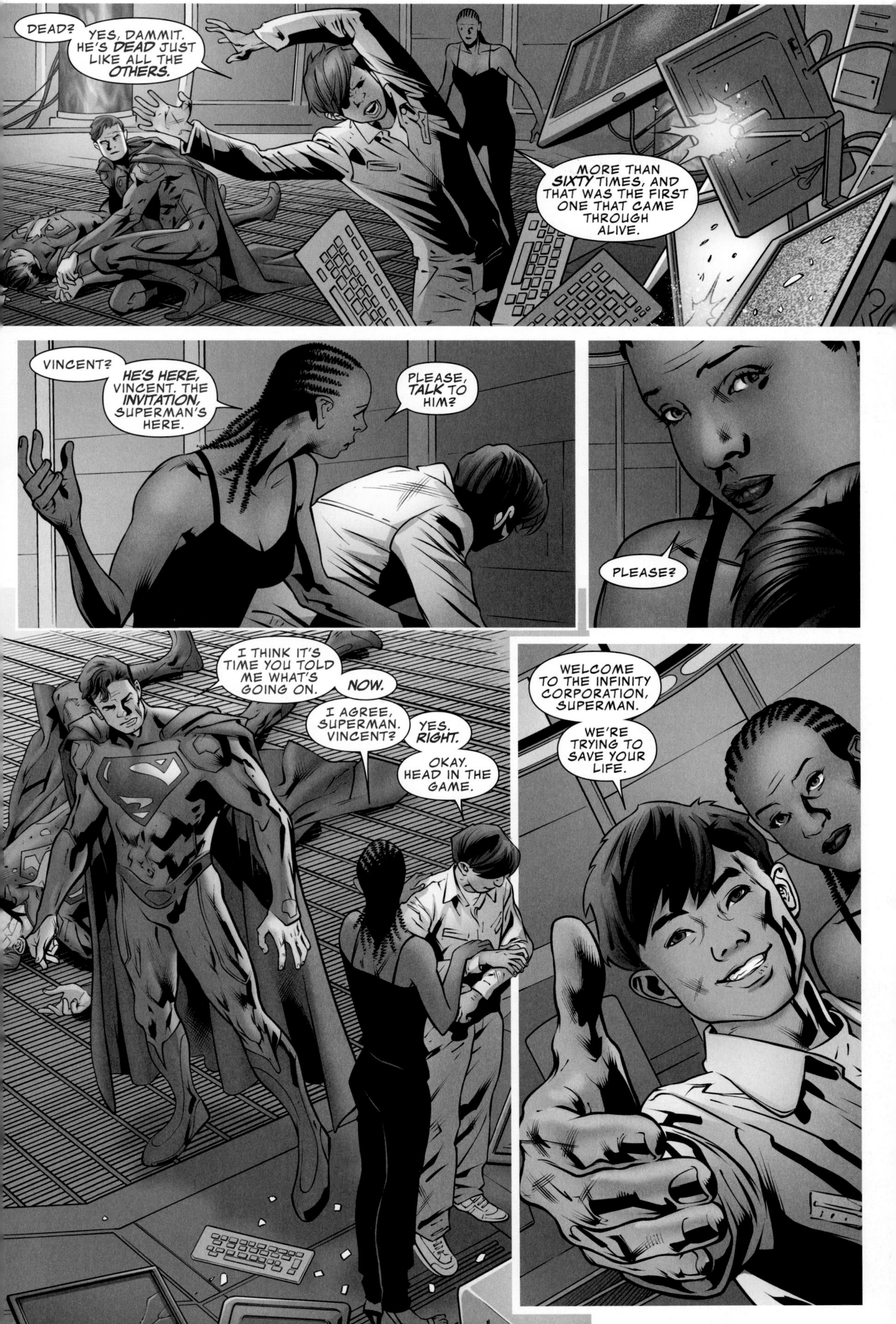
DEAD?
YES, DAMMIT. HE'S DEAD JUST LIKE ALL THE OTHERS.
MORE THAN SIXTY TIMES, AND THAT WAS THE FIRST ONE THAT CAME THROUGH ALIVE.
VINCENT?
HE'S HERE, VINCENT. THE INVITATION, SUPERMAN'S HERE.
PLEASE, TALK TO HIM?
PLEASE?
I THINK IT'S TIME YOU TOLD ME WHAT'S GOING ON.
NOW.
I AGREE, SUPERMAN. VINCENT?
YES. RIGHT.
OKAY. HEAD IN THE GAME.
WELCOME TO THE INFINITY CORPORATION, SUPERMAN.
WE'RE TRYING TO SAVE YOUR LIFE.

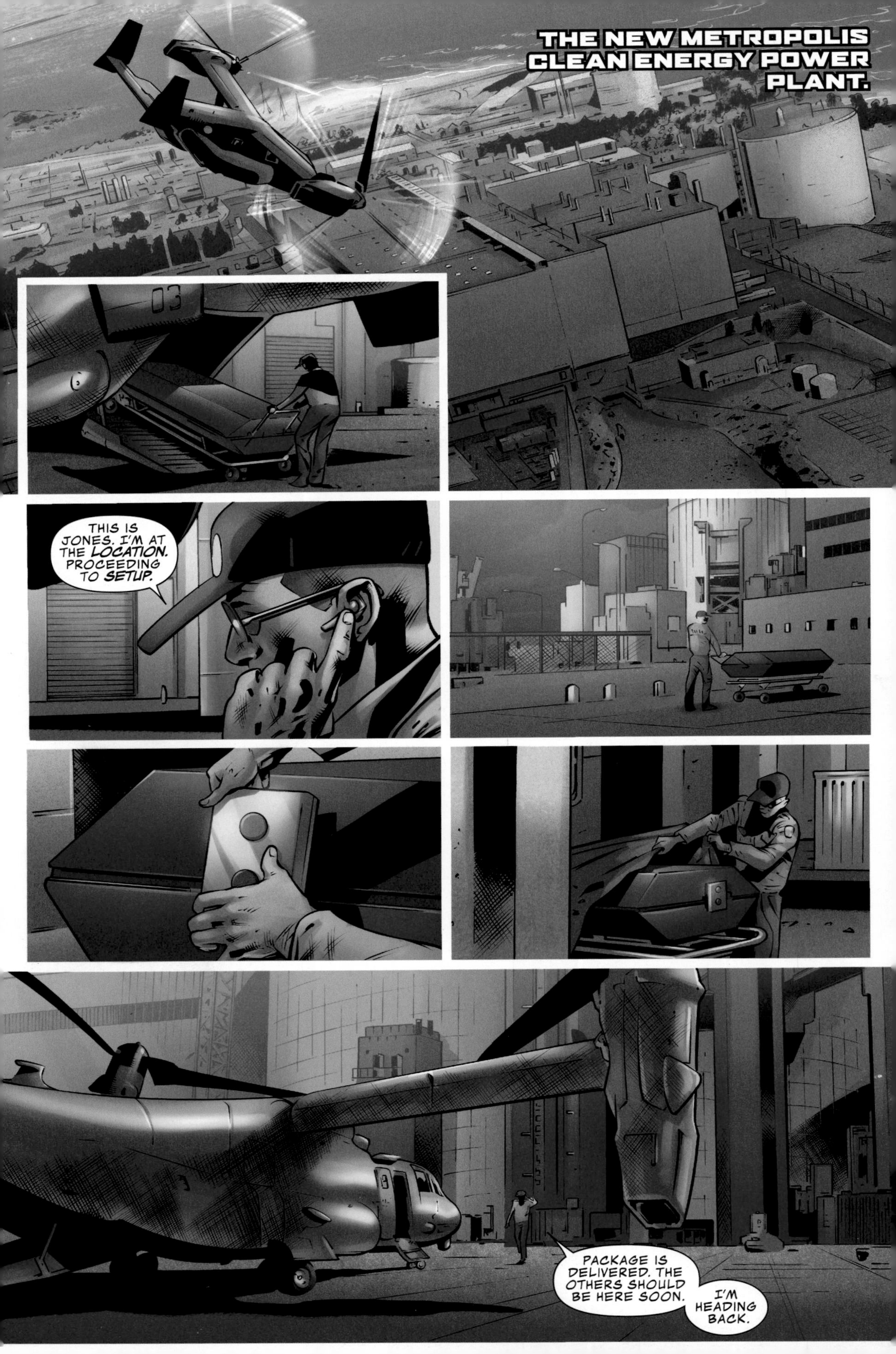
THE NEW METROPOLIS CLEAN ENERGY POWER PLANT.
03
THIS IS JONES. I'M AT THE LOCATION. PROCEEDING TO SETUP.
PACKAGE IS DELIVERED. THE OTHERS SHOULD BE HERE SOON.
I'M HEADING BACK.

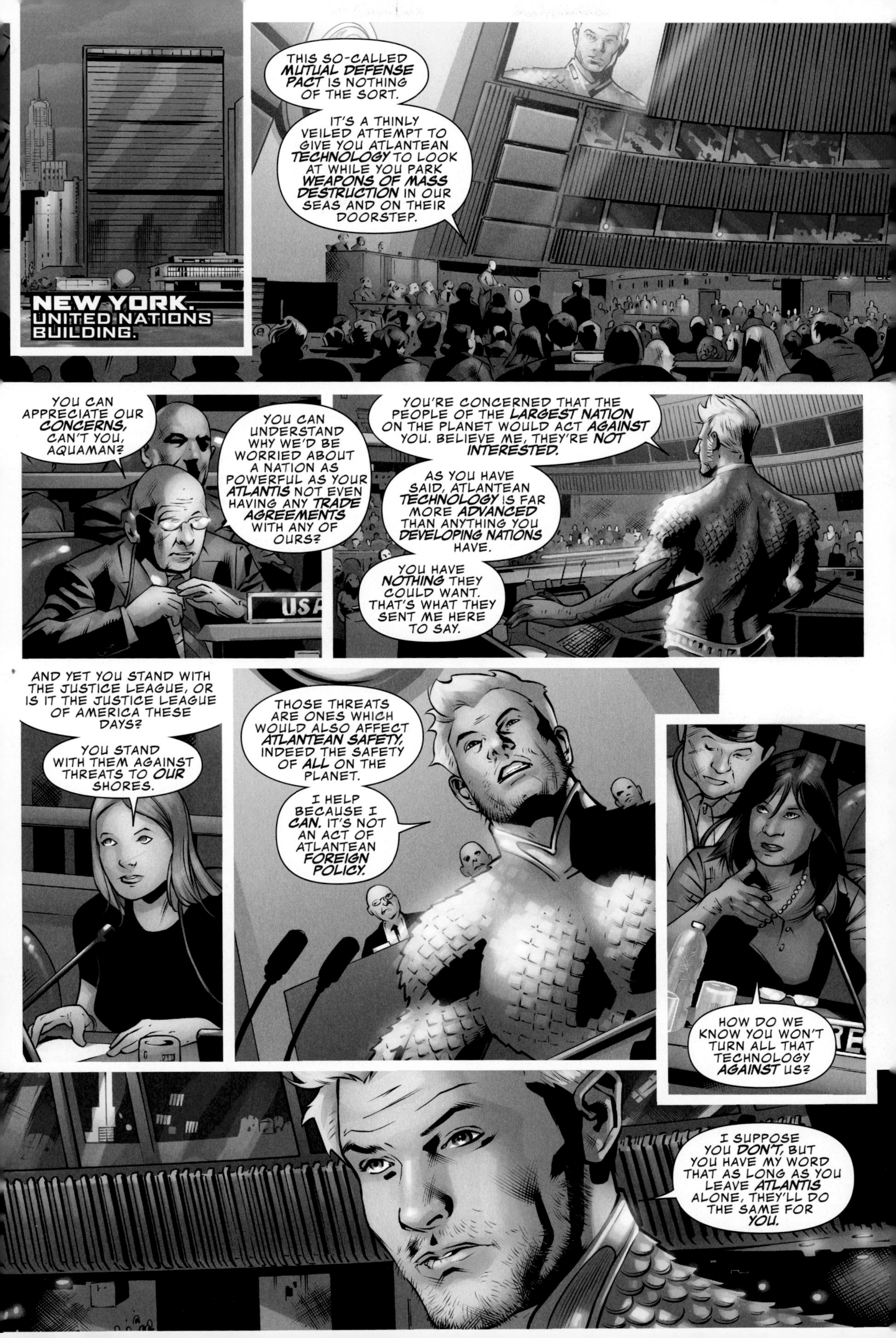
NEW YORK. UNITED NATIONS BUILDING.
THIS SO-CALLED MUTUAL DEFENSE PACT IS NOTHING OF THE SORT.
IT'S A THINLY VEILED ATTEMPT TO GIVE YOU ATLANTEAN TECHNOLOGY TO LOOK AT WHILE YOU PARK WEAPONS OF MASS DESTRUCTION IN OUR SEAS AND ON THEIR DOORSTEP.
YOU CAN APPRECIATE OUR CONCERNS, CAN'T YOU, AQUAMAN?
YOU CAN UNDERSTAND WHY WE'D BE WORRIED ABOUT A NATION AS POWERFUL AS YOUR ATLANTIS NOT EVEN HAVING ANY TRADE AGREEMENTS WITH ANY OF OURS?
USA
YOU'RE CONCERNED THAT THE PEOPLE OF THE LARGEST NATION ON THE PLANET WOULD ACT AGAINST YOU. BELIEVE ME, THEY'RE NOT INTERESTED.
AS YOU HAVE SAID, ATLANTEAN TECHNOLOGY IS FAR MORE ADVANCED THAN ANYTHING YOU DEVELOPING NATIONS HAVE.
YOU HAVE NOTHING THEY COULD WANT. THAT'S WHAT THEY SENT ME HERE TO SAY.
AND YET YOU STAND WITH THE JUSTICE LEAGUE, OR IS IT THE JUSTICE LEAGUE OF AMERICA THESE DAYS?
YOU STAND WITH THEM AGAINST THREATS TO OUR SHORES.
THOSE THREATS ARE ONES WHICH WOULD ALSO AFFECT ATLANTEAN SAFETY, INDEED THE SAFETY OF ALL ON THE PLANET.
I HELP BECAUSE I CAN. IT'S NOT AN ACT OF ATLANTEAN FOREIGN POLICY.
HOW DO WE KNOW YOU WON'T TURN ALL THAT TECHNOLOGY AGAINST US?
I SUPPOSE YOU DON'T, BUT YOU HAVE MY WORD THAT AS LONG AS YOU LEAVE ATLANTIS ALONE, THEY'LL DO THE SAME FOR YOU.

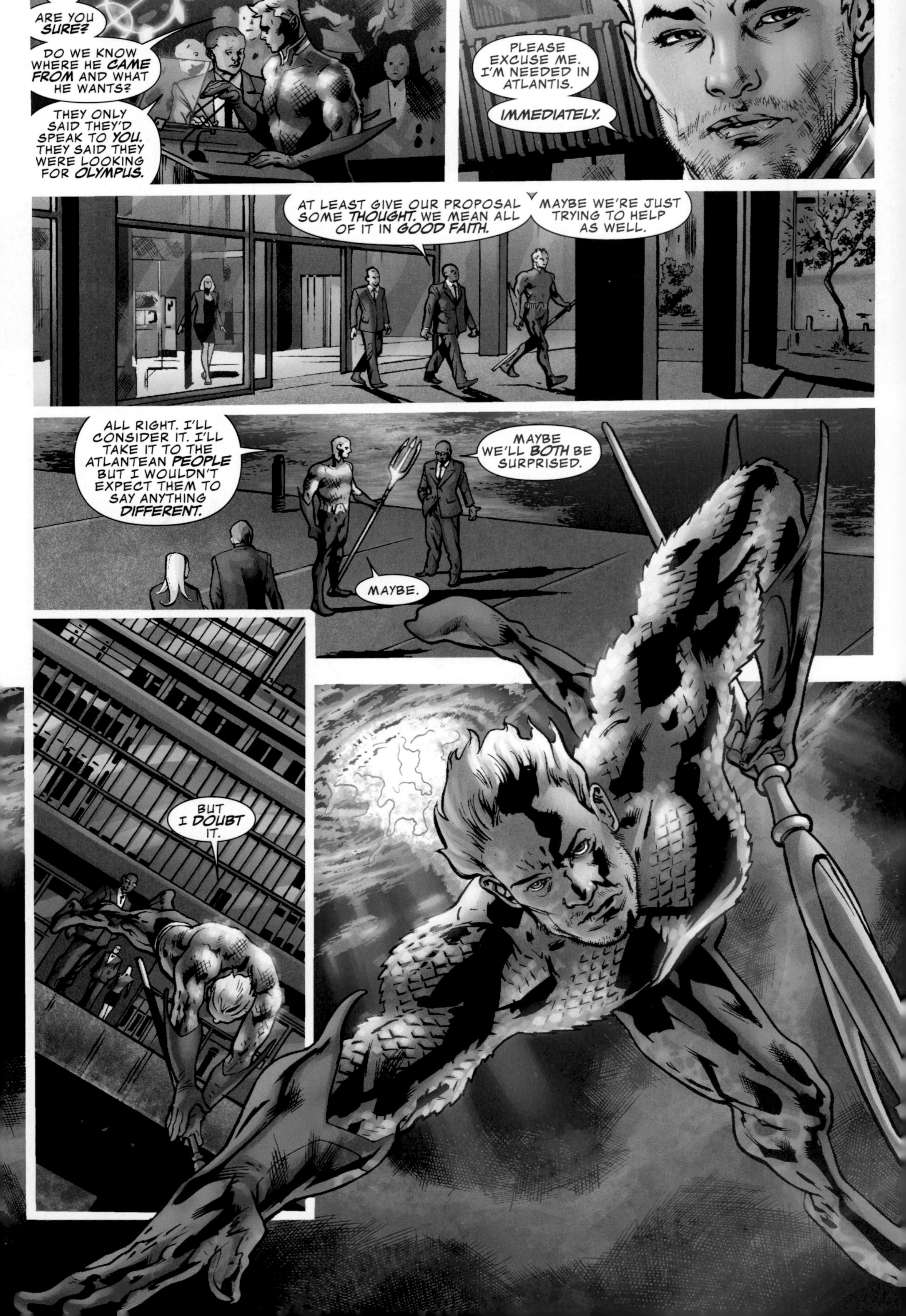
...
ARE YOU SURE?
DO WE KNOW WHERE HE CAME FROM AND WHAT HE WANTS?
THEY ONLY SAID THEY'D SPEAK TO YOU. THEY SAID THEY WERE LOOKING FOR OLYMPUS.
PLEASE EXCUSE ME. I'M NEEDED IN ATLANTIS.
IMMEDIATELY.
AT LEAST GIVE OUR PROPOSAL SOME THOUGHT. WE MEAN ALL OF IT IN GOOD FAITH.
MAYBE WE'RE JUST TRYING TO HELP AS WELL.
ALL RIGHT. I'LL CONSIDER IT. I'LL TAKE IT TO THE ATLANTEAN PEOPLE BUT I WOULDN'T EXPECT THEM TO SAY ANYTHING DIFFERENT.
MAYBE WE'LL BOTH BE SURPRISED.
MAYBE.
BUT I DOUBT IT.

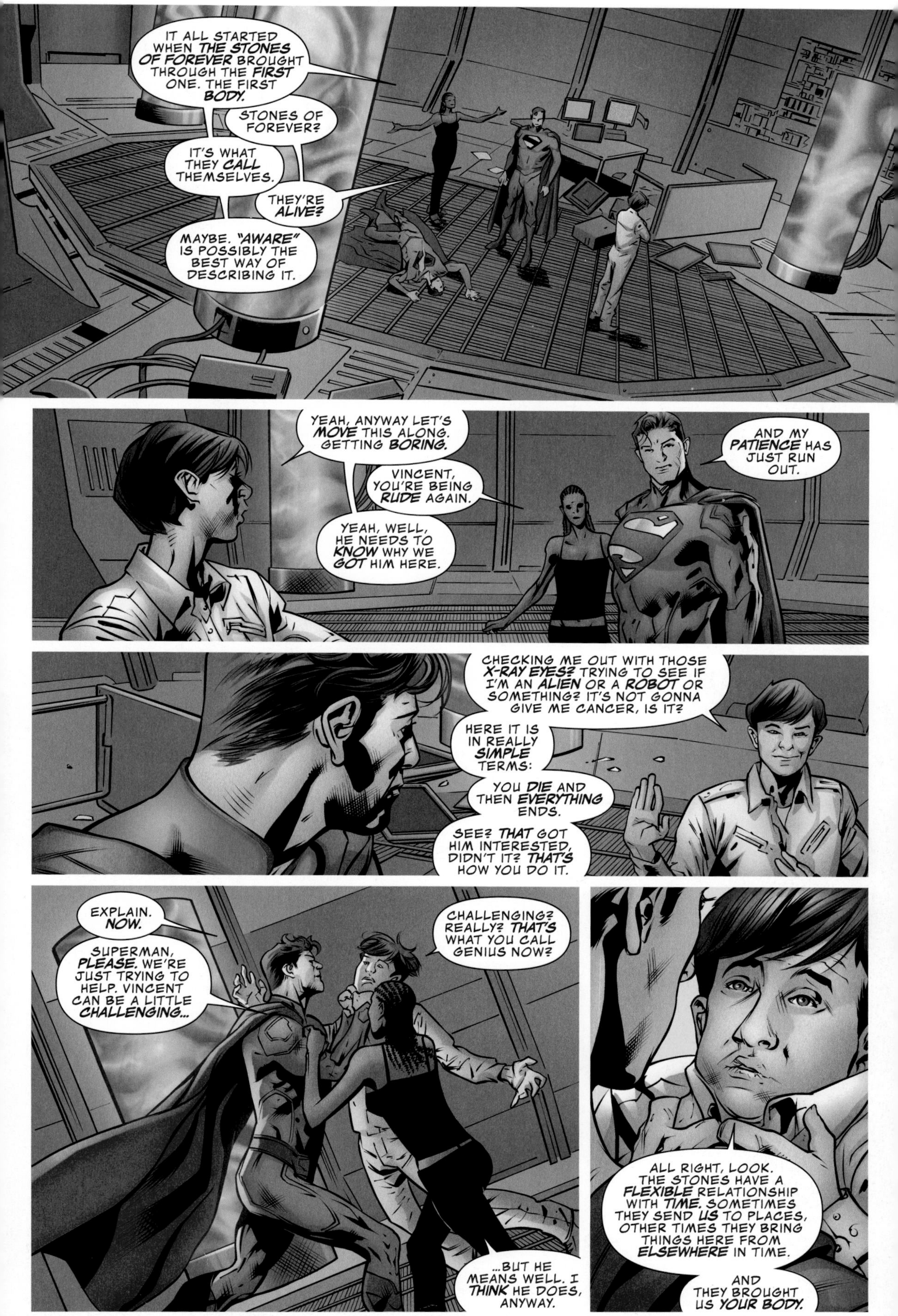
IT ALL STARTED WHEN THE STONES OF FOREVER BROUGHT THROUGH THE FIRST ONE. THE FIRST BODY.
STONES OF FOREVER?
IT'S WHAT THEY CALL THEMSELVES.
THEY'RE ALIVE?
MAYBE. "AWARE" IS POSSIBLY THE BEST WAY OF DESCRIBING IT.
YEAH, ANYWAY LET'S MOVE THIS ALONG. GETTING BORING.
VINCENT, YOU'RE BEING RUDE AGAIN.
YEAH, WELL, HE NEEDS TO KNOW WHY WE GOT HIM HERE.
AND MY PATIENCE HAS JUST RUN OUT.
CHECKING ME OUT WITH THOSE X-RAY EYES? TRYING TO SEE IF I'M AN ALIEN OR A ROBOT OR SOMETHING? IT'S NOT GONNA GIVE ME CANCER, IS IT?
HERE IT IS IN REALLY SIMPLE TERMS:
YOU DIE AND THEN EVERYTHING ENDS.
SEE? THAT GOT HIM INTERESTED, DIDN'T IT? THAT'S HOW YOU DO IT.
EXPLAIN. NOW.
SUPERMAN, PLEASE. WE'RE JUST TRYING TO HELP. VINCENT CAN BE A LITTLE CHALLENGING...
CHALLENGING? REALLY? THAT'S WHAT YOU CALL GENIUS NOW?
...BUT HE MEANS WELL. I THINK HE DOES, ANYWAY.
ALL RIGHT, LOOK. THE STONES HAVE A FLEXIBLE RELATIONSHIP WITH TIME. SOMETIMES THEY SEND US TO PLACES, OTHER TIMES THEY BRING THINGS HERE FROM ELSEWHERE IN TIME.
AND THEY BROUGHT US YOUR BODY.

THAT ROOM WAS *FILLED* WITH BODIES. *MY* BODIES.

FROM ACROSS MANY *DIFFERENT TIMELINES.* IT'S AS THOUGH THE STONES WERE TRYING TO *TEST* A CERTAINTY OR FIND WAYS OF TELLING US WHAT'S *GOING* TO HAPPEN.

YOU AREN'T TELLING ME EVERYTHING.

OF COURSE I'M NOT. I DON'T *KNOW* EVERYTHING.

DO YOU KNOW *HOW* I DIE?

NO.

WHEN?

NO.

THEN YOU HAVE *NOTHING* TO TELL ME.

I'M TELLING YOU WHAT I'M *SURE* OF.

I CAN TELL YOU THAT THE *WHOLE FUTURE* IS GOING TO END. WHATEVER IS COMING IS GOING TO *CHANGE EVERYTHING.* THE FUTURE, THE PRESENT *AND* THE PAST.

IT'S *ALREADY* HAPPENING. WE ARE ALREADY *PART* OF IT. YOUR DEATH IS TIED UP IN THIS LIKE A *FIXED BEACON* IN TIME, ACROSS *ALL* TIME.

A *UNIVERSAL* EXTINCTION LEVEL EVENT AND THE SHOCKWAVE REACHES BACK TO THE *BEGINNING OF TIME.*

THOSE OTHER BODIES ARE JUST *RIPPLES,* SUPERMAN. WHATEVER IS GOING TO HAPPEN WILL HAPPEN *HERE.* THIS PLACE. *THIS* TIME. TO YOU, TO ALL OF US. *THAT'S* WHY WE INVITED YOU HERE, TO *TELL* YOU.

HOW CAN YOU *KNOW* THE FUTURE IS GONE?

I DON'T, BUT *THEY* DO.

THE STONES. THEY TOLD YOU?

WE HAVE A *SPECIAL* RELATIONSHIP.

I'M SURE YOU DO.

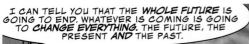

TIME IS *CONSTANTLY* IN FLUX, IT'S FAR MORE *FLUID* THAN YOU COULD IMAGINE.

IT'S NOT A *STREAM,* SUPERMAN, IT'S A ROILING *OCEAN* IN A CONSTANT *STORM.* THE PAST ISN'T FIXED AND THE FUTURE ISN'T WRITTEN. THE ONLY TIME THAT MATTERS, THE ONLY MOMENT THAT COUNTS, IS ALWAYS THE *NOW.*

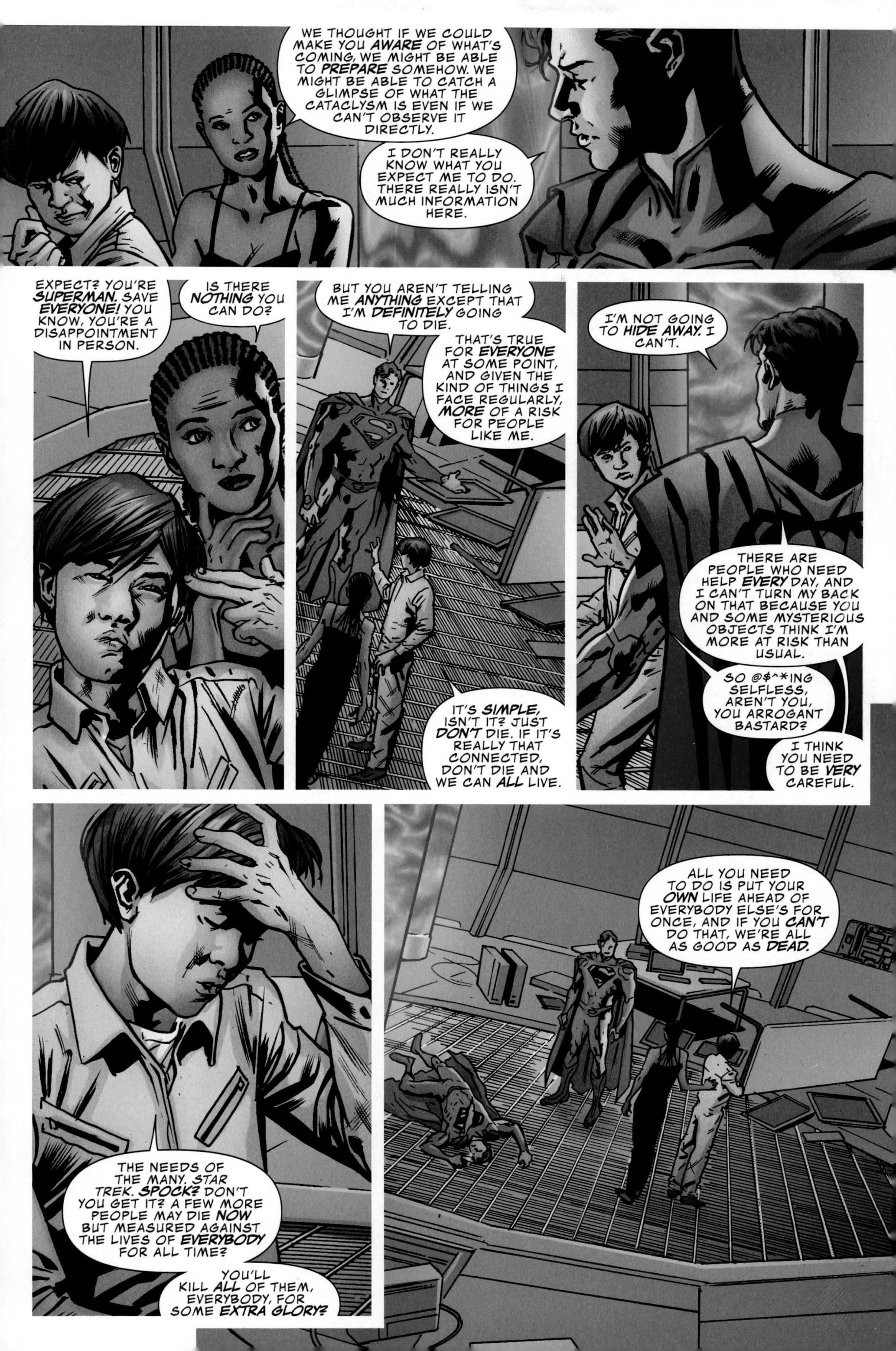
WE THOUGHT IF WE COULD MAKE YOU AWARE OF WHAT'S COMING, WE MIGHT BE ABLE TO PREPARE SOMEHOW. WE MIGHT BE ABLE TO CATCH A GLIMPSE OF WHAT THE CATACLYSM IS EVEN IF WE CAN'T OBSERVE IT DIRECTLY.
I DON'T REALLY KNOW WHAT YOU EXPECT ME TO DO. THERE REALLY ISN'T MUCH INFORMATION HERE.
EXPECT? YOU'RE SUPERMAN. SAVE EVERYONE! YOU KNOW, YOU'RE A DISAPPOINTMENT IN PERSON.
IS THERE NOTHING YOU CAN DO?
BUT YOU AREN'T TELLING ME ANYTHING EXCEPT THAT I'M DEFINITELY GOING TO DIE.
THAT'S TRUE FOR EVERYONE AT SOME POINT, AND GIVEN THE KIND OF THINGS I FACE REGULARLY, MORE OF A RISK FOR PEOPLE LIKE ME.
IT'S SIMPLE, ISN'T IT? JUST DON'T DIE. IF IT'S REALLY THAT CONNECTED, DON'T DIE AND WE CAN ALL LIVE.
I'M NOT GOING TO HIDE AWAY. I CAN'T.
THERE ARE PEOPLE WHO NEED HELP EVERY DAY, AND I CAN'T TURN MY BACK ON THAT BECAUSE YOU AND SOME MYSTERIOUS OBJECTS THINK I'M MORE AT RISK THAN USUAL.
SO @$^*ING SELFLESS, AREN'T YOU, YOU ARROGANT BASTARD?
I THINK YOU NEED TO BE VERY CAREFUL.
THE NEEDS OF THE MANY. STAR TREK. SPOCK? DON'T YOU GET IT? A FEW MORE PEOPLE MAY DIE NOW BUT MEASURED AGAINST THE LIVES OF EVERYBODY FOR ALL TIME?
YOU'LL KILL ALL OF THEM, EVERYBODY, FOR SOME EXTRA GLORY?
ALL YOU NEED TO DO IS PUT YOUR OWN LIFE AHEAD OF EVERYBODY ELSE'S FOR ONCE, AND IF YOU CAN'T DO THAT, WE'RE ALL AS GOOD AS DEAD.

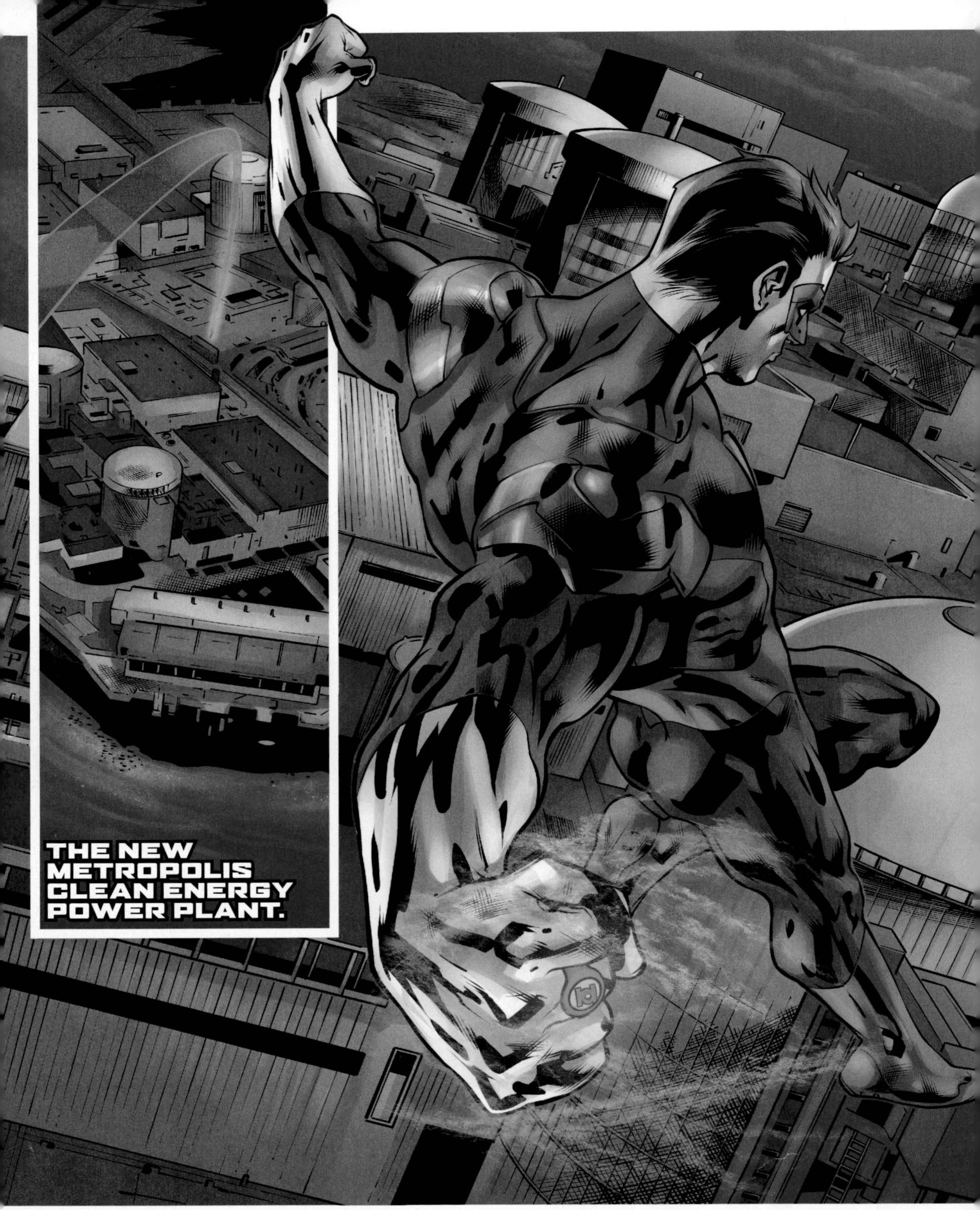
THE NEW METROPOLIS CLEAN ENERGY POWER PLANT.

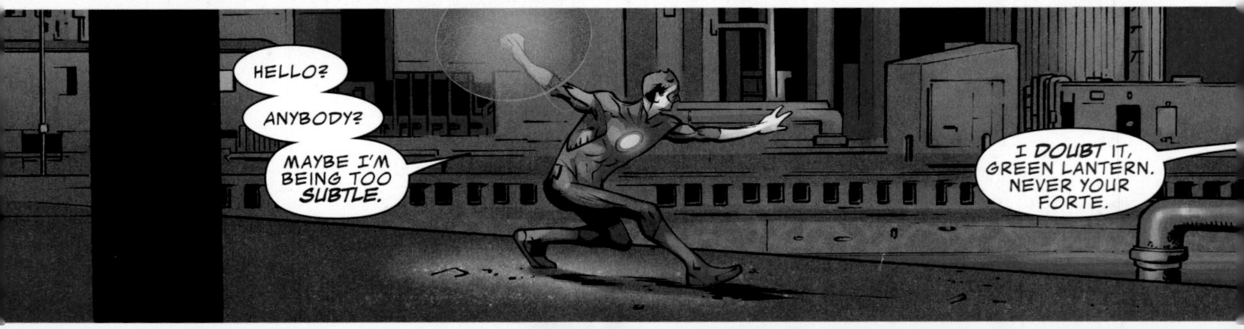
HELLO?
ANYBODY?
MAYBE I'M BEING TOO SUBTLE.
I DOUBT IT, GREEN LANTERN. NEVER YOUR FORTE.

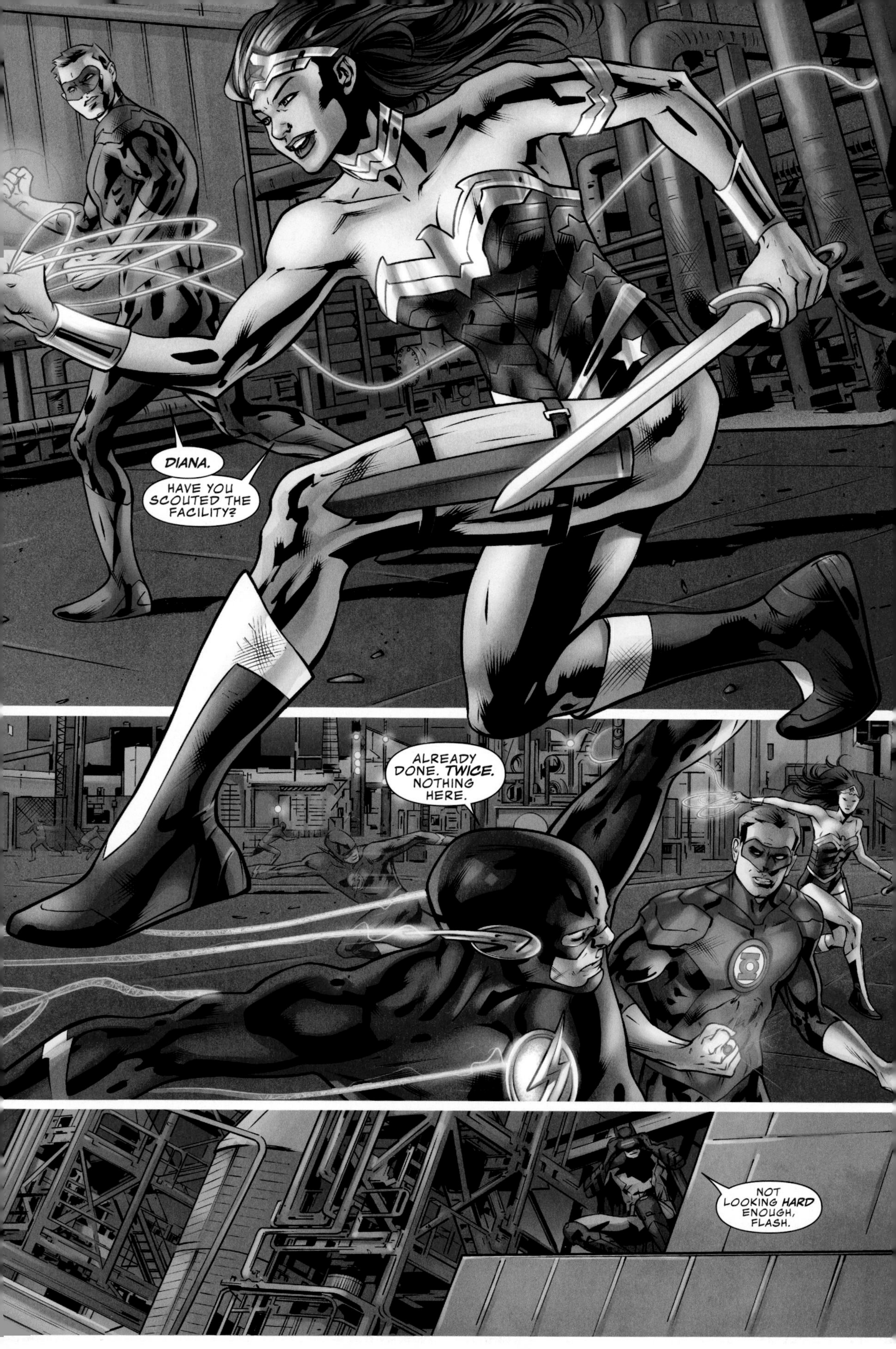
DIANA.
HAVE YOU SCOUTED THE FACILITY?
ALREADY DONE. TWICE. NOTHING HERE.
NOT LOOKING HARD ENOUGH, FLASH.

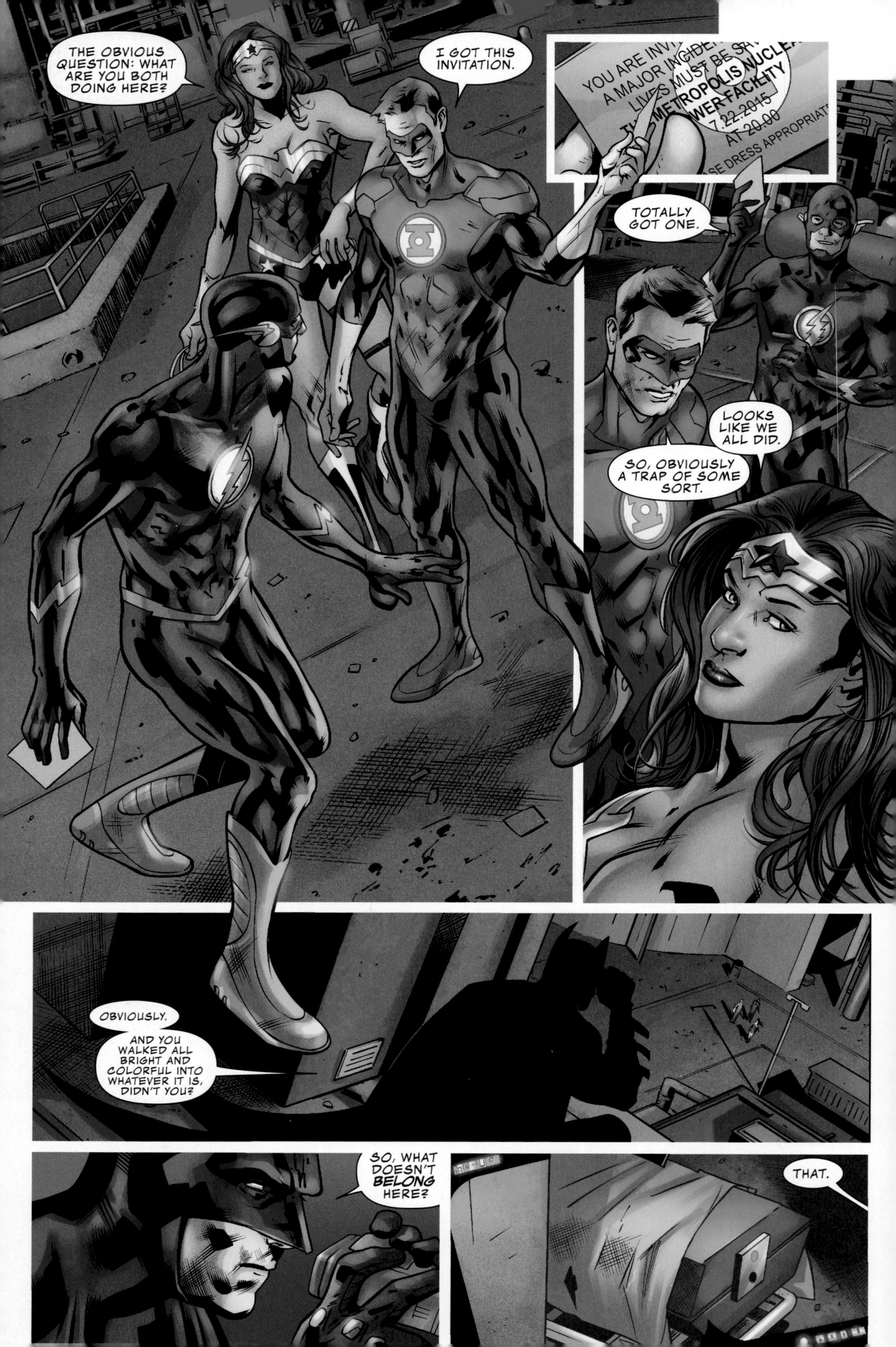
THE OBVIOUS QUESTION: WHAT ARE YOU BOTH DOING HERE?
I GOT THIS INVITATION.
YOU ARE INVI
A MAJOR INCIDEN
LIVES MUST BE SA
METROPOLIS NUCLEA
WER FACILITY
7.22.2015
AT 20.00
SE DRESS APPROPRIAT
TOTALLY GOT ONE.
LOOKS LIKE WE ALL DID.
SO, OBVIOUSLY A TRAP OF SOME SORT.
OBVIOUSLY.
AND YOU WALKED ALL BRIGHT AND COLORFUL INTO WHATEVER IT IS, DIDN'T YOU?
SO, WHAT DOESN'T BELONG HERE?
THAT.

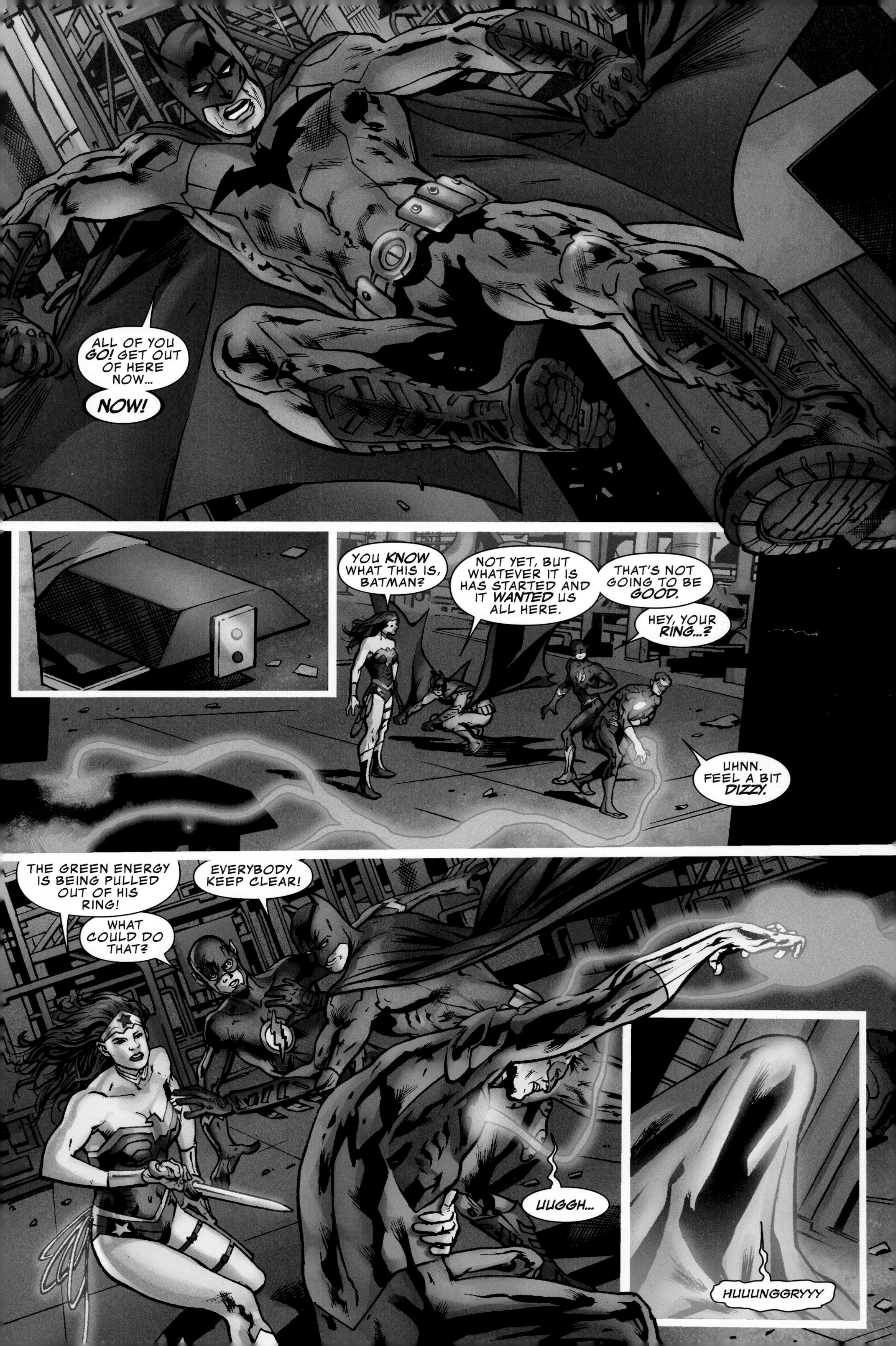
ALL OF YOU GO! GET OUT OF HERE NOW... NOW!
YOU KNOW WHAT THIS IS, BATMAN?
NOT YET, BUT WHATEVER IT IS HAS STARTED AND IT WANTED US ALL HERE.
THAT'S NOT GOING TO BE GOOD.
HEY, YOUR RING...?
UHNN. FEEL A BIT DIZZY.
THE GREEN ENERGY IS BEING PULLED OUT OF HIS RING!
WHAT COULD DO THAT?
EVERYBODY KEEP CLEAR!
UUGGH...
HUUUNGGRYYY

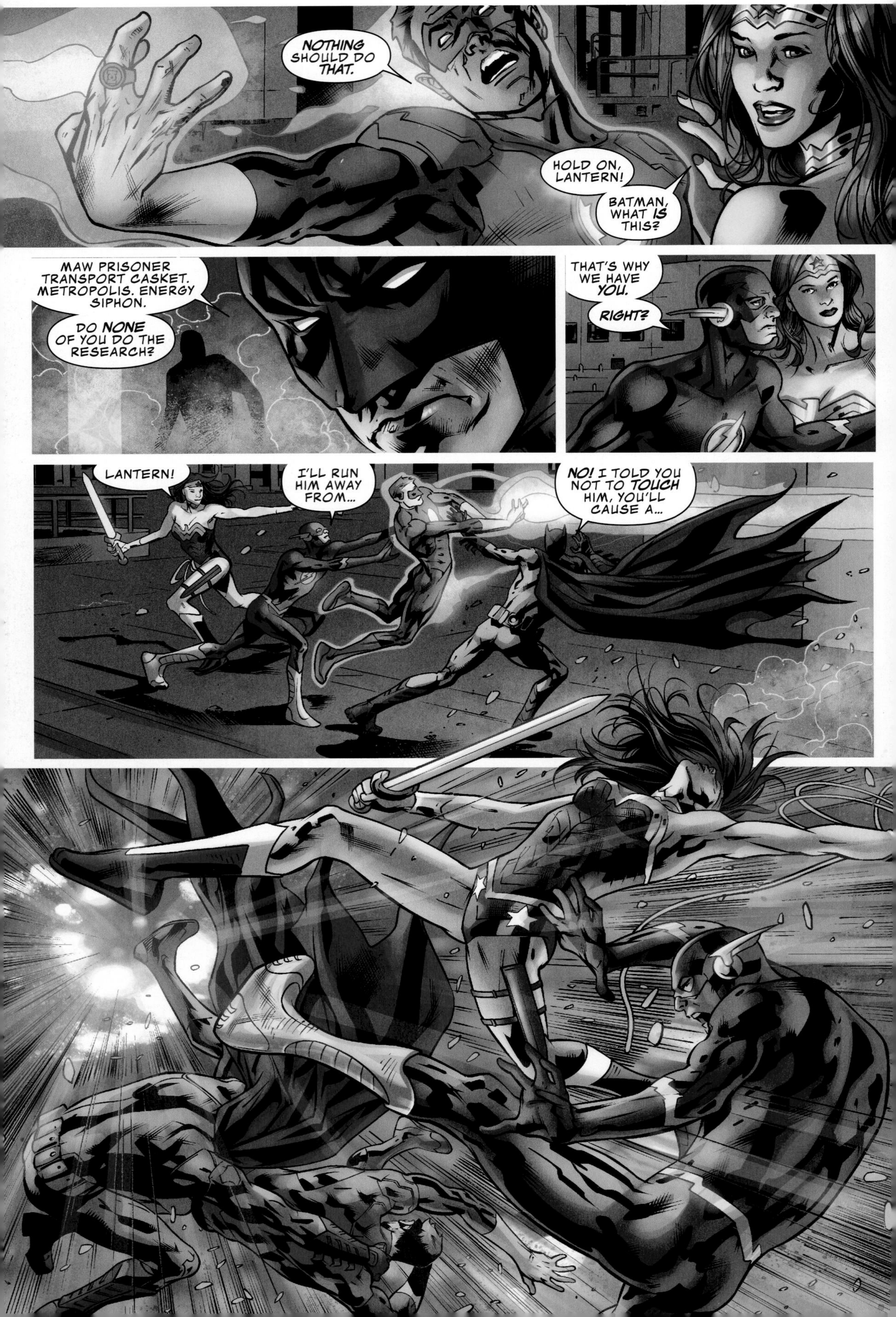

NOTHING SHOULD DO THAT.
HOLD ON, LANTERN!
BATMAN, WHAT IS THIS?
MAW PRISONER TRANSPORT CASKET. METROPOLIS. ENERGY SIPHON.
DO NONE OF YOU DO THE RESEARCH?
THAT'S WHY WE HAVE YOU.
RIGHT?
LANTERN!
I'LL RUN HIM AWAY FROM...
NO! I TOLD YOU NOT TO TOUCH HIM, YOU'LL CAUSE A...

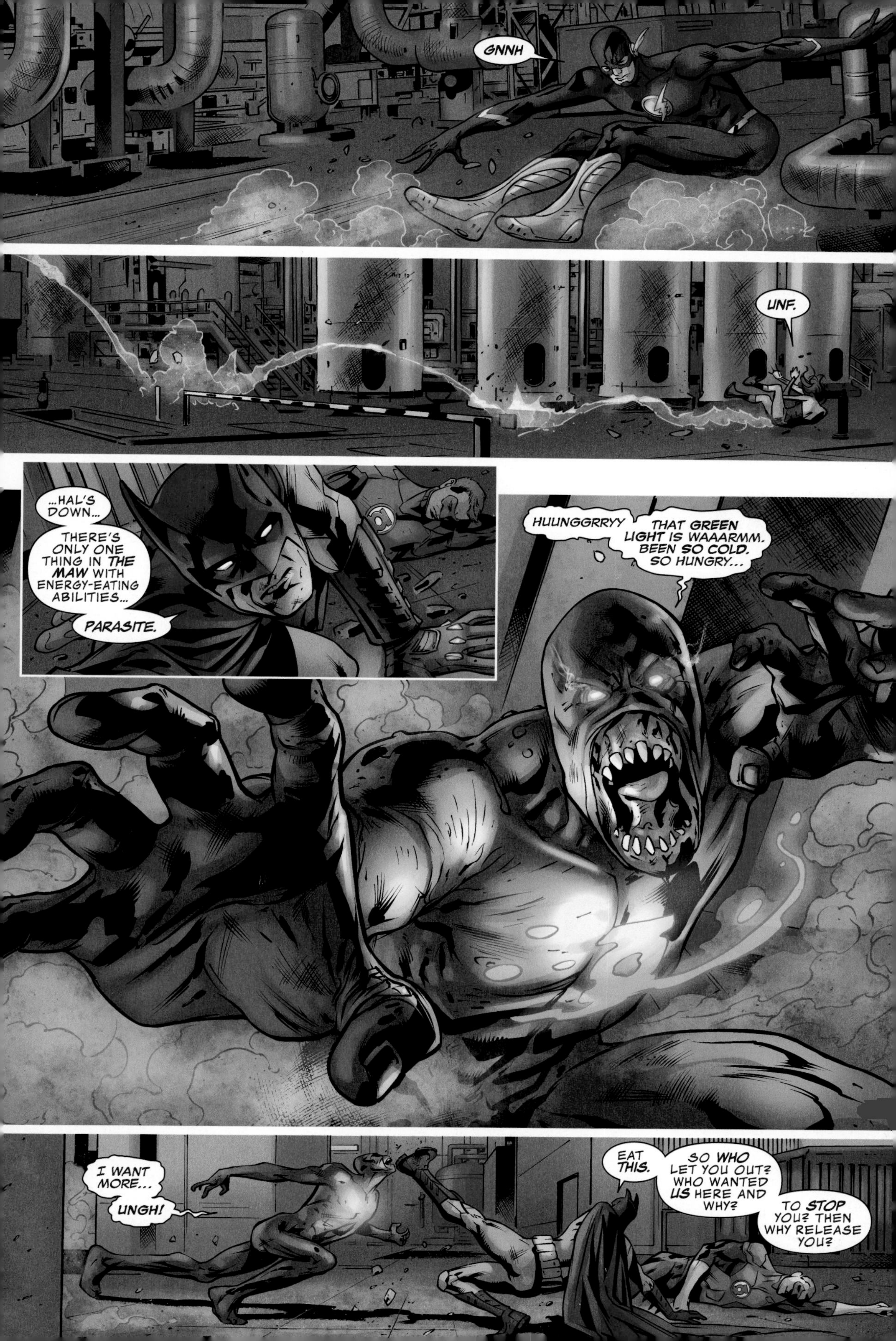
GNNH
UNF.
...HAL'S DOWN...
THERE'S ONLY ONE THING IN THE MAW WITH ENERGY-EATING ABILITIES...
PARASITE.
HUUNGGRRYY
THAT GREEN LIGHT IS WAAARMM. BEEN SO COLD. SO HUNGRY...
I WANT MORE...
UNGH!
EAT THIS.
SO WHO LET YOU OUT? WHO WANTED US HERE AND WHY?
TO STOP YOU? THEN WHY RELEASE YOU?

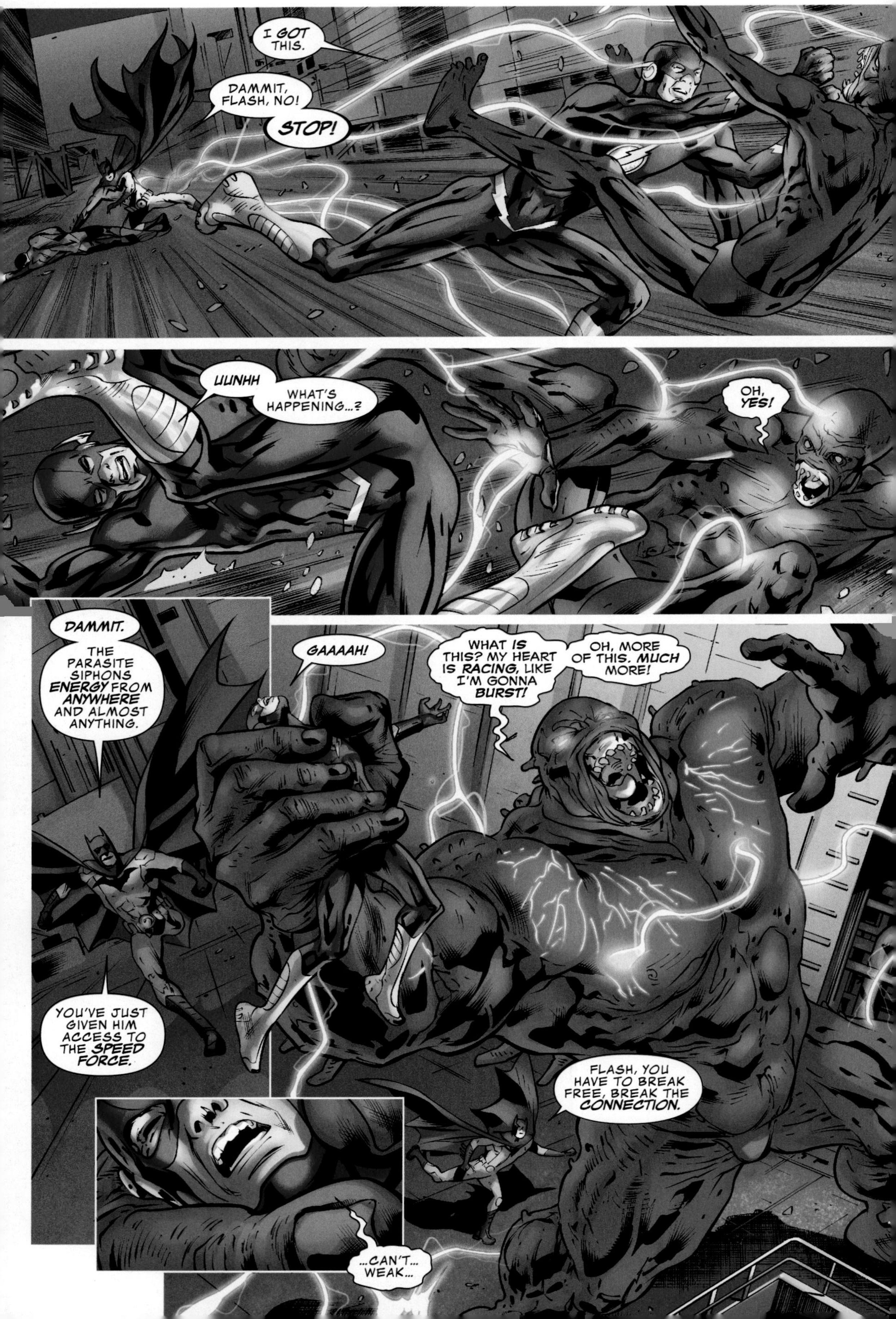
I GOT THIS.
DAMMIT, FLASH, NO!
STOP!
UUNHH
WHAT'S HAPPENING...?
OH, YES!
DAMMIT.
THE PARASITE SIPHONS ENERGY FROM ANYWHERE AND ALMOST ANYTHING.
GAAAAH!
WHAT IS THIS? MY HEART IS RACING, LIKE I'M GONNA BURST!
OH, MORE OF THIS. MUCH MORE!
YOU'VE JUST GIVEN HIM ACCESS TO THE SPEED FORCE.
FLASH, YOU HAVE TO BREAK FREE, BREAK THE CONNECTION.
...CAN'T... WEAK...

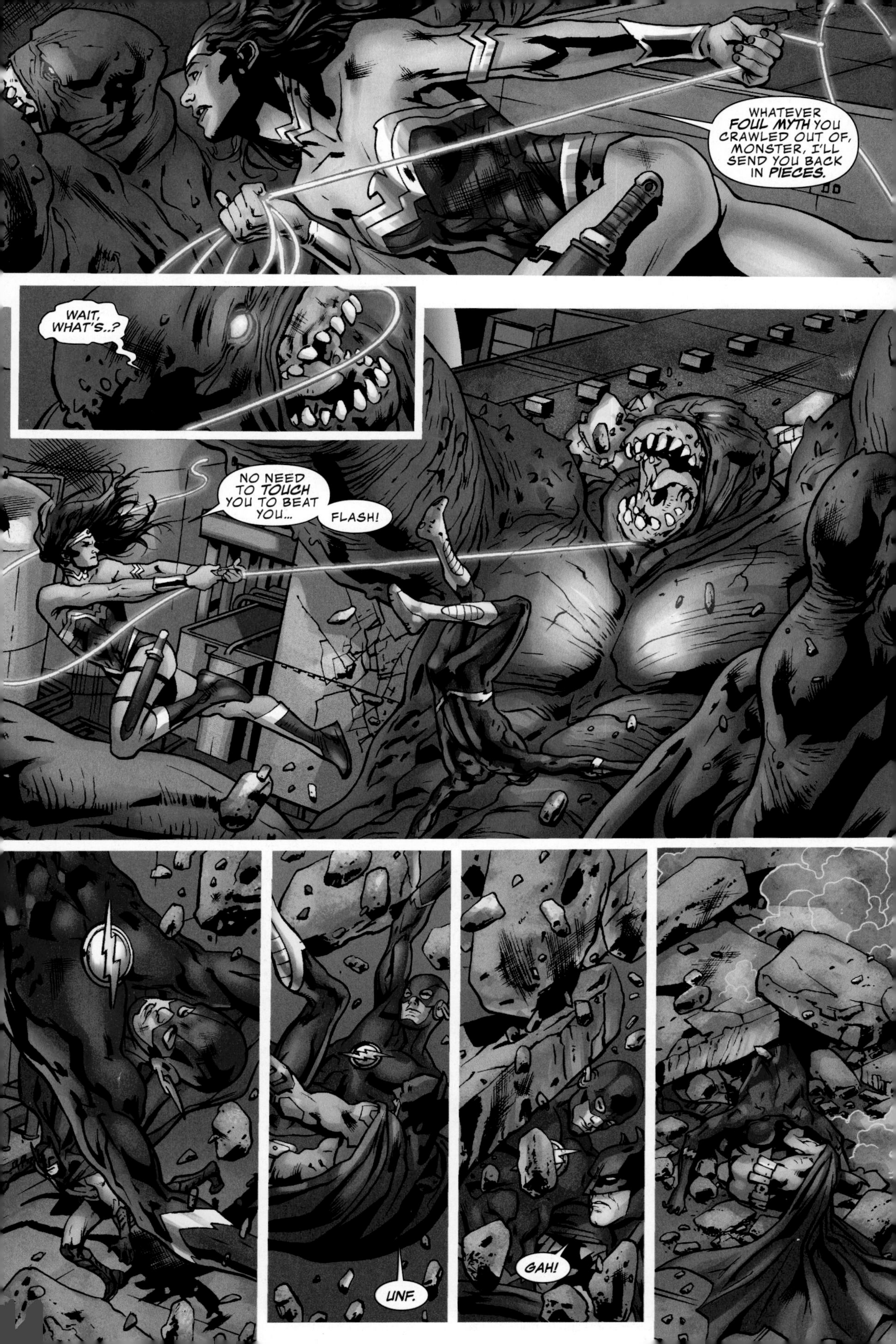
WHATEVER FOUL MYTH YOU CRAWLED OUT OF, MONSTER, I'LL SEND YOU BACK IN PIECES.
WAIT, WHAT'S..?
NO NEED TO TOUCH YOU TO BEAT YOU...
FLASH!
UNF.
GAH!

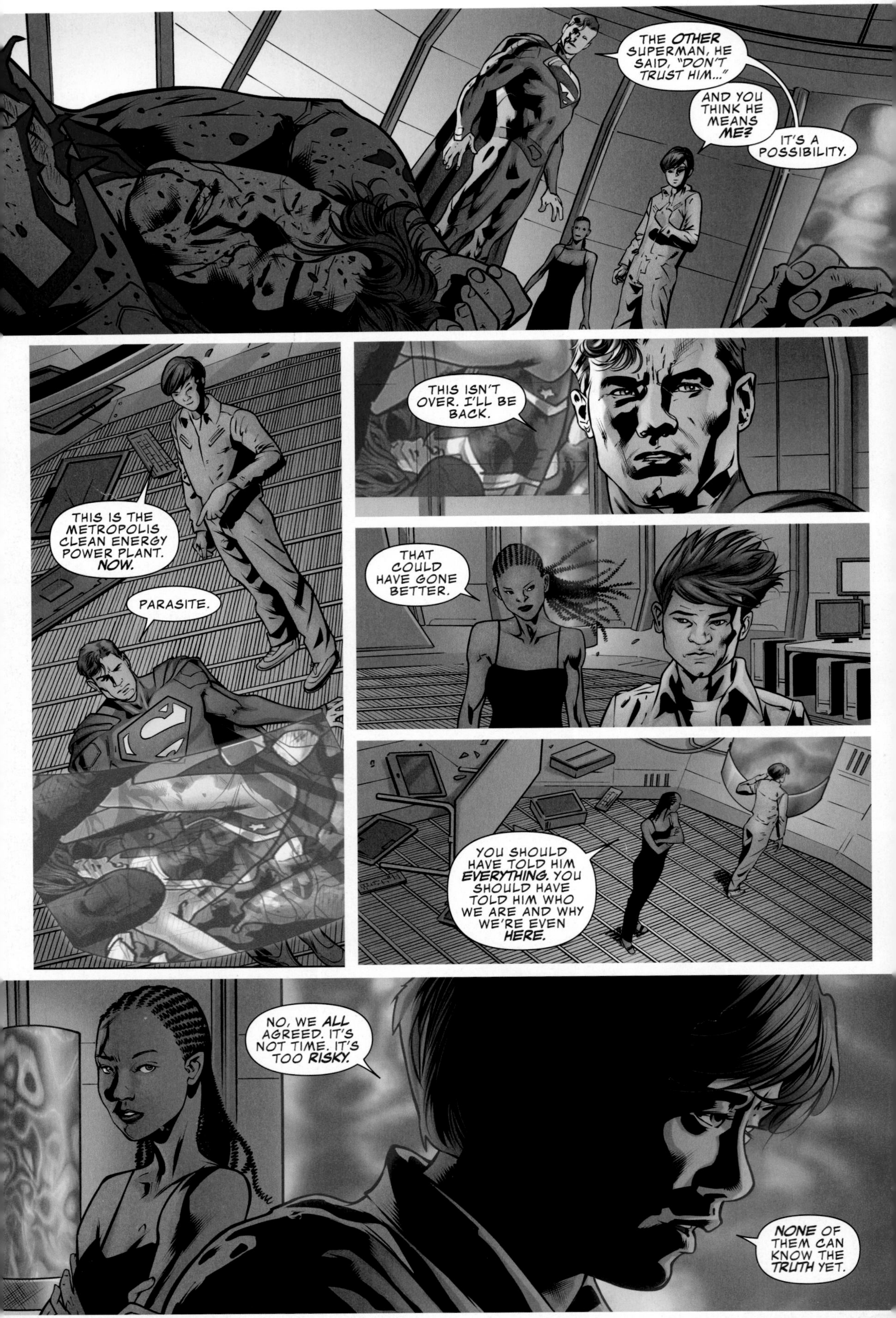
THE OTHER SUPERMAN, HE SAID, "DON'T TRUST HIM..."
AND YOU THINK HE MEANS ME?
IT'S A POSSIBILITY.
THIS IS THE METROPOLIS CLEAN ENERGY POWER PLANT. NOW.
PARASITE.
THIS ISN'T OVER. I'LL BE BACK.
THAT COULD HAVE GONE BETTER.
YOU SHOULD HAVE TOLD HIM EVERYTHING. YOU SHOULD HAVE TOLD HIM WHO WE ARE AND WHY WE'RE EVEN HERE.
NO, WE ALL AGREED. IT'S NOT TIME. IT'S TOO RISKY.
NONE OF THEM CAN KNOW THE TRUTH YET.

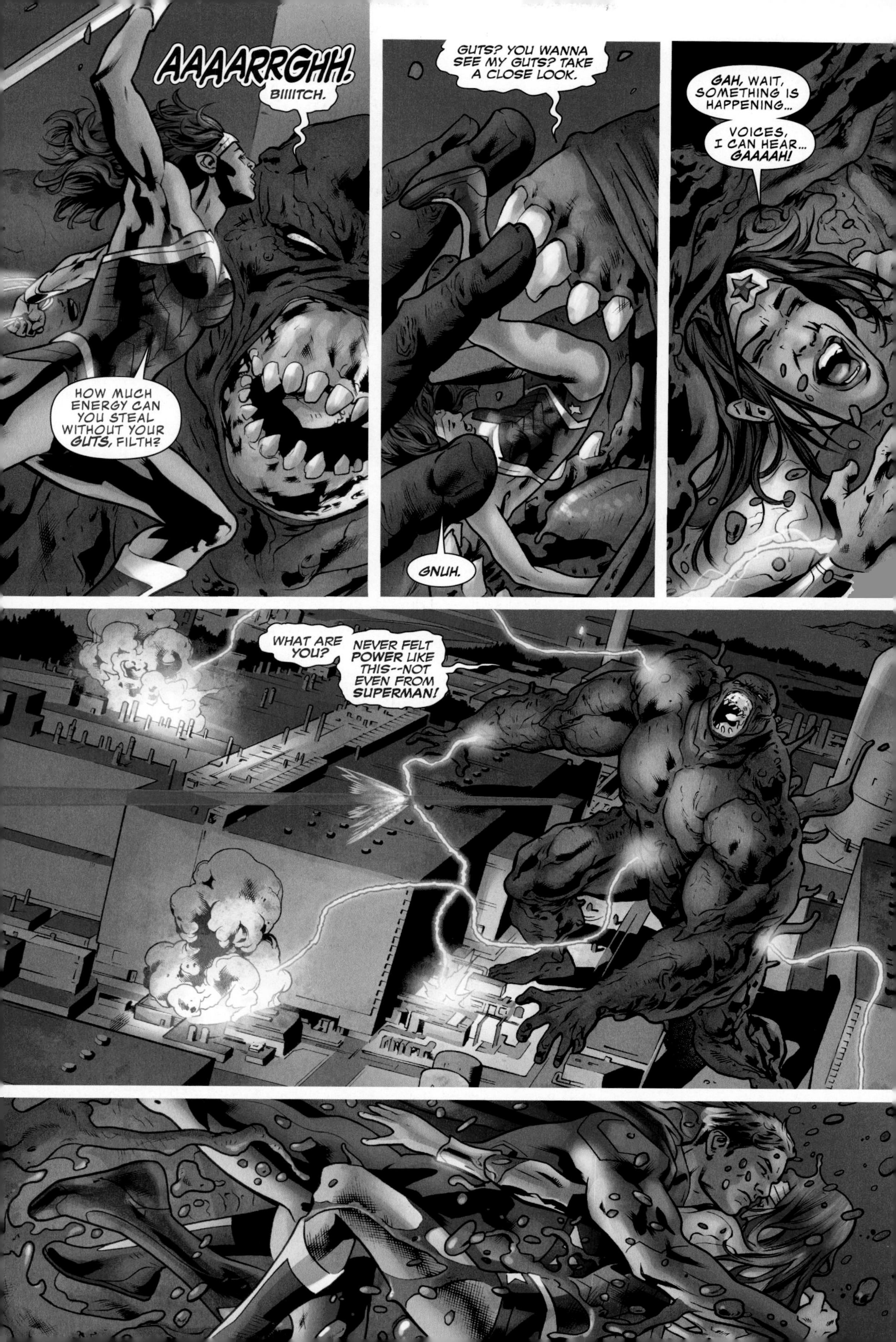
AAAARRGHH.
BIIIITCH.
HOW MUCH ENERGY CAN YOU STEAL WITHOUT YOUR GUTS, FILTH?
GUTS? YOU WANNA SEE MY GUTS? TAKE A CLOSE LOOK.
GNUH.
GAH, WAIT, SOMETHING IS HAPPENING...
VOICES, I CAN HEAR... GAAAAH!
WHAT ARE YOU?
NEVER FELT POWER LIKE THIS--NOT EVEN FROM SUPERMAN!

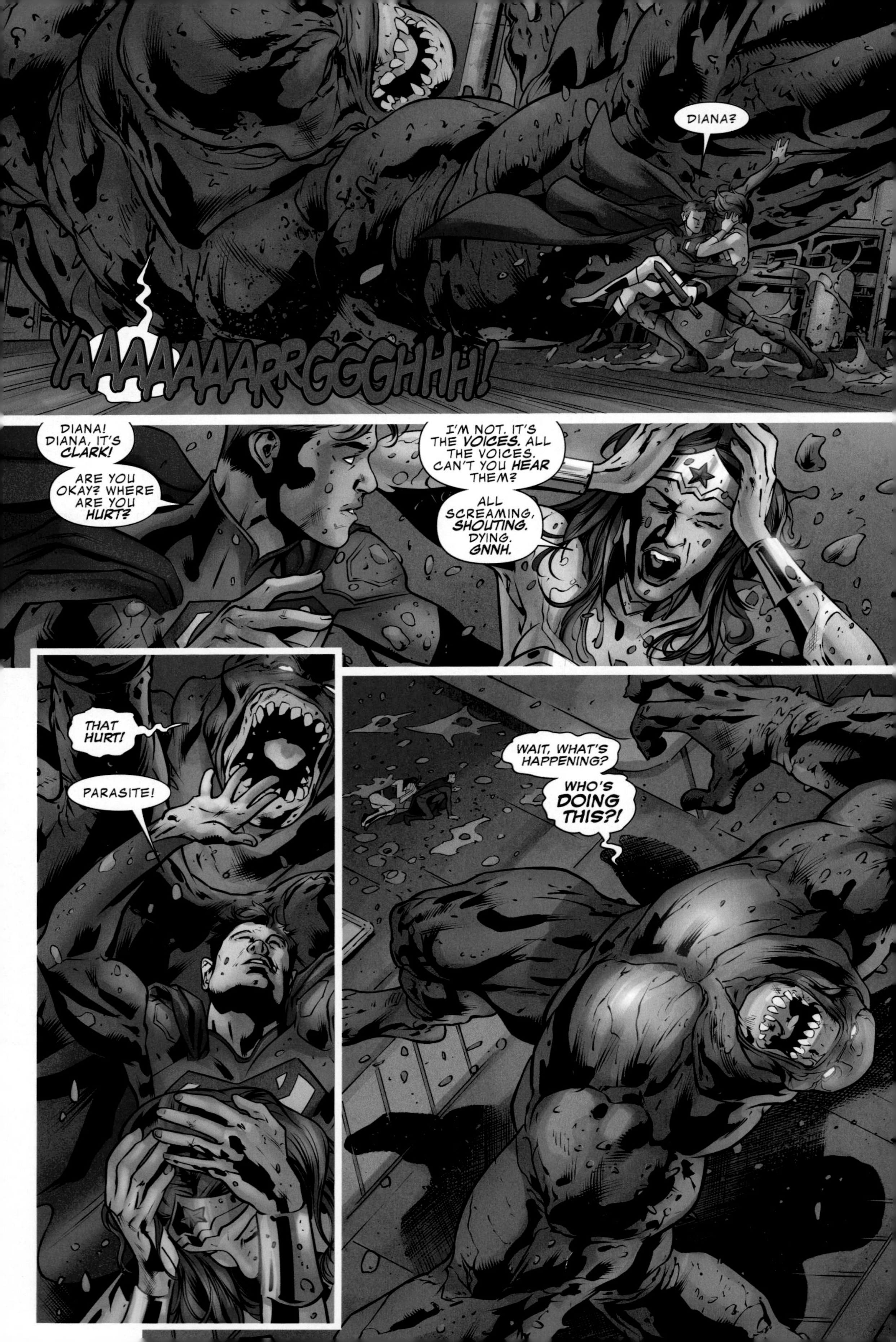
DIANA?
YAAAAAAARRGGGHHH!
DIANA! DIANA, IT'S CLARK!
ARE YOU OKAY? WHERE ARE YOU HURT?
I'M NOT. IT'S THE VOICES. ALL THE VOICES. CAN'T YOU HEAR THEM?
ALL SCREAMING, SHOUTING. DYING. GNNH.
THAT HURT!
PARASITE!
WAIT, WHAT'S HAPPENING?
WHO'S DOING THIS?!

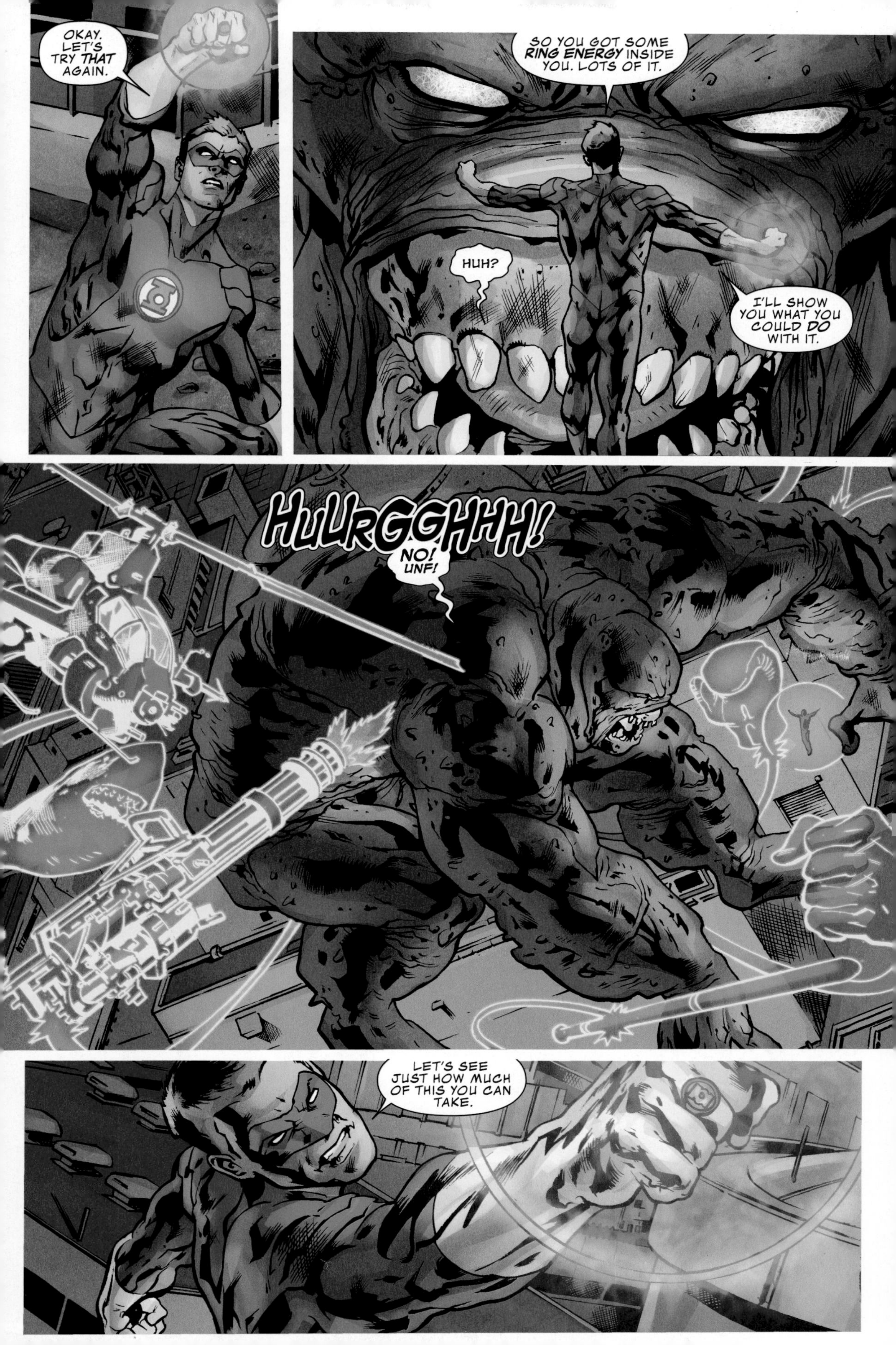
OKAY. LET'S TRY THAT AGAIN.
SO YOU GOT SOME RING ENERGY INSIDE YOU. LOTS OF IT.
HUH?
I'LL SHOW YOU WHAT YOU COULD DO WITH IT.
HUURGGHHH!
NO! UNF!
LET'S SEE JUST HOW MUCH OF THIS YOU CAN TAKE.

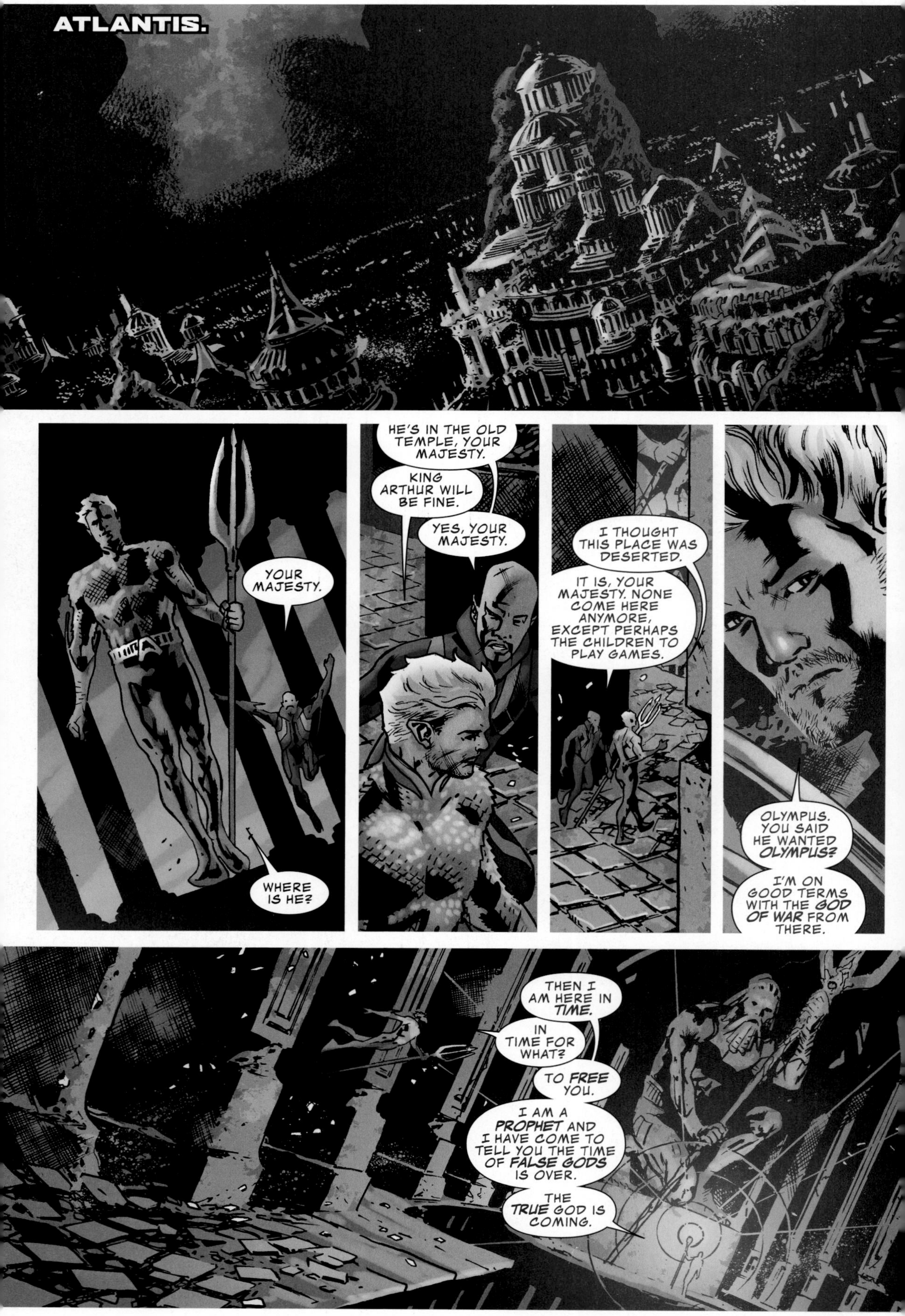
ATLANTIS.
YOUR MAJESTY.
WHERE IS HE?
HE'S IN THE OLD TEMPLE, YOUR MAJESTY.
KING ARTHUR WILL BE FINE.
YES, YOUR MAJESTY.
I THOUGHT THIS PLACE WAS DESERTED.
IT IS, YOUR MAJESTY. NONE COME HERE ANYMORE, EXCEPT PERHAPS THE CHILDREN TO PLAY GAMES.
OLYMPUS. YOU SAID HE WANTED OLYMPUS?
I'M ON GOOD TERMS WITH THE GOD OF WAR FROM THERE.
THEN I AM HERE IN TIME.
IN TIME FOR WHAT?
TO FREE YOU.
I AM A PROPHET AND I HAVE COME TO TELL YOU THE TIME OF FALSE GODS IS OVER.
THE TRUE GOD IS COMING.

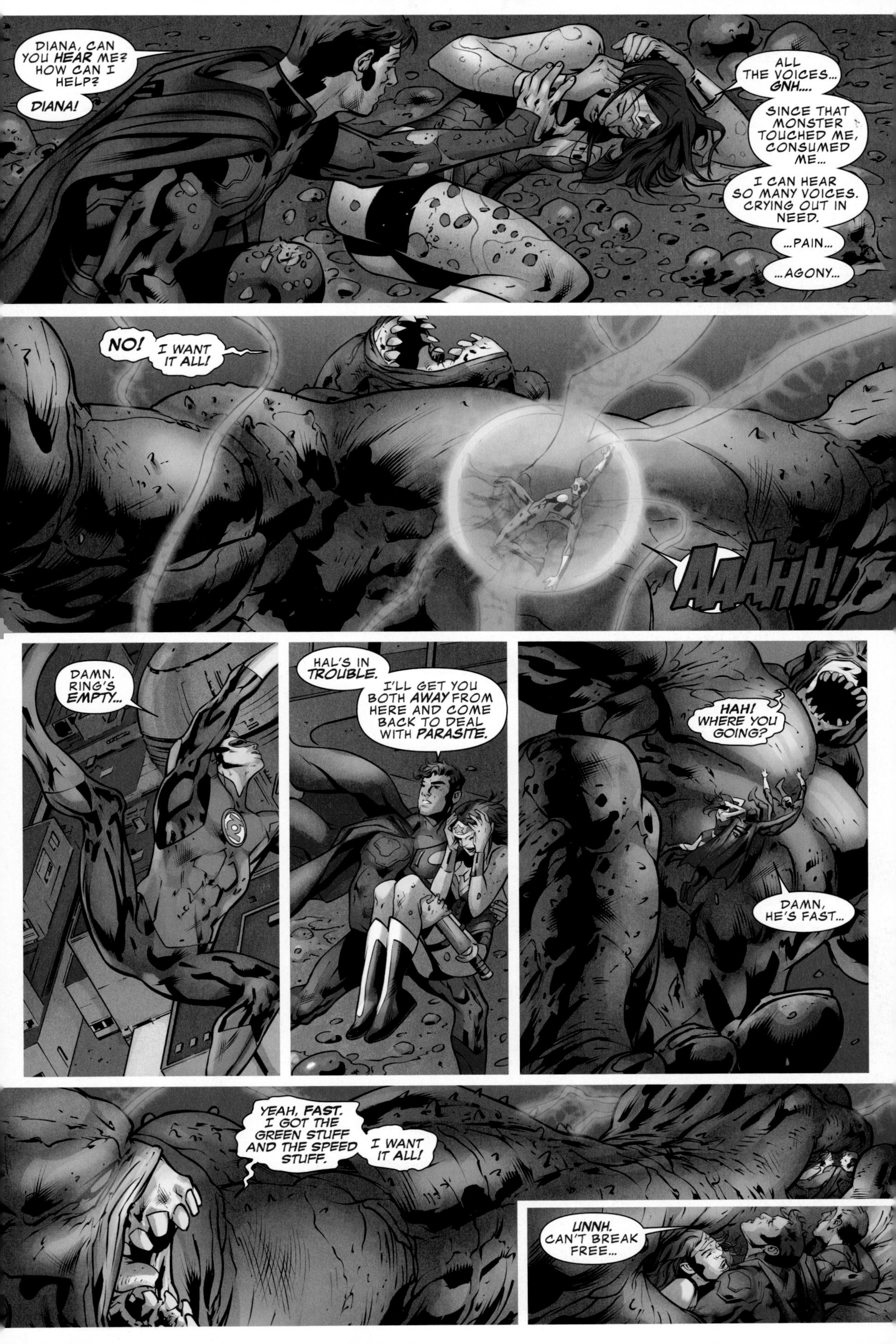
DIANA, CAN YOU HEAR ME? HOW CAN I HELP?
DIANA!
ALL THE VOICES... GNH....
SINCE THAT MONSTER TOUCHED ME, CONSUMED ME...
I CAN HEAR SO MANY VOICES. CRYING OUT IN NEED.
...PAIN...
...AGONY...
NO!
I WANT IT ALL!
AAAHH!
DAMN. RING'S EMPTY...
HAL'S IN TROUBLE.
I'LL GET YOU BOTH AWAY FROM HERE AND COME BACK TO DEAL WITH PARASITE.
HAH! WHERE YOU GOING?
DAMN, HE'S FAST...
YEAH, FAST. I GOT THE GREEN STUFF AND THE SPEED STUFF.
I WANT IT ALL!
UNNH. CAN'T BREAK FREE...

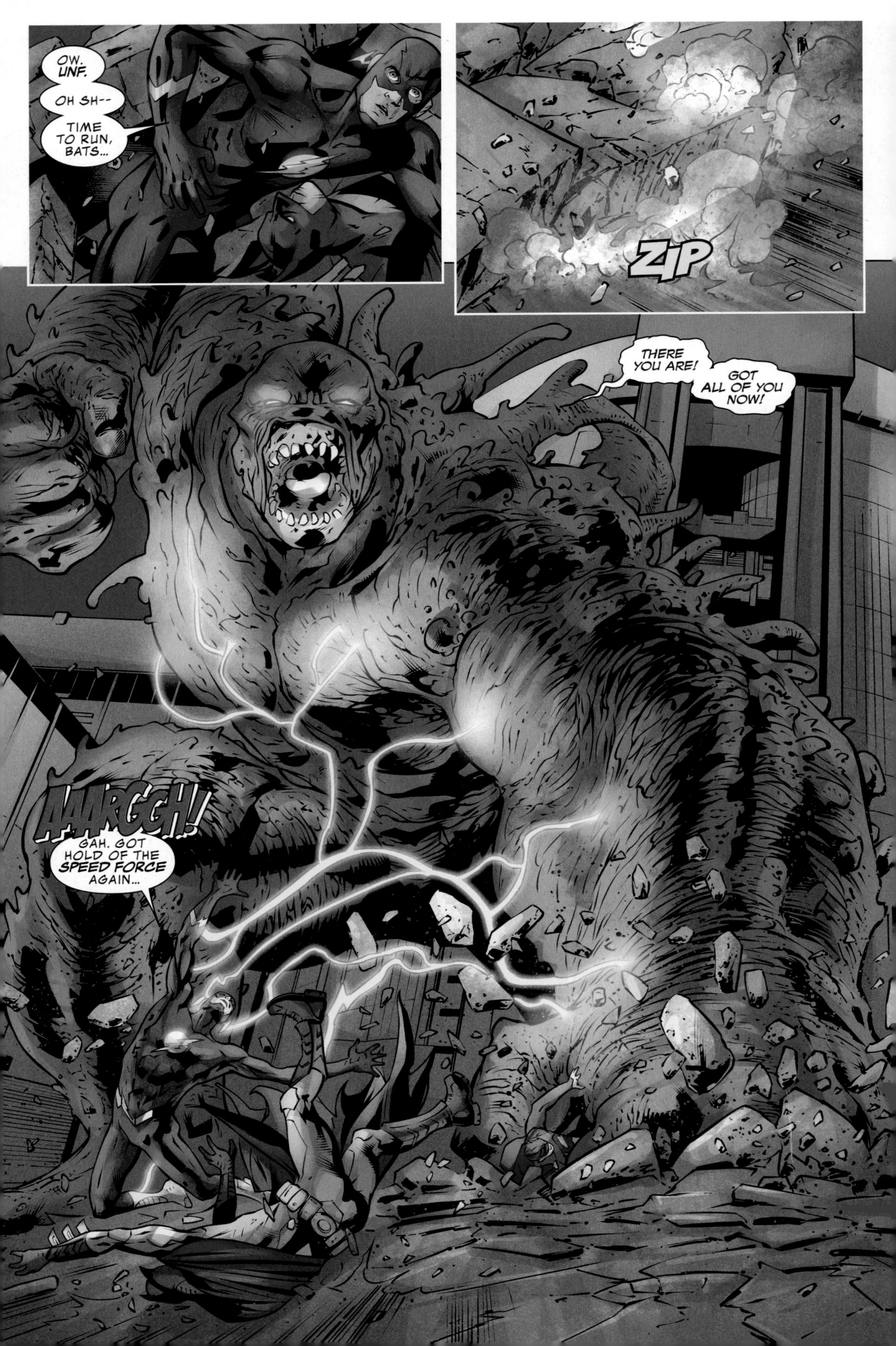
OW. UNF.
OH SH--
TIME TO RUN, BATS...
ZIP
THERE YOU ARE!
GOT ALL OF YOU NOW!
AAARGGH!
GAH. GOT HOLD OF THE SPEED FORCE AGAIN...

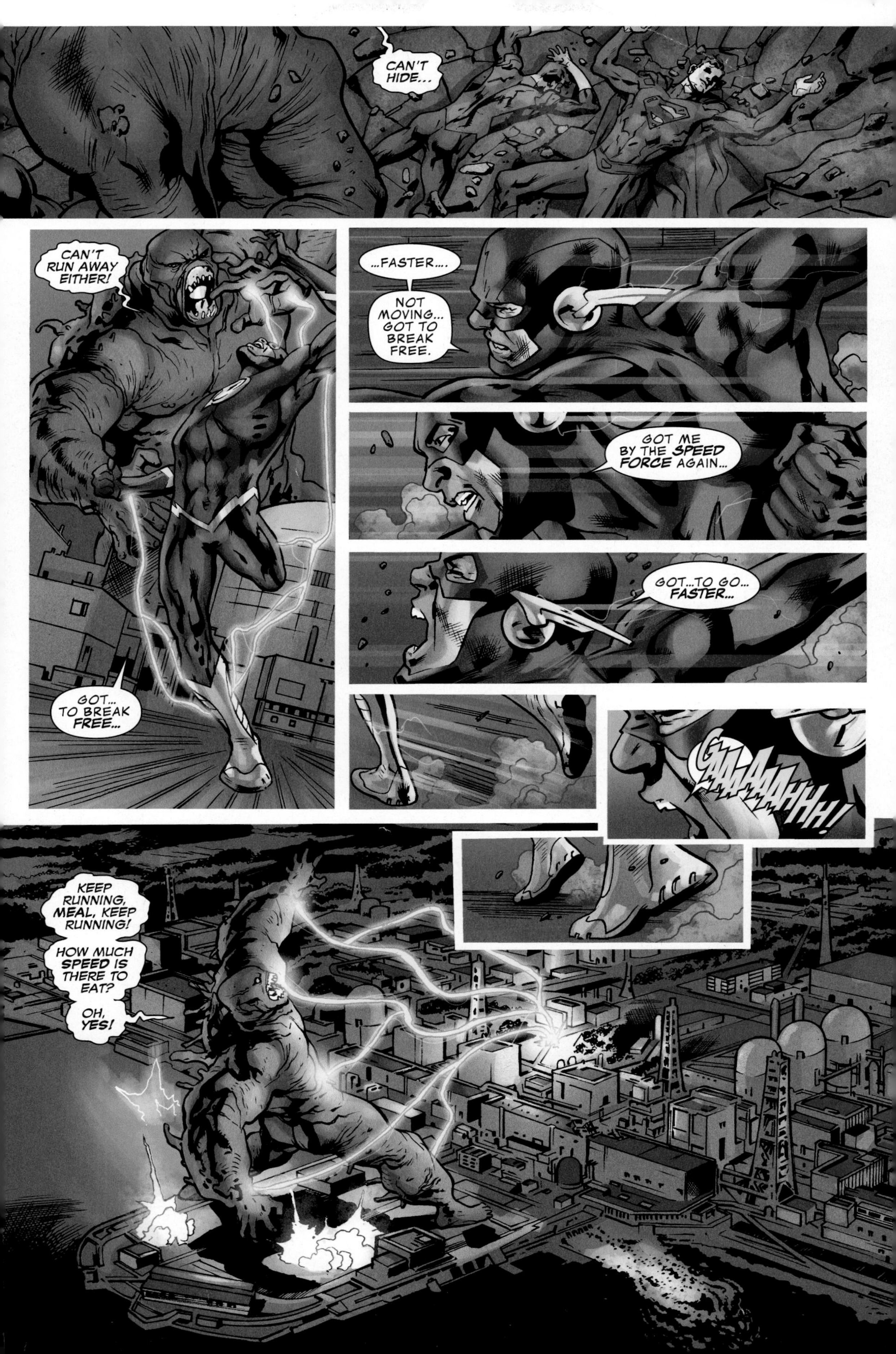

CAN'T HIDE...
CAN'T RUN AWAY EITHER!
GOT... TO BREAK FREE...
...FASTER....
NOT MOVING... GOT TO BREAK FREE.
GOT ME BY THE SPEED FORCE AGAIN...
GOT...TO GO... FASTER...
GAAAAAAHHH!
KEEP RUNNING, MEAL, KEEP RUNNING!
HOW MUCH SPEED IS THERE TO EAT?
OH, YES!

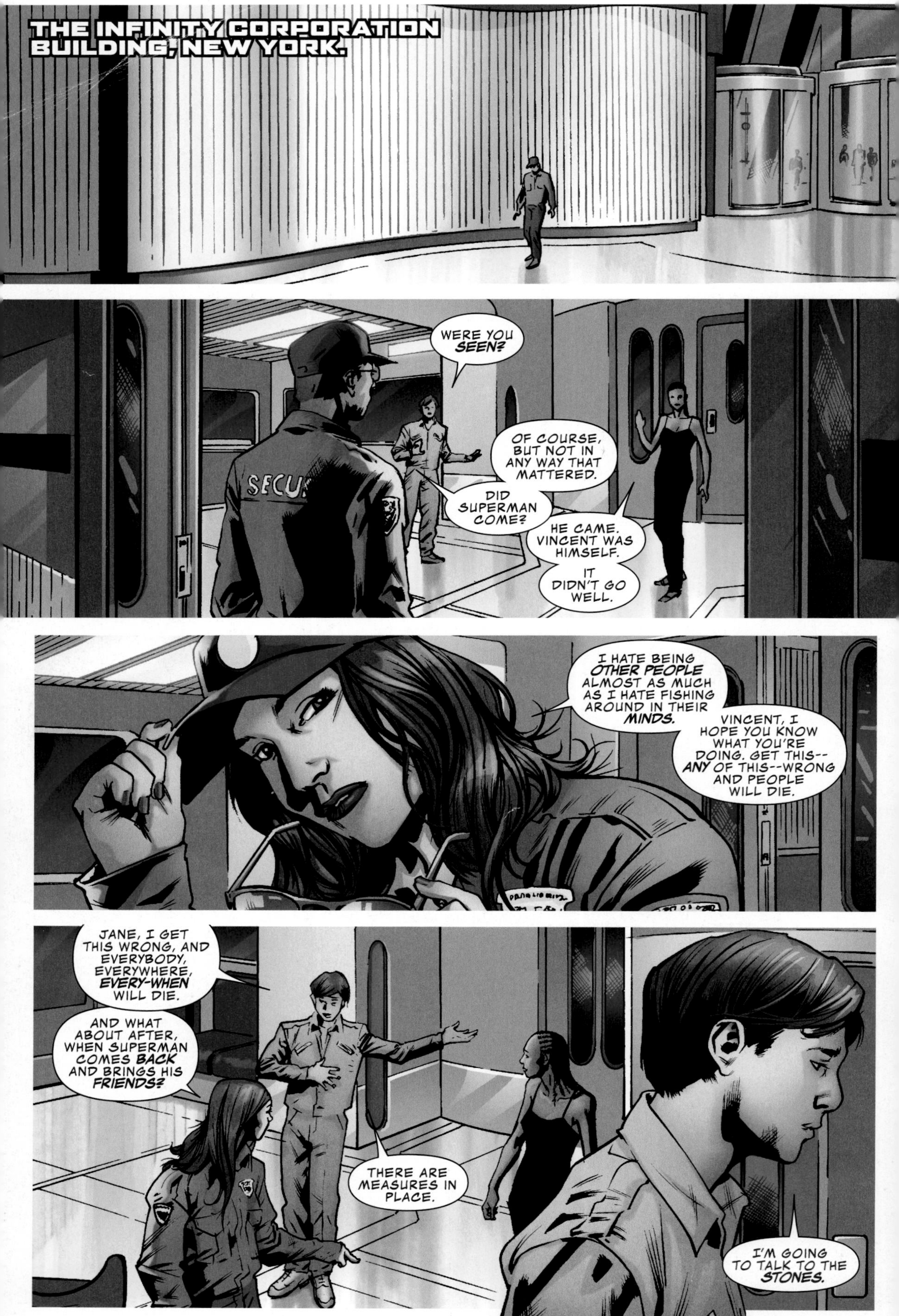
THE INFINITY CORPORATION BUILDING, NEW YORK.
WERE YOU SEEN?
OF COURSE, BUT NOT IN ANY WAY THAT MATTERED.
DID SUPERMAN COME?
HE CAME. VINCENT WAS HIMSELF.
IT DIDN'T GO WELL.
I HATE BEING OTHER PEOPLE ALMOST AS MUCH AS I HATE FISHING AROUND IN THEIR MINDS.
VINCENT, I HOPE YOU KNOW WHAT YOU'RE DOING. GET THIS--ANY OF THIS--WRONG AND PEOPLE WILL DIE.
JANE, I GET THIS WRONG, AND EVERYBODY, EVERYWHERE, EVERY-WHEN WILL DIE.
AND WHAT ABOUT AFTER, WHEN SUPERMAN COMES BACK AND BRINGS HIS FRIENDS?
THERE ARE MEASURES IN PLACE.
I'M GOING TO TALK TO THE STONES.

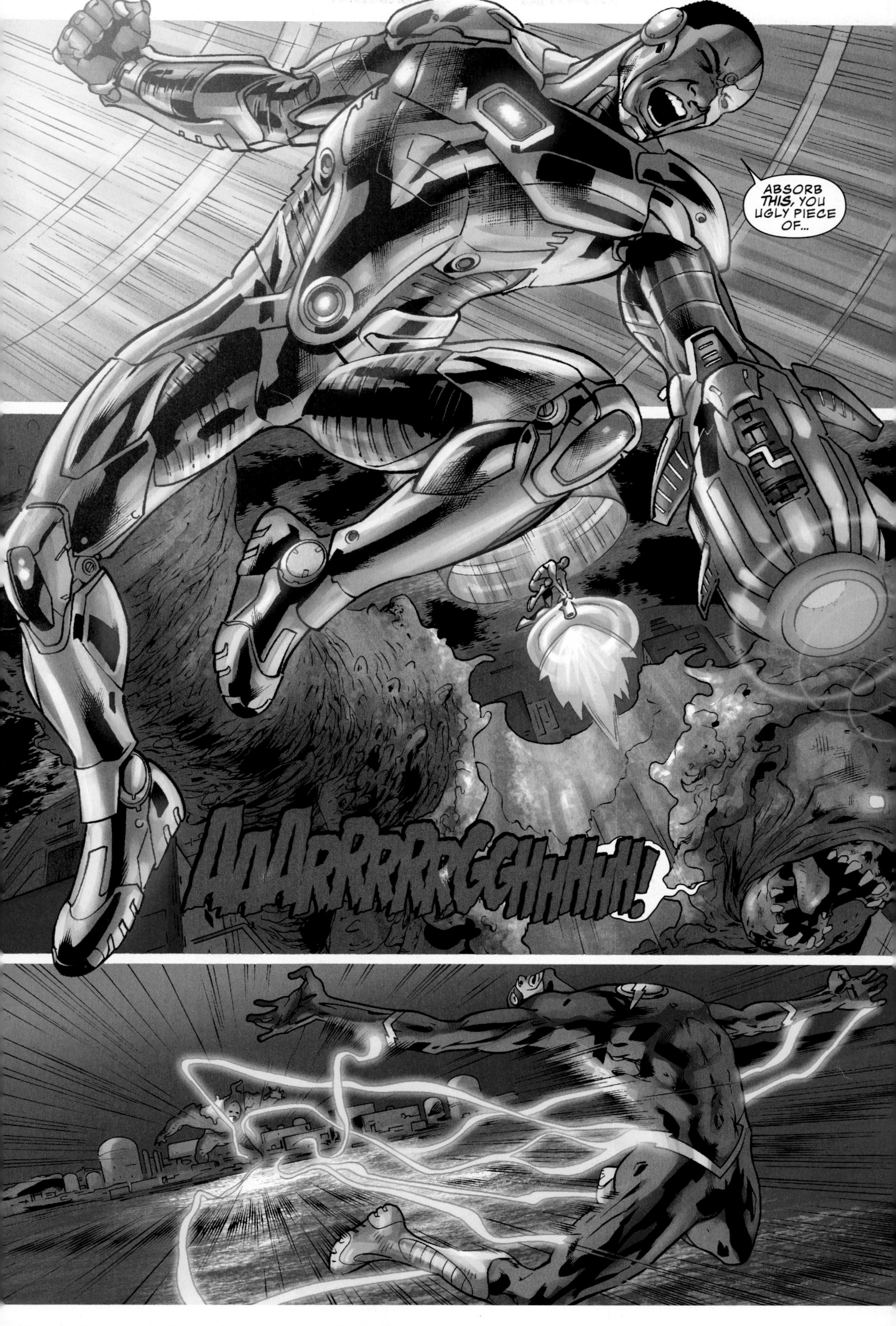
ABSORB THIS, YOU UGLY PIECE OF...
AAARRRRRRGHHHHH!

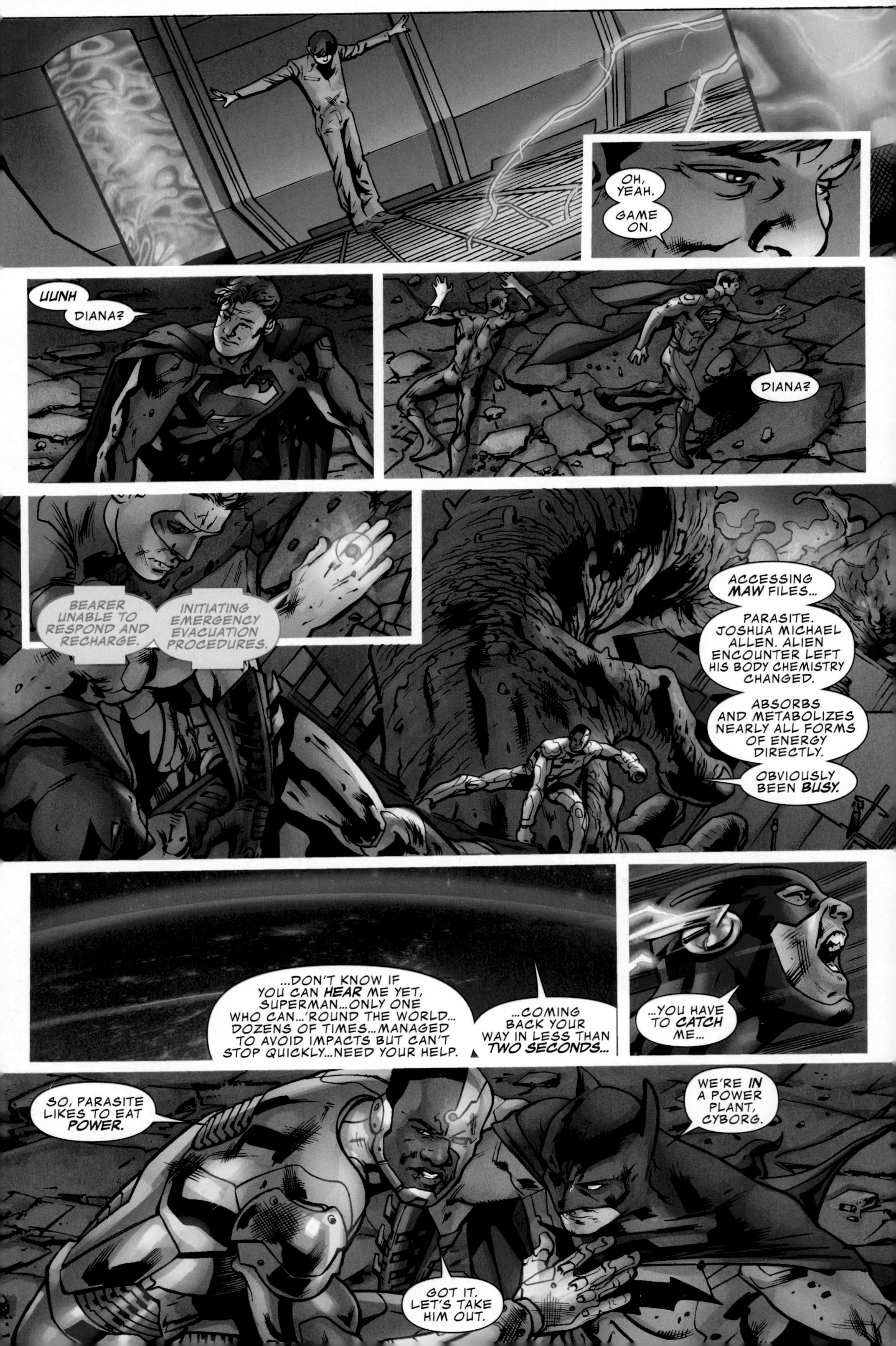
OH, YEAH.
GAME ON.
UUNH
DIANA?
DIANA?
BEARER UNABLE TO RESPOND AND RECHARGE.
INITIATING EMERGENCY EVACUATION PROCEDURES.
ACCESSING MAW FILES...
PARASITE. JOSHUA MICHAEL ALLEN. ALIEN ENCOUNTER LEFT HIS BODY CHEMISTRY CHANGED.
ABSORBS AND METABOLIZES NEARLY ALL FORMS OF ENERGY DIRECTLY.
OBVIOUSLY BEEN BUSY.
...DON'T KNOW IF YOU CAN HEAR ME YET, SUPERMAN...ONLY ONE WHO CAN...'ROUND THE WORLD... DOZENS OF TIMES...MANAGED TO AVOID IMPACTS BUT CAN'T STOP QUICKLY...NEED YOUR HELP.
...COMING BACK YOUR WAY IN LESS THAN TWO SECONDS...
...YOU HAVE TO CATCH ME...
SO, PARASITE LIKES TO EAT POWER.
WE'RE IN A POWER PLANT, CYBORG.
GOT IT. LET'S TAKE HIM OUT.

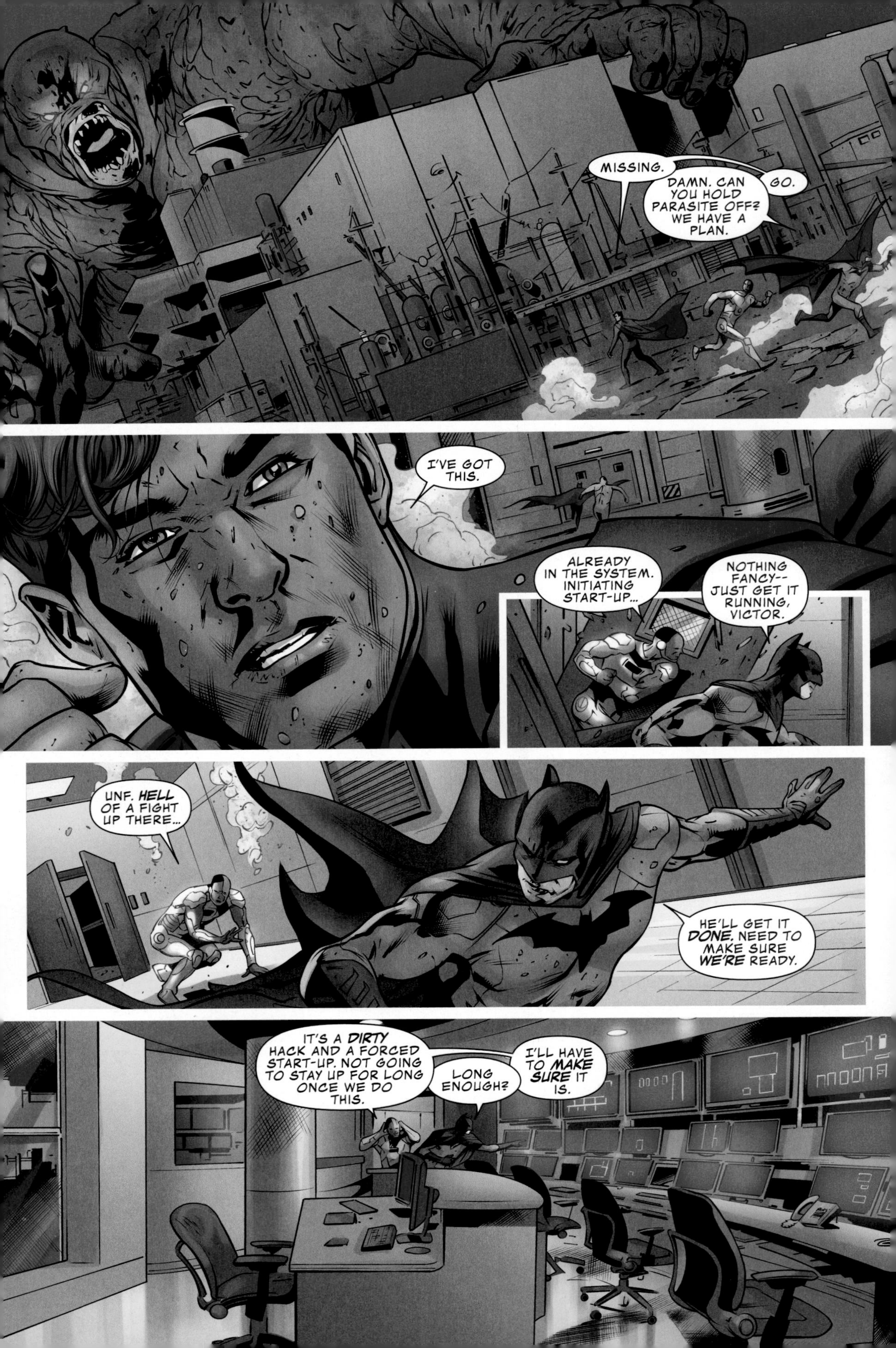
MISSING.
DAMN. CAN YOU HOLD PARASITE OFF? WE HAVE A PLAN.
GO.
I'VE GOT THIS.
ALREADY IN THE SYSTEM. INITIATING START-UP...
NOTHING FANCY-- JUST GET IT RUNNING, VICTOR.
UNF. HELL OF A FIGHT UP THERE...
HE'LL GET IT DONE. NEED TO MAKE SURE WE'RE READY.
IT'S A DIRTY HACK AND A FORCED START-UP. NOT GOING TO STAY UP FOR LONG ONCE WE DO THIS.
LONG ENOUGH?
I'LL HAVE TO MAKE SURE IT IS.

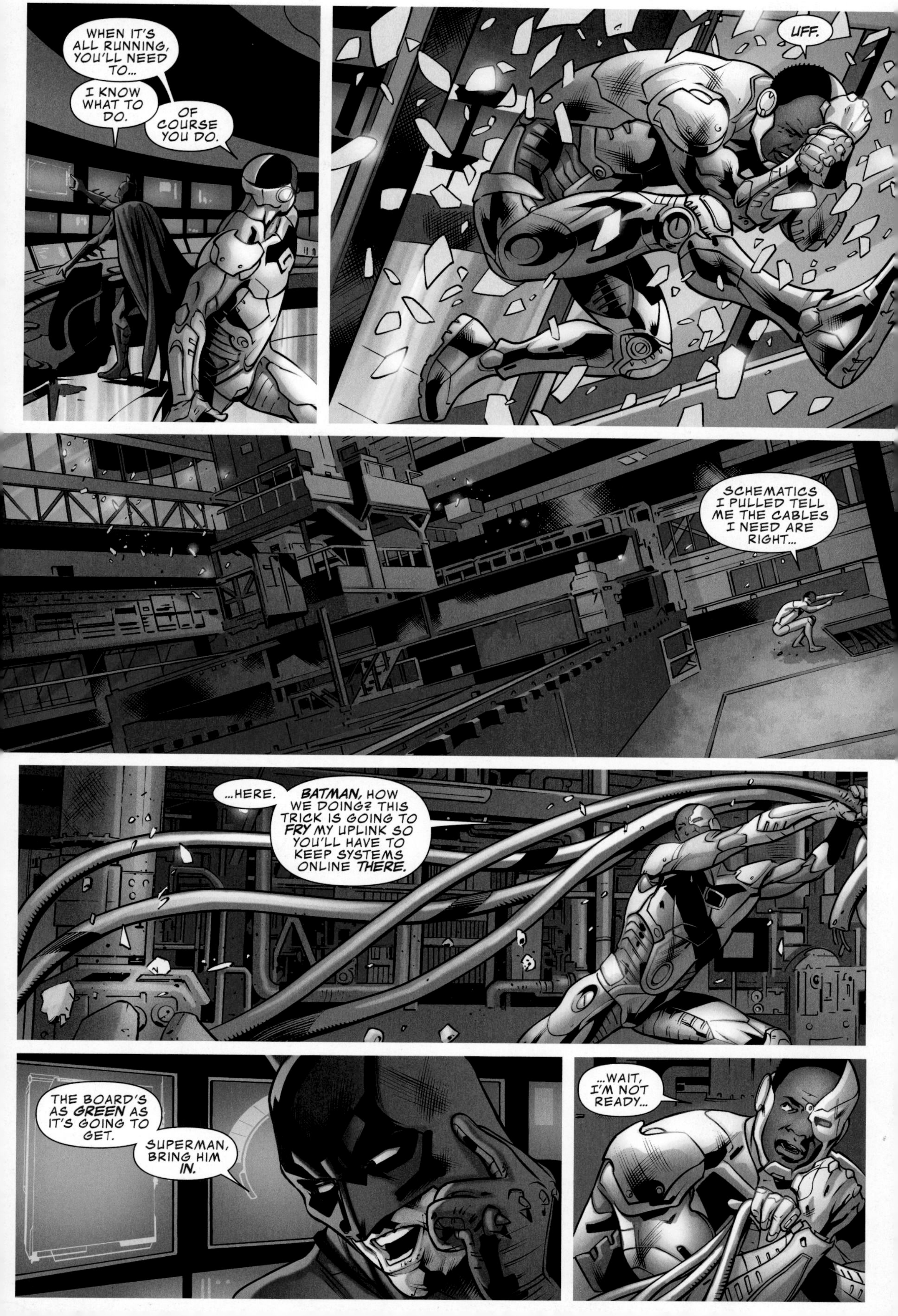
WHEN IT'S ALL RUNNING, YOU'LL NEED TO...
I KNOW WHAT TO DO.
OF COURSE YOU DO.
UFF.
SCHEMATICS I PULLED TELL ME THE CABLES I NEED ARE RIGHT...
...HERE.
BATMAN, HOW WE DOING? THIS TRICK IS GOING TO FRY MY UPLINK SO YOU'LL HAVE TO KEEP SYSTEMS ONLINE THERE.
THE BOARD'S AS GREEN AS IT'S GOING TO GET.
SUPERMAN, BRING HIM IN.
...WAIT, I'M NOT READY...

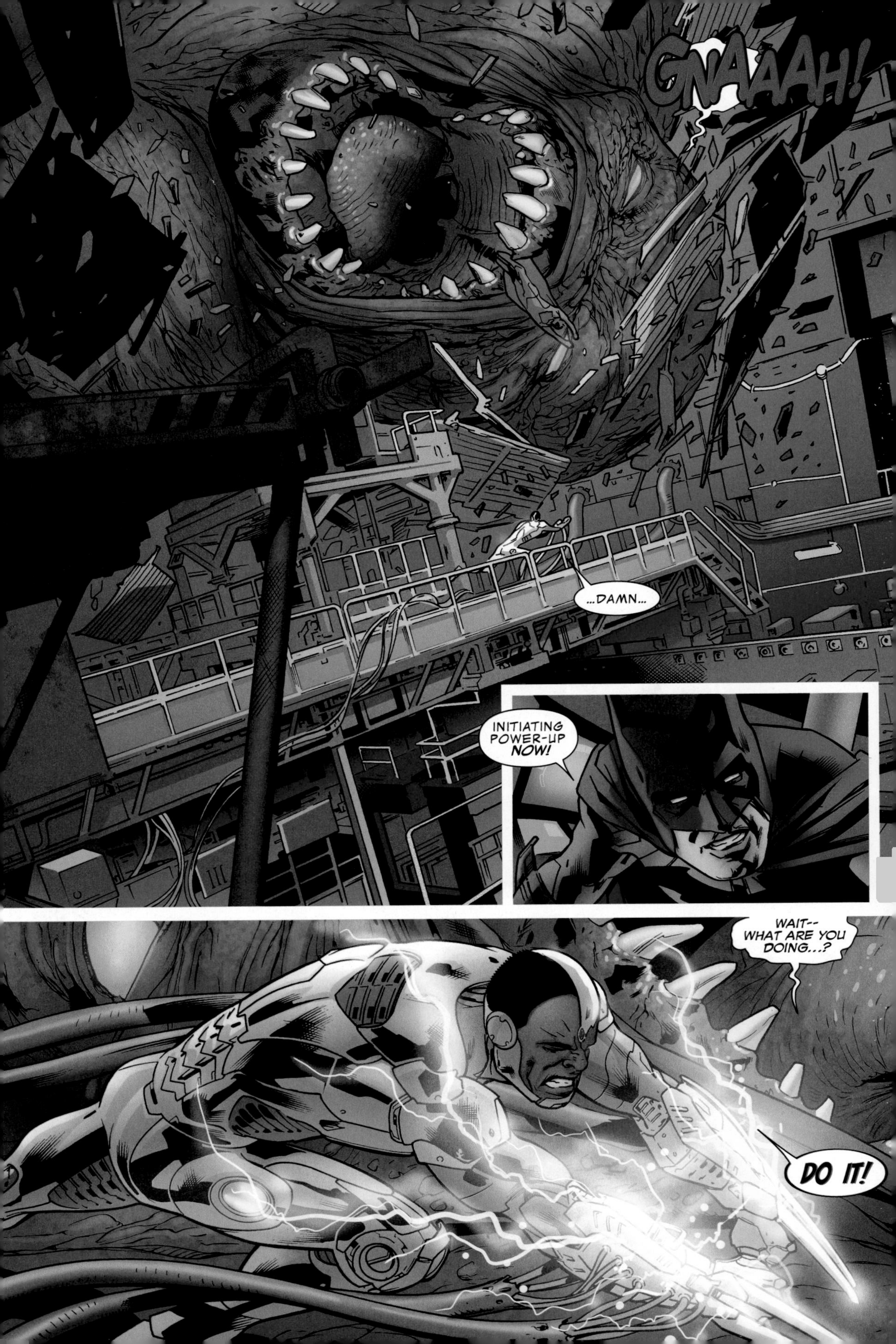
GNAAAH!
...DAMN...
INITIATING POWER-UP NOW!
WAIT-- WHAT ARE YOU DOING...?
DO IT!

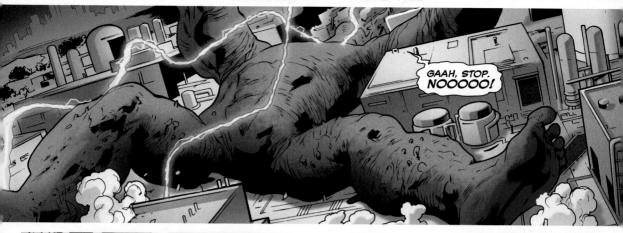

GAAH, STOP. NOOOOO!

SYSTEM'S BLOWING!

VICTOR, YOU'LL HAVE TO HOLD IT TOGETHER!

UNFF!

NOOO. PLEASE!

YOU'RE TAKING ALL THE POWER AWAY!

...AND DUMPING IT ALL INTO THE NATIONAL GRID...

GNAAAAAAHHHH!

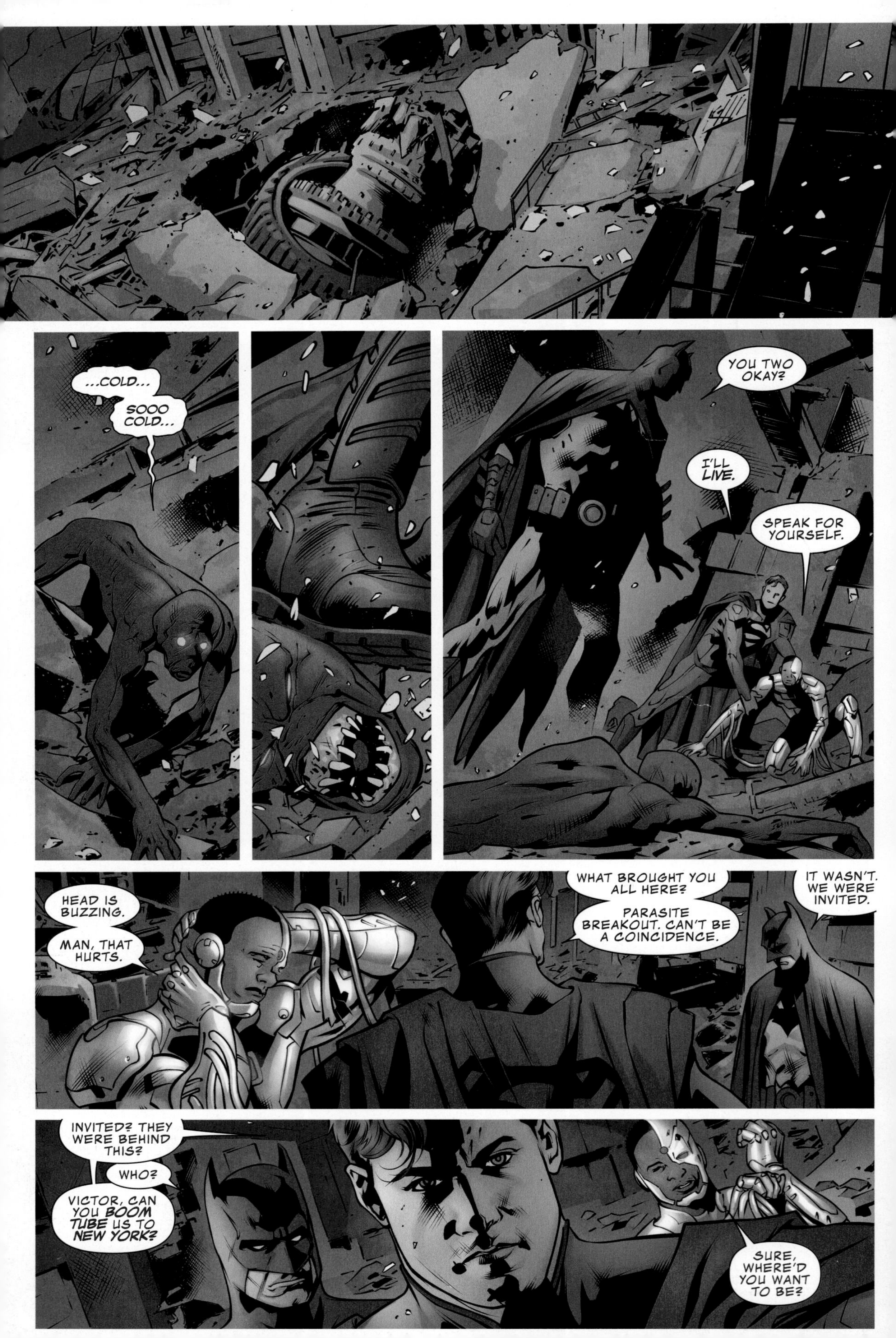
...COLD...
SOOO COLD...
YOU TWO OKAY?
I'LL LIVE.
SPEAK FOR YOURSELF.
HEAD IS BUZZING.
MAN, THAT HURTS.
WHAT BROUGHT YOU ALL HERE?
PARASITE BREAKOUT. CAN'T BE A COINCIDENCE.
IT WASN'T. WE WERE INVITED.
INVITED? THEY WERE BEHIND THIS?
WHO?
VICTOR, CAN YOU BOOM TUBE US TO NEW YORK?
SURE, WHERE'D YOU WANT TO BE?

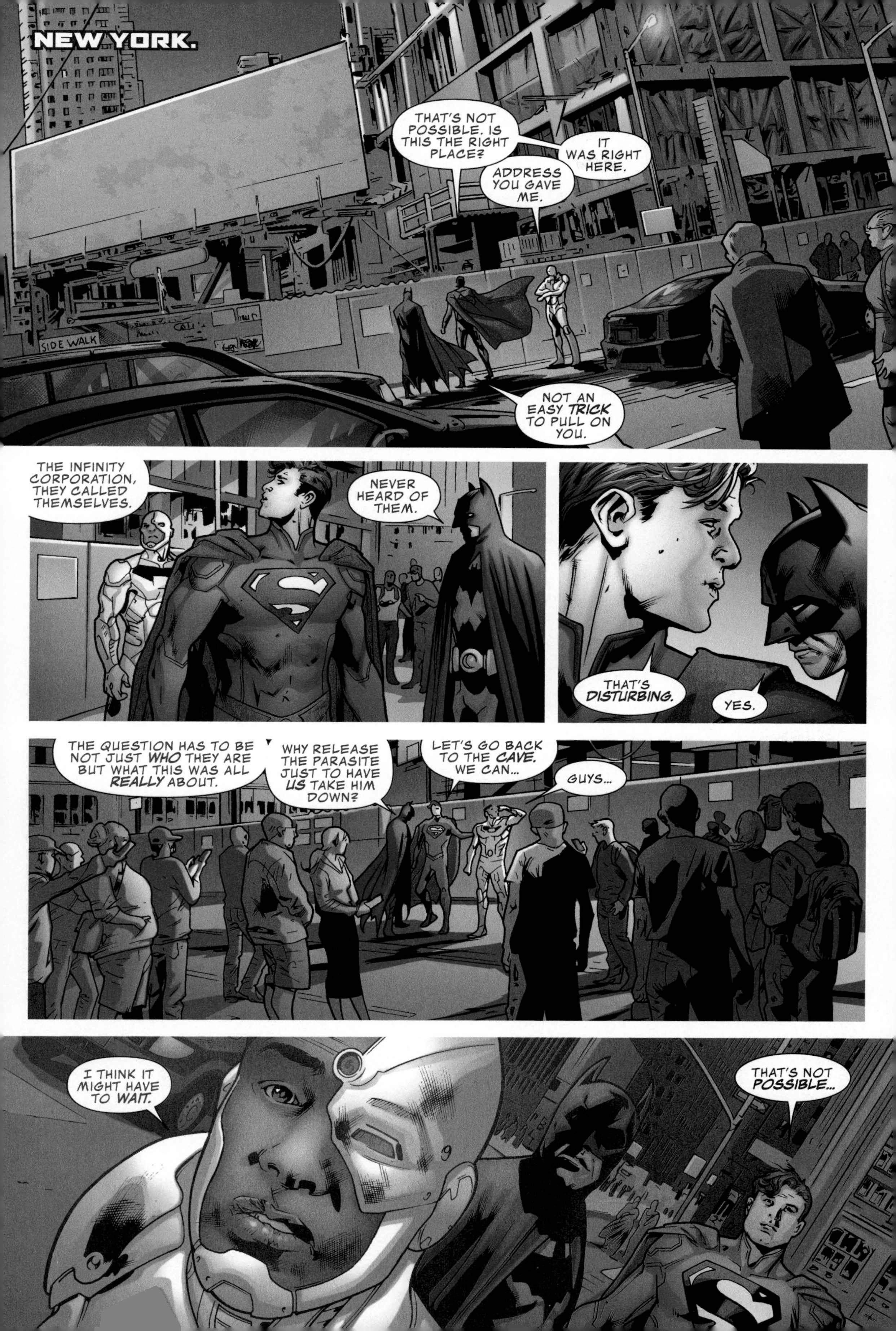
NEW YORK.
THAT'S NOT POSSIBLE. IS THIS THE RIGHT PLACE?
IT WAS RIGHT HERE.
ADDRESS YOU GAVE ME.
SIDE WALK
NOT AN EASY TRICK TO PULL ON YOU.
THE INFINITY CORPORATION, THEY CALLED THEMSELVES.
NEVER HEARD OF THEM.
THAT'S DISTURBING.
YES.
THE QUESTION HAS TO BE NOT JUST WHO THEY ARE BUT WHAT THIS WAS ALL REALLY ABOUT.
WHY RELEASE THE PARASITE JUST TO HAVE US TAKE HIM DOWN?
LET'S GO BACK TO THE CAVE. WE CAN...
GUYS...
I THINK IT MIGHT HAVE TO WAIT.
THAT'S NOT POSSIBLE...

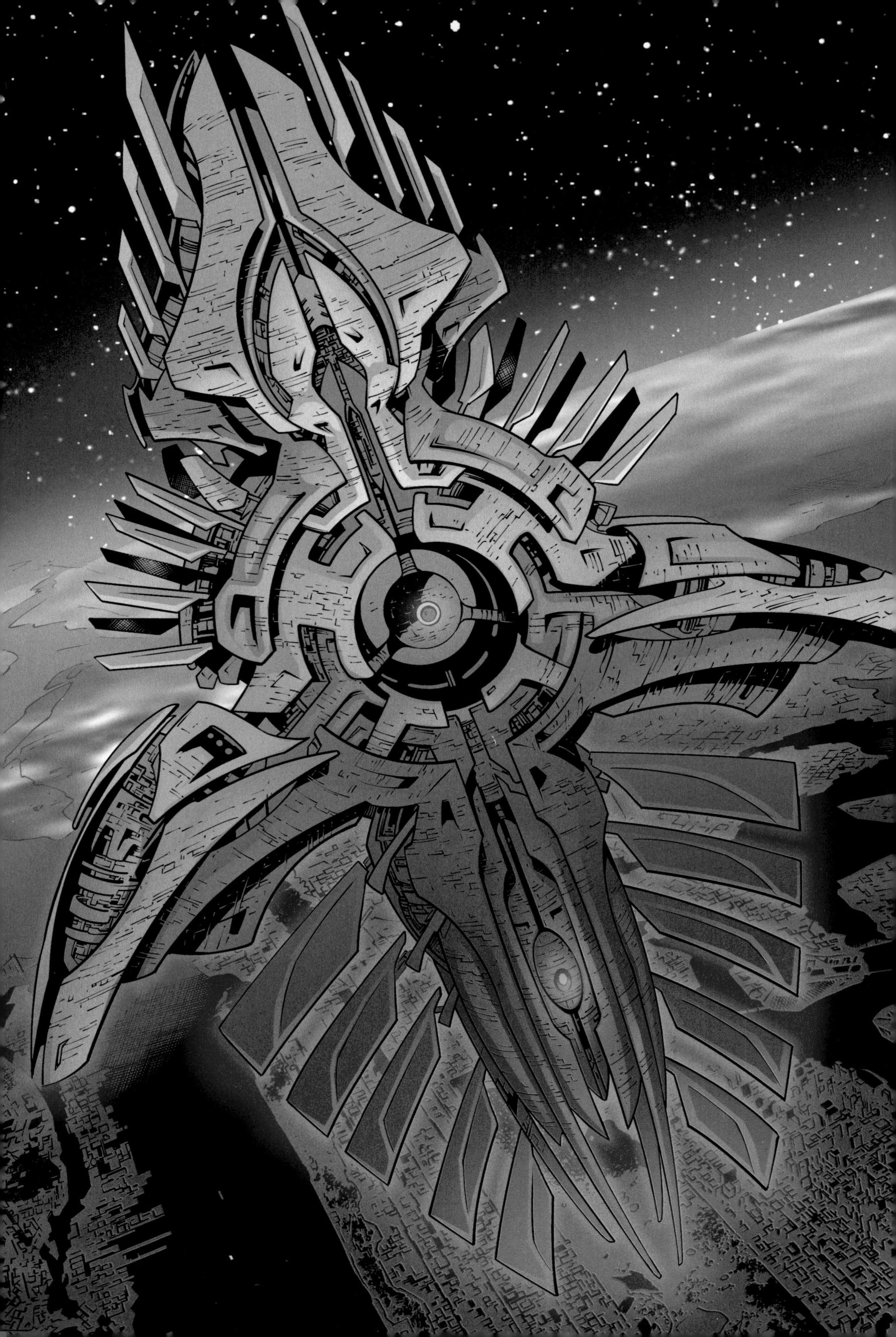

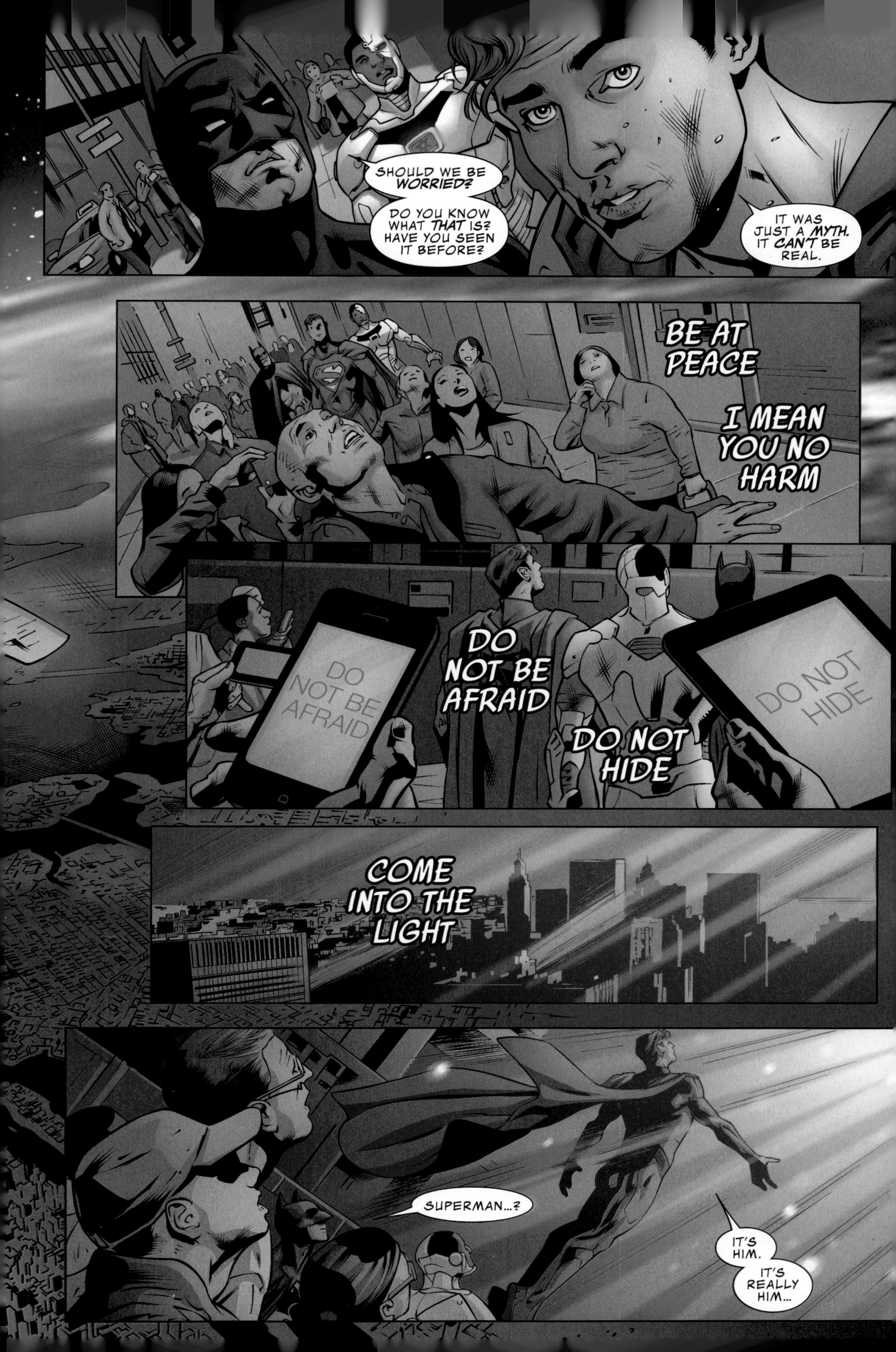

SHOULD WE BE WORRIED?
DO YOU KNOW WHAT THAT IS? HAVE YOU SEEN IT BEFORE?
IT WAS JUST A MYTH. IT CAN'T BE REAL.
BE AT PEACE
I MEAN YOU NO HARM
DO NOT BE AFRAID
DO NOT BE AFRAID
DO NOT HIDE
DO NOT HIDE
COME INTO THE LIGHT
SUPERMAN...?
IT'S HIM.
IT'S REALLY HIM...

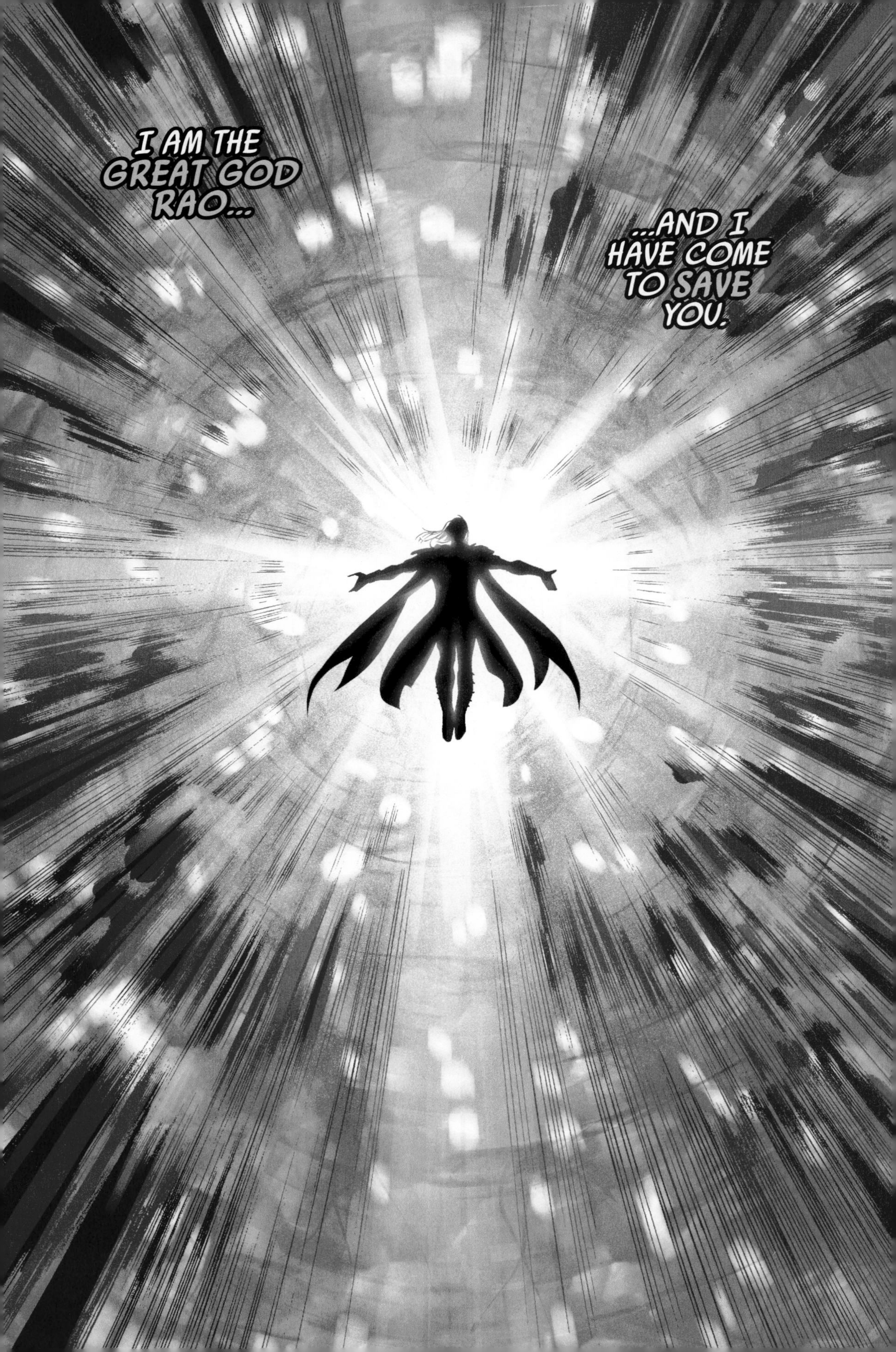
I AM THE GREAT GOD RAO...
...AND I HAVE COME TO SAVE YOU.

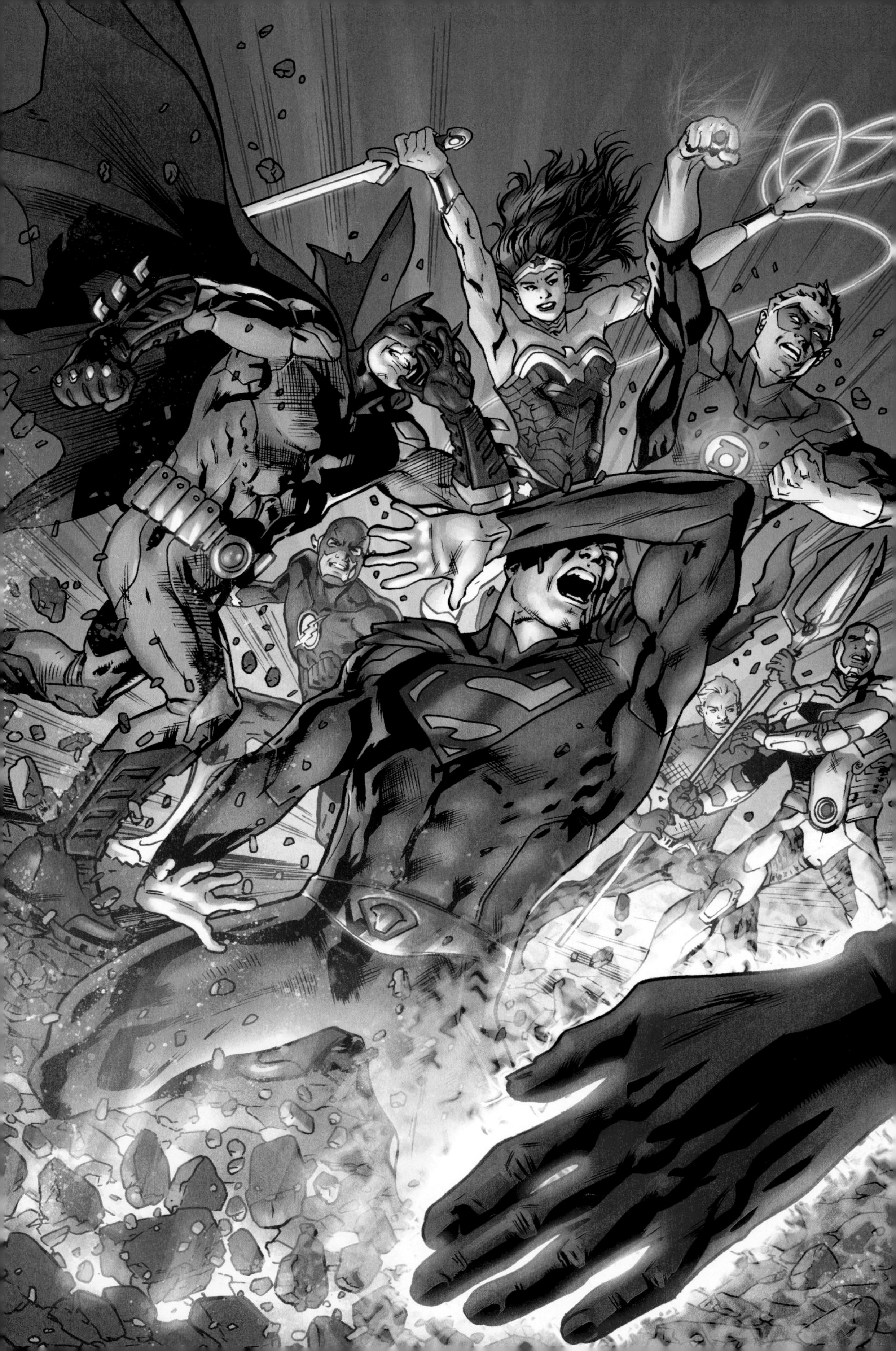

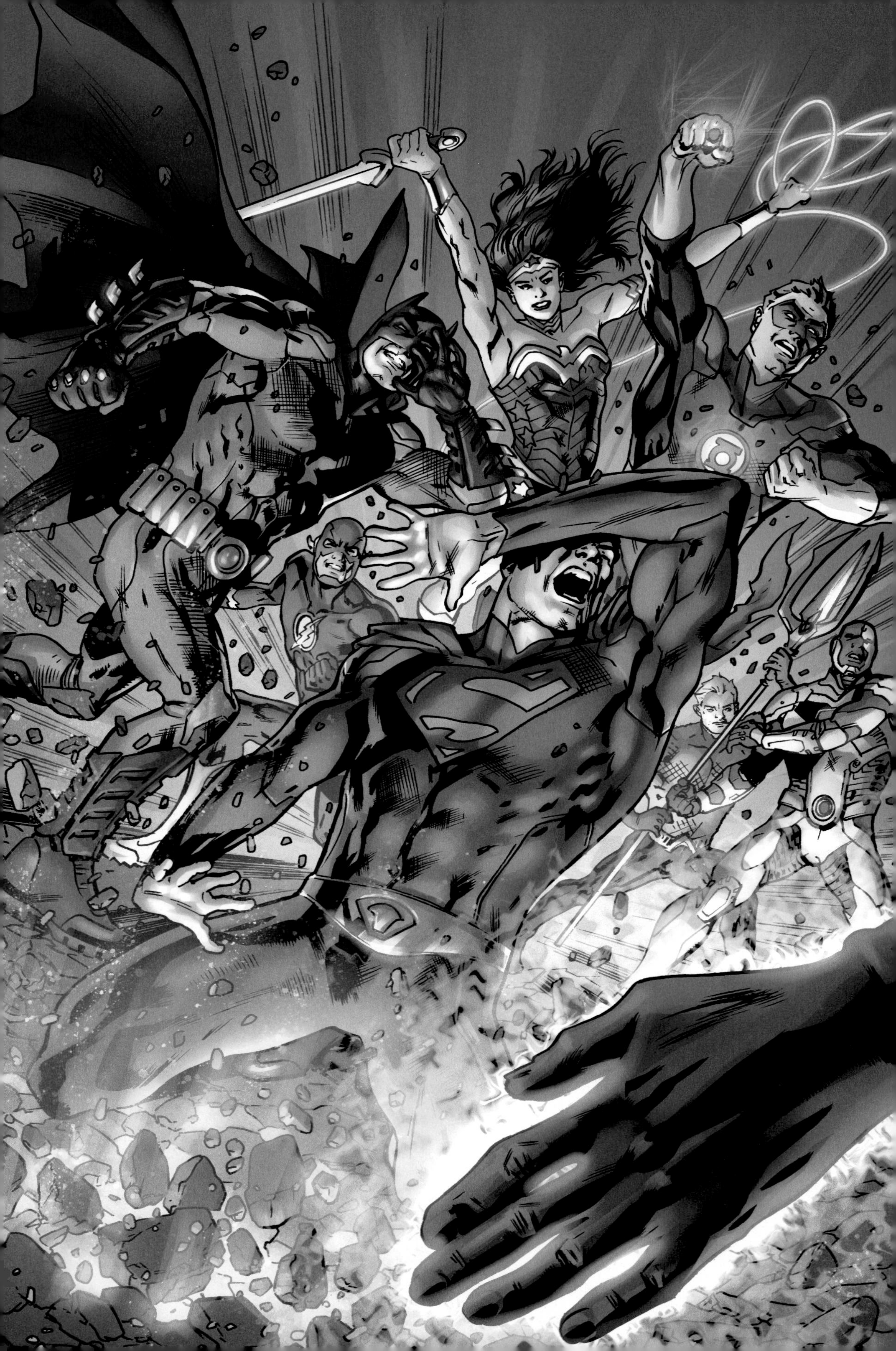

DC COMICS PRESENTS

THE JUSTICE LEAGUE OF AMERICA

POWER AND GLORY

PART TWO

BY **BRYAN HITCH**

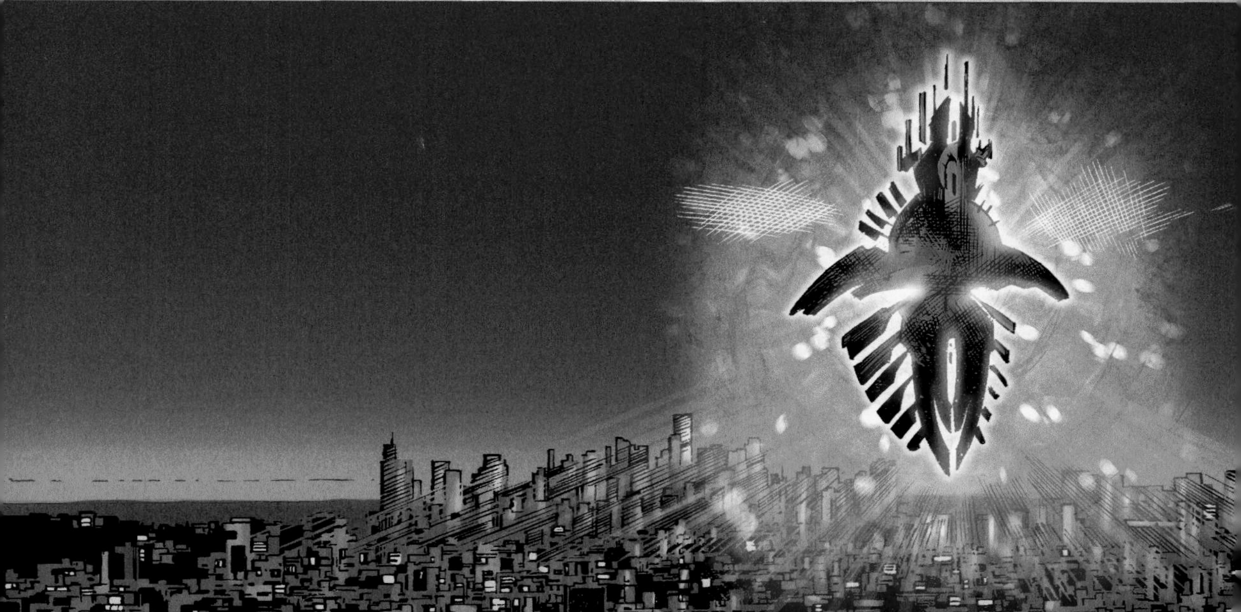

INKS BY **DANIEL HENRIQUES, ANDREW CURRIE & BRYAN HITCH**
COLORS BY **ALEX SINCLAIR**
LETTERS BY **CHRIS ELIOPOULOS**
ASSISTS BY **AMEDEO TURTURRO**
EDITS BY **BRIAN CUNNINGHAM**

COVER BY **BRYAN HITCH** AND **ALEX SINCLAIR**

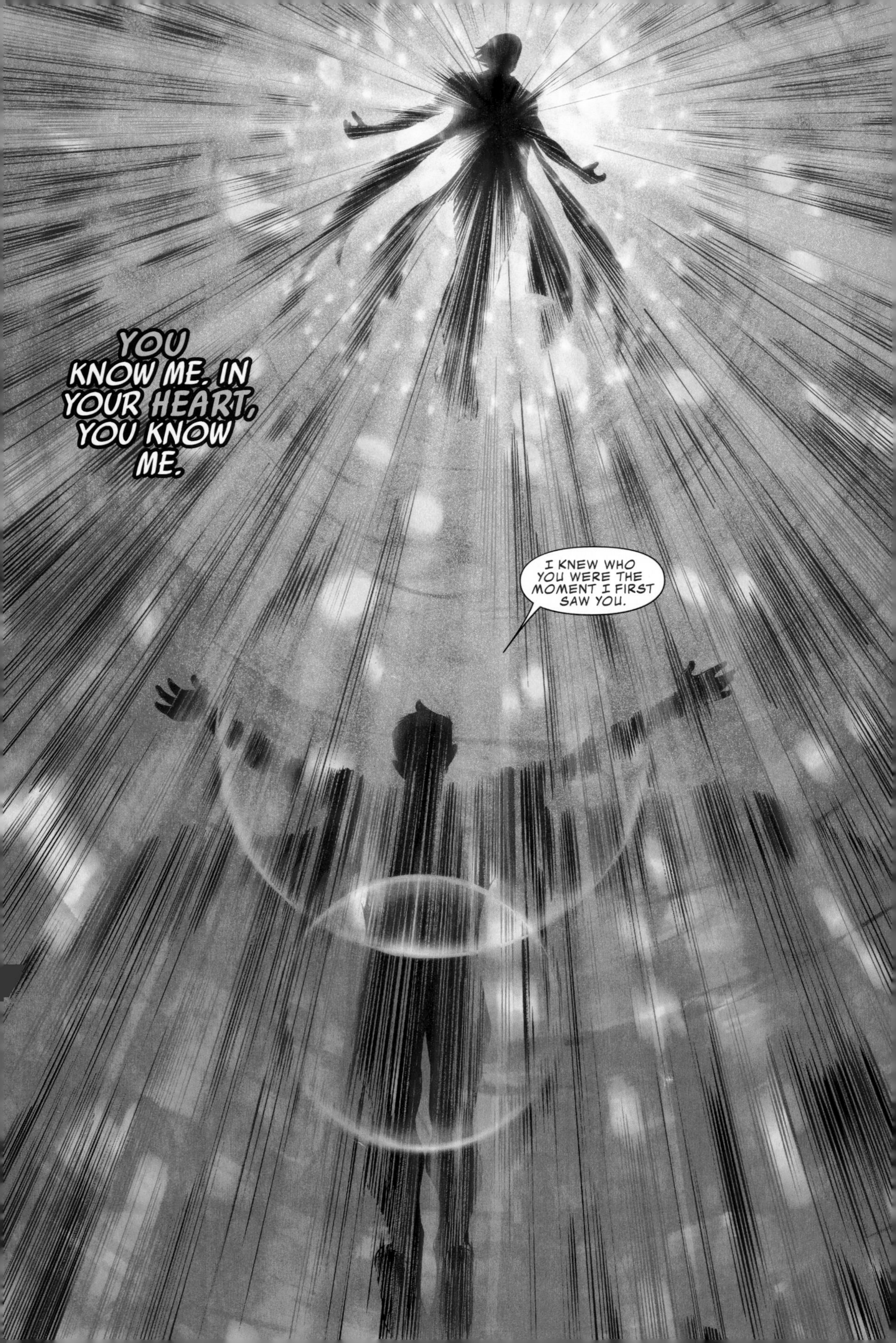
YOU KNOW ME. IN YOUR HEART, YOU KNOW ME.
I KNEW WHO YOU WERE THE MOMENT I FIRST SAW YOU.

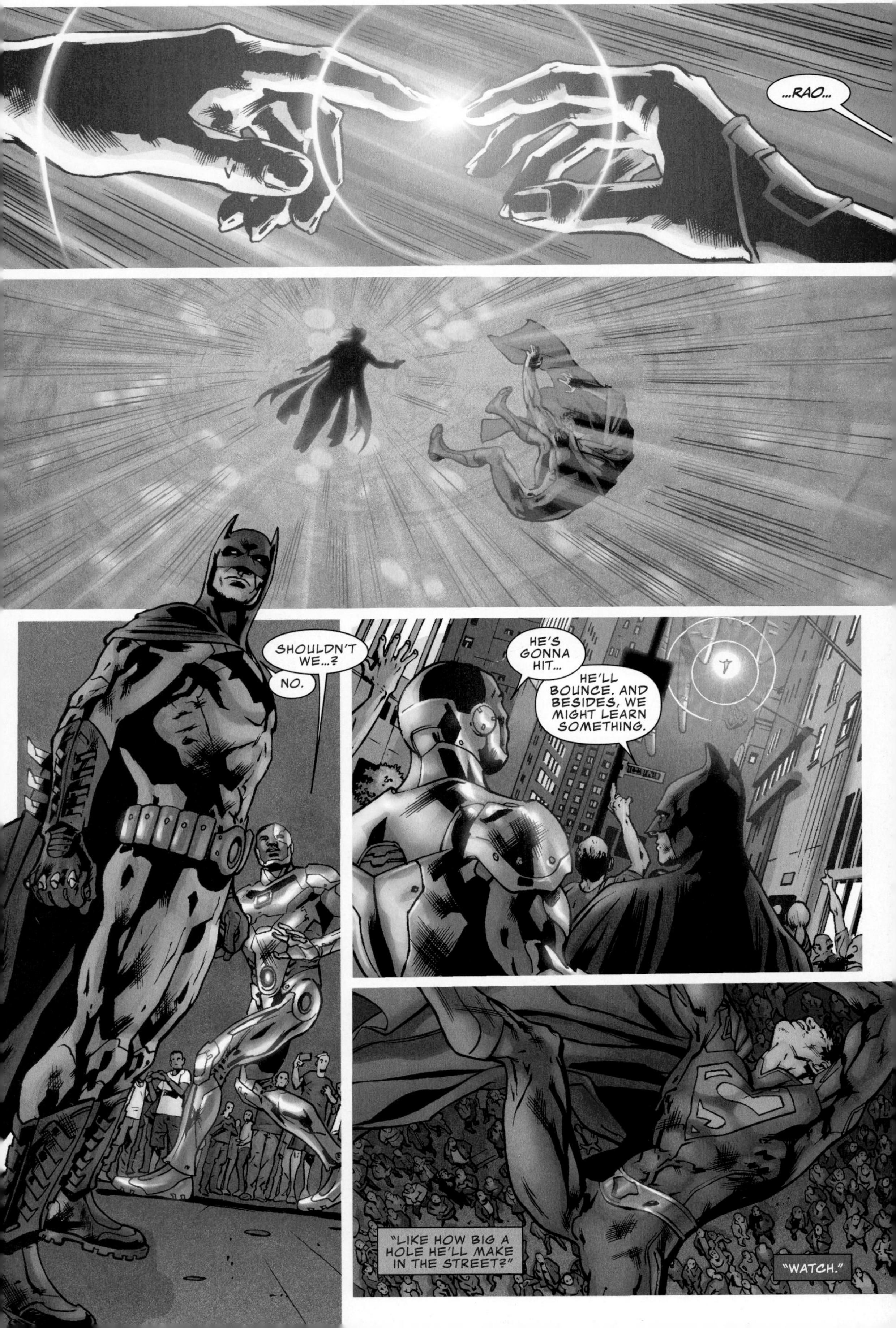
...RAO...
SHOULDN'T WE...?
NO.
HE'S GONNA HIT...
HE'LL BOUNCE. AND BESIDES, WE MIGHT LEARN SOMETHING.
"LIKE HOW BIG A HOLE HE'LL MAKE IN THE STREET?"
"WATCH."

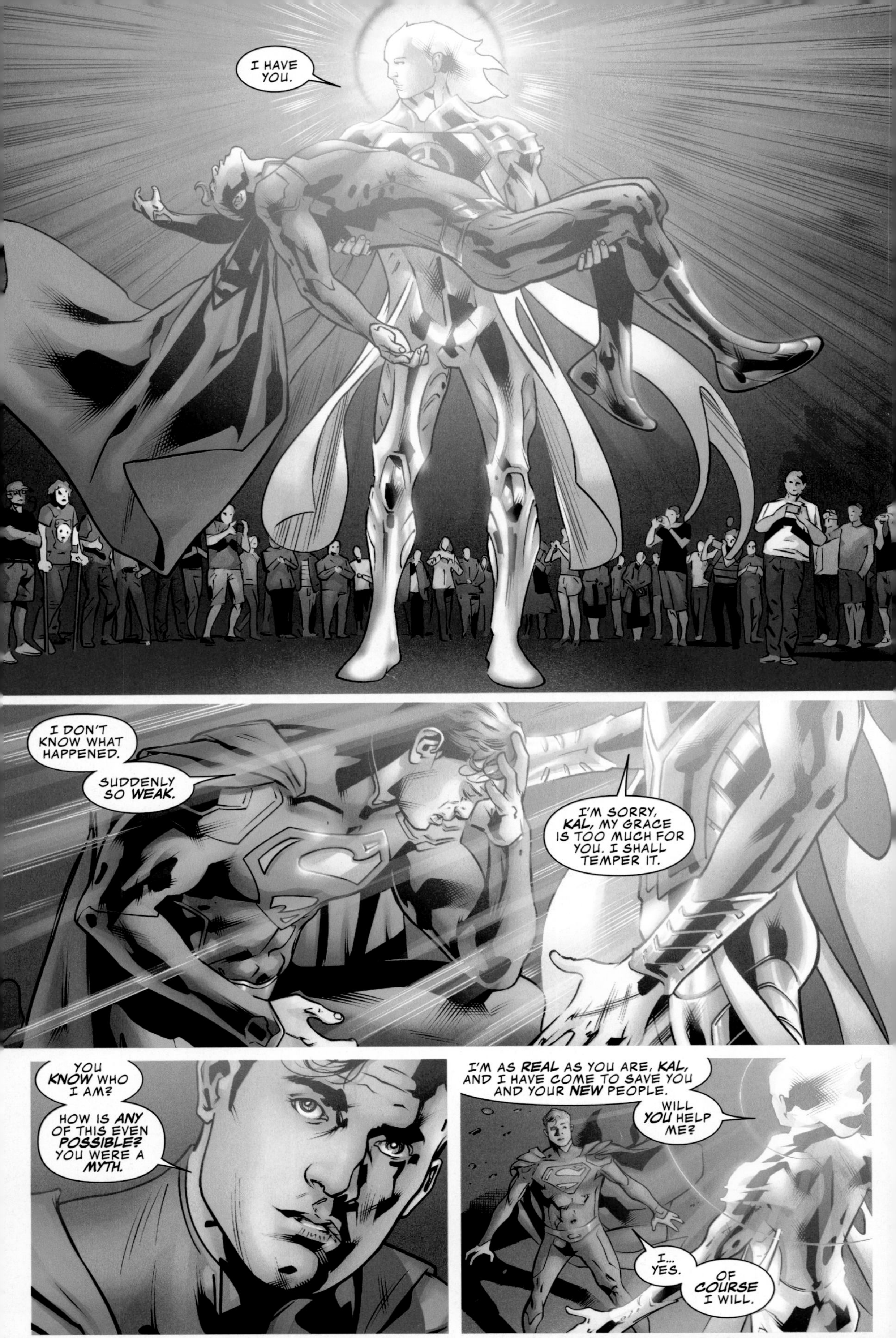
I HAVE YOU.
I DON'T KNOW WHAT HAPPENED.
SUDDENLY SO WEAK.
I'M SORRY, KAL, MY GRACE IS TOO MUCH FOR YOU. I SHALL TEMPER IT.
YOU KNOW WHO I AM?
HOW IS ANY OF THIS EVEN POSSIBLE? YOU WERE A MYTH.
I'M AS REAL AS YOU ARE, KAL, AND I HAVE COME TO SAVE YOU AND YOUR NEW PEOPLE.
WILL YOU HELP ME?
I... YES.
OF COURSE I WILL.

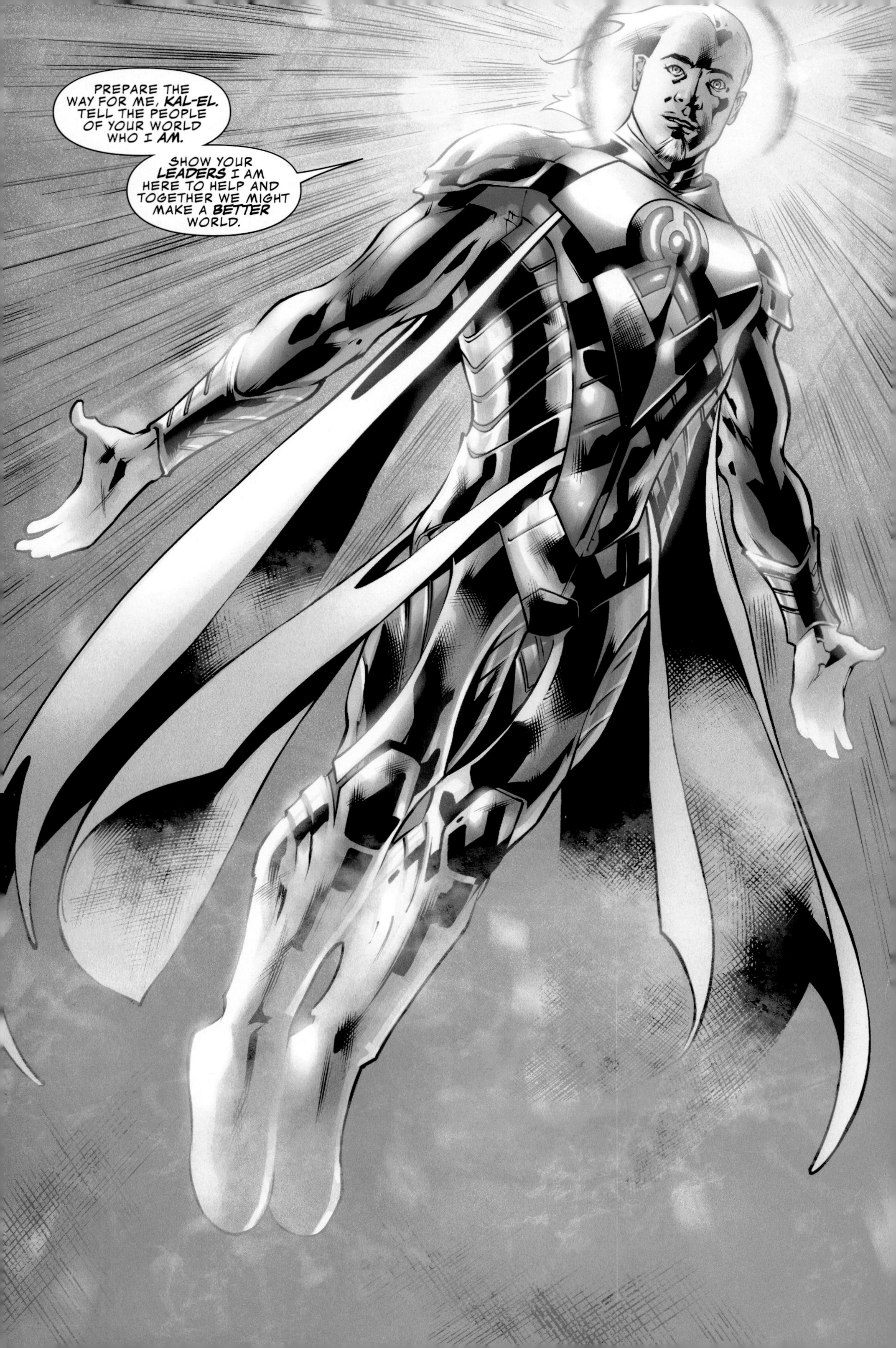
PREPARE THE WAY FOR ME, KAL-EL. TELL THE PEOPLE OF YOUR WORLD WHO I AM.
SHOW YOUR LEADERS I AM HERE TO HELP AND TOGETHER WE MIGHT MAKE A BETTER WORLD.

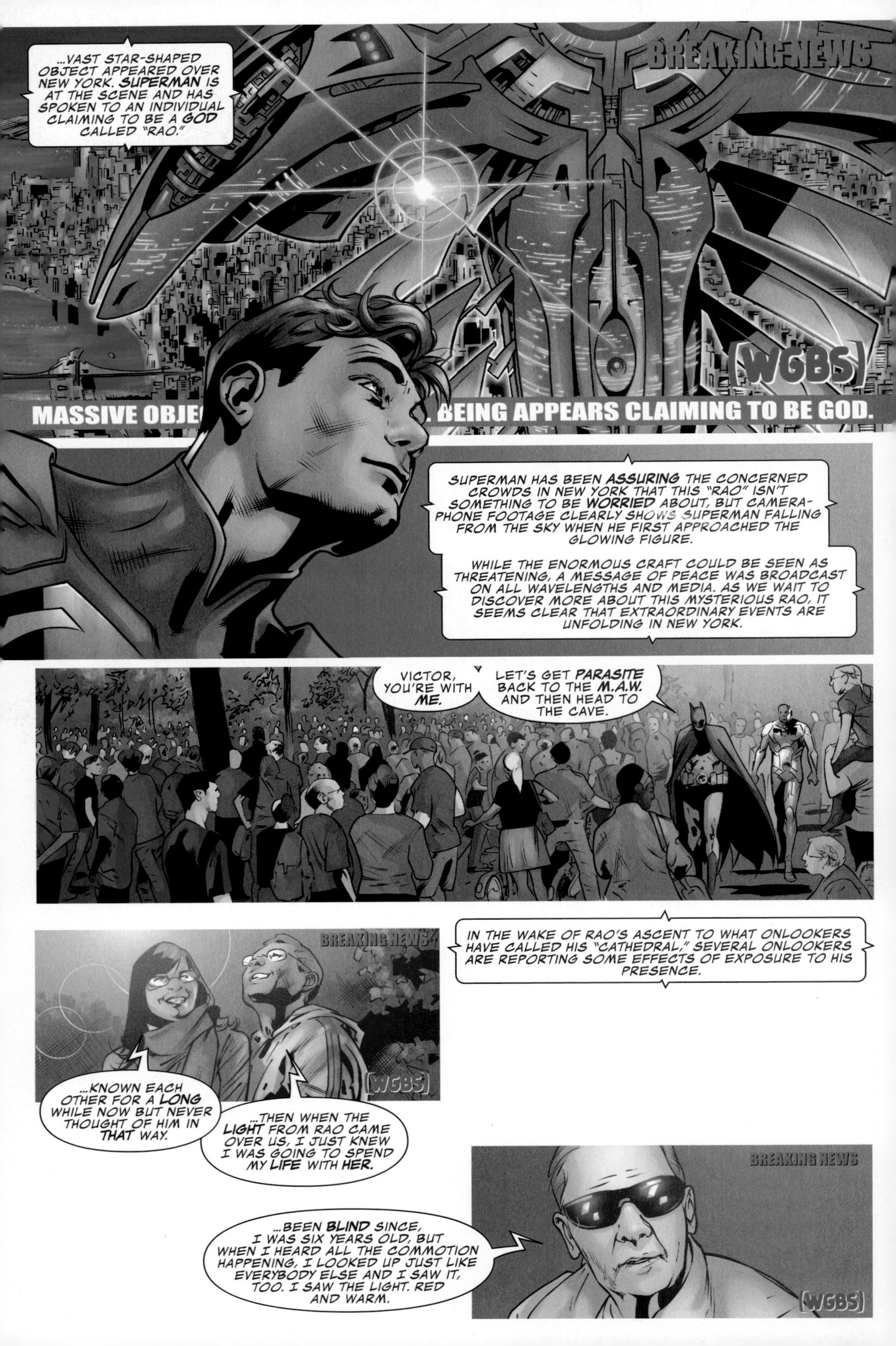
...VAST STAR-SHAPED OBJECT APPEARED OVER NEW YORK. SUPERMAN IS AT THE SCENE AND HAS SPOKEN TO AN INDIVIDUAL CLAIMING TO BE A GOD CALLED "RAO."
BREAKING NEWS
(WGBS)
MASSIVE OBJE... BEING APPEARS CLAIMING TO BE GOD.
SUPERMAN HAS BEEN ASSURING THE CONCERNED CROWDS IN NEW YORK THAT THIS "RAO" ISN'T SOMETHING TO BE WORRIED ABOUT, BUT CAMERA-PHONE FOOTAGE CLEARLY SHOWS SUPERMAN FALLING FROM THE SKY WHEN HE FIRST APPROACHED THE GLOWING FIGURE.
WHILE THE ENORMOUS CRAFT COULD BE SEEN AS THREATENING, A MESSAGE OF PEACE WAS BROADCAST ON ALL WAVELENGTHS AND MEDIA. AS WE WAIT TO DISCOVER MORE ABOUT THIS MYSTERIOUS RAO, IT SEEMS CLEAR THAT EXTRAORDINARY EVENTS ARE UNFOLDING IN NEW YORK.
VICTOR, YOU'RE WITH ME.
LET'S GET PARASITE BACK TO THE M.A.W. AND THEN HEAD TO THE CAVE.
BREAKING NEWS
(WGBS)
IN THE WAKE OF RAO'S ASCENT TO WHAT ONLOOKERS HAVE CALLED HIS "CATHEDRAL," SEVERAL ONLOOKERS ARE REPORTING SOME EFFECTS OF EXPOSURE TO HIS PRESENCE.
...KNOWN EACH OTHER FOR A LONG WHILE NOW BUT NEVER THOUGHT OF HIM IN THAT WAY.
...THEN WHEN THE LIGHT FROM RAO CAME OVER US, I JUST KNEW I WAS GOING TO SPEND MY LIFE WITH HER.
BREAKING NEWS
(WGBS)
...BEEN BLIND SINCE, I WAS SIX YEARS OLD, BUT WHEN I HEARD ALL THE COMMOTION HAPPENING, I LOOKED UP JUST LIKE EVERYBODY ELSE AND I SAW IT, TOO. I SAW THE LIGHT. RED AND WARM.

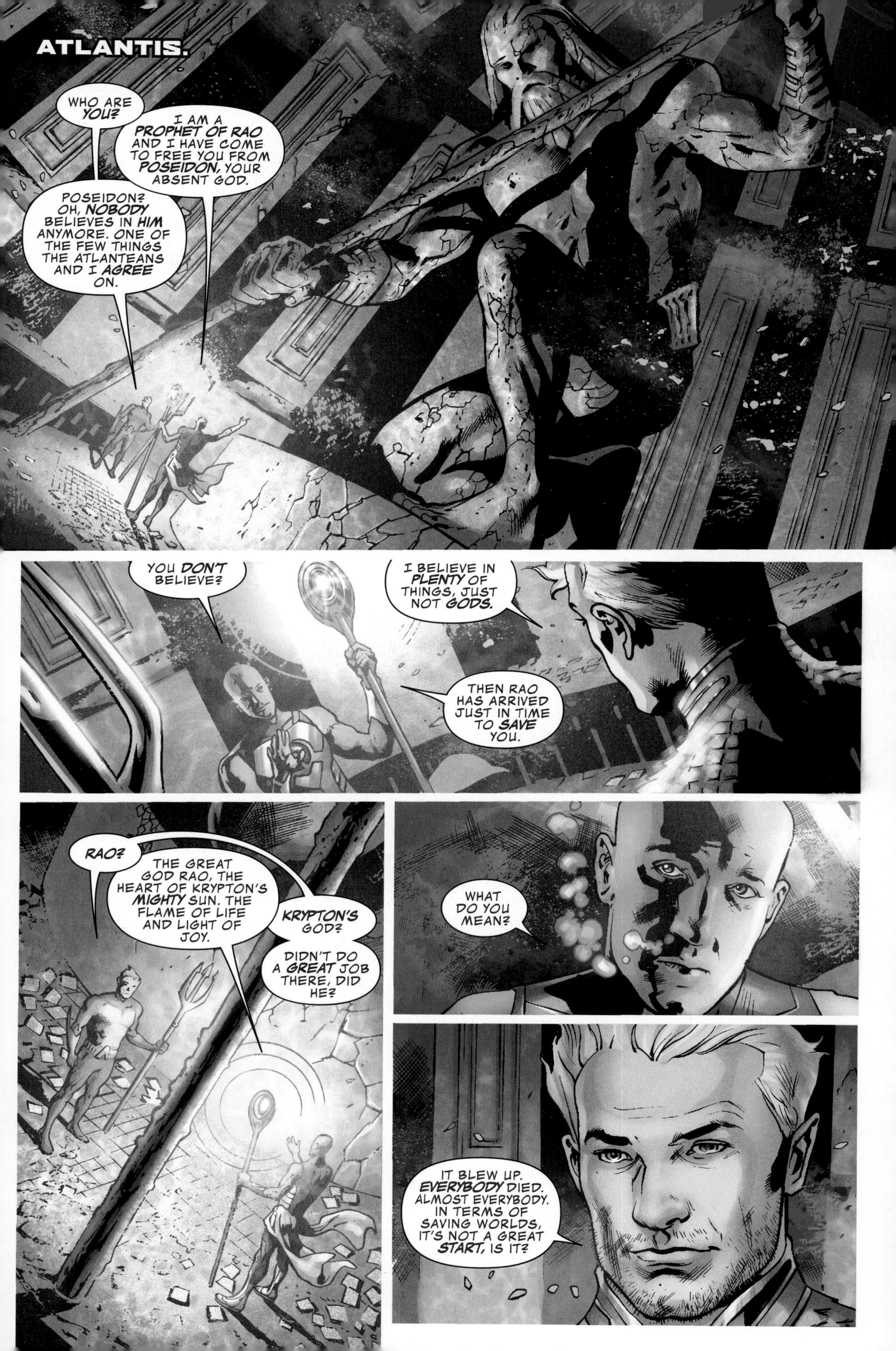
ATLANTIS.
WHO ARE YOU?
I AM A PROPHET OF RAO AND I HAVE COME TO FREE YOU FROM POSEIDON, YOUR ABSENT GOD.
POSEIDON? OH, NOBODY BELIEVES IN HIM ANYMORE. ONE OF THE FEW THINGS THE ATLANTEANS AND I AGREE ON.
YOU DON'T BELIEVE?
I BELIEVE IN PLENTY OF THINGS, JUST NOT GODS.
THEN RAO HAS ARRIVED JUST IN TIME TO SAVE YOU.
RAO?
THE GREAT GOD RAO, THE HEART OF KRYPTON'S MIGHTY SUN. THE FLAME OF LIFE AND LIGHT OF JOY.
KRYPTON'S GOD?
DIDN'T DO A GREAT JOB THERE, DID HE?
WHAT DO YOU MEAN?
IT BLEW UP. EVERYBODY DIED. ALMOST EVERYBODY. IN TERMS OF SAVING WORLDS, IT'S NOT A GREAT START, IS IT?

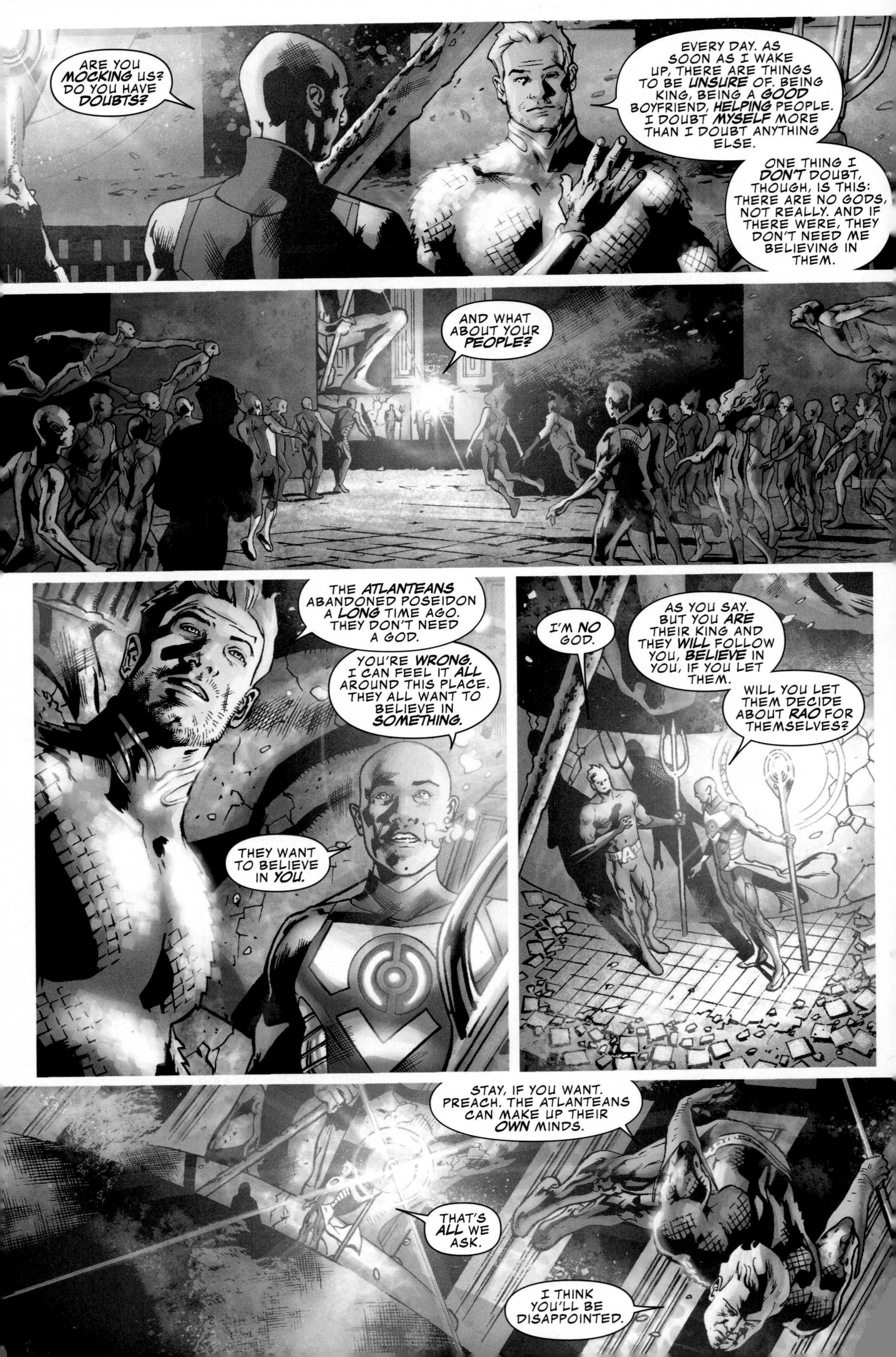
ARE YOU MOCKING US? DO YOU HAVE DOUBTS?
EVERY DAY. AS SOON AS I WAKE UP, THERE ARE THINGS TO BE UNSURE OF. BEING KING, BEING A GOOD BOYFRIEND, HELPING PEOPLE. I DOUBT MYSELF MORE THAN I DOUBT ANYTHING ELSE.
ONE THING I DON'T DOUBT, THOUGH, IS THIS: THERE ARE NO GODS, NOT REALLY. AND IF THERE WERE, THEY DON'T NEED ME BELIEVING IN THEM.
AND WHAT ABOUT YOUR PEOPLE?
THE ATLANTEANS ABANDONED POSEIDON A LONG TIME AGO. THEY DON'T NEED A GOD.
YOU'RE WRONG. I CAN FEEL IT ALL AROUND THIS PLACE. THEY ALL WANT TO BELIEVE IN SOMETHING.
THEY WANT TO BELIEVE IN YOU.
I'M NO GOD.
AS YOU SAY. BUT YOU ARE THEIR KING AND THEY WILL FOLLOW YOU, BELIEVE IN YOU, IF YOU LET THEM.
WILL YOU LET THEM DECIDE ABOUT RAO FOR THEMSELVES?
STAY, IF YOU WANT. PREACH. THE ATLANTEANS CAN MAKE UP THEIR OWN MINDS.
THAT'S ALL WE ASK.
I THINK YOU'LL BE DISAPPOINTED.

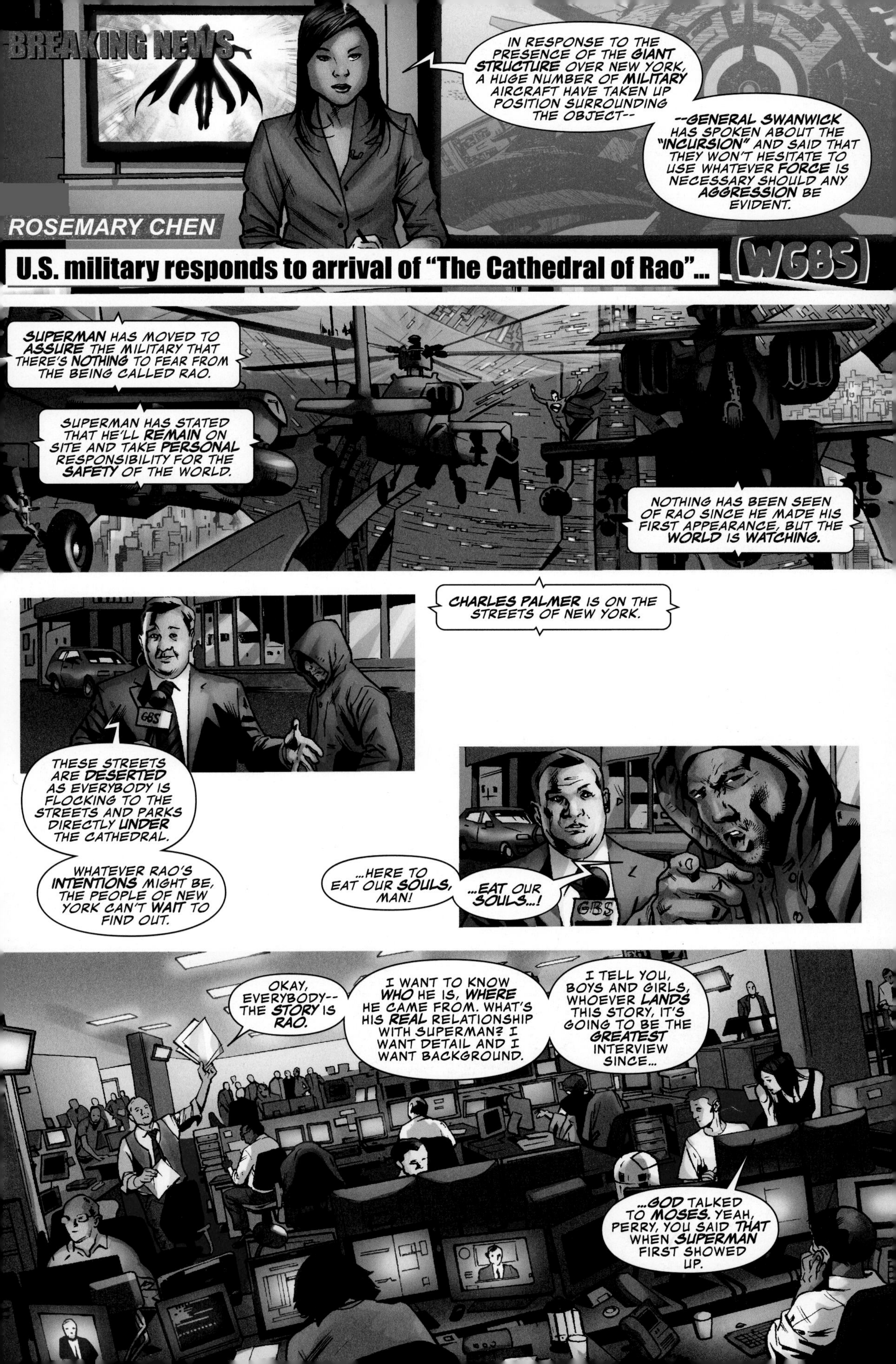
BREAKING NEWS
IN RESPONSE TO THE PRESENCE OF THE GIANT STRUCTURE OVER NEW YORK, A HUGE NUMBER OF MILITARY AIRCRAFT HAVE TAKEN UP POSITION SURROUNDING THE OBJECT--
--GENERAL SWANWICK HAS SPOKEN ABOUT THE "INCURSION" AND SAID THAT THEY WON'T HESITATE TO USE WHATEVER FORCE IS NECESSARY SHOULD ANY AGGRESSION BE EVIDENT.
ROSEMARY CHEN
U.S. military responds to arrival of "The Cathedral of Rao"...
WGBS
SUPERMAN HAS MOVED TO ASSURE THE MILITARY THAT THERE'S NOTHING TO FEAR FROM THE BEING CALLED RAO.
SUPERMAN HAS STATED THAT HE'LL REMAIN ON SITE AND TAKE PERSONAL RESPONSIBILITY FOR THE SAFETY OF THE WORLD.
NOTHING HAS BEEN SEEN OF RAO SINCE HE MADE HIS FIRST APPEARANCE, BUT THE WORLD IS WATCHING.
CHARLES PALMER IS ON THE STREETS OF NEW YORK.
GBS
THESE STREETS ARE DESERTED AS EVERYBODY IS FLOCKING TO THE STREETS AND PARKS DIRECTLY UNDER THE CATHEDRAL.
WHATEVER RAO'S INTENTIONS MIGHT BE, THE PEOPLE OF NEW YORK CAN'T WAIT TO FIND OUT.
...HERE TO EAT OUR SOULS, MAN!
...EAT OUR SOULS...!
GBS
OKAY, EVERYBODY-- THE STORY IS RAO.
I WANT TO KNOW WHO HE IS, WHERE HE CAME FROM. WHAT'S HIS REAL RELATIONSHIP WITH SUPERMAN? I WANT DETAIL AND I WANT BACKGROUND.
I TELL YOU, BOYS AND GIRLS, WHOEVER LANDS THIS STORY, IT'S GOING TO BE THE GREATEST INTERVIEW SINCE...
...GOD TALKED TO MOSES. YEAH, PERRY, YOU SAID THAT WHEN SUPERMAN FIRST SHOWED UP.

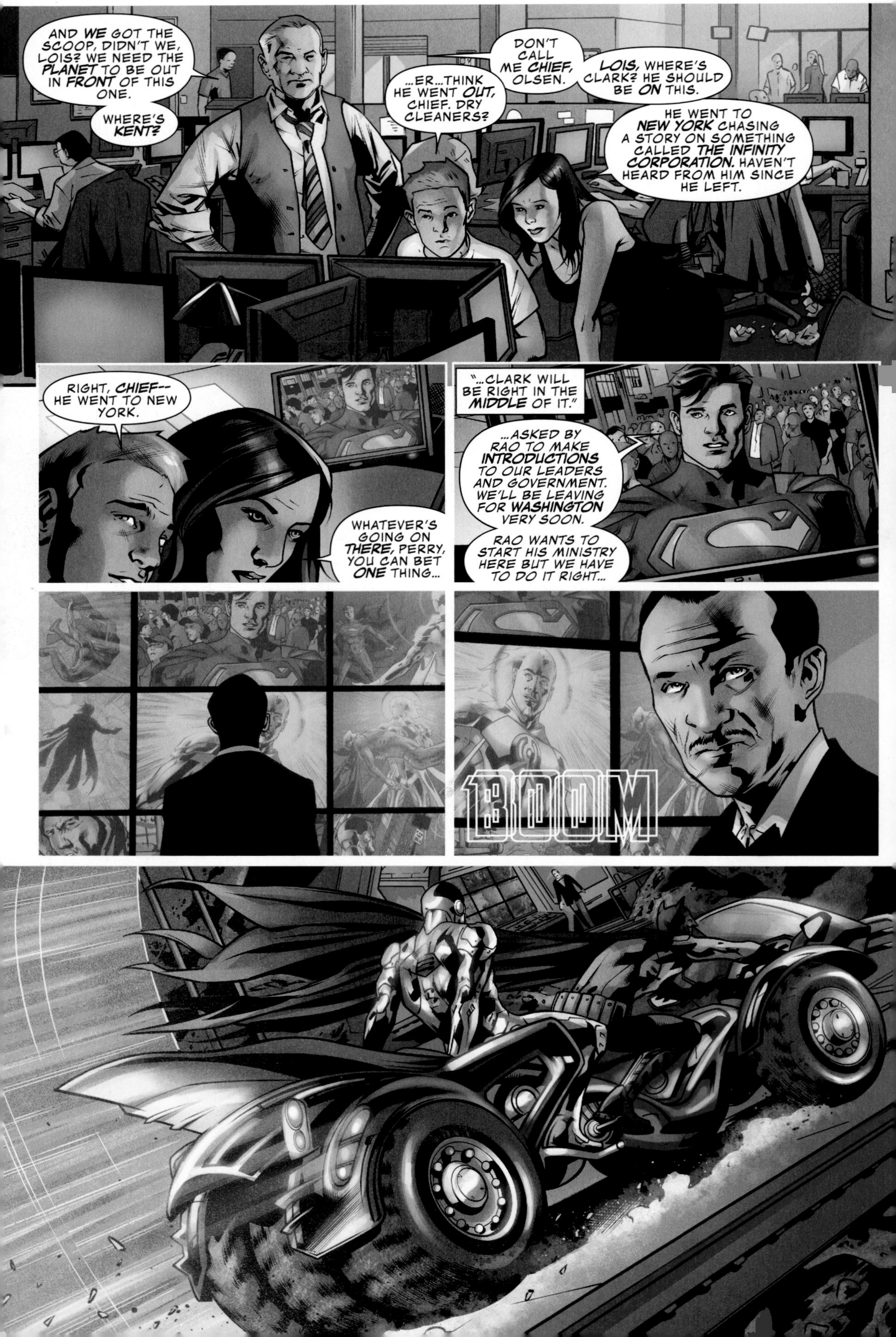

AND WE GOT THE SCOOP, DIDN'T WE, LOIS? WE NEED THE PLANET TO BE OUT IN FRONT OF THIS ONE.
WHERE'S KENT?
...ER...THINK HE WENT OUT, CHIEF. DRY CLEANERS?
DON'T CALL ME CHIEF, OLSEN.
LOIS, WHERE'S CLARK? HE SHOULD BE ON THIS.
HE WENT TO NEW YORK CHASING A STORY ON SOMETHING CALLED THE INFINITY CORPORATION. HAVEN'T HEARD FROM HIM SINCE HE LEFT.
RIGHT, CHIEF-- HE WENT TO NEW YORK.
WHATEVER'S GOING ON THERE, PERRY, YOU CAN BET ONE THING...
"...CLARK WILL BE RIGHT IN THE MIDDLE OF IT."
...ASKED BY RAO TO MAKE INTRODUCTIONS TO OUR LEADERS AND GOVERNMENT. WE'LL BE LEAVING FOR WASHINGTON VERY SOON.
RAO WANTS TO START HIS MINISTRY HERE BUT WE HAVE TO DO IT RIGHT...
BOOM

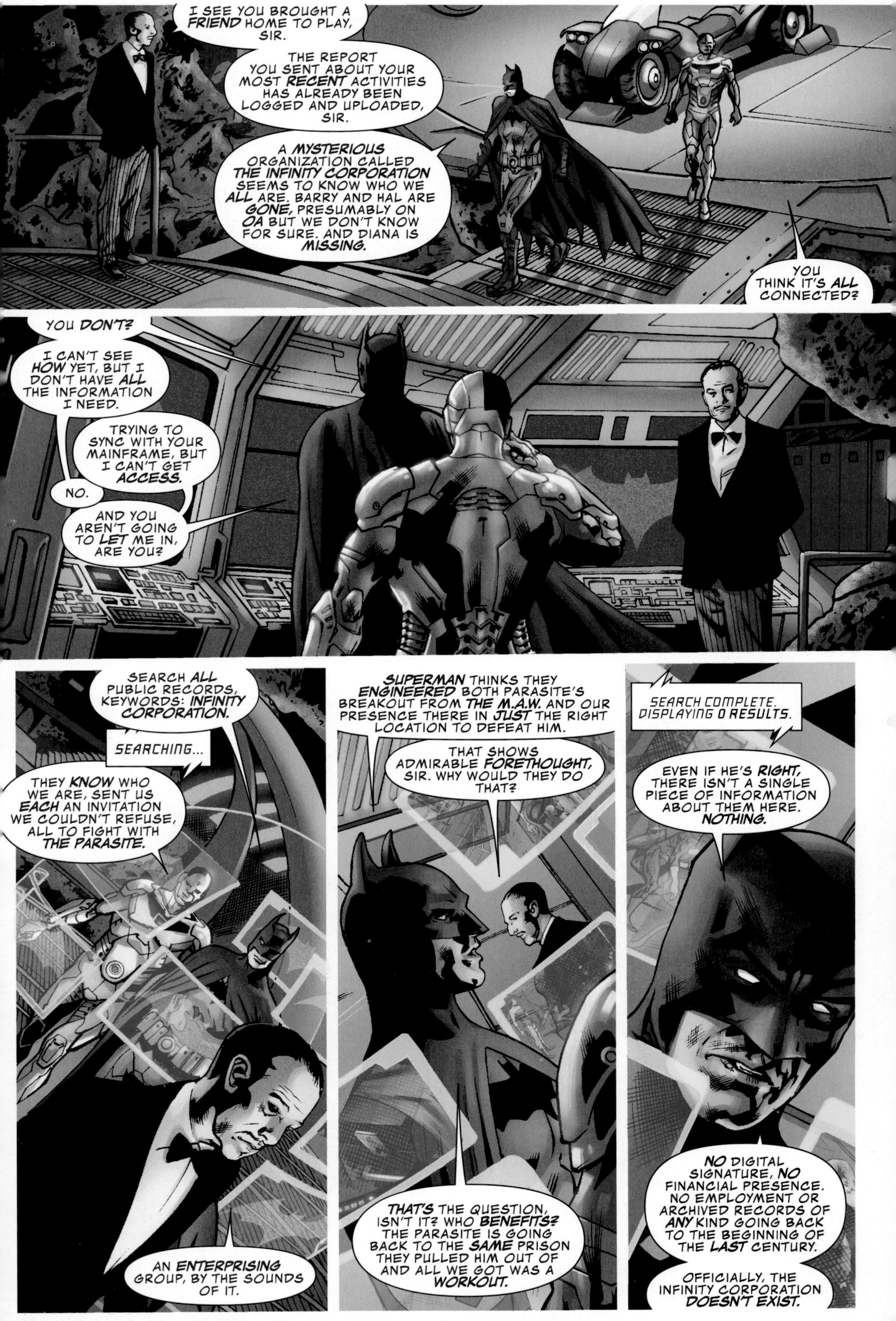

I SEE YOU BROUGHT A FRIEND HOME TO PLAY, SIR.
THE REPORT YOU SENT ABOUT YOUR MOST RECENT ACTIVITIES HAS ALREADY BEEN LOGGED AND UPLOADED, SIR.
A MYSTERIOUS ORGANIZATION CALLED THE INFINITY CORPORATION SEEMS TO KNOW WHO WE ALL ARE. BARRY AND HAL ARE GONE, PRESUMABLY ON OA BUT WE DON'T KNOW FOR SURE. AND DIANA IS MISSING.
YOU THINK IT'S ALL CONNECTED?
YOU DON'T?
I CAN'T SEE HOW YET, BUT I DON'T HAVE ALL THE INFORMATION I NEED.
TRYING TO SYNC WITH YOUR MAINFRAME, BUT I CAN'T GET ACCESS.
NO.
AND YOU AREN'T GOING TO LET ME IN, ARE YOU?
SEARCH ALL PUBLIC RECORDS, KEYWORDS: INFINITY CORPORATION.
SEARCHING...
THEY KNOW WHO WE ARE, SENT US EACH AN INVITATION WE COULDN'T REFUSE, ALL TO FIGHT WITH THE PARASITE.
AN ENTERPRISING GROUP, BY THE SOUNDS OF IT.
SUPERMAN THINKS THEY ENGINEERED BOTH PARASITE'S BREAKOUT FROM THE M.A.W. AND OUR PRESENCE THERE IN JUST THE RIGHT LOCATION TO DEFEAT HIM.
THAT SHOWS ADMIRABLE FORETHOUGHT, SIR. WHY WOULD THEY DO THAT?
THAT'S THE QUESTION, ISN'T IT? WHO BENEFITS? THE PARASITE IS GOING BACK TO THE SAME PRISON THEY PULLED HIM OUT OF AND ALL WE GOT WAS A WORKOUT.
SEARCH COMPLETE. DISPLAYING 0 RESULTS.
EVEN IF HE'S RIGHT, THERE ISN'T A SINGLE PIECE OF INFORMATION ABOUT THEM HERE. NOTHING.
NO DIGITAL SIGNATURE, NO FINANCIAL PRESENCE. NO EMPLOYMENT OR ARCHIVED RECORDS OF ANY KIND GOING BACK TO THE BEGINNING OF THE LAST CENTURY.
OFFICIALLY, THE INFINITY CORPORATION DOESN'T EXIST.

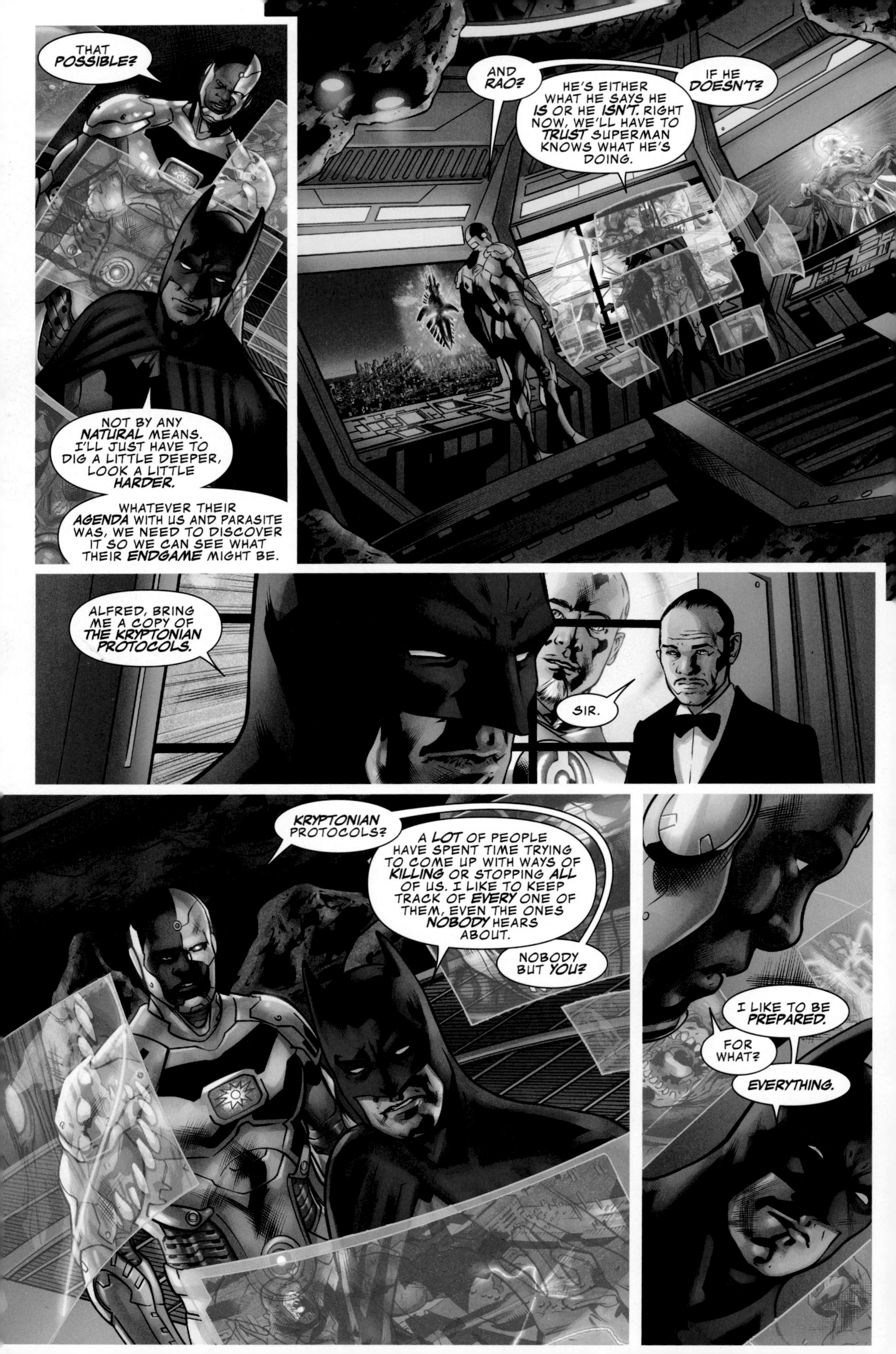

THAT POSSIBLE?
NOT BY ANY NATURAL MEANS. I'LL JUST HAVE TO DIG A LITTLE DEEPER, LOOK A LITTLE HARDER.
WHATEVER THEIR AGENDA WITH US AND PARASITE WAS, WE NEED TO DISCOVER IT SO WE CAN SEE WHAT THEIR ENDGAME MIGHT BE.
AND RAO?
HE'S EITHER WHAT HE SAYS HE IS OR HE ISN'T. RIGHT NOW, WE'LL HAVE TO TRUST SUPERMAN KNOWS WHAT HE'S DOING.
IF HE DOESN'T?
ALFRED, BRING ME A COPY OF THE KRYPTONIAN PROTOCOLS.
SIR.
KRYPTONIAN PROTOCOLS?
A LOT OF PEOPLE HAVE SPENT TIME TRYING TO COME UP WITH WAYS OF KILLING OR STOPPING ALL OF US. I LIKE TO KEEP TRACK OF EVERY ONE OF THEM, EVEN THE ONES NOBODY HEARS ABOUT.
NOBODY BUT YOU?
I LIKE TO BE PREPARED.
FOR WHAT?
EVERYTHING.

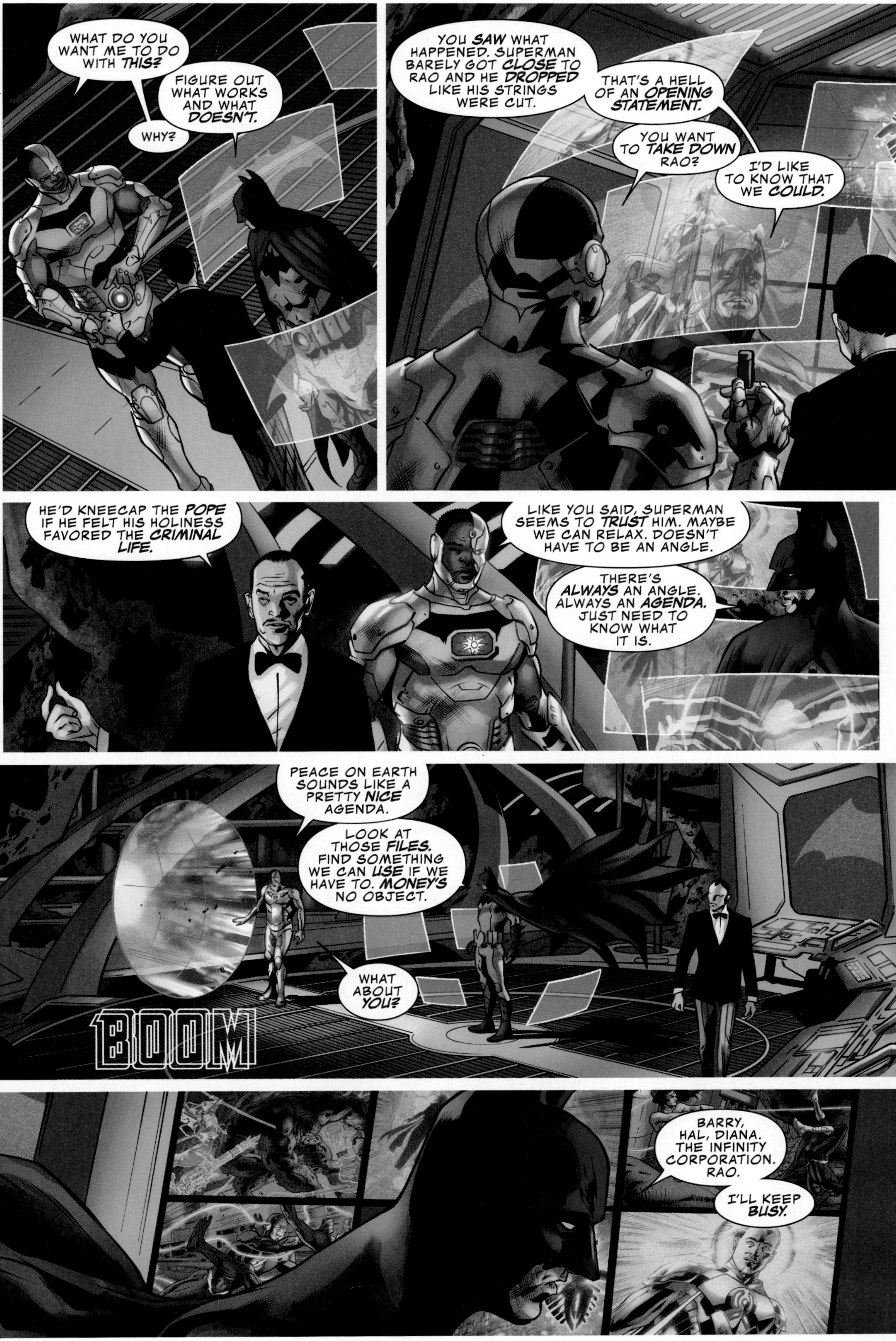
WHAT DO YOU WANT ME TO DO WITH THIS?
FIGURE OUT WHAT WORKS AND WHAT DOESN'T.
WHY?
YOU SAW WHAT HAPPENED. SUPERMAN BARELY GOT CLOSE TO RAO AND HE DROPPED LIKE HIS STRINGS WERE CUT.
THAT'S A HELL OF AN OPENING STATEMENT.
YOU WANT TO TAKE DOWN RAO?
I'D LIKE TO KNOW THAT WE COULD.
HE'D KNEECAP THE POPE IF HE FELT HIS HOLINESS FAVORED THE CRIMINAL LIFE.
LIKE YOU SAID, SUPERMAN SEEMS TO TRUST HIM. MAYBE WE CAN RELAX. DOESN'T HAVE TO BE AN ANGLE.
THERE'S ALWAYS AN ANGLE. ALWAYS AN AGENDA. JUST NEED TO KNOW WHAT IT IS.
PEACE ON EARTH SOUNDS LIKE A PRETTY NICE AGENDA.
LOOK AT THOSE FILES. FIND SOMETHING WE CAN USE IF WE HAVE TO. MONEY'S NO OBJECT.
WHAT ABOUT YOU?
BOOM
BARRY, HAL, DIANA. THE INFINITY CORPORATION. RAO.
I'LL KEEP BUSY.

DO WE NEED ANOTHER GOD?

By Lois Lane

Over the course of the last day, we have seen something that may truly change the world.

A god has come to Earth.

Superman says he's Rao, the lost god of Krypton, a physical embodiment of their ancient Red Sun. A being that brought an end to war and ushered in a golden age of peace and unity.

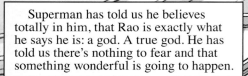

Superman has told us he believes totally in him, that Rao is exactly what he says he is: a god. A true god. He has told us there's nothing to fear and that something wonderful is going to happen.

But there are questions to ask about Rao and why he's come here.

What does a being like Rao hope to gain here, where every culture has its own faith, its own churches and its own gods?

What do you believe in? Here, it isn't about faith; Rao can be seen and touched, can be touched by, but what does that mean for all of us?

Wars are still fought in the names of gods and religions; innocents are still gunned down in the name of faith. We think ourselves enlightened, but this is still a world shaped too much by which god or church we choose to say is our own.

We live in a modern world still mapped by ancient beliefs.

We have seen gods walk the Earth before. The Justice League has an Olympian God of War in Wonder Woman which, by implication, says the Gods of Olympus are real. Will we see Thor outside of movies?

It sounds ridiculous, but New Gods have come and reigned fire on us and the Justice League have saved us. We live in an age of heroes and legends, but is this now a new age, one of gods?

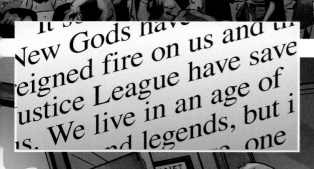

It s... New Gods have reigned fire on us and th... ustice League have save ...s. We live in an age of ...d legends, but i ...one

One last question that's worth asking is this: If one Kryptonian man, one SUPER man can bring us such hope and wonder, what can a Kryptonian GOD do?

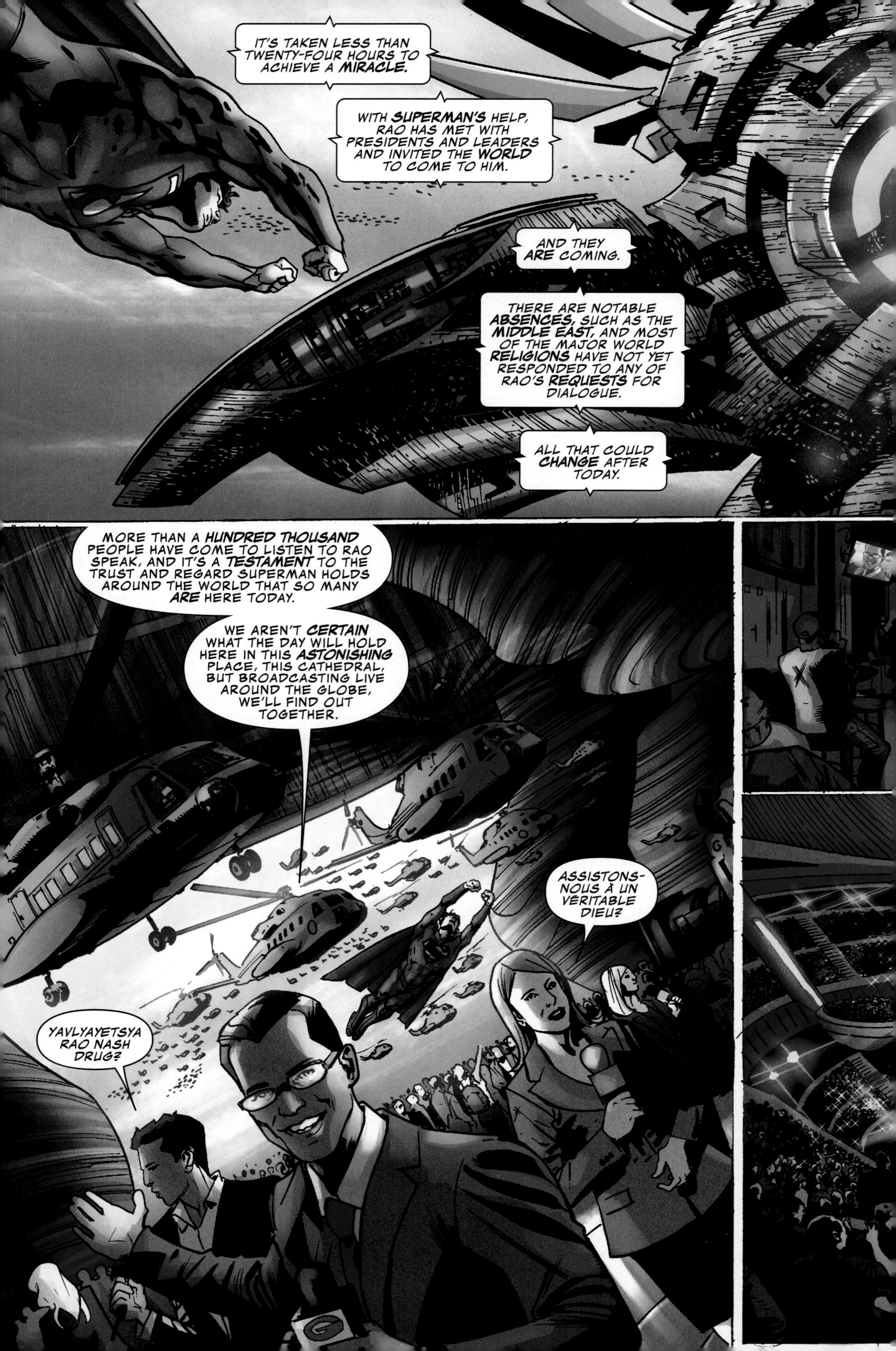
IT'S TAKEN LESS THAN TWENTY-FOUR HOURS TO ACHIEVE A MIRACLE.
WITH SUPERMAN'S HELP, RAO HAS MET WITH PRESIDENTS AND LEADERS AND INVITED THE WORLD TO COME TO HIM.
AND THEY ARE COMING.
THERE ARE NOTABLE ABSENCES, SUCH AS THE MIDDLE EAST, AND MOST OF THE MAJOR WORLD RELIGIONS HAVE NOT YET RESPONDED TO ANY OF RAO'S REQUESTS FOR DIALOGUE.
ALL THAT COULD CHANGE AFTER TODAY.
MORE THAN A HUNDRED THOUSAND PEOPLE HAVE COME TO LISTEN TO RAO SPEAK, AND IT'S A TESTAMENT TO THE TRUST AND REGARD SUPERMAN HOLDS AROUND THE WORLD THAT SO MANY ARE HERE TODAY.
WE AREN'T CERTAIN WHAT THE DAY WILL HOLD HERE IN THIS ASTONISHING PLACE, THIS CATHEDRAL, BUT BROADCASTING LIVE AROUND THE GLOBE, WE'LL FIND OUT TOGETHER.
ASSISTONS-NOUS À UN VÉRITABLE DIEU?
YAVLYAYETSYA RAO NASH DRUG?

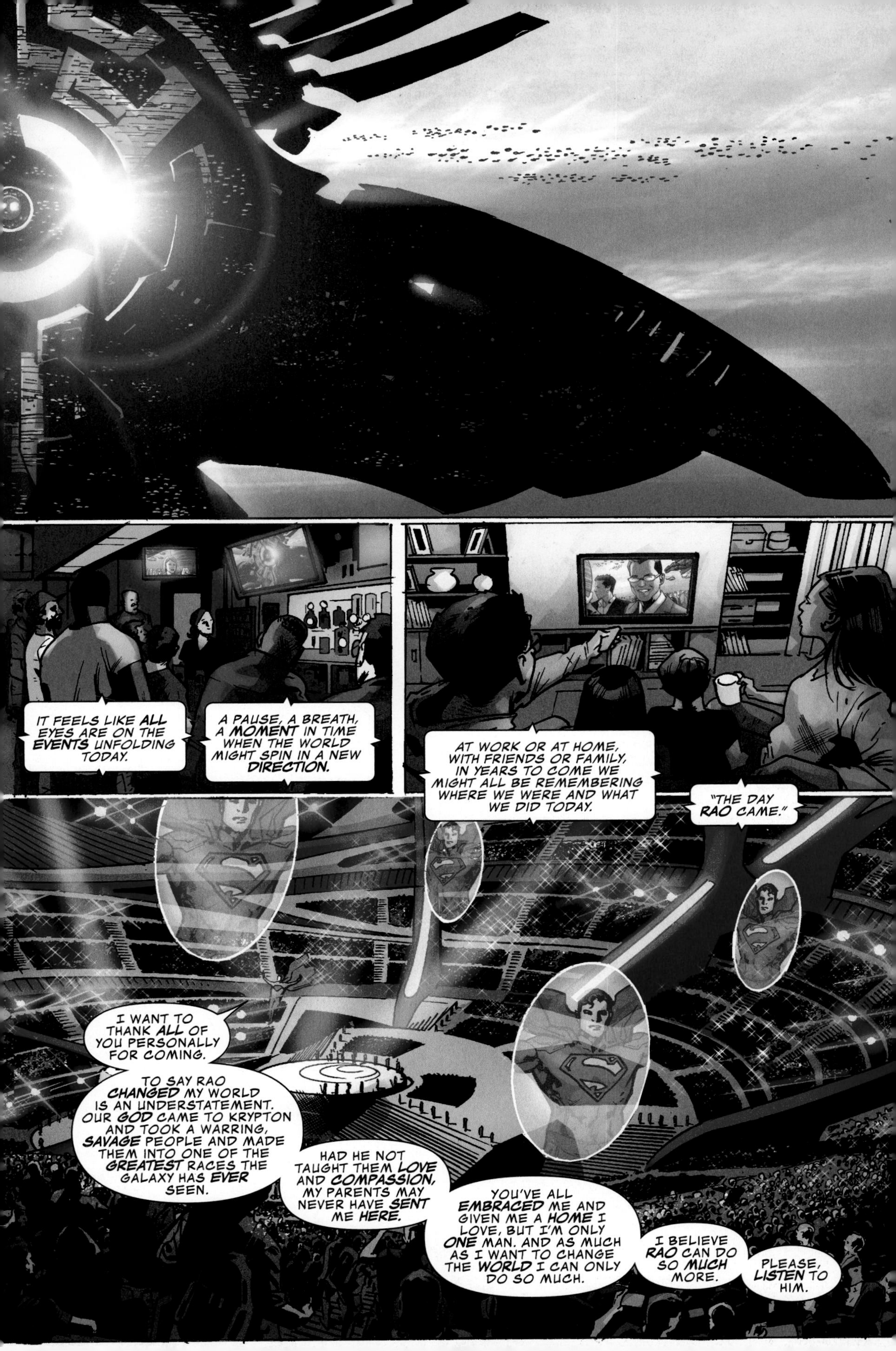
IT FEELS LIKE ALL EYES ARE ON THE EVENTS UNFOLDING TODAY.
A PAUSE, A BREATH, A MOMENT IN TIME WHEN THE WORLD MIGHT SPIN IN A NEW DIRECTION.
AT WORK OR AT HOME, WITH FRIENDS OR FAMILY, IN YEARS TO COME WE MIGHT ALL BE REMEMBERING WHERE WE WERE AND WHAT WE DID TODAY.
"THE DAY RAO CAME."
I WANT TO THANK ALL OF YOU PERSONALLY FOR COMING.
TO SAY RAO CHANGED MY WORLD IS AN UNDERSTATEMENT. OUR GOD CAME TO KRYPTON AND TOOK A WARRING, SAVAGE PEOPLE AND MADE THEM INTO ONE OF THE GREATEST RACES THE GALAXY HAS EVER SEEN.
HAD HE NOT TAUGHT THEM LOVE AND COMPASSION, MY PARENTS MAY NEVER HAVE SENT ME HERE.
YOU'VE ALL EMBRACED ME AND GIVEN ME A HOME I LOVE, BUT I'M ONLY ONE MAN. AND AS MUCH AS I WANT TO CHANGE THE WORLD I CAN ONLY DO SO MUCH.
I BELIEVE RAO CAN DO SO MUCH MORE.
PLEASE, LISTEN TO HIM.

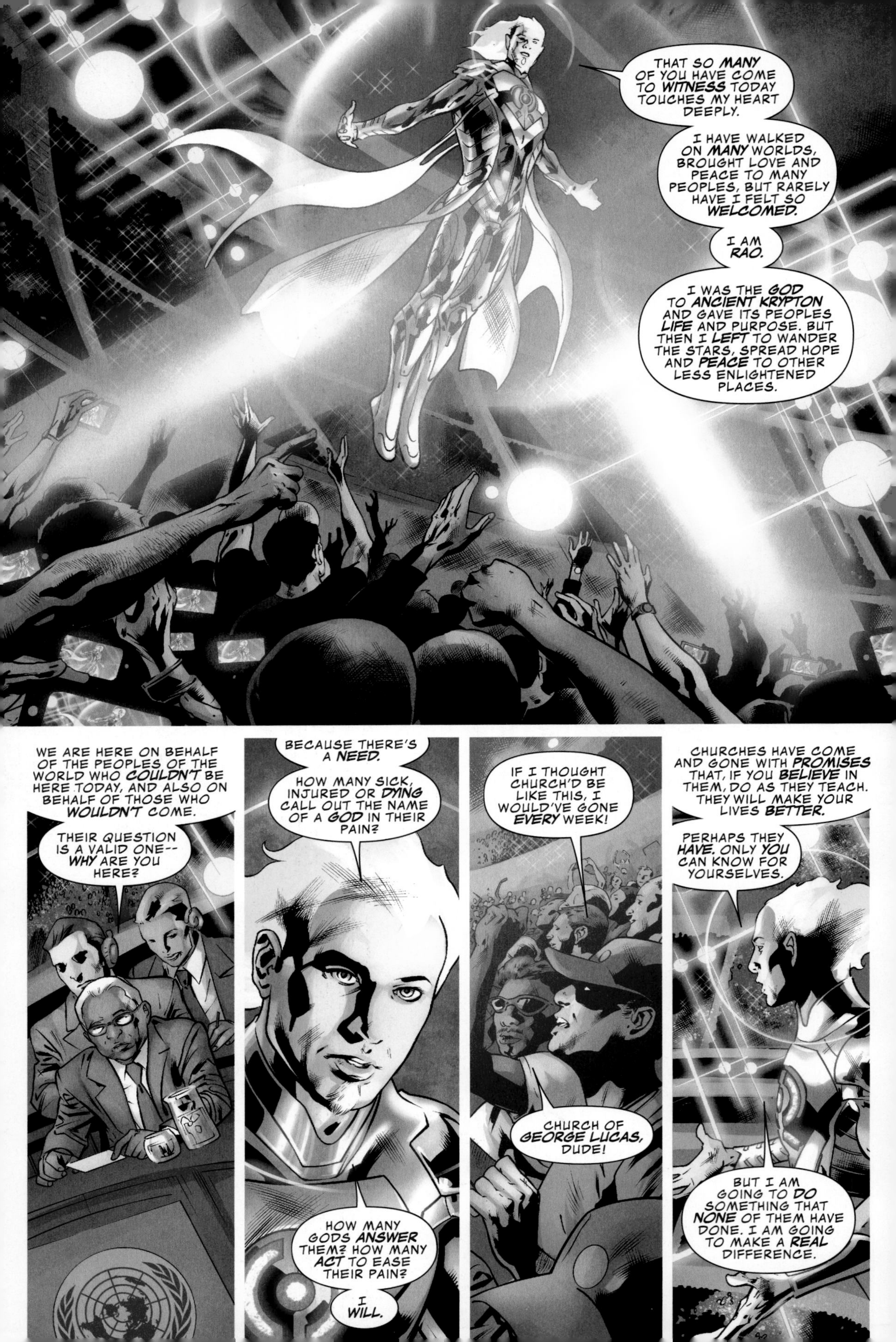
THAT SO MANY OF YOU HAVE COME TO WITNESS TODAY TOUCHES MY HEART DEEPLY.
I HAVE WALKED ON MANY WORLDS, BROUGHT LOVE AND PEACE TO MANY PEOPLES, BUT RARELY HAVE I FELT SO WELCOMED.
I AM RAO.
I WAS THE GOD TO ANCIENT KRYPTON AND GAVE ITS PEOPLES LIFE AND PURPOSE. BUT THEN I LEFT TO WANDER THE STARS, SPREAD HOPE AND PEACE TO OTHER LESS ENLIGHTENED PLACES.
WE ARE HERE ON BEHALF OF THE PEOPLES OF THE WORLD WHO COULDN'T BE HERE TODAY, AND ALSO ON BEHALF OF THOSE WHO WOULDN'T COME.
THEIR QUESTION IS A VALID ONE-- WHY ARE YOU HERE?
BECAUSE THERE'S A NEED.
HOW MANY SICK, INJURED OR DYING CALL OUT THE NAME OF A GOD IN THEIR PAIN?
HOW MANY GODS ANSWER THEM? HOW MANY ACT TO EASE THEIR PAIN?
I WILL.
IF I THOUGHT CHURCH'D BE LIKE THIS, I WOULD'VE GONE EVERY WEEK!
CHURCH OF GEORGE LUCAS, DUDE!
CHURCHES HAVE COME AND GONE WITH PROMISES THAT, IF YOU BELIEVE IN THEM, DO AS THEY TEACH. THEY WILL MAKE YOUR LIVES BETTER.
PERHAPS THEY HAVE. ONLY YOU CAN KNOW FOR YOURSELVES.
BUT I AM GOING TO DO SOMETHING THAT NONE OF THEM HAVE DONE. I AM GOING TO MAKE A REAL DIFFERENCE.

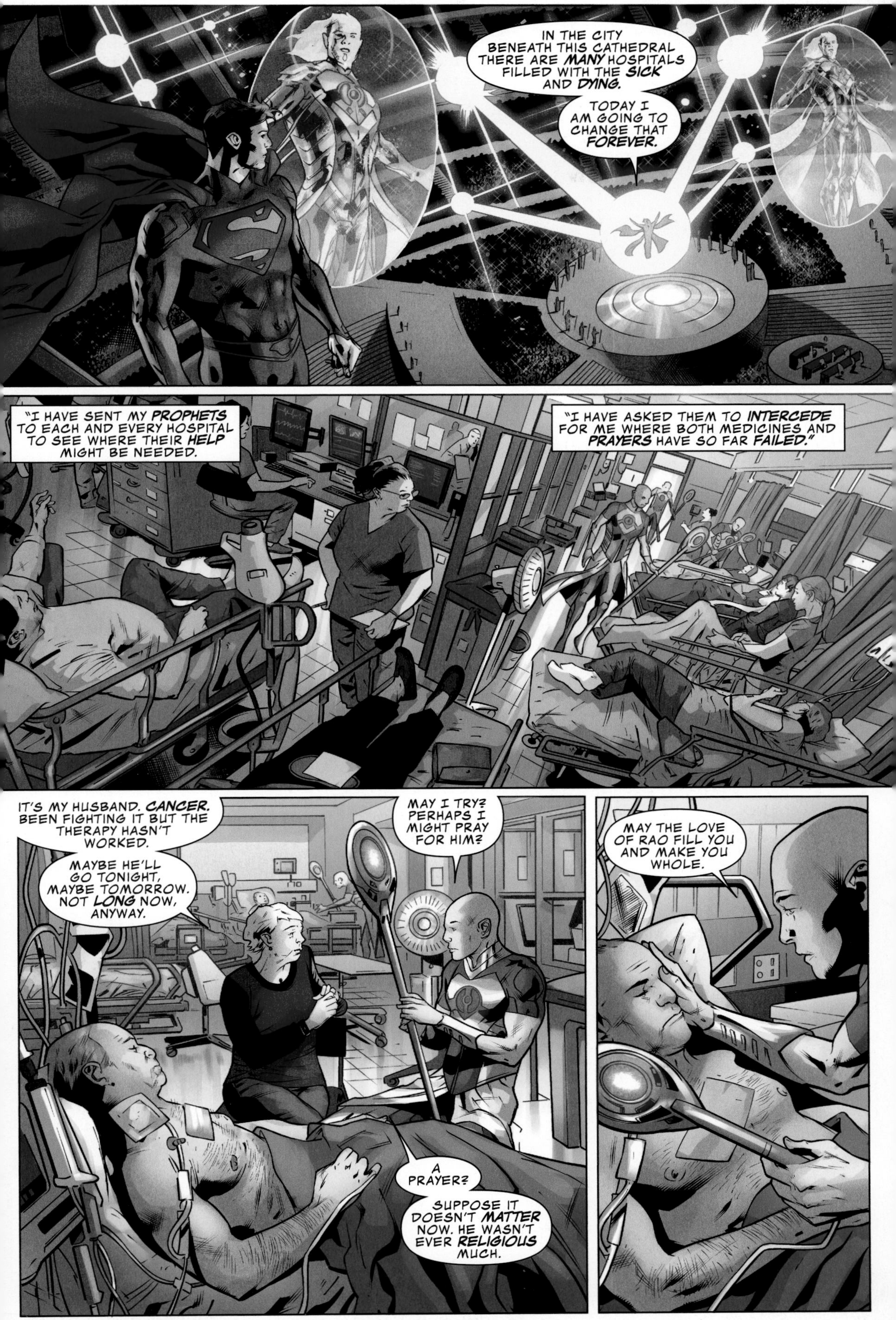
IN THE CITY BENEATH THIS CATHEDRAL THERE ARE MANY HOSPITALS FILLED WITH THE SICK AND DYING.
TODAY I AM GOING TO CHANGE THAT FOREVER.
"I HAVE SENT MY PROPHETS TO EACH AND EVERY HOSPITAL TO SEE WHERE THEIR HELP MIGHT BE NEEDED.
"I HAVE ASKED THEM TO INTERCEDE FOR ME WHERE BOTH MEDICINES AND PRAYERS HAVE SO FAR FAILED."
IT'S MY HUSBAND. CANCER. BEEN FIGHTING IT BUT THE THERAPY HASN'T WORKED.
MAYBE HE'LL GO TONIGHT, MAYBE TOMORROW. NOT LONG NOW, ANYWAY.
MAY I TRY? PERHAPS I MIGHT PRAY FOR HIM?
A PRAYER?
SUPPOSE IT DOESN'T MATTER NOW. HE WASN'T EVER RELIGIOUS MUCH.
MAY THE LOVE OF RAO FILL YOU AND MAKE YOU WHOLE.

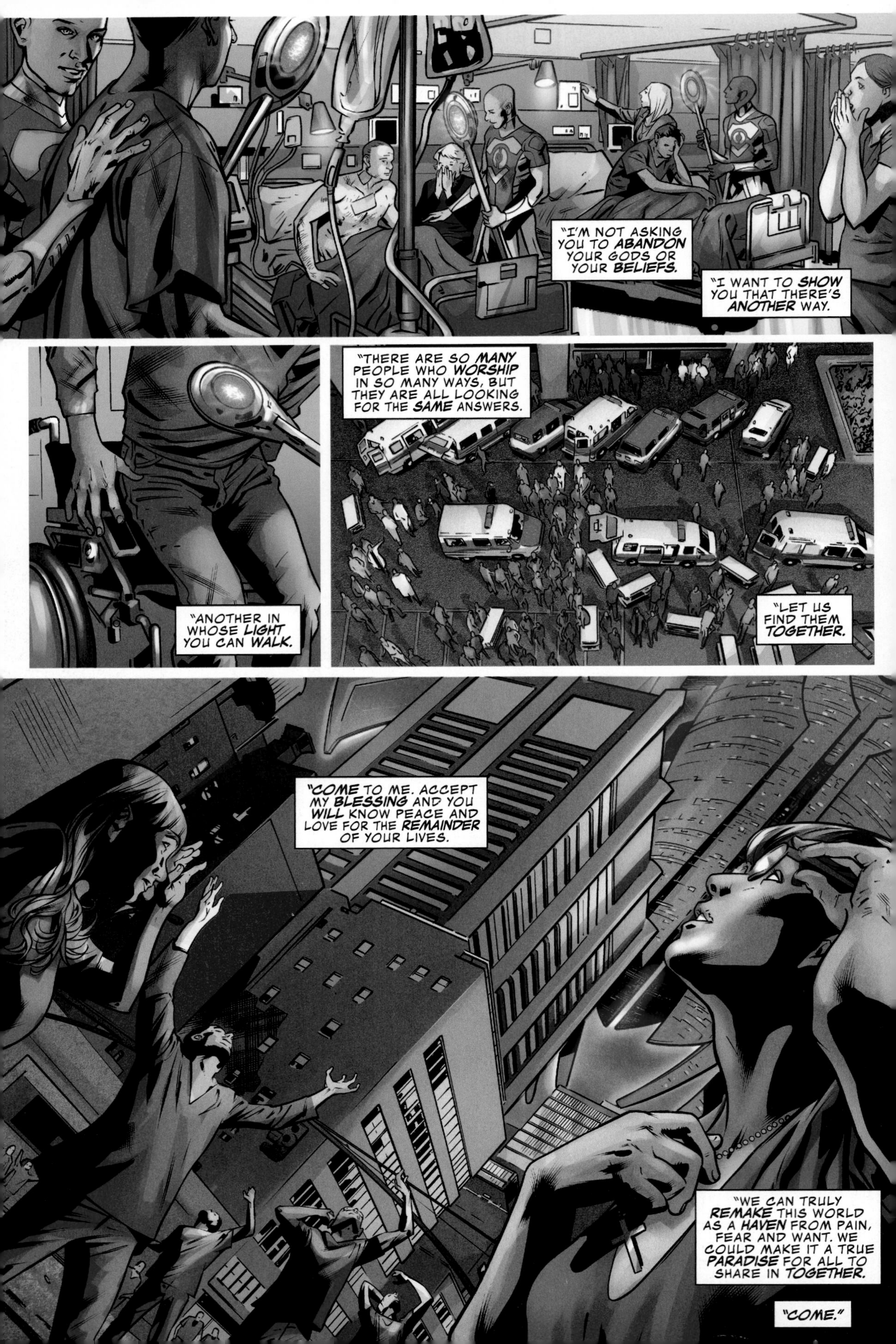
"I'M NOT ASKING YOU TO ABANDON YOUR GODS OR YOUR BELIEFS.
"I WANT TO SHOW YOU THAT THERE'S ANOTHER WAY.
"ANOTHER IN WHOSE LIGHT YOU CAN WALK.
"THERE ARE SO MANY PEOPLE WHO WORSHIP IN SO MANY WAYS, BUT THEY ARE ALL LOOKING FOR THE SAME ANSWERS.
"LET US FIND THEM TOGETHER.
"COME TO ME. ACCEPT MY BLESSING AND YOU WILL KNOW PEACE AND LOVE FOR THE REMAINDER OF YOUR LIVES.
"WE CAN TRULY REMAKE THIS WORLD AS A HAVEN FROM PAIN, FEAR AND WANT. WE COULD MAKE IT A TRUE PARADISE FOR ALL TO SHARE IN TOGETHER.
"COME."

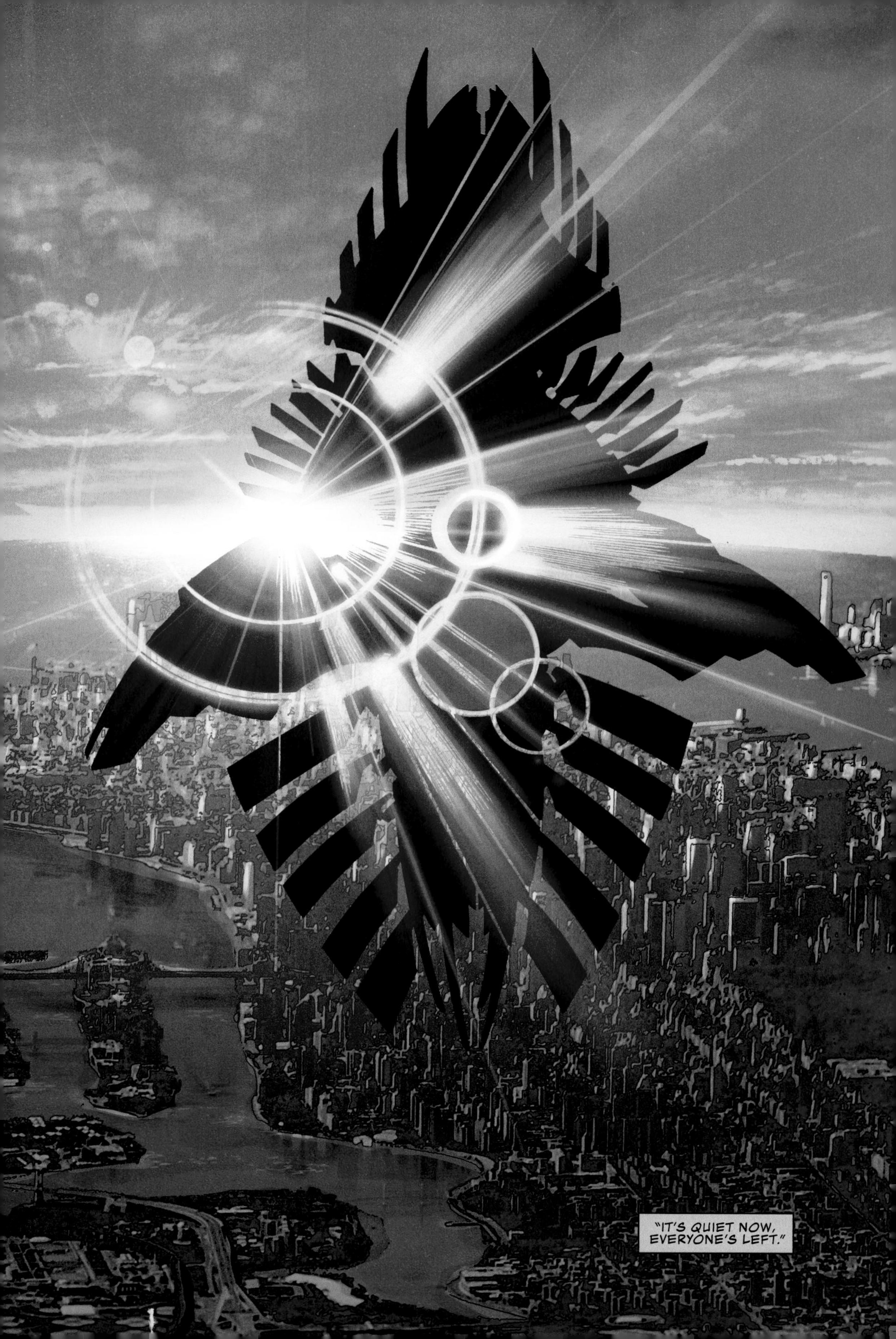
"IT'S QUIET NOW, EVERYONE'S LEFT."

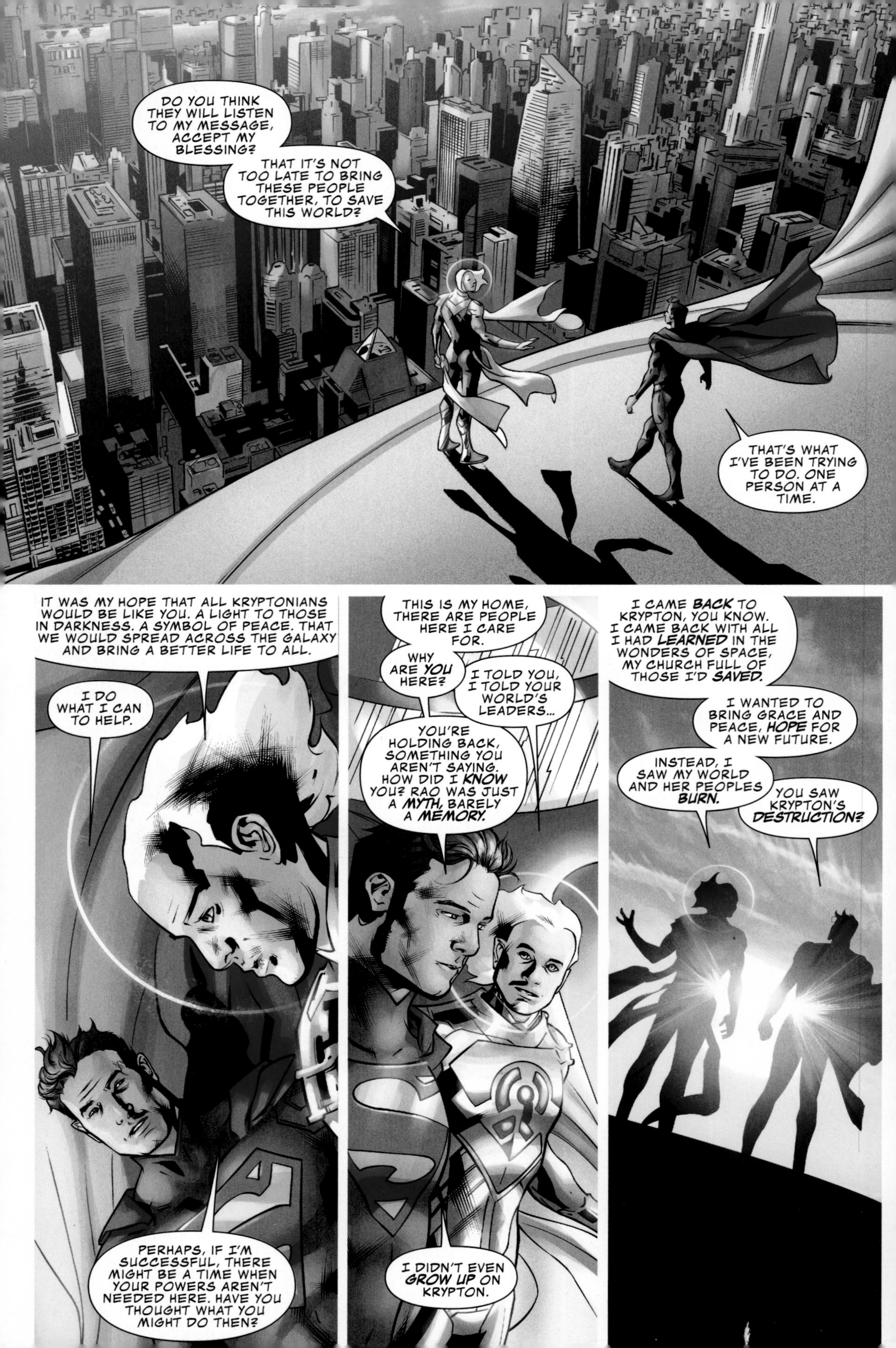
DO YOU THINK THEY WILL LISTEN TO MY MESSAGE, ACCEPT MY BLESSING?
THAT IT'S NOT TOO LATE TO BRING THESE PEOPLE TOGETHER, TO SAVE THIS WORLD?
THAT'S WHAT I'VE BEEN TRYING TO DO. ONE PERSON AT A TIME.
IT WAS MY HOPE THAT ALL KRYPTONIANS WOULD BE LIKE YOU. A LIGHT TO THOSE IN DARKNESS. A SYMBOL OF PEACE. THAT WE WOULD SPREAD ACROSS THE GALAXY AND BRING A BETTER LIFE TO ALL.
I DO WHAT I CAN TO HELP.
PERHAPS, IF I'M SUCCESSFUL, THERE MIGHT BE A TIME WHEN YOUR POWERS AREN'T NEEDED HERE. HAVE YOU THOUGHT WHAT YOU MIGHT DO THEN?
THIS IS MY HOME, THERE ARE PEOPLE HERE I CARE FOR.
WHY ARE YOU HERE?
I TOLD YOU, I TOLD YOUR WORLD'S LEADERS...
YOU'RE HOLDING BACK, SOMETHING YOU AREN'T SAYING. HOW DID I KNOW YOU? RAO WAS JUST A MYTH, BARELY A MEMORY.
I DIDN'T EVEN GROW UP ON KRYPTON.
I CAME BACK TO KRYPTON, YOU KNOW. I CAME BACK WITH ALL I HAD LEARNED IN THE WONDERS OF SPACE, MY CHURCH FULL OF THOSE I'D SAVED.
I WANTED TO BRING GRACE AND PEACE, HOPE FOR A NEW FUTURE.
INSTEAD, I SAW MY WORLD AND HER PEOPLES BURN.
YOU SAW KRYPTON'S DESTRUCTION?

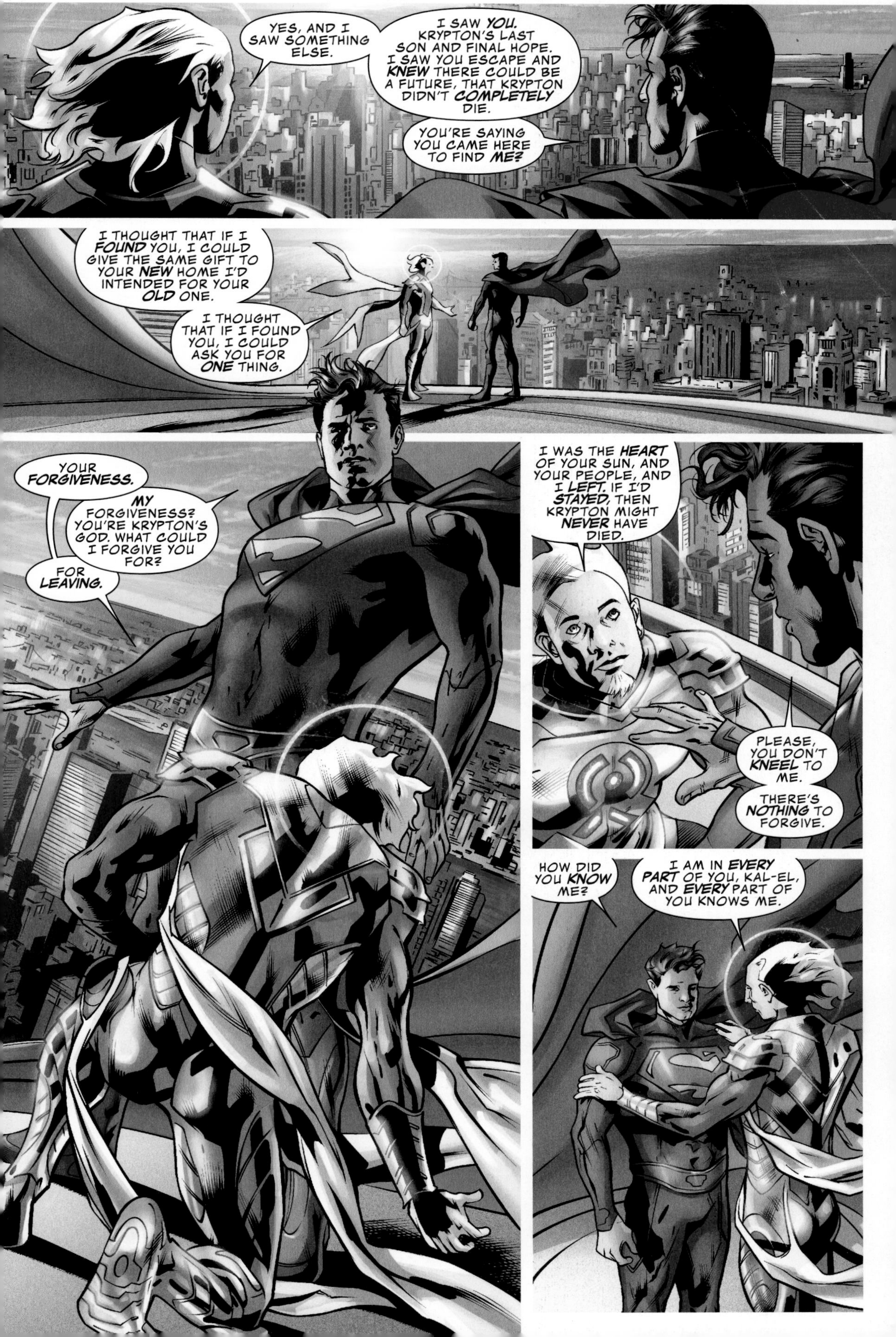
YES, AND I SAW SOMETHING ELSE.
I SAW YOU. KRYPTON'S LAST SON AND FINAL HOPE. I SAW YOU ESCAPE AND KNEW THERE COULD BE A FUTURE, THAT KRYPTON DIDN'T COMPLETELY DIE.
YOU'RE SAYING YOU CAME HERE TO FIND ME?
I THOUGHT THAT IF I FOUND YOU, I COULD GIVE THE SAME GIFT TO YOUR NEW HOME I'D INTENDED FOR YOUR OLD ONE.
I THOUGHT THAT IF I FOUND YOU, I COULD ASK YOU FOR ONE THING.
YOUR FORGIVENESS.
MY FORGIVENESS? YOU'RE KRYPTON'S GOD. WHAT COULD I FORGIVE YOU FOR?
FOR LEAVING.
I WAS THE HEART OF YOUR SUN, AND YOUR PEOPLE, AND I LEFT. IF I'D STAYED, THEN KRYPTON MIGHT NEVER HAVE DIED.
PLEASE, YOU DON'T KNEEL TO ME.
THERE'S NOTHING TO FORGIVE.
HOW DID YOU KNOW ME?
I AM IN EVERY PART OF YOU, KAL-EL, AND EVERY PART OF YOU KNOWS ME.

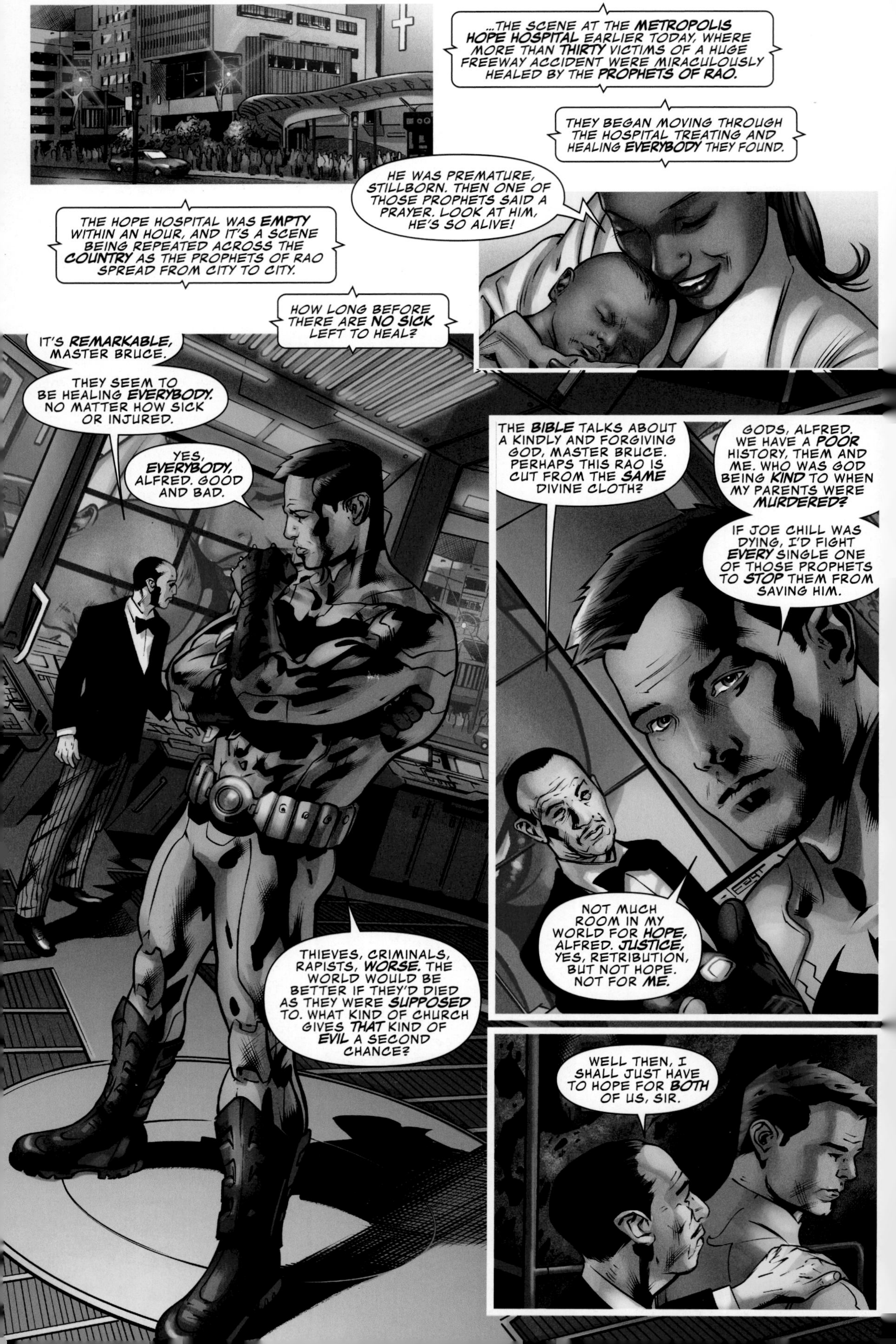

...THE SCENE AT THE METROPOLIS HOPE HOSPITAL EARLIER TODAY, WHERE MORE THAN THIRTY VICTIMS OF A HUGE FREEWAY ACCIDENT WERE MIRACULOUSLY HEALED BY THE PROPHETS OF RAO.
THEY BEGAN MOVING THROUGH THE HOSPITAL TREATING AND HEALING EVERYBODY THEY FOUND.
HE WAS PREMATURE, STILLBORN. THEN ONE OF THOSE PROPHETS SAID A PRAYER. LOOK AT HIM, HE'S SO ALIVE!
THE HOPE HOSPITAL WAS EMPTY WITHIN AN HOUR, AND IT'S A SCENE BEING REPEATED ACROSS THE COUNTRY AS THE PROPHETS OF RAO SPREAD FROM CITY TO CITY.
HOW LONG BEFORE THERE ARE NO SICK LEFT TO HEAL?
IT'S REMARKABLE, MASTER BRUCE.
THEY SEEM TO BE HEALING EVERYBODY. NO MATTER HOW SICK OR INJURED.
YES, EVERYBODY, ALFRED. GOOD AND BAD.
THIEVES, CRIMINALS, RAPISTS, WORSE. THE WORLD WOULD BE BETTER IF THEY'D DIED AS THEY WERE SUPPOSED TO. WHAT KIND OF CHURCH GIVES THAT KIND OF EVIL A SECOND CHANCE?
THE BIBLE TALKS ABOUT A KINDLY AND FORGIVING GOD, MASTER BRUCE. PERHAPS THIS RAO IS CUT FROM THE SAME DIVINE CLOTH?
GODS, ALFRED. WE HAVE A POOR HISTORY, THEM AND ME. WHO WAS GOD BEING KIND TO WHEN MY PARENTS WERE MURDERED?
IF JOE CHILL WAS DYING, I'D FIGHT EVERY SINGLE ONE OF THOSE PROPHETS TO STOP THEM FROM SAVING HIM.
NOT MUCH ROOM IN MY WORLD FOR HOPE, ALFRED. JUSTICE, YES, RETRIBUTION, BUT NOT HOPE. NOT FOR ME.
WELL THEN, I SHALL JUST HAVE TO HOPE FOR BOTH OF US, SIR.

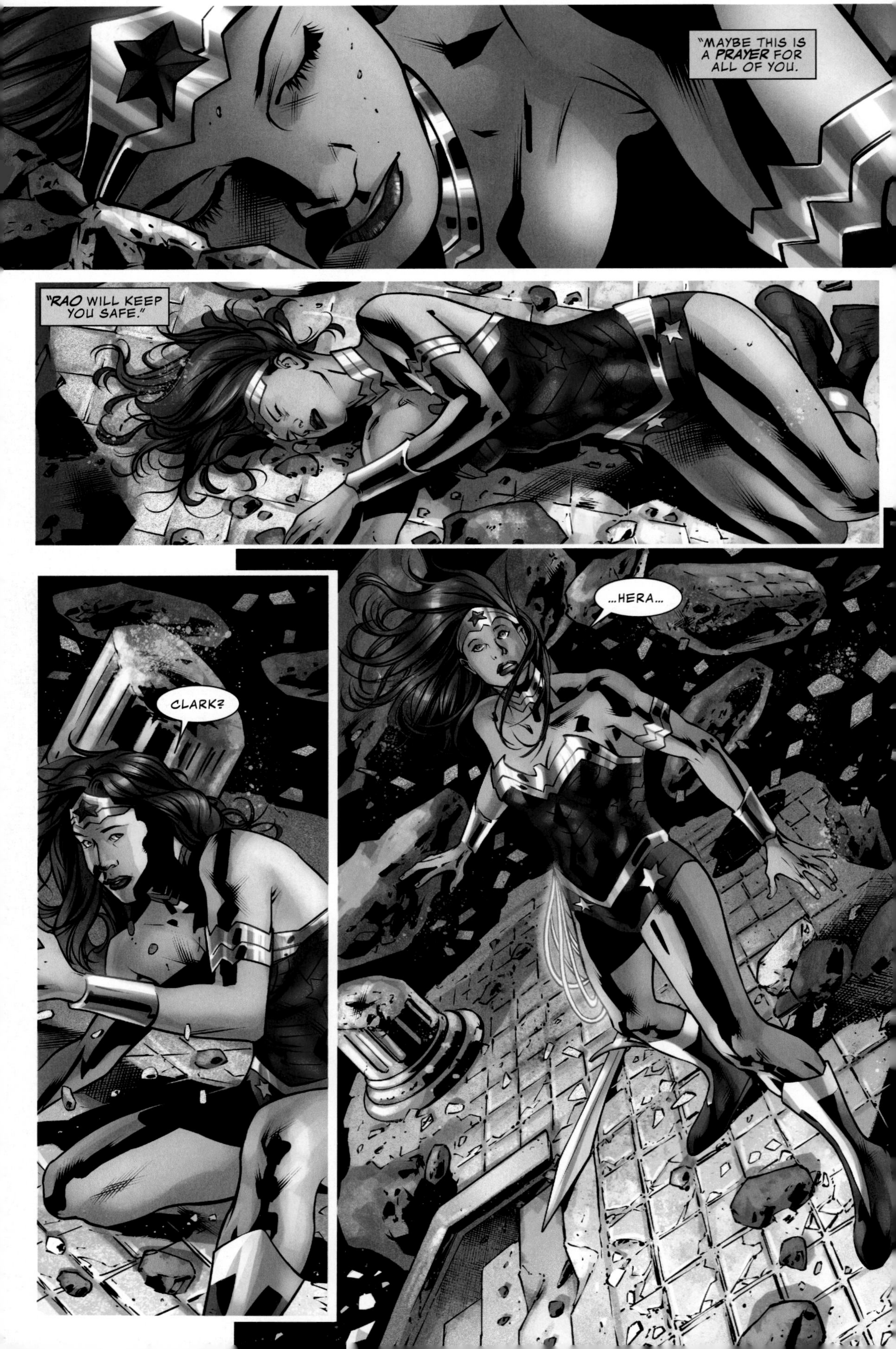
"MAYBE THIS IS A PRAYER FOR ALL OF YOU.
"RAO WILL KEEP YOU SAFE."
CLARK?
...HERA...

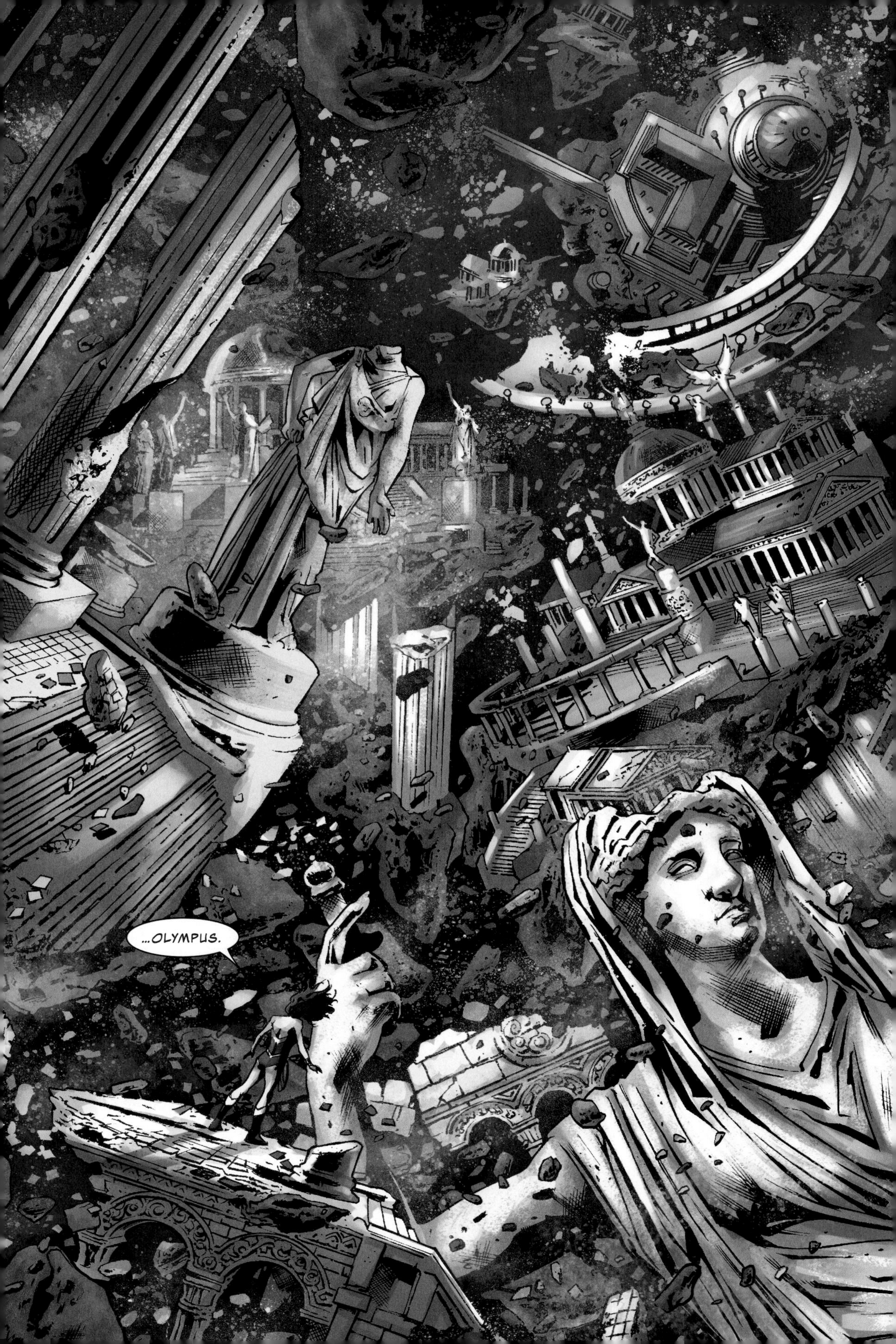
...OLYMPUS.

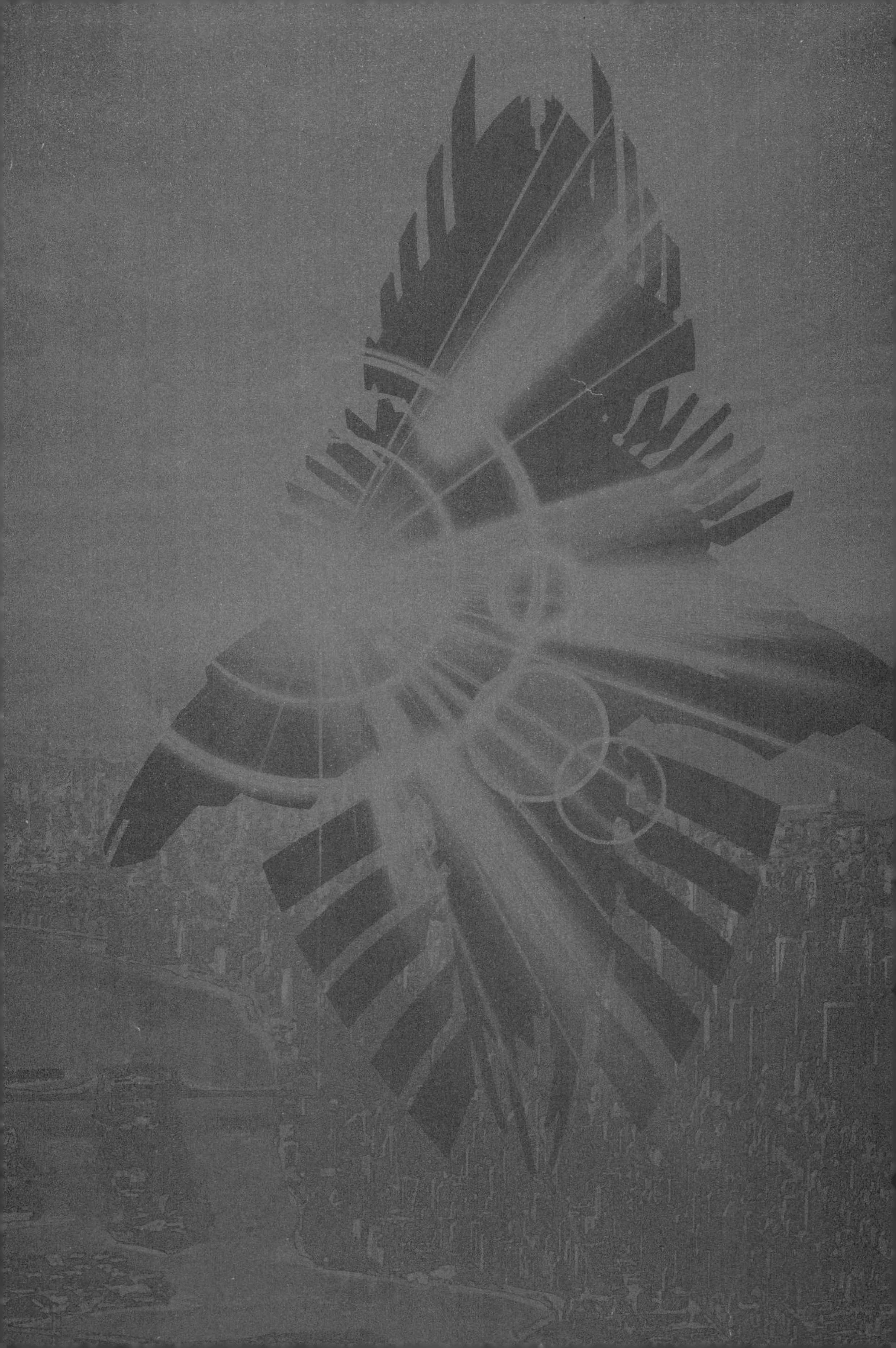

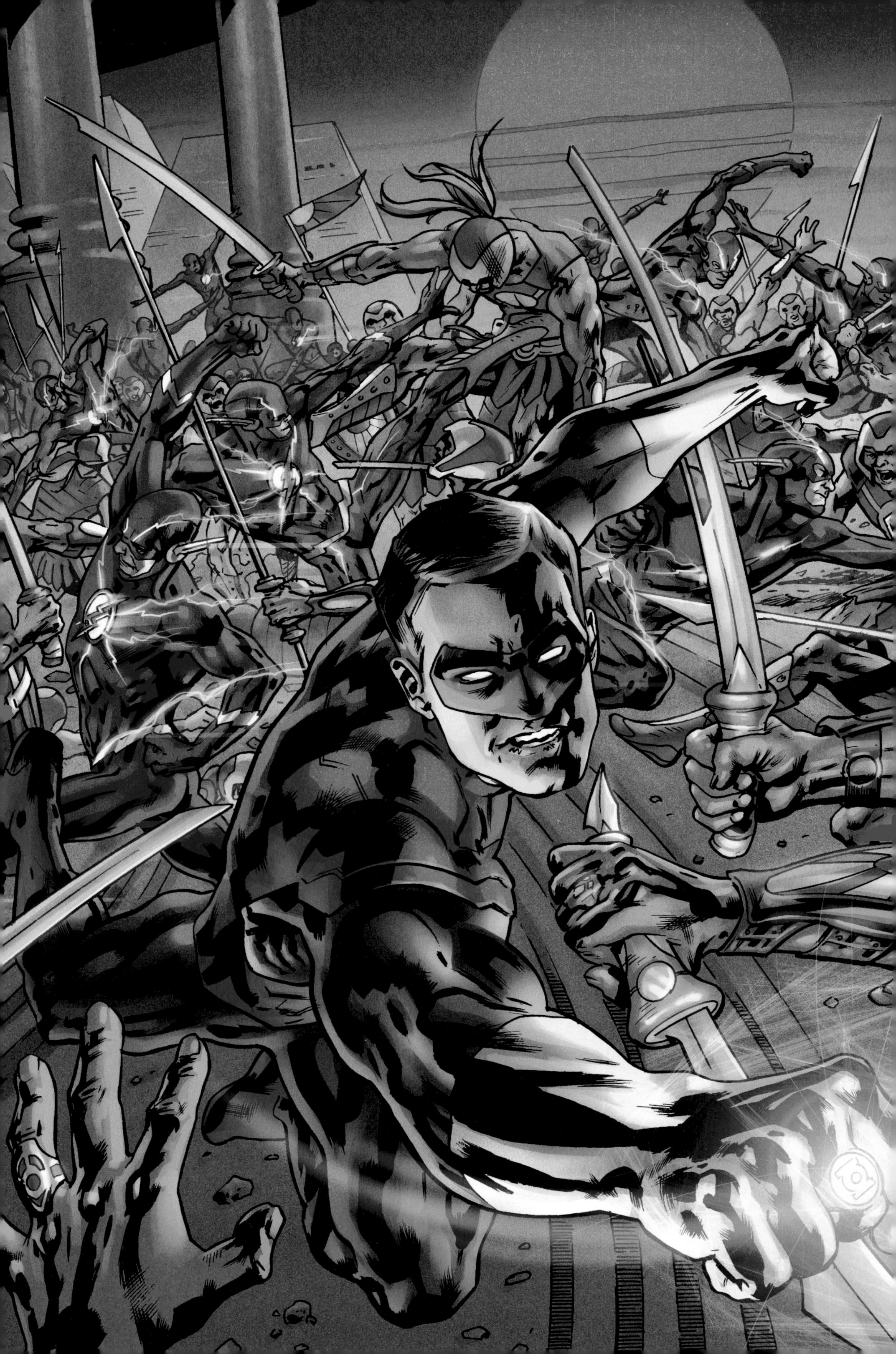

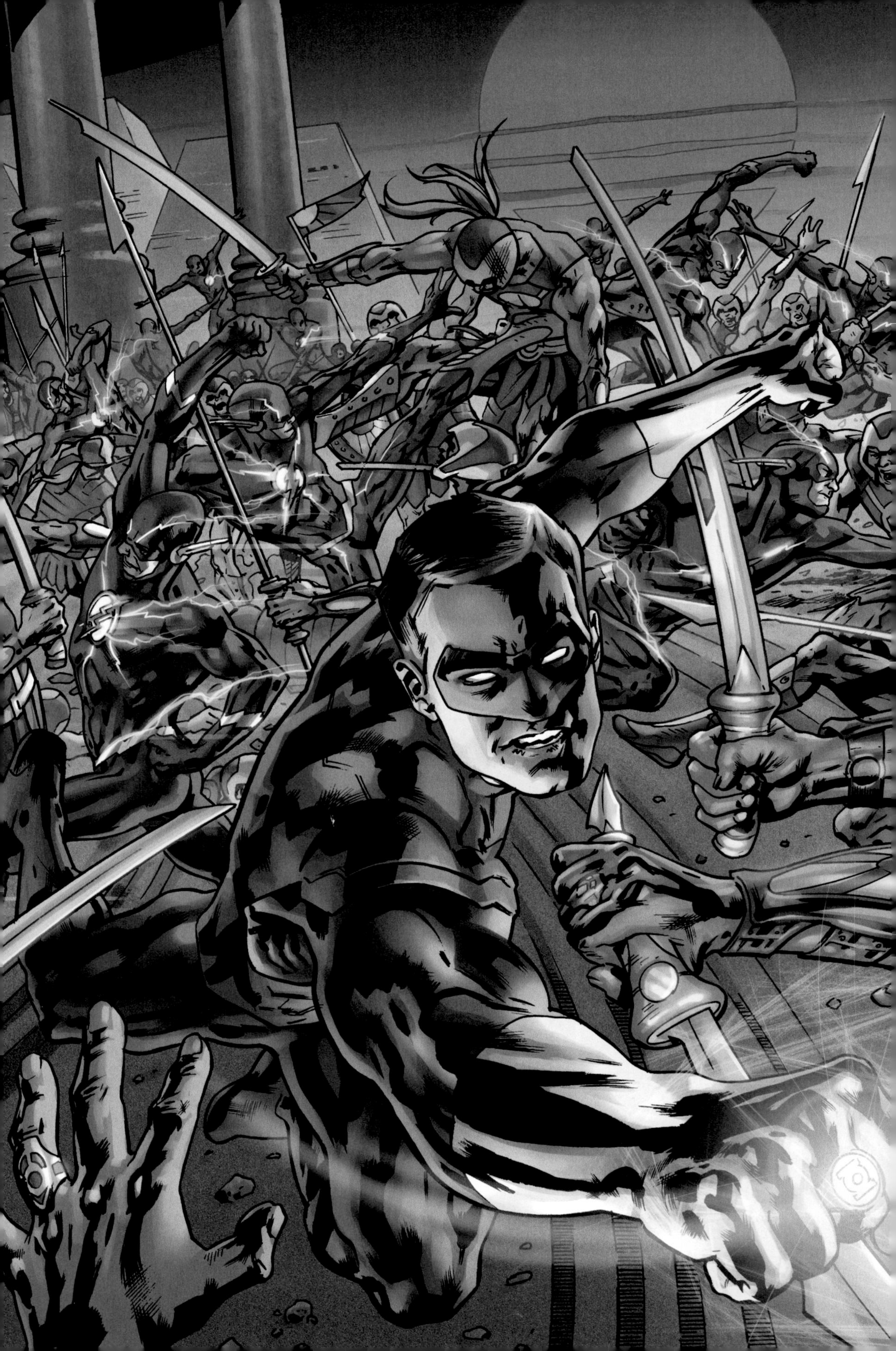

DC COMICS PRESENTS

THE JUSTICE LEAGUE OF AMERICA

POWER AND GLORY

PART THREE

BY BRYAN HITCH

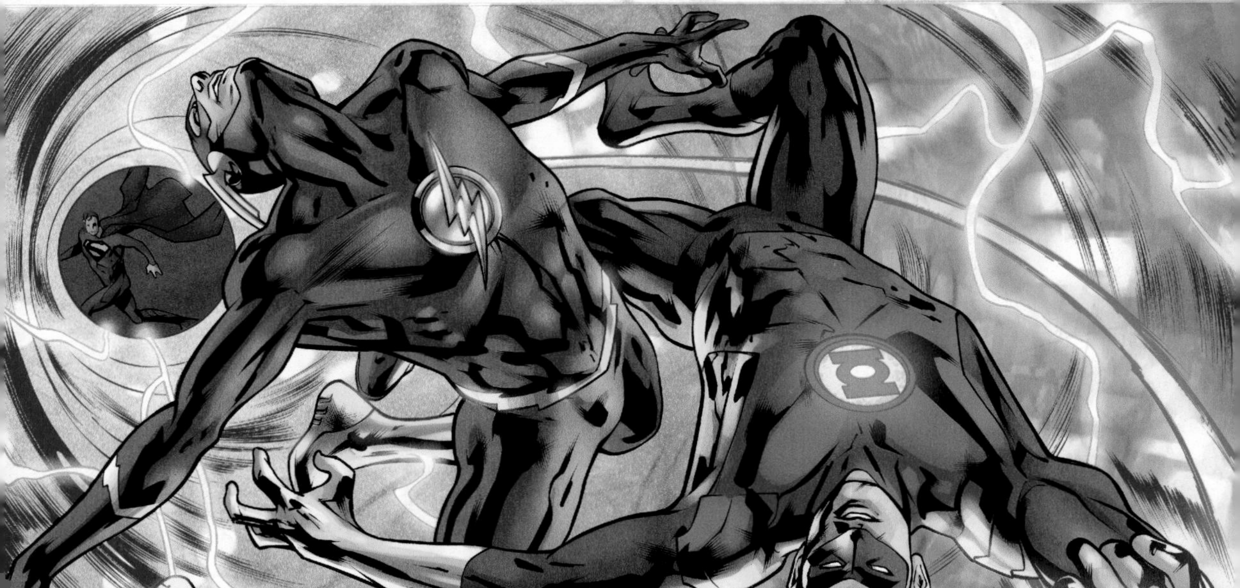

INKS BY DANIEL HENRIQUES
COLORS BY ALEX SINCLAIR
LETTERS BY CHRIS ELIOPOULOS
ASSISTS BY AMEDEO TURTURRO
EDITS BY BRIAN CUNNINGHAM

COVER BY BRYAN HITCH AND ALEX SINCLAIR

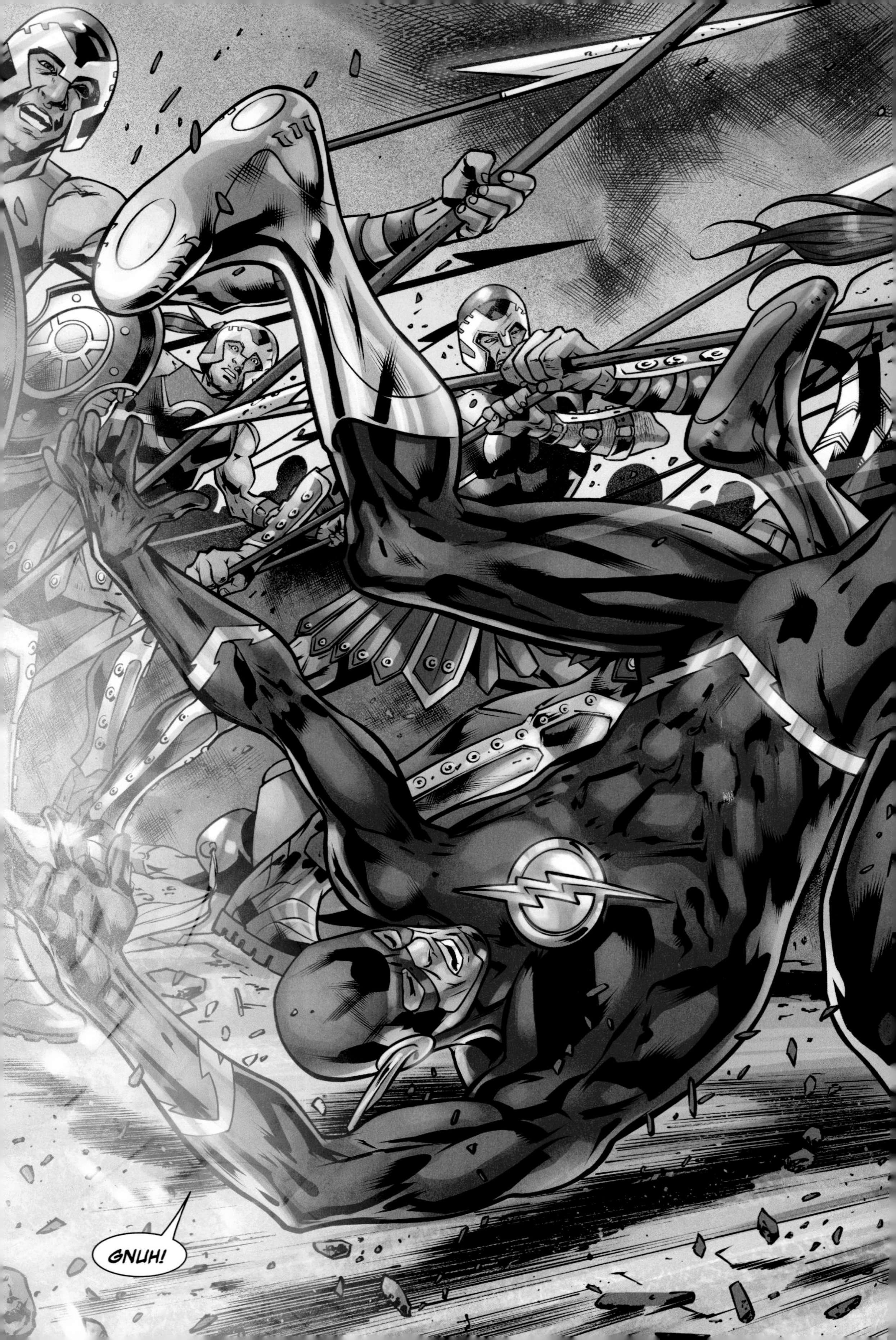
GNUH!

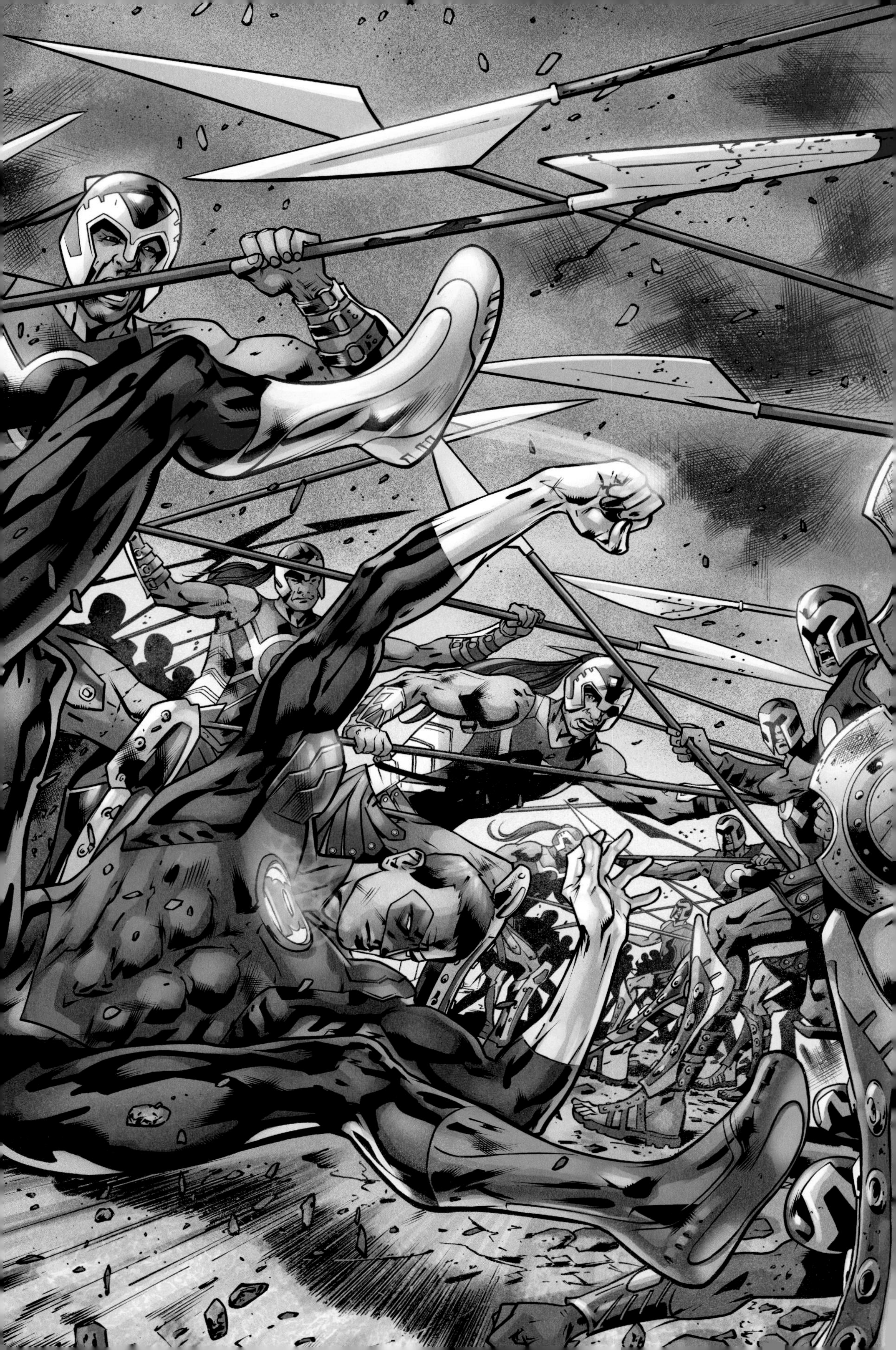

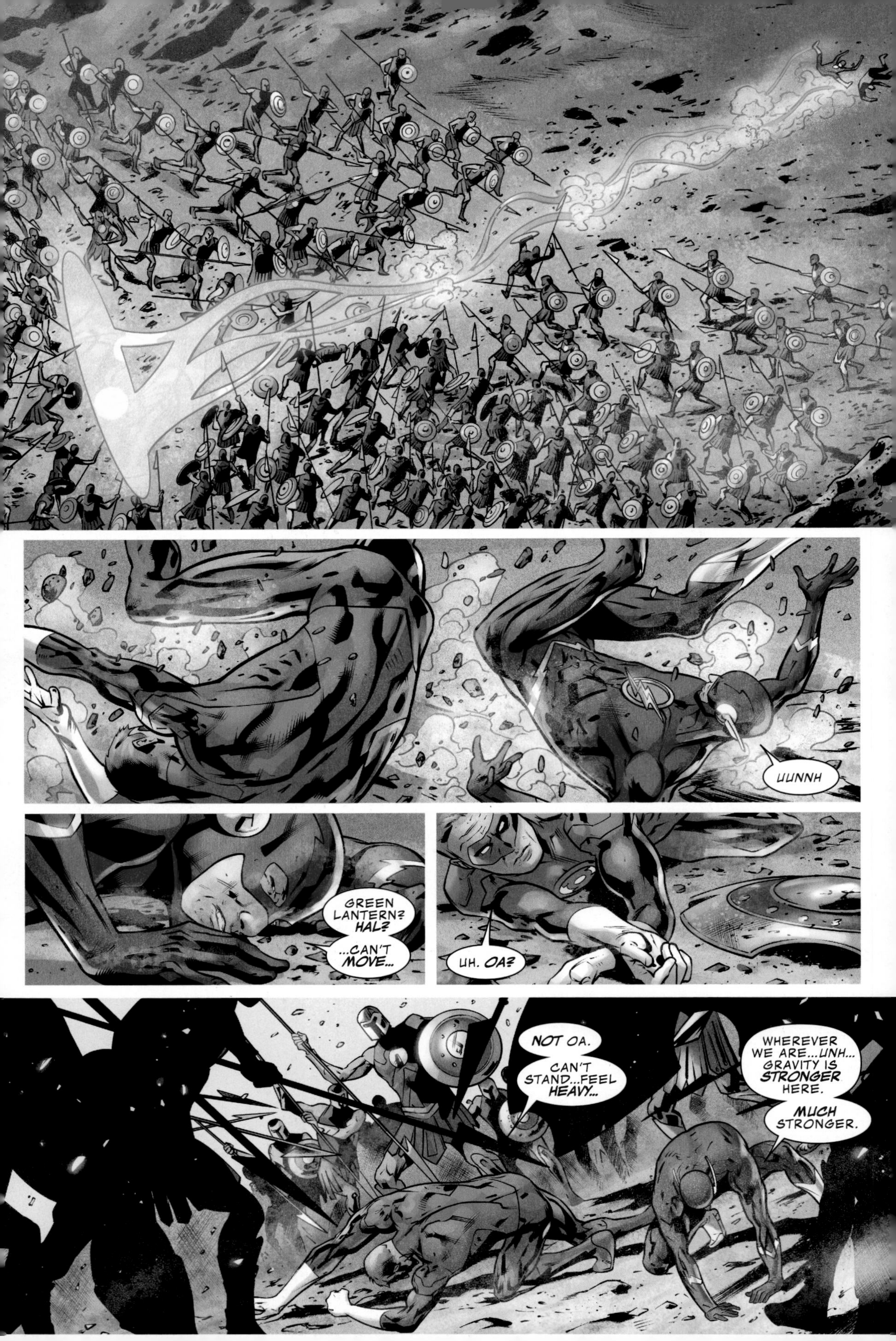
UUNNH
GREEN LANTERN? HAL?
...CAN'T MOVE...
UH. OA?
NOT OA.
CAN'T STAND...FEEL HEAVY...
WHEREVER WE ARE...UNH... GRAVITY IS STRONGER HERE.
MUCH STRONGER.

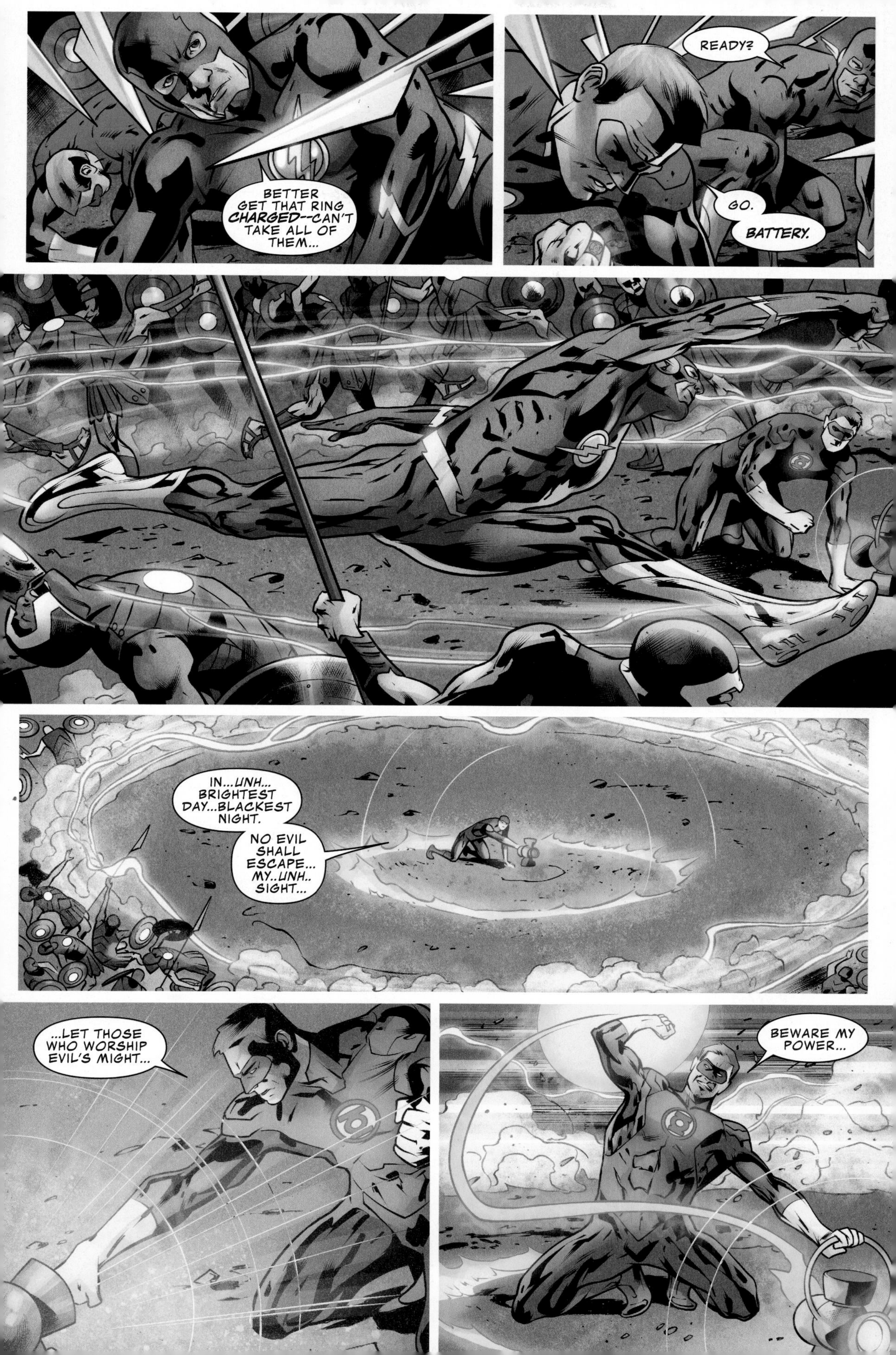
BETTER GET THAT RING CHARGED--CAN'T TAKE ALL OF THEM...
READY?
GO.
BATTERY.
IN...UNH... BRIGHTEST DAY...BLACKEST NIGHT.
NO EVIL SHALL ESCAPE... MY..UNH.. SIGHT...
...LET THOSE WHO WORSHIP EVIL'S MIGHT...
BEWARE MY POWER...

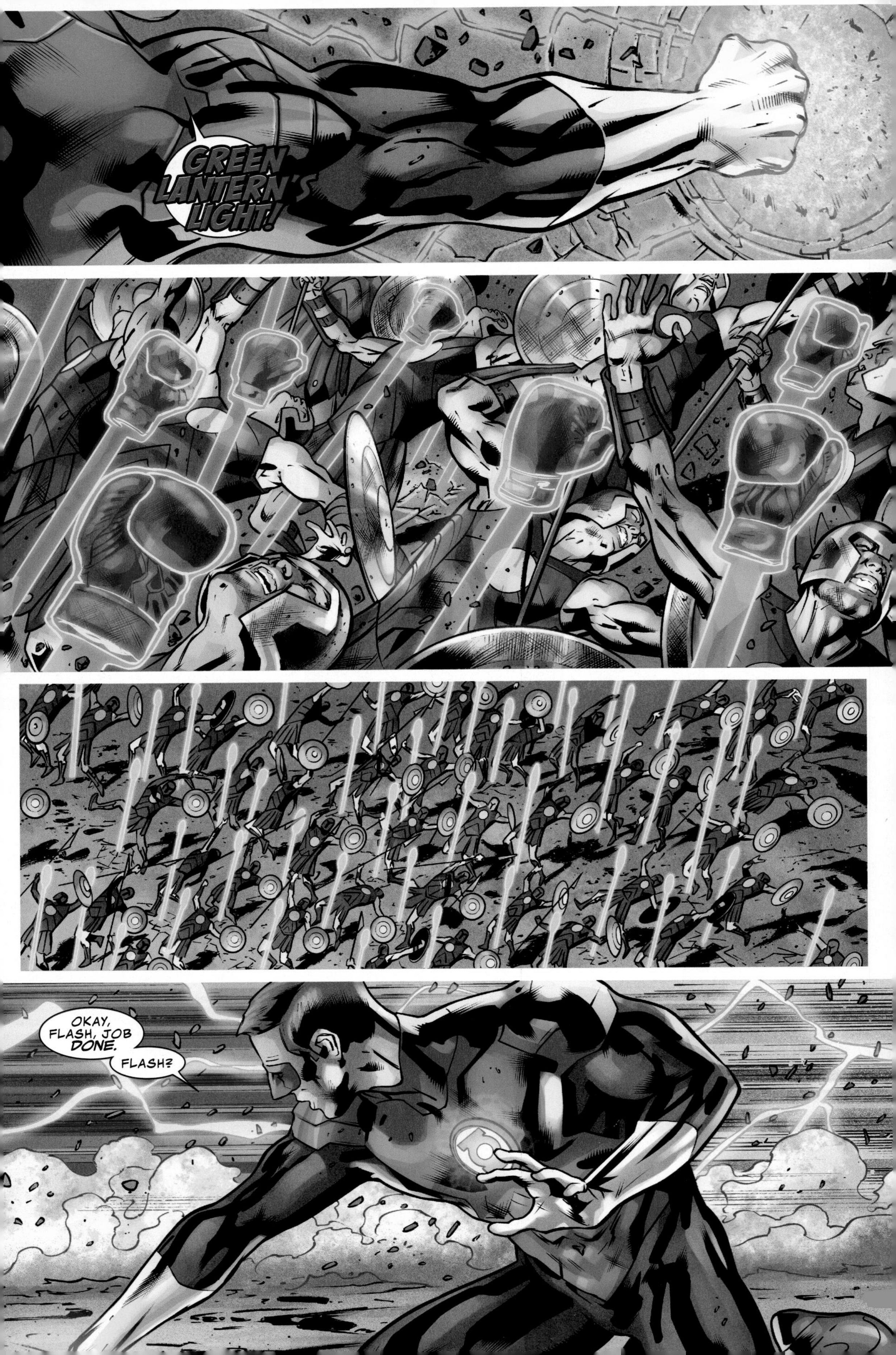
GREEN LANTERN'S LIGHT!
OKAY, FLASH, JOB DONE.
FLASH?

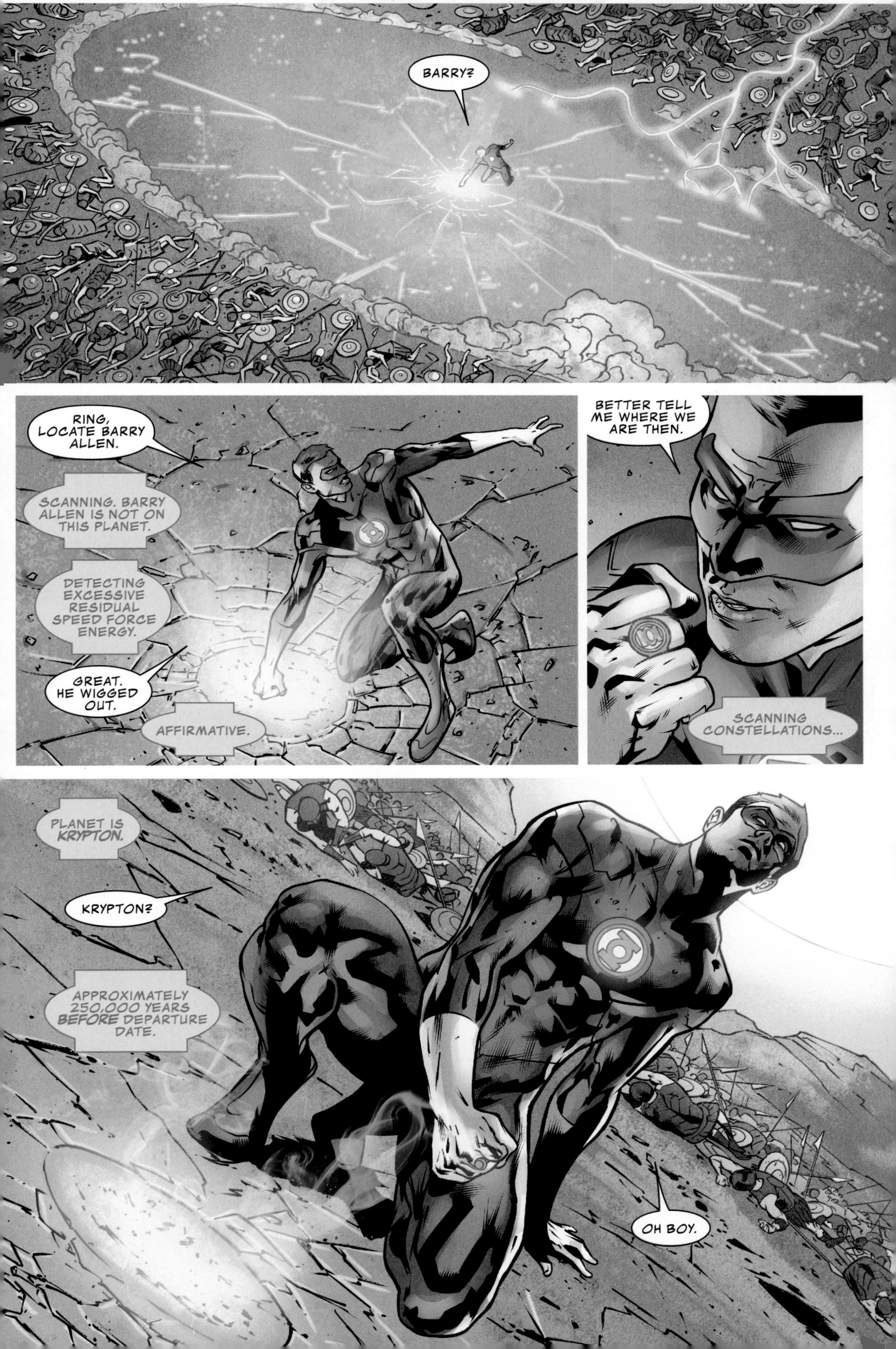

BARRY?
RING, LOCATE BARRY ALLEN.
SCANNING. BARRY ALLEN IS NOT ON THIS PLANET.
DETECTING EXCESSIVE RESIDUAL SPEED FORCE ENERGY.
GREAT. HE WIGGED OUT.
AFFIRMATIVE.
BETTER TELL ME WHERE WE ARE THEN.
SCANNING CONSTELLATIONS...
PLANET IS KRYPTON.
KRYPTON?
APPROXIMATELY 250,000 YEARS BEFORE DEPARTURE DATE.
OH BOY.

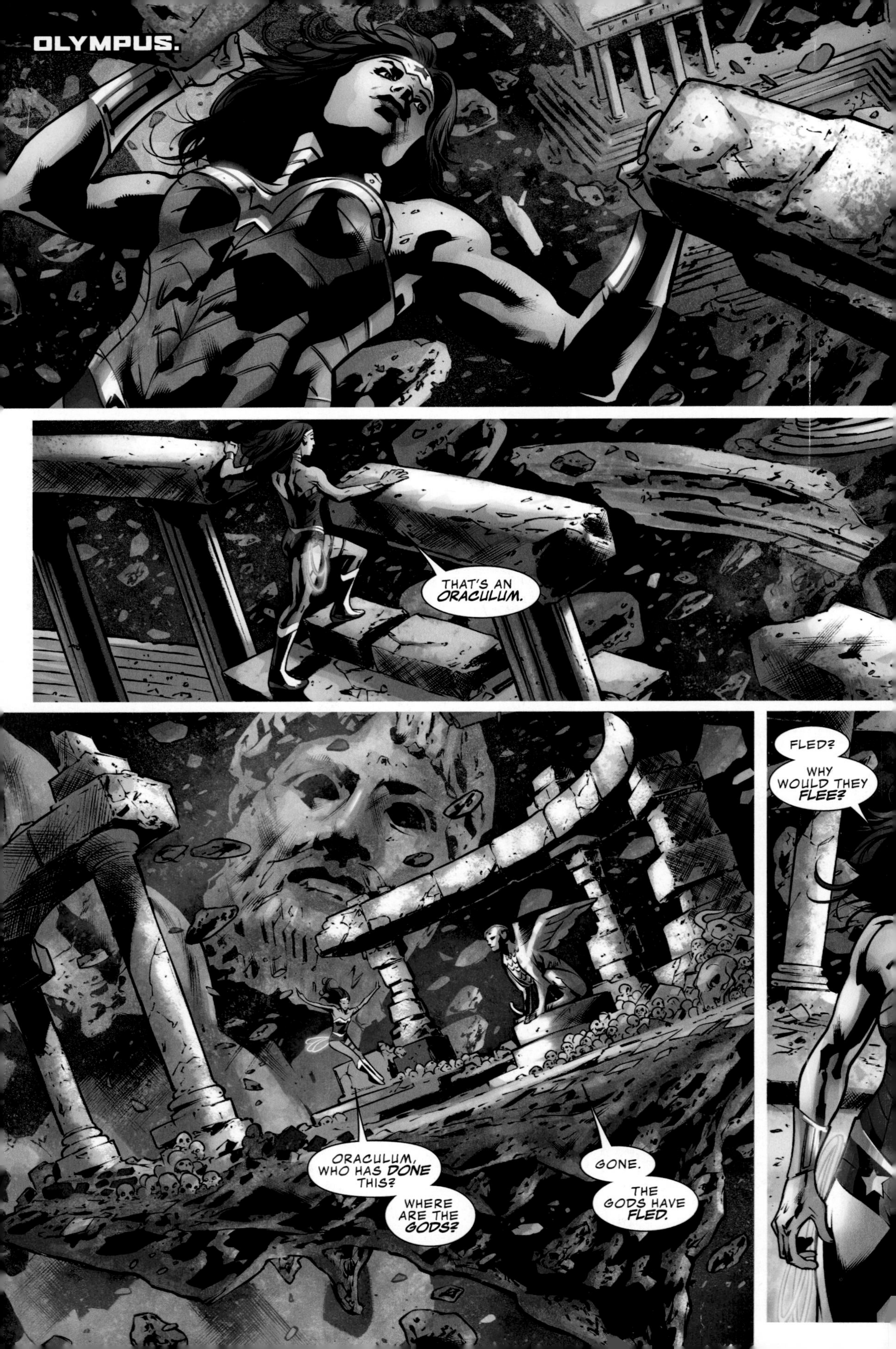
OLYMPUS.
THAT'S AN ORACULUM.
ORACULUM, WHO HAS DONE THIS?
WHERE ARE THE GODS?
GONE.
THE GODS HAVE FLED.
FLED?
WHY WOULD THEY FLEE?

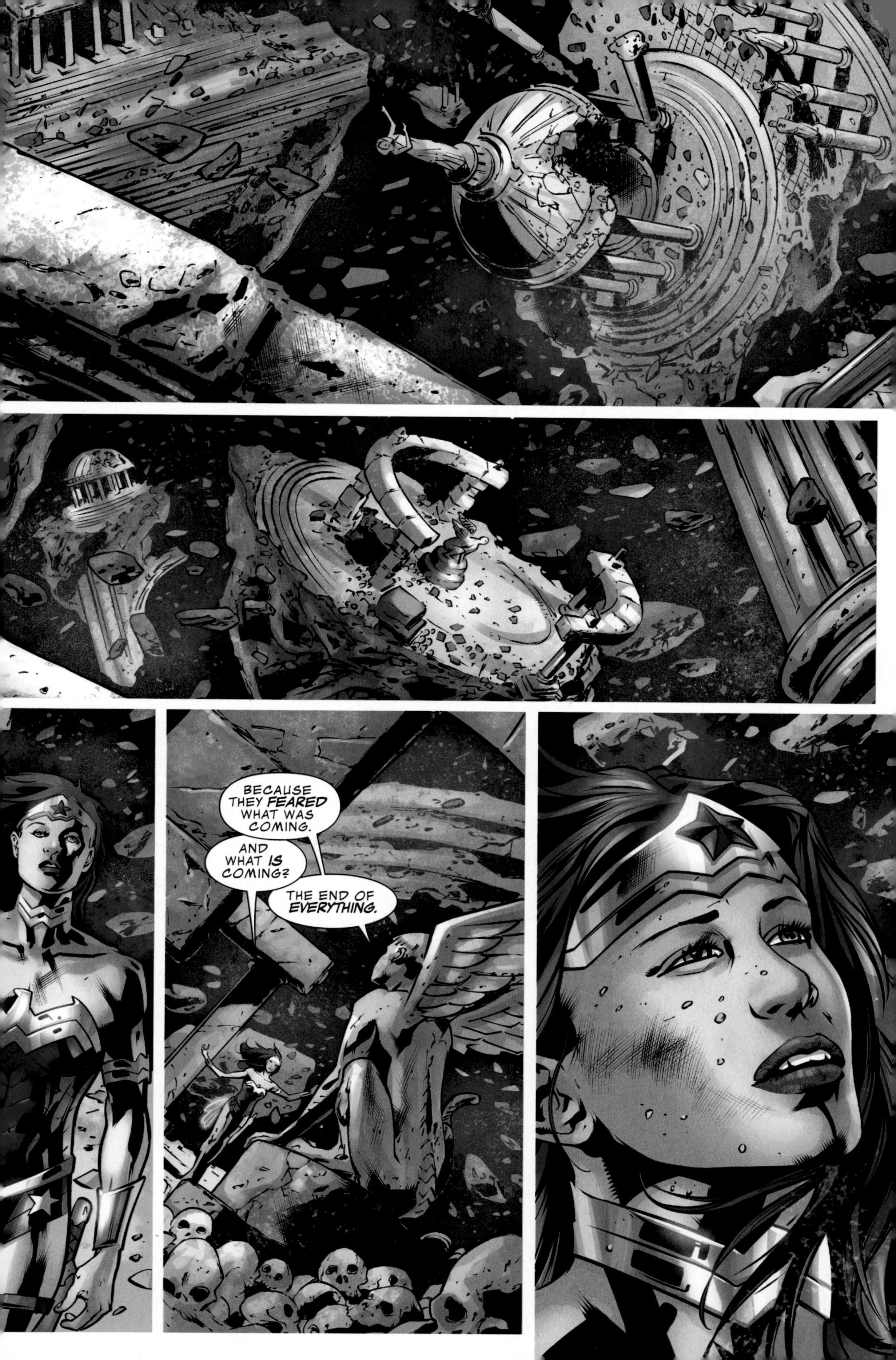
BECAUSE THEY FEARED WHAT WAS COMING.
AND WHAT IS COMING?
THE END OF EVERYTHING.

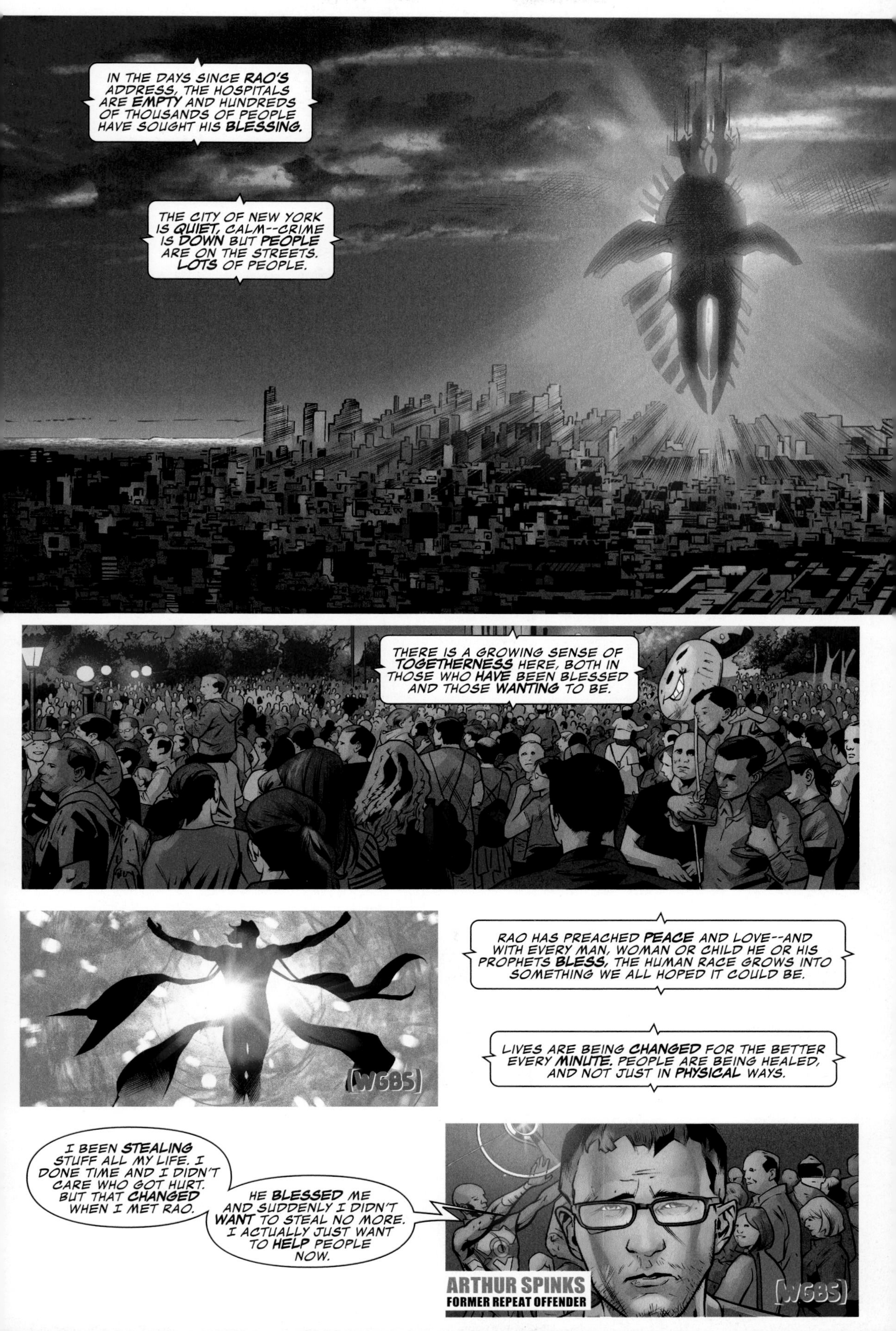
IN THE DAYS SINCE RAO'S ADDRESS, THE HOSPITALS ARE EMPTY AND HUNDREDS OF THOUSANDS OF PEOPLE HAVE SOUGHT HIS BLESSING.
THE CITY OF NEW YORK IS QUIET, CALM--CRIME IS DOWN BUT PEOPLE ARE ON THE STREETS. LOTS OF PEOPLE.
THERE IS A GROWING SENSE OF TOGETHERNESS HERE, BOTH IN THOSE WHO HAVE BEEN BLESSED AND THOSE WANTING TO BE.
[WGBS]
RAO HAS PREACHED PEACE AND LOVE--AND WITH EVERY MAN, WOMAN OR CHILD HE OR HIS PROPHETS BLESS, THE HUMAN RACE GROWS INTO SOMETHING WE ALL HOPED IT COULD BE.
LIVES ARE BEING CHANGED FOR THE BETTER EVERY MINUTE. PEOPLE ARE BEING HEALED, AND NOT JUST IN PHYSICAL WAYS.
I BEEN STEALING STUFF ALL MY LIFE. I DONE TIME AND I DIDN'T CARE WHO GOT HURT. BUT THAT CHANGED WHEN I MET RAO.
HE BLESSED ME AND SUDDENLY I DIDN'T WANT TO STEAL NO MORE. I ACTUALLY JUST WANT TO HELP PEOPLE NOW.
ARTHUR SPINKS
FORMER REPEAT OFFENDER
[WGBS]

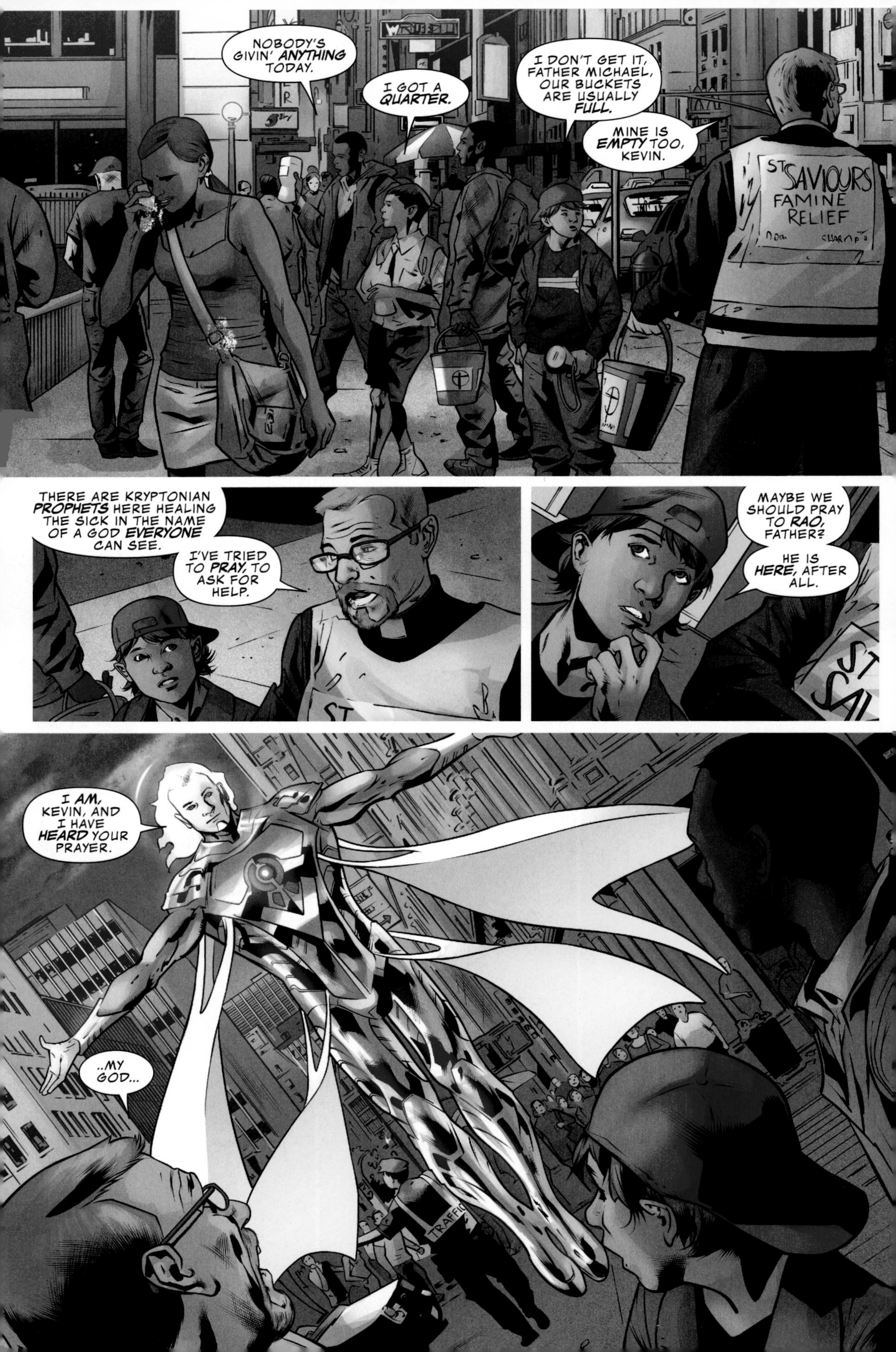
NOBODY'S GIVIN' ANYTHING TODAY.
I GOT A QUARTER.
I DON'T GET IT, FATHER MICHAEL, OUR BUCKETS ARE USUALLY FULL.
MINE IS EMPTY TOO, KEVIN.
ST SAVIOURS FAMINE RELIEF
THERE ARE KRYPTONIAN PROPHETS HERE HEALING THE SICK IN THE NAME OF A GOD EVERYONE CAN SEE.
I'VE TRIED TO PRAY, TO ASK FOR HELP.
MAYBE WE SHOULD PRAY TO RAO, FATHER?
HE IS HERE, AFTER ALL.
I AM, KEVIN, AND I HAVE HEARD YOUR PRAYER.
..MY GOD...

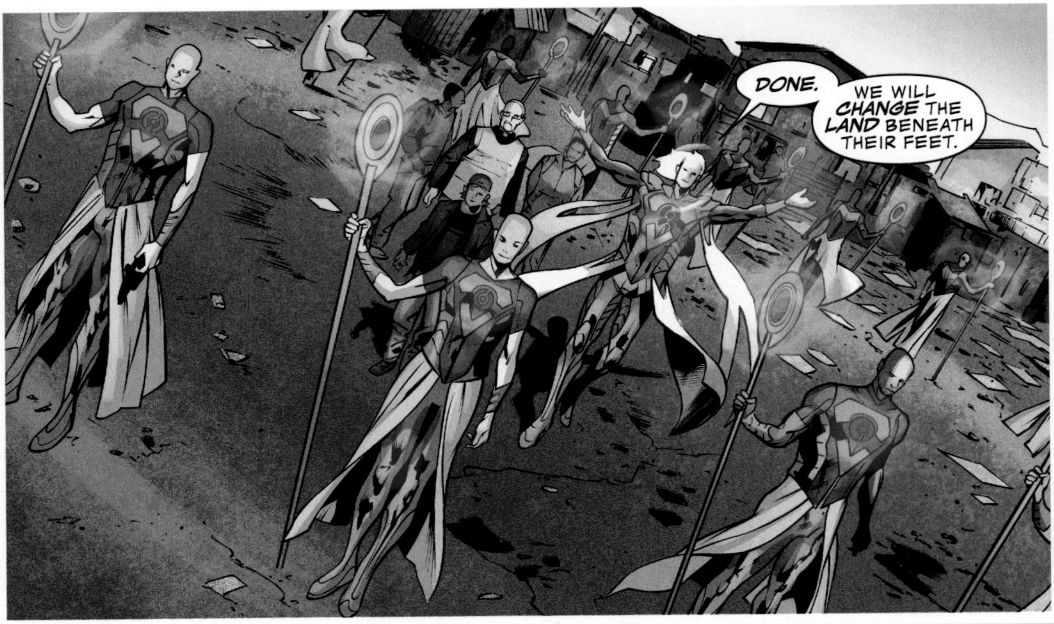
DONE.
WE WILL CHANGE THE LAND BENEATH THEIR FEET.

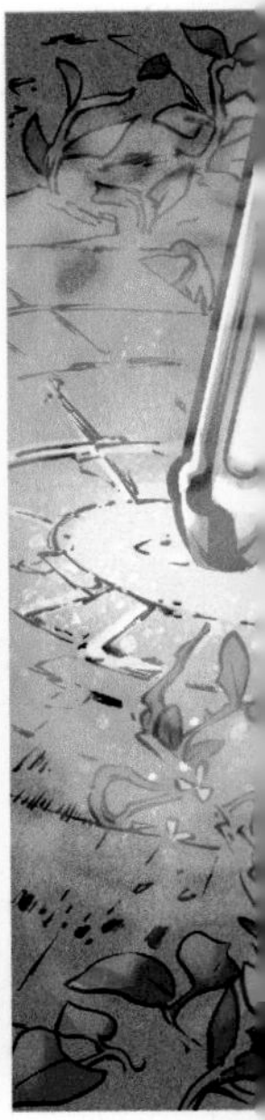

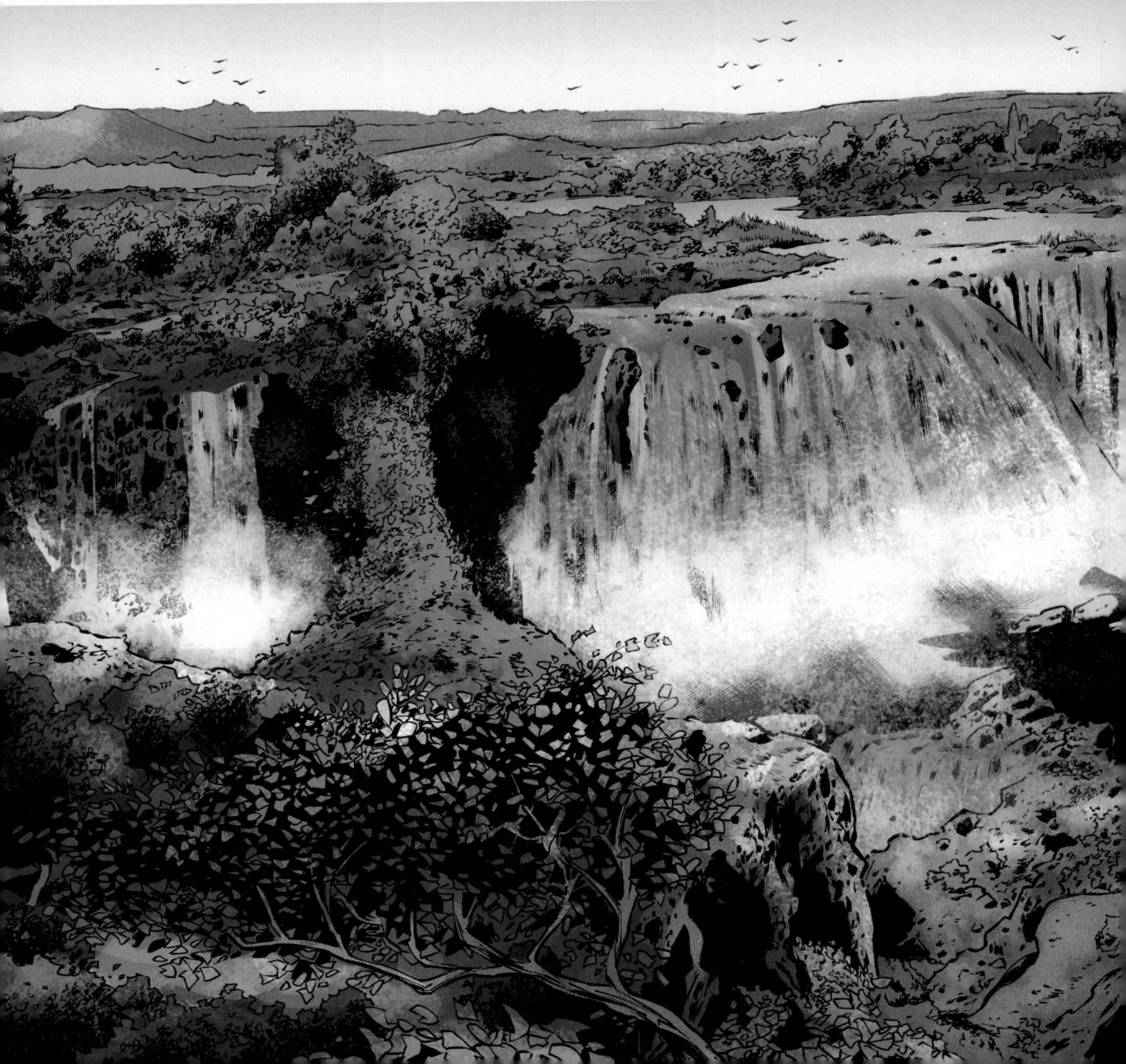

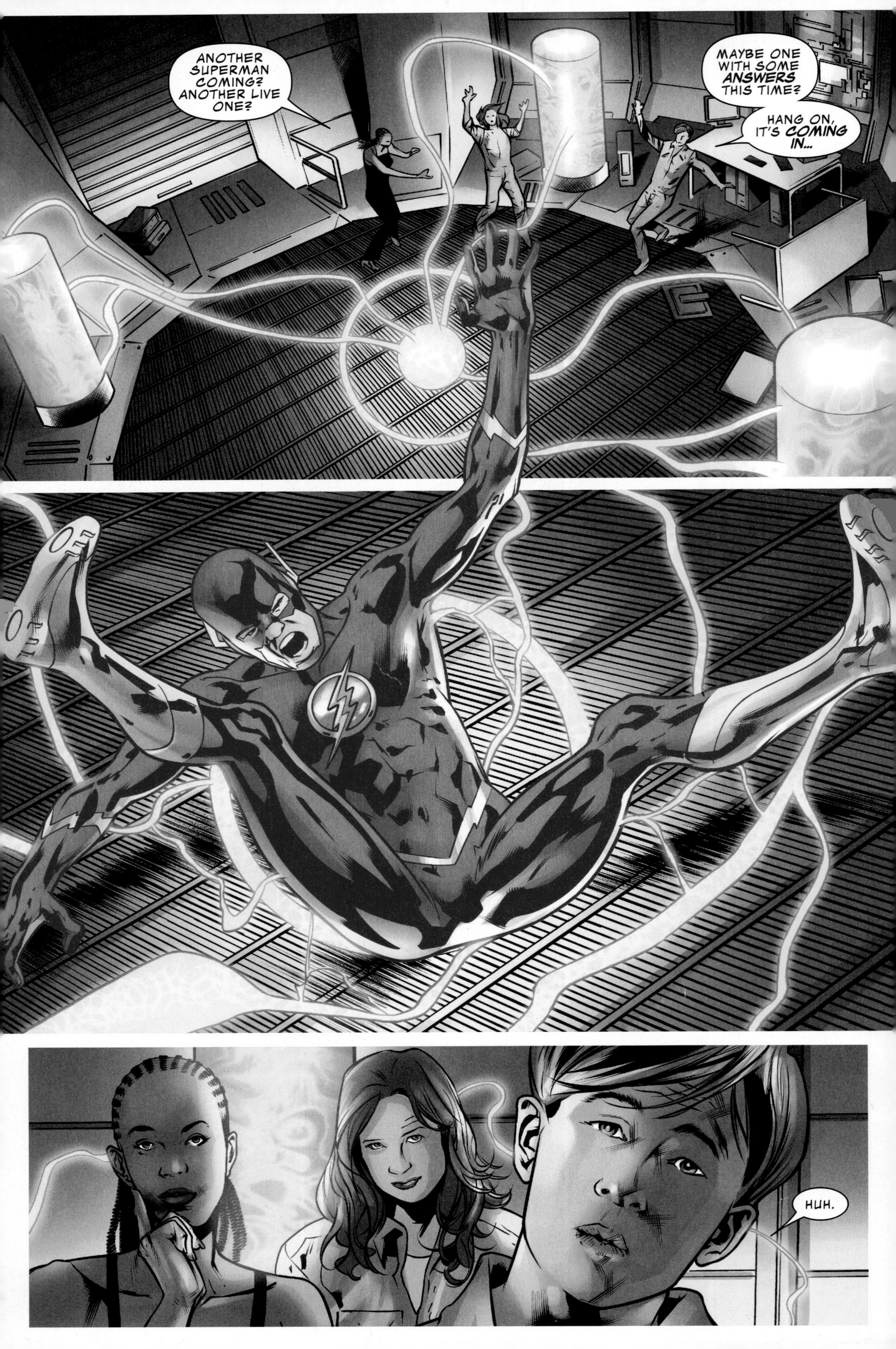
ANOTHER SUPERMAN COMING? ANOTHER LIVE ONE?
MAYBE ONE WITH SOME **ANSWERS** THIS TIME?
HANG ON, IT'S **COMING IN...**
HUH.

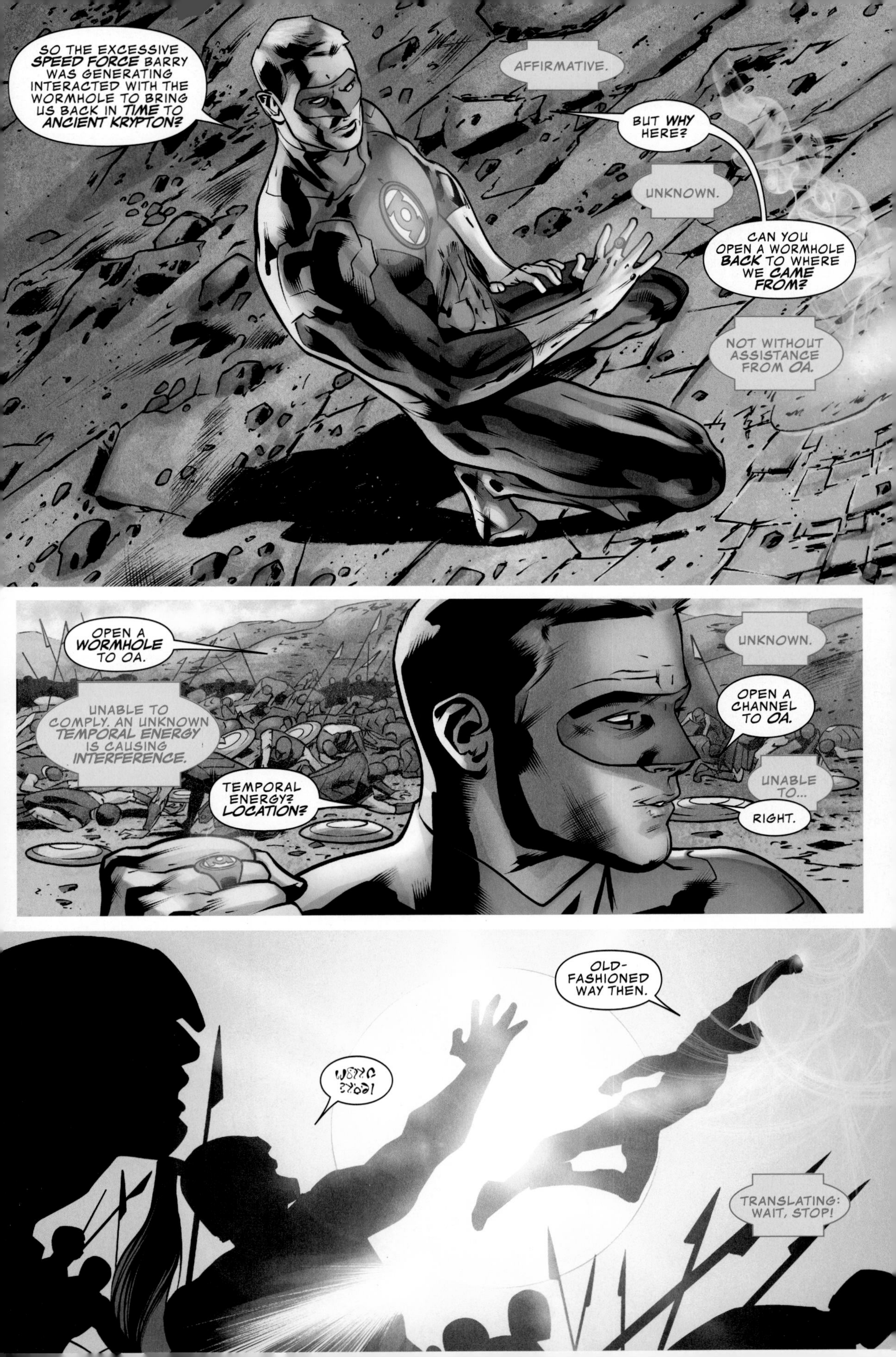
SO THE EXCESSIVE SPEED FORCE BARRY WAS GENERATING INTERACTED WITH THE WORMHOLE TO BRING US BACK IN TIME TO ANCIENT KRYPTON?
AFFIRMATIVE.
BUT WHY HERE?
UNKNOWN.
CAN YOU OPEN A WORMHOLE BACK TO WHERE WE CAME FROM?
NOT WITHOUT ASSISTANCE FROM OA.
OPEN A WORMHOLE TO OA.
UNABLE TO COMPLY. AN UNKNOWN TEMPORAL ENERGY IS CAUSING INTERFERENCE.
TEMPORAL ENERGY? LOCATION?
UNKNOWN.
OPEN A CHANNEL TO OA.
UNABLE TO...
RIGHT.
OLD-FASHIONED WAY THEN.
TRANSLATING: WAIT, STOP!

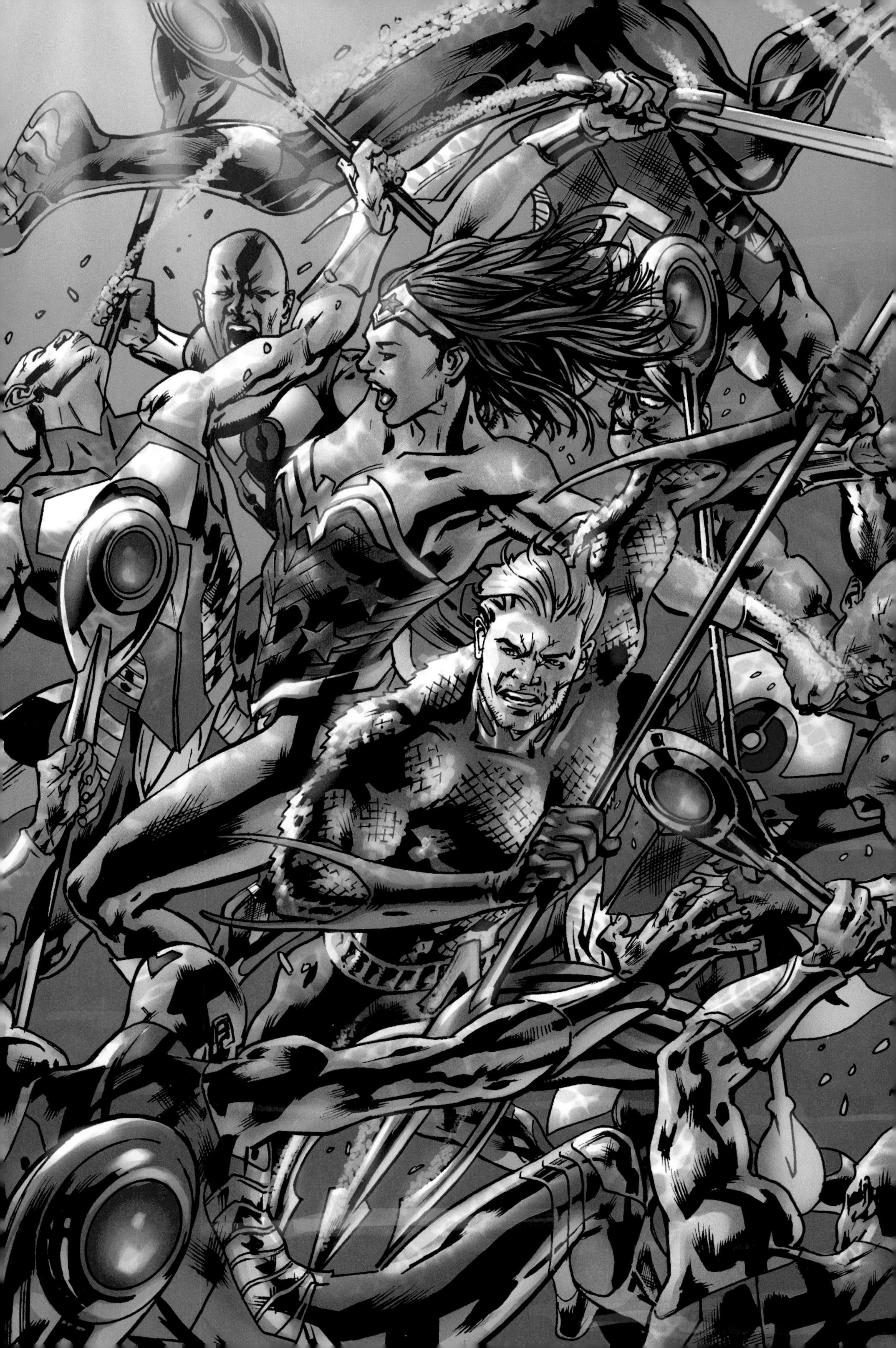

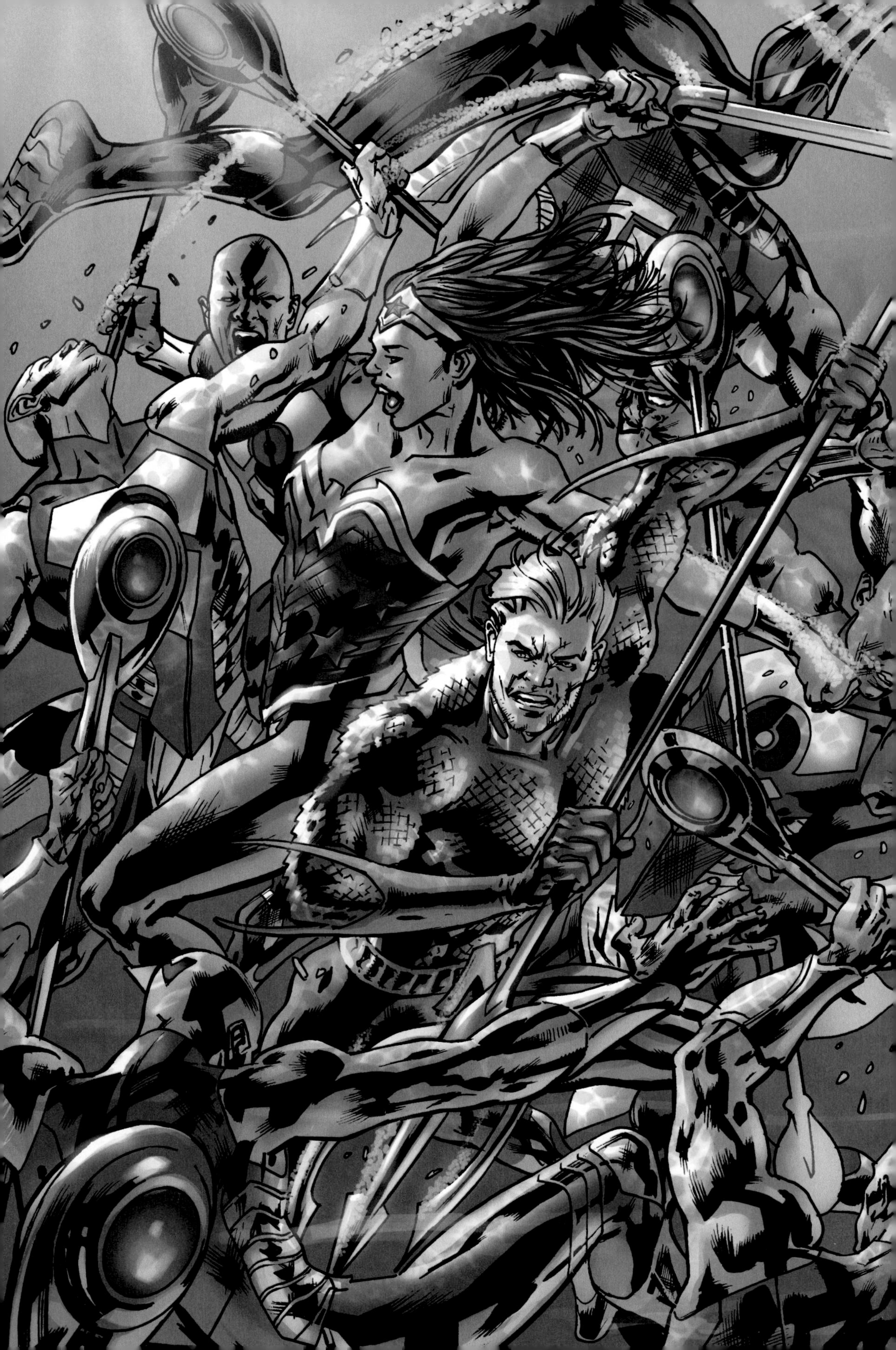

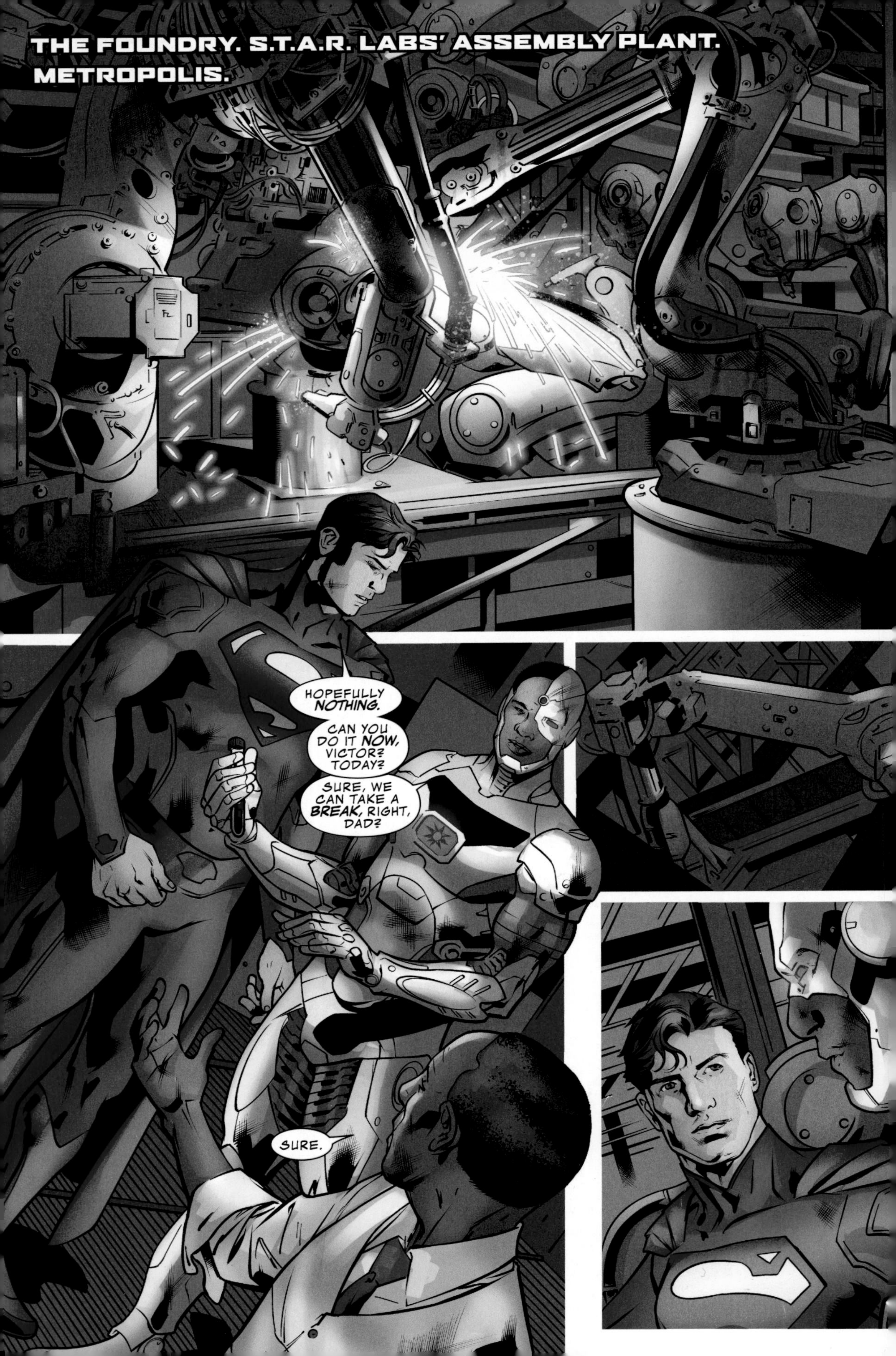
THE FOUNDRY. S.T.A.R. LABS' ASSEMBLY PLANT. METROPOLIS.
HOPEFULLY NOTHING.
CAN YOU DO IT NOW, VICTOR? TODAY?
SURE, WE CAN TAKE A BREAK, RIGHT, DAD?
SURE.

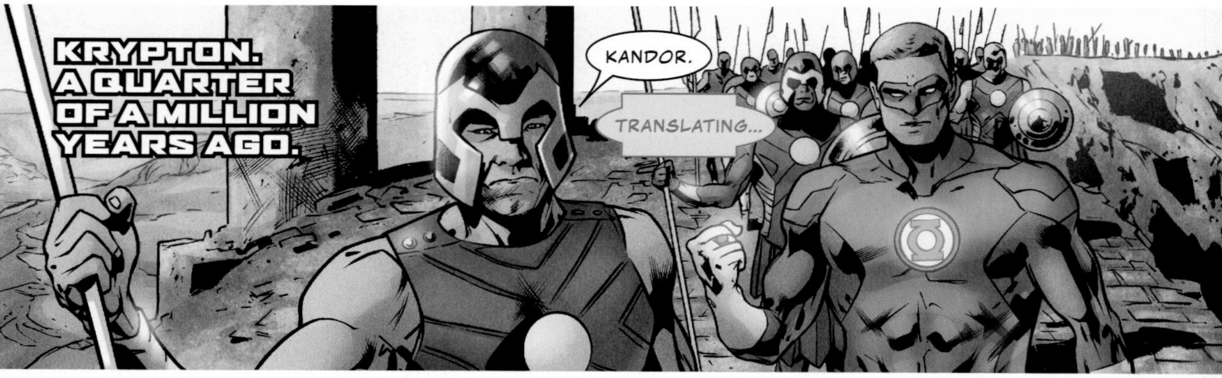
KRYPTON. A QUARTER OF A MILLION YEARS AGO.
KANDOR.
TRANSLATING...

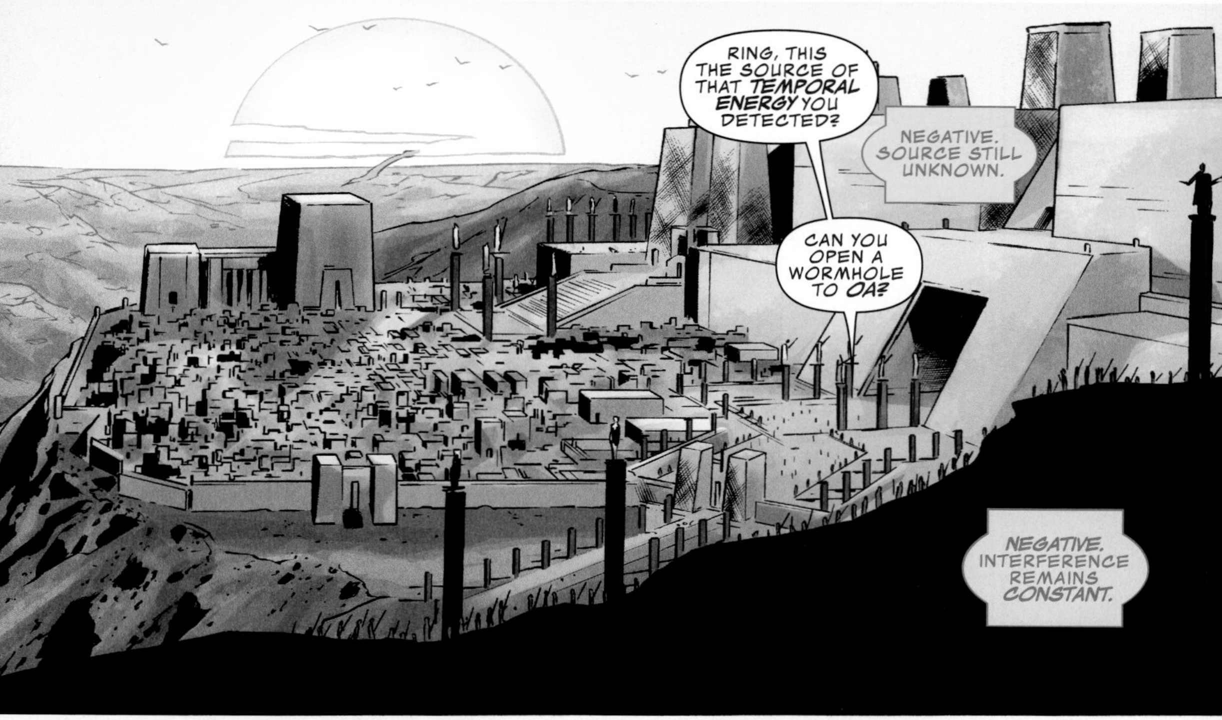
RING, THIS THE SOURCE OF THAT TEMPORAL ENERGY YOU DETECTED?
NEGATIVE. SOURCE STILL UNKNOWN.
CAN YOU OPEN A WORMHOLE TO OA?
NEGATIVE. INTERFERENCE REMAINS CONSTANT.

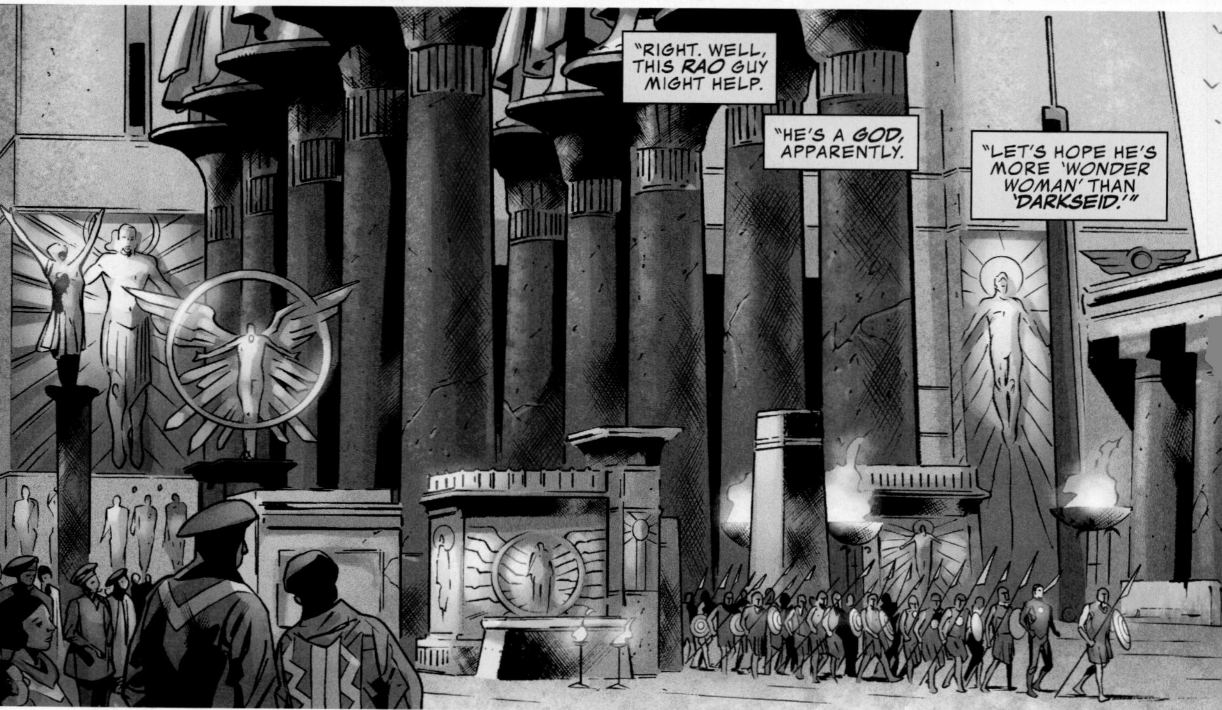
"RIGHT. WELL, THIS RAO GUY MIGHT HELP.
"HE'S A GOD, APPARENTLY.
"LET'S HOPE HE'S MORE 'WONDER WOMAN' THAN 'DARKSEID.'"

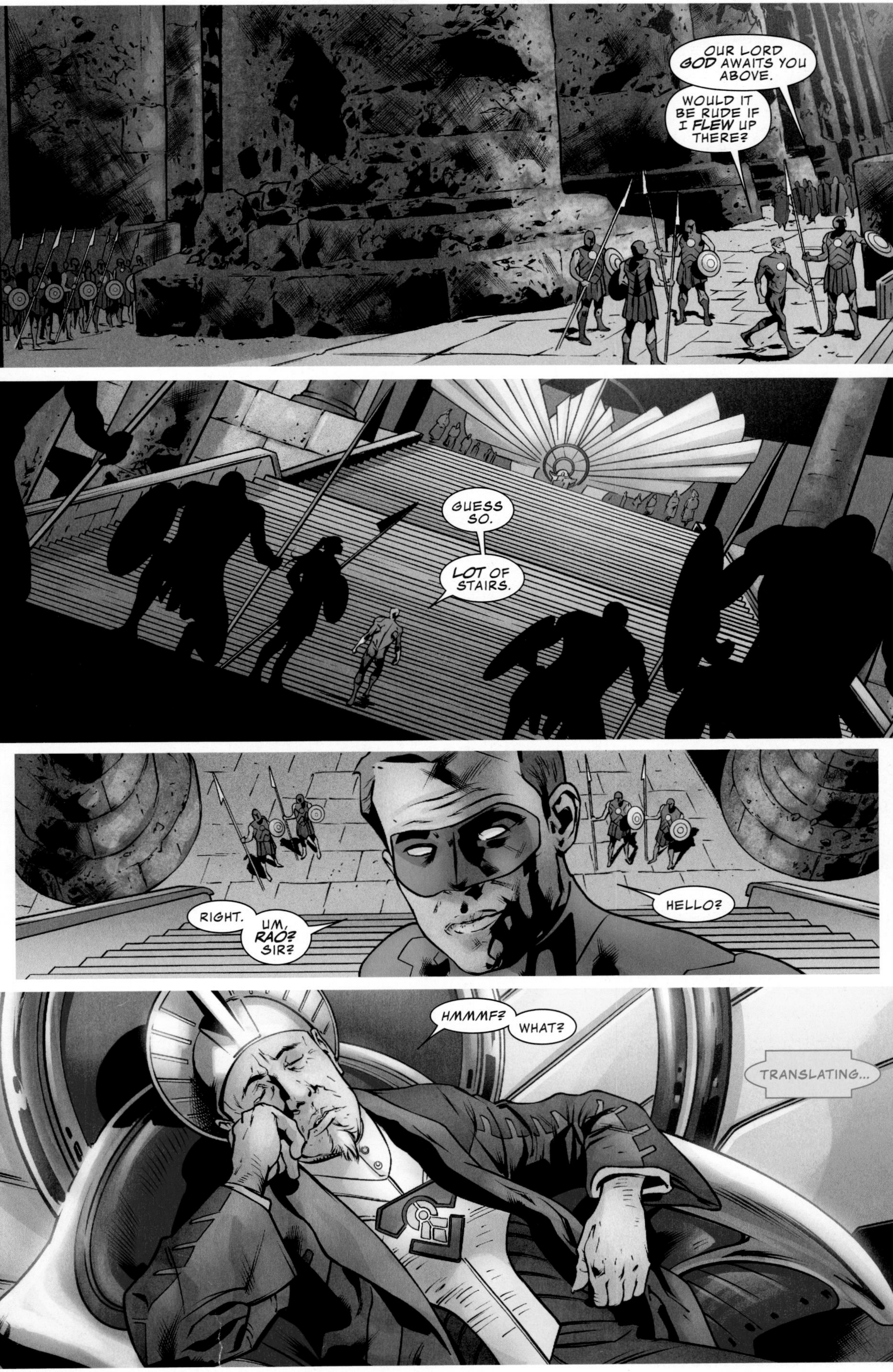

OUR LORD GOD AWAITS YOU ABOVE.
WOULD IT BE RUDE IF I FLEW UP THERE?
GUESS SO.
LOT OF STAIRS.
RIGHT.
UM, RAO? SIR?
HELLO?
HMMMF?
WHAT?
TRANSLATING...

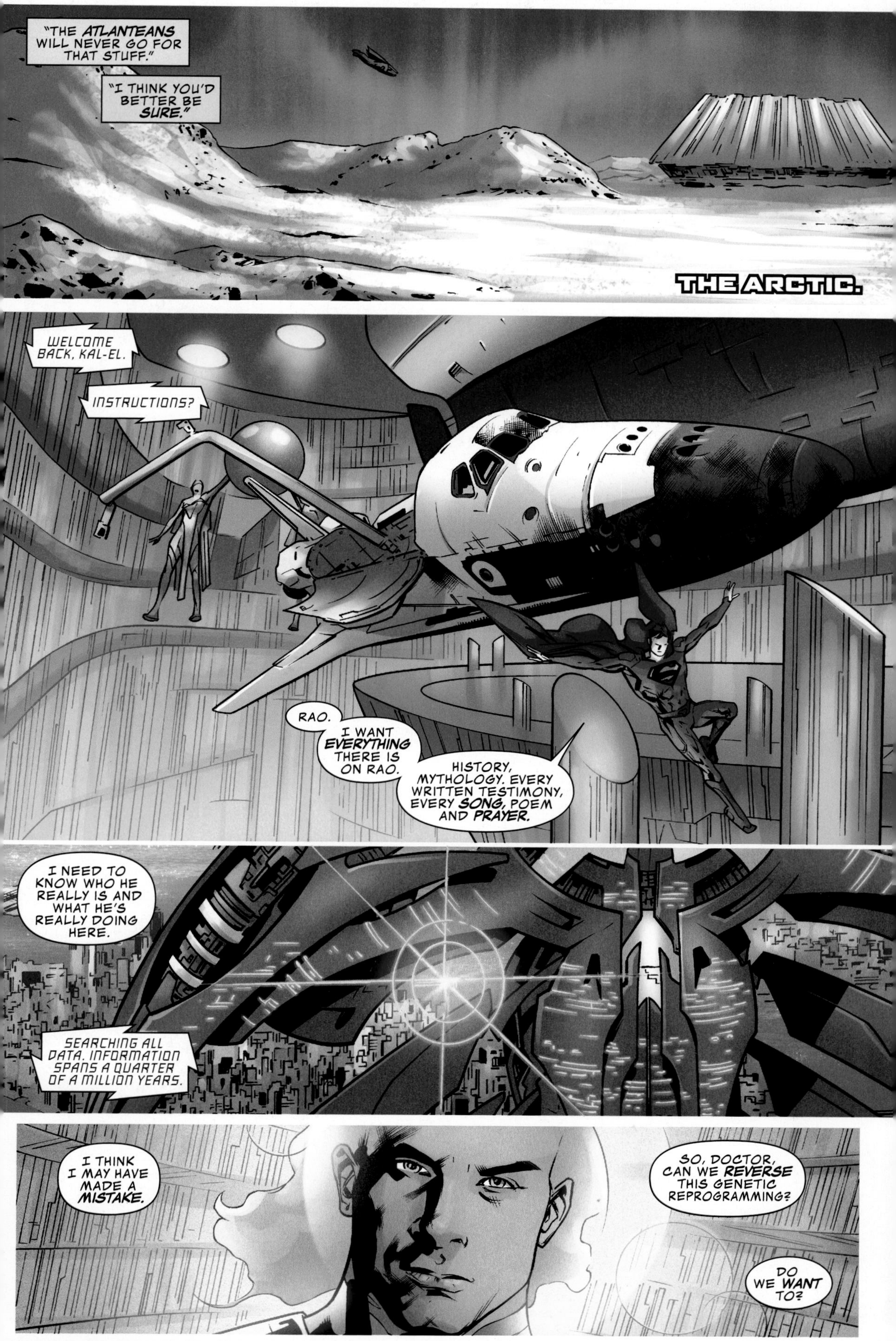
"THE ATLANTEANS WILL NEVER GO FOR THAT STUFF."
"I THINK YOU'D BETTER BE SURE."
THE ARCTIC.
WELCOME BACK, KAL-EL.
INSTRUCTIONS?
RAO.
I WANT EVERYTHING THERE IS ON RAO.
HISTORY, MYTHOLOGY. EVERY WRITTEN TESTIMONY, EVERY SONG, POEM AND PRAYER.
I NEED TO KNOW WHO HE REALLY IS AND WHAT HE'S REALLY DOING HERE.
SEARCHING ALL DATA. INFORMATION SPANS A QUARTER OF A MILLION YEARS.
I THINK I MAY HAVE MADE A MISTAKE.
SO, DOCTOR, CAN WE REVERSE THIS GENETIC REPROGRAMMING?
DO WE WANT TO?

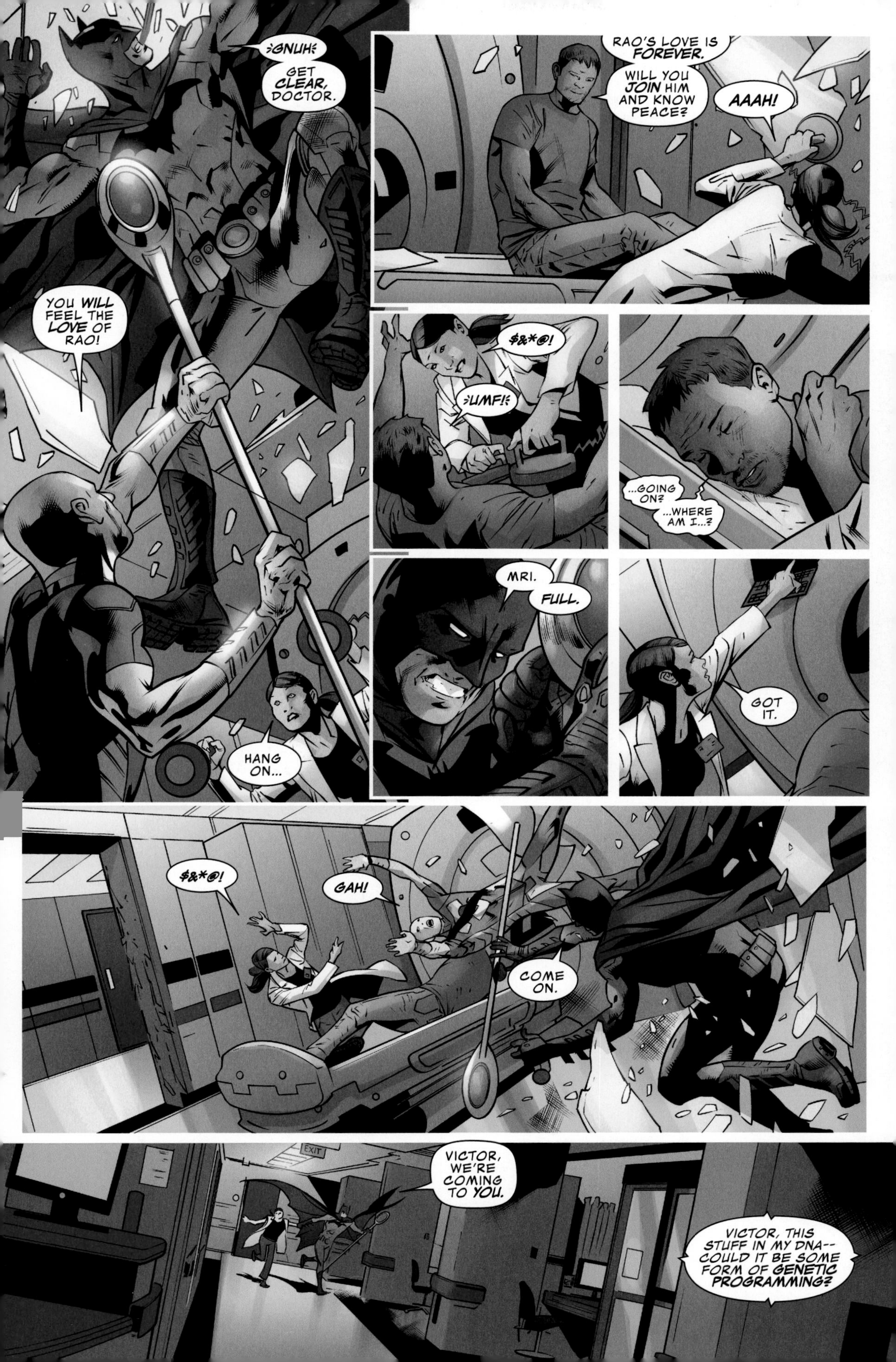
GNUH
GET CLEAR, DOCTOR.
YOU WILL FEEL THE LOVE OF RAO!
HANG ON...
RAO'S LOVE IS FOREVER.
WILL YOU JOIN HIM AND KNOW PEACE?
AAAH!
$&*@!
UMF!
...GOING ON?
...WHERE AM I...?
MRI.
FULL.
GOT IT.
$&*@!
GAH!
COME ON.
VICTOR, WE'RE COMING TO YOU.
EXIT
VICTOR, THIS STUFF IN MY DNA--COULD IT BE SOME FORM OF GENETIC PROGRAMMING?

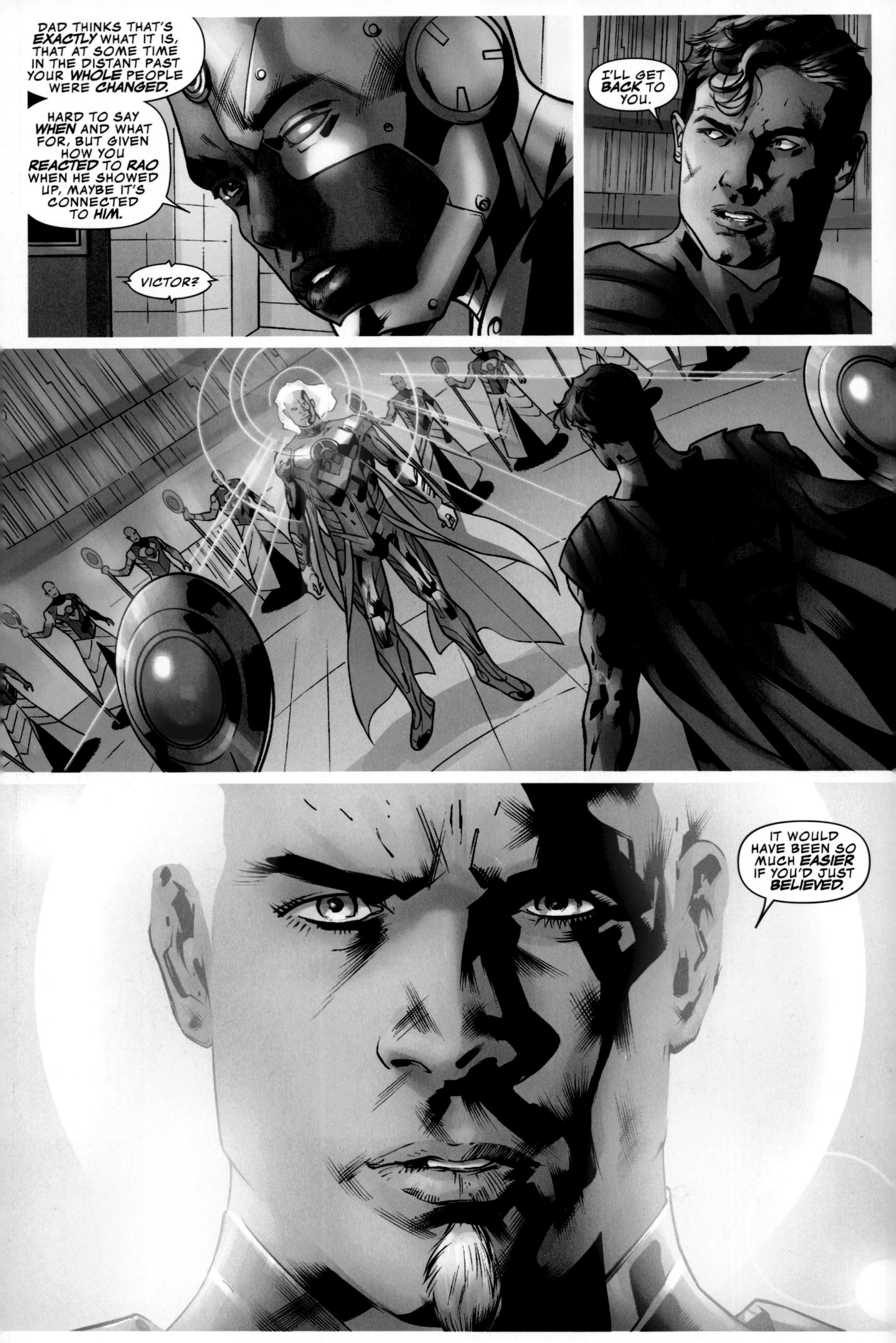
DAD THINKS THAT'S EXACTLY WHAT IT IS, THAT AT SOME TIME IN THE DISTANT PAST YOUR WHOLE PEOPLE WERE CHANGED.
HARD TO SAY WHEN AND WHAT FOR, BUT GIVEN HOW YOU REACTED TO RAO WHEN HE SHOWED UP, MAYBE IT'S CONNECTED TO HIM.
VICTOR?
I'LL GET BACK TO YOU.
IT WOULD HAVE BEEN SO MUCH EASIER IF YOU'D JUST BELIEVED.

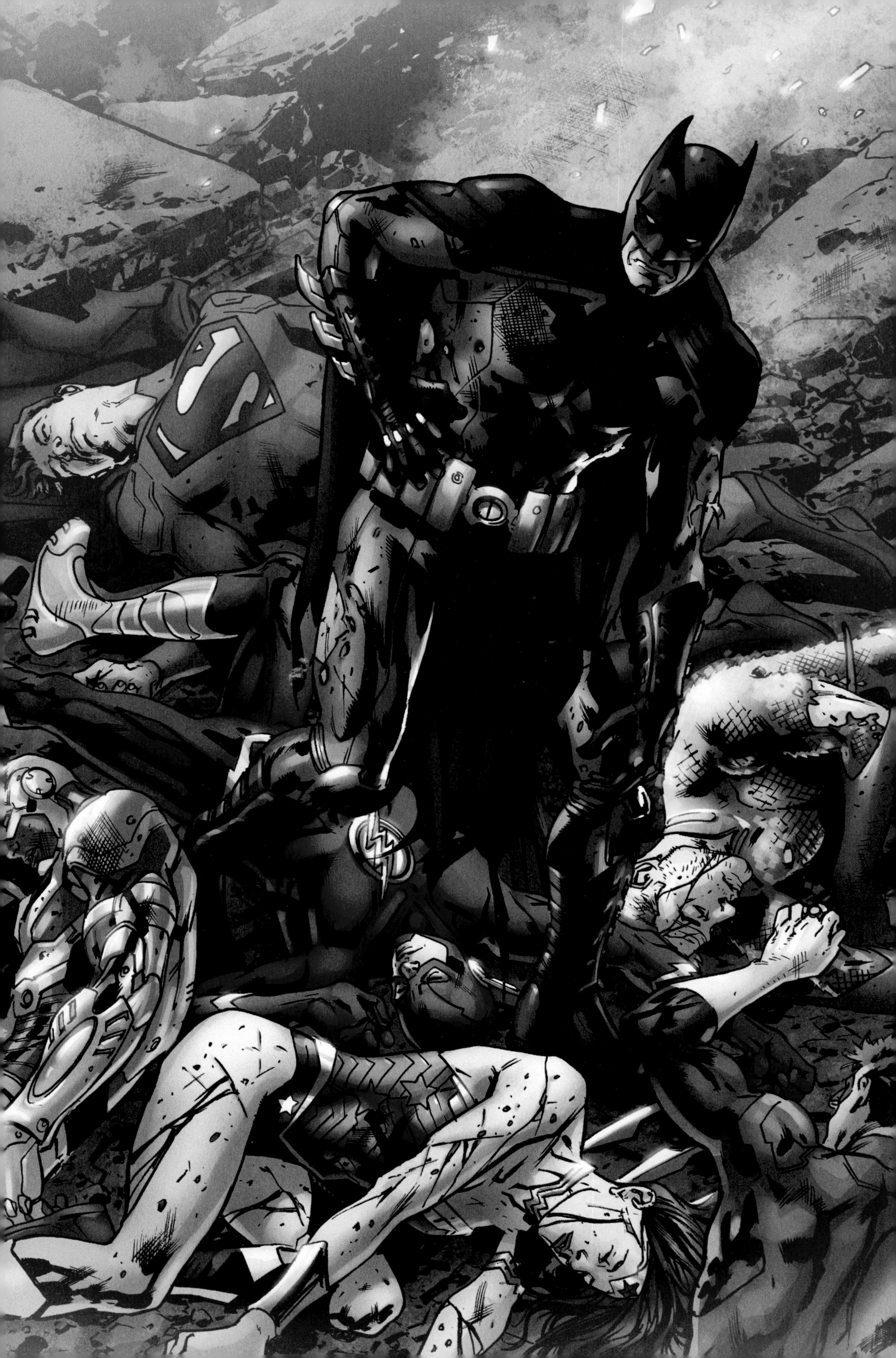

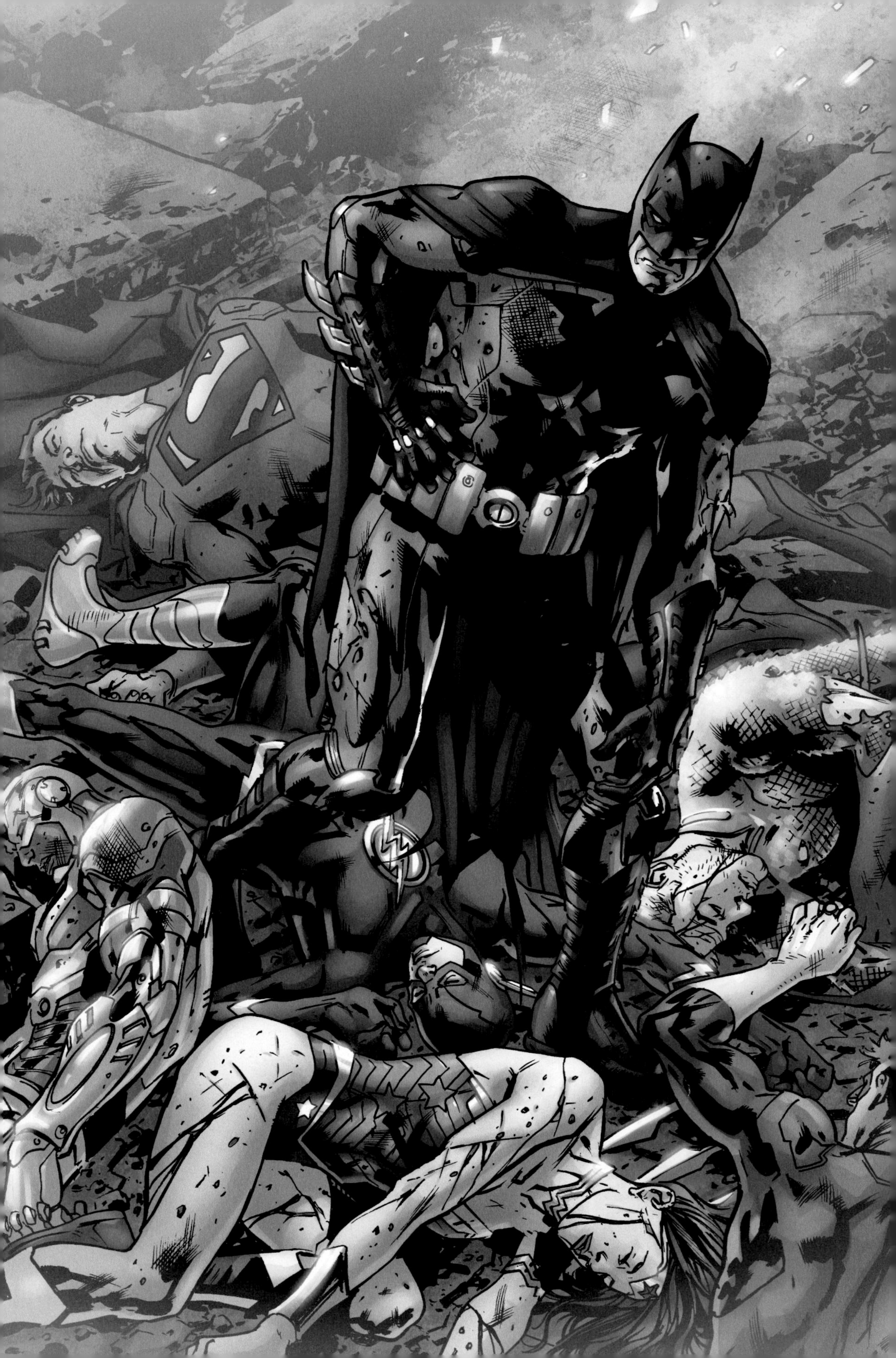

DC COMICS PRESENTS
THE JUSTICE LEAGUE OF AMERICA
POWER AND GLORY
PART FIVE
BY BRYAN HITCH

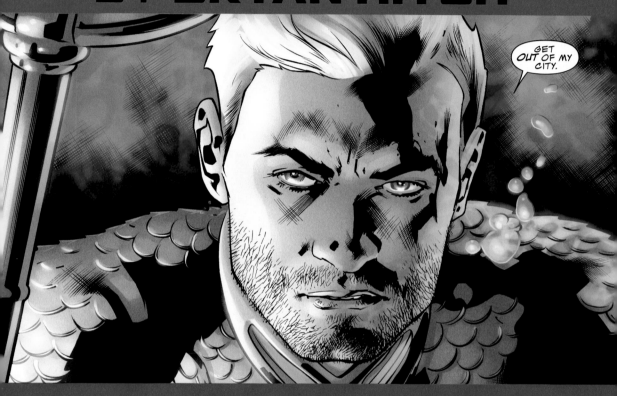

GET OUT OF MY CITY.

INKS BY DANIEL HENRIQUES,
ANDREW CURRIE & BRYAN HITCH
COLORS BY ALEX SINCLAIR
LETTERS BY CHRIS ELIOPOULOS
ASSISTS BY AMEDEO TURTURRO
EDITS BY BRIAN CUNNINGHAM
COVER BY BRYAN HITCH AND ALEX SINCLAIR

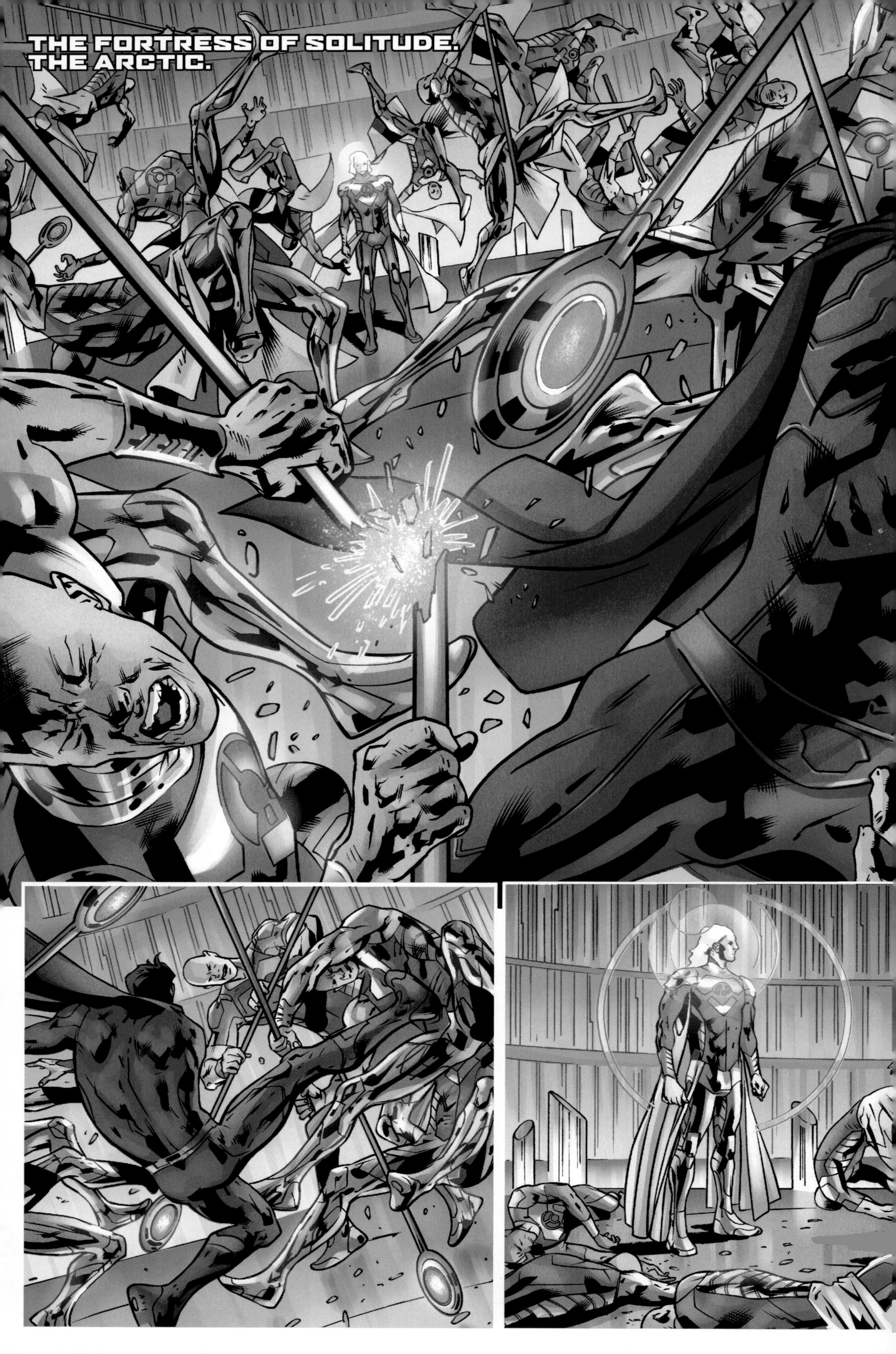
THE FORTRESS OF SOLITUDE. THE ARCTIC.

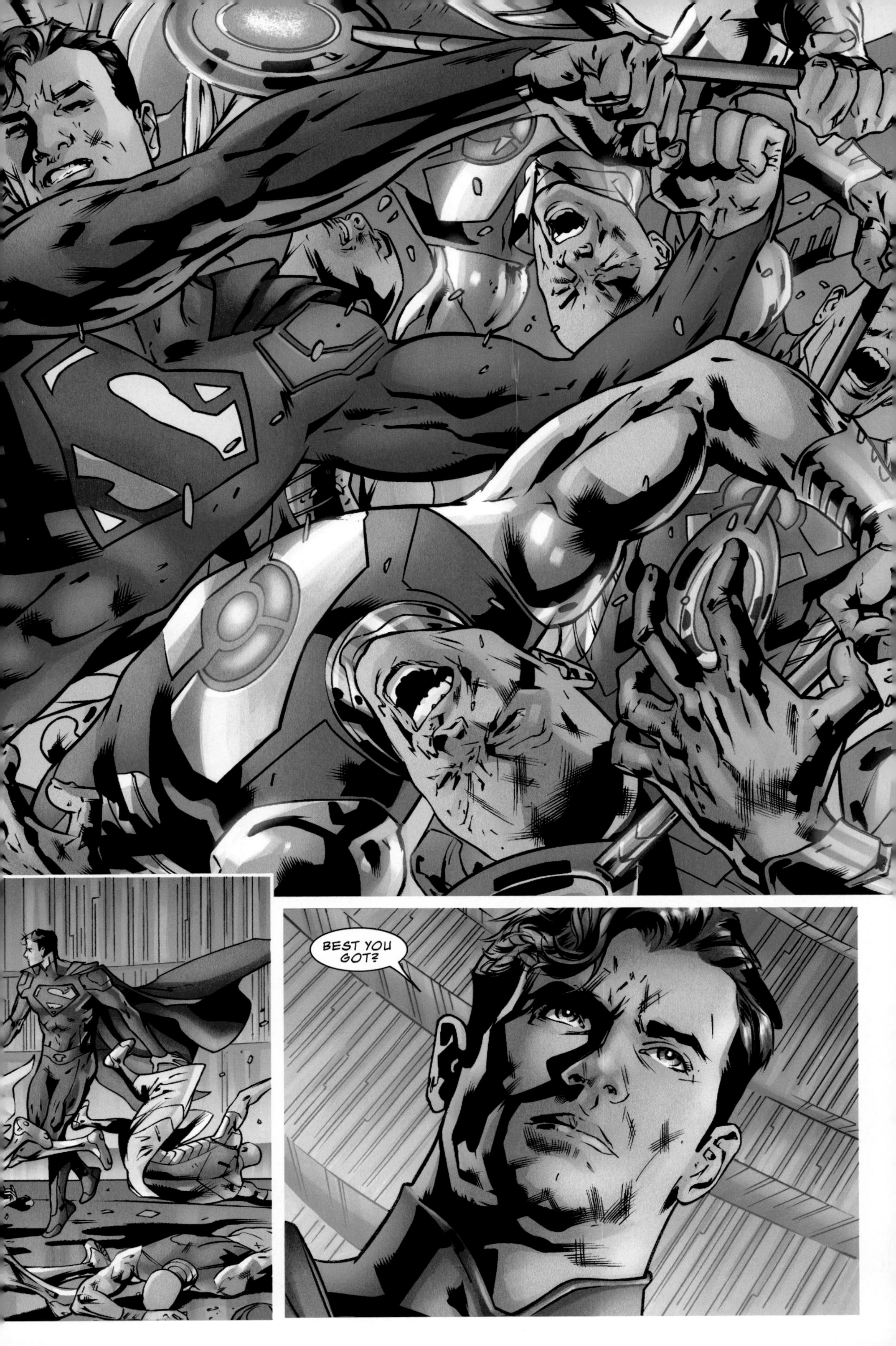
BEST YOU GOT?

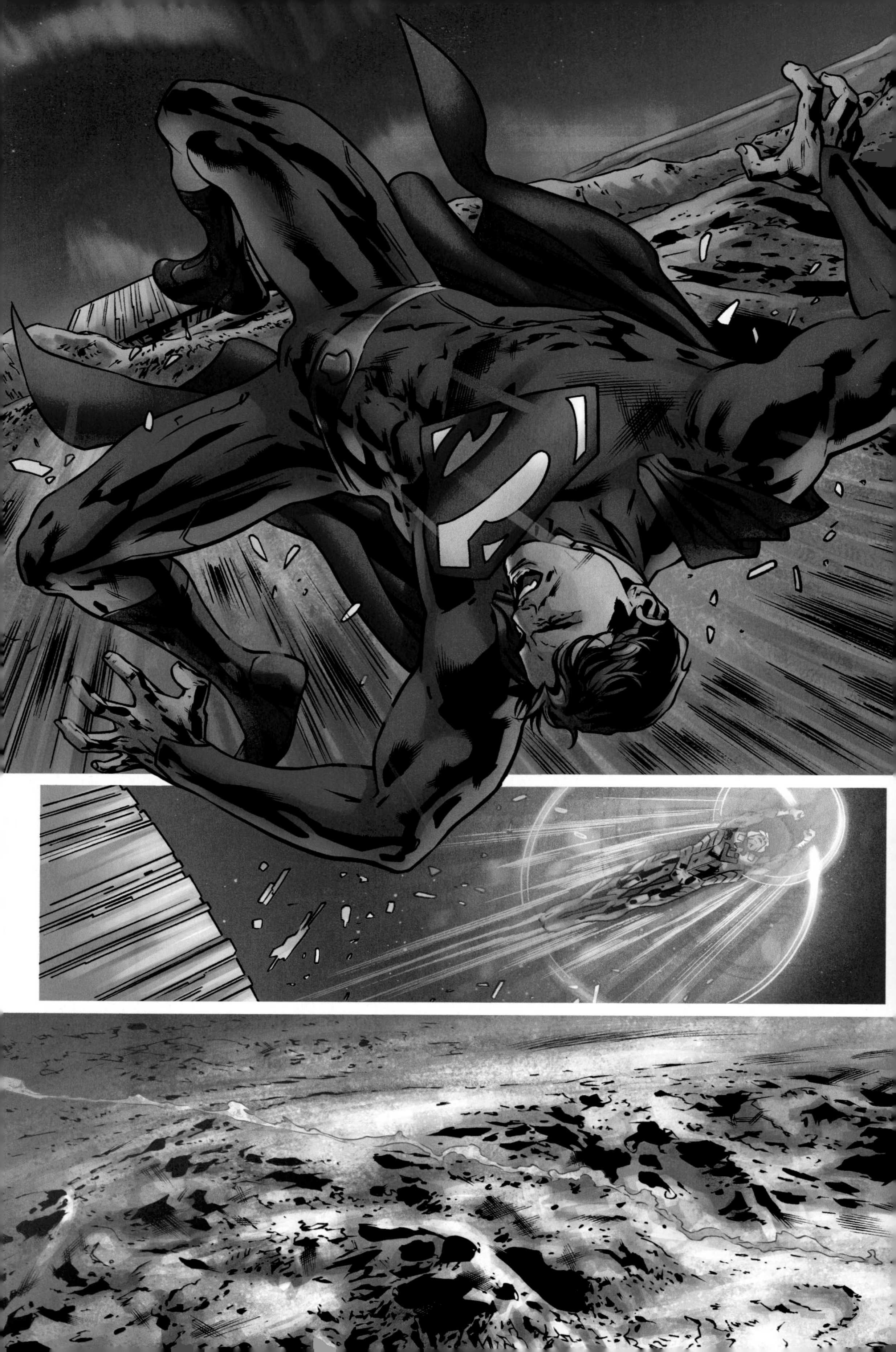

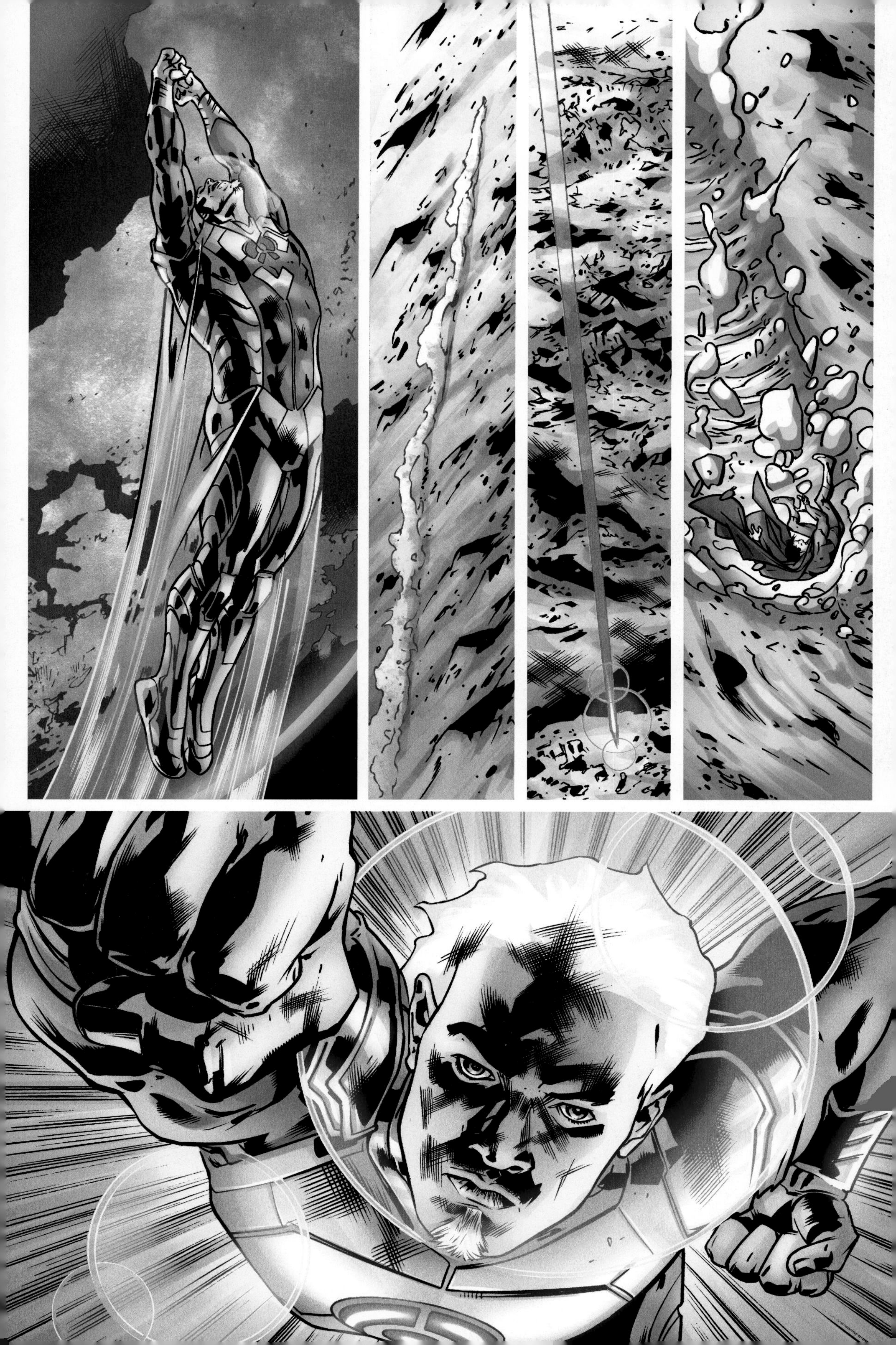

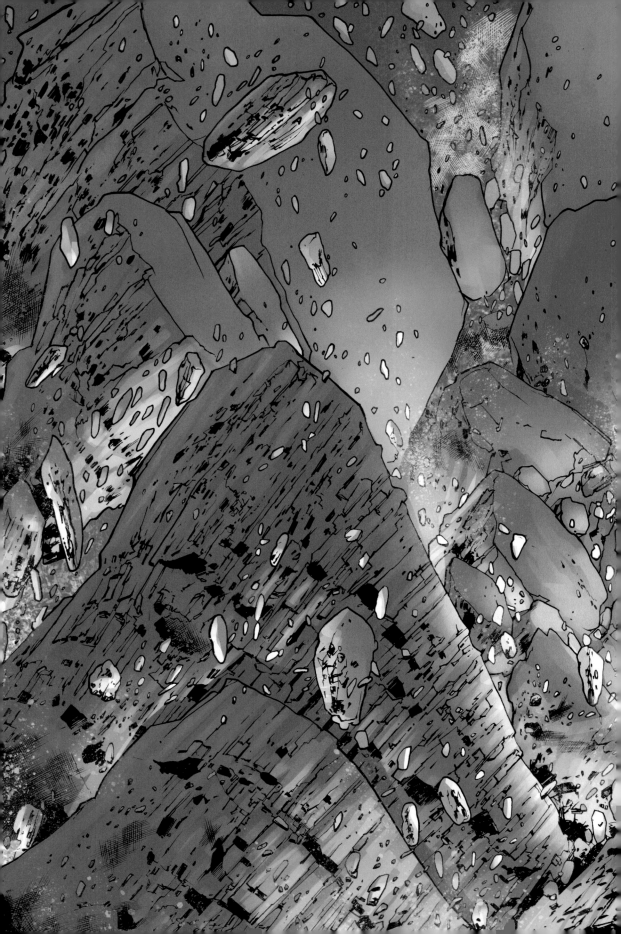

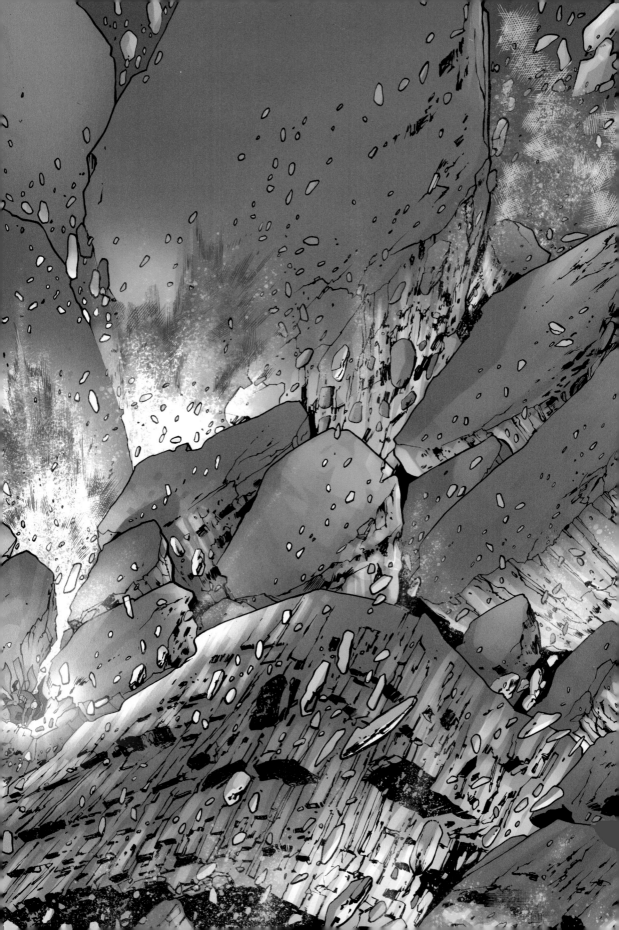

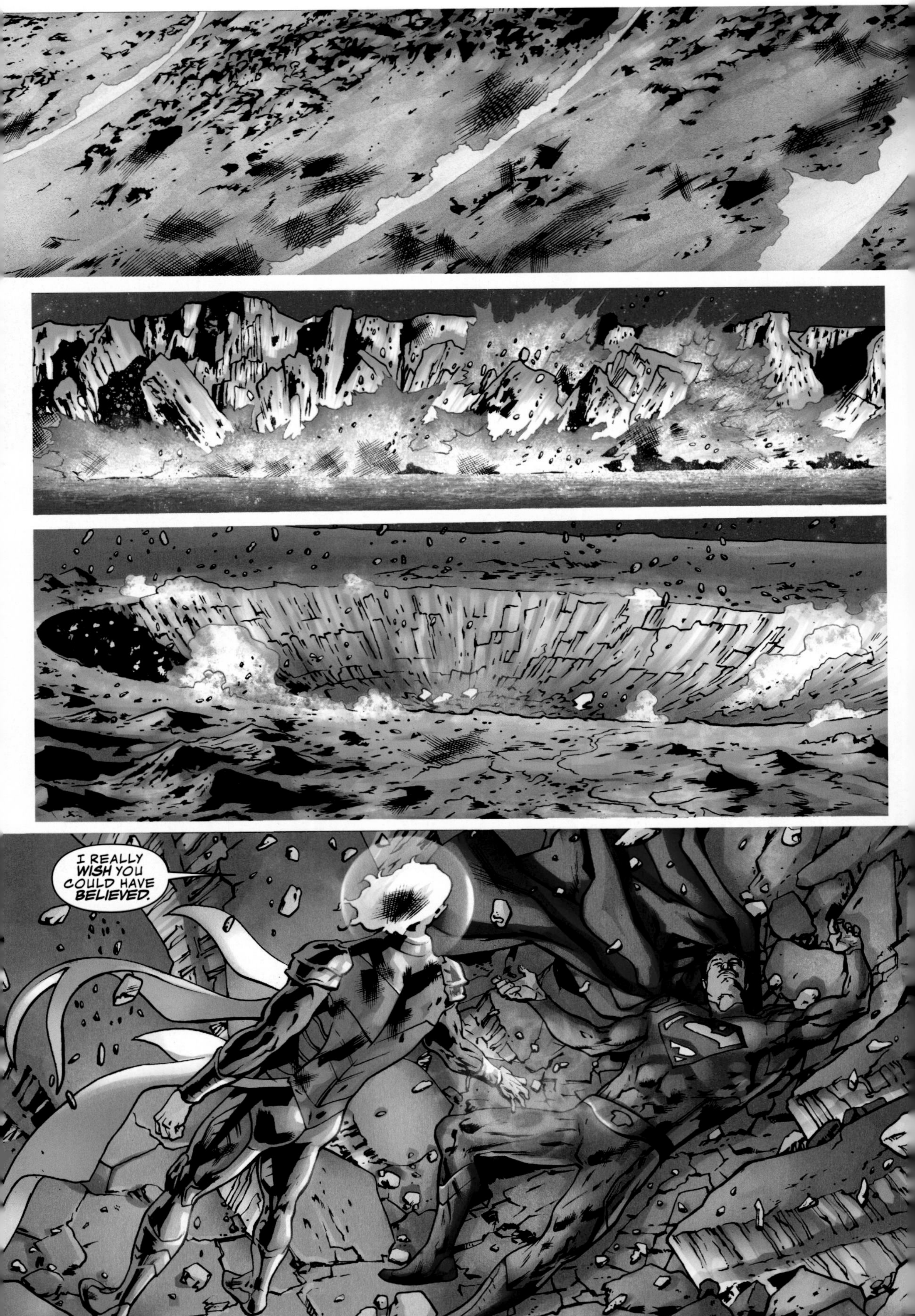
I REALLY WISH YOU COULD HAVE BELIEVED.

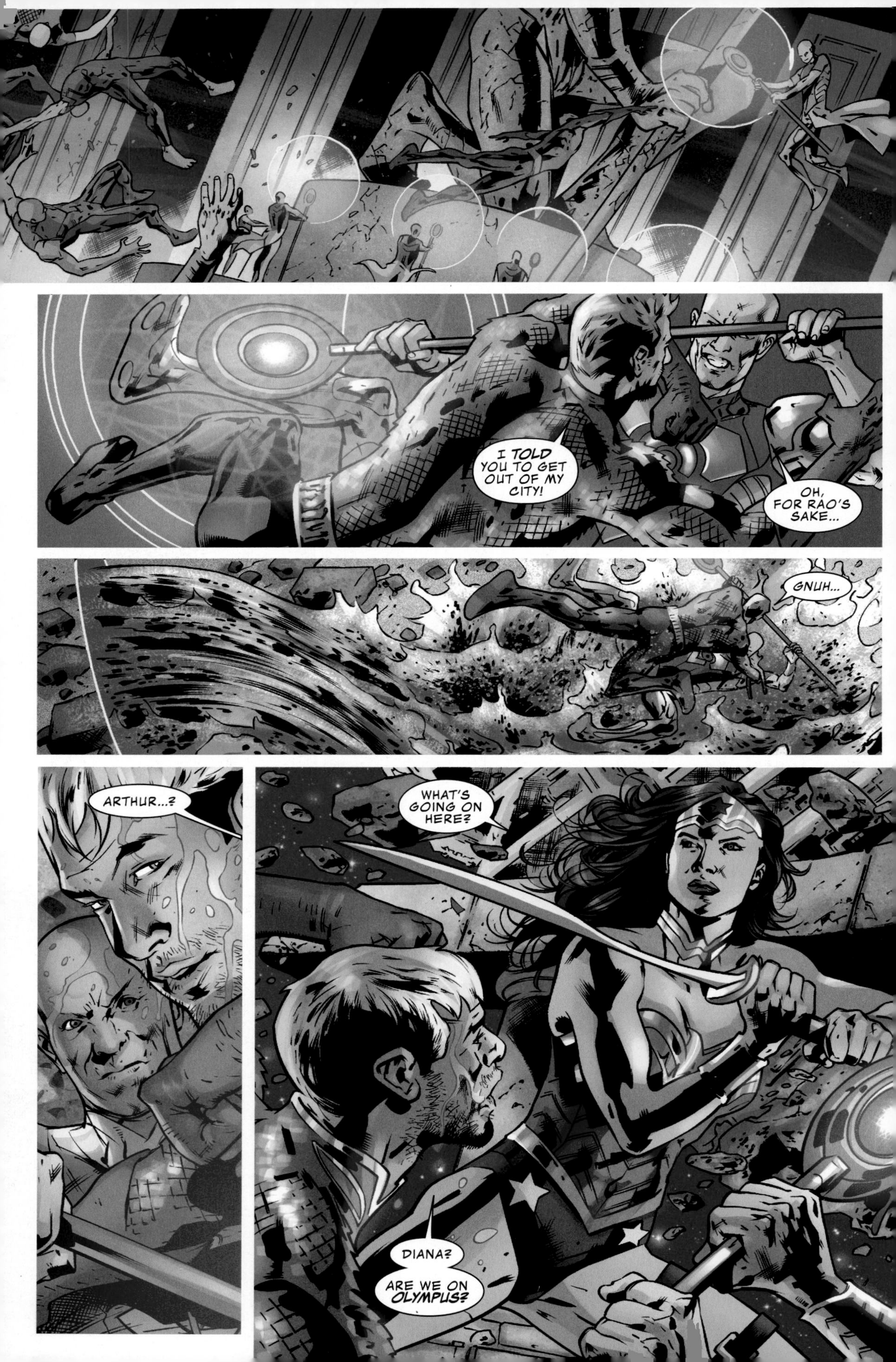
I TOLD YOU TO GET OUT OF MY CITY!
OH, FOR RAO'S SAKE...
GNUH...
ARTHUR...?
WHAT'S GOING ON HERE?
DIANA?
ARE WE ON OLYMPUS?

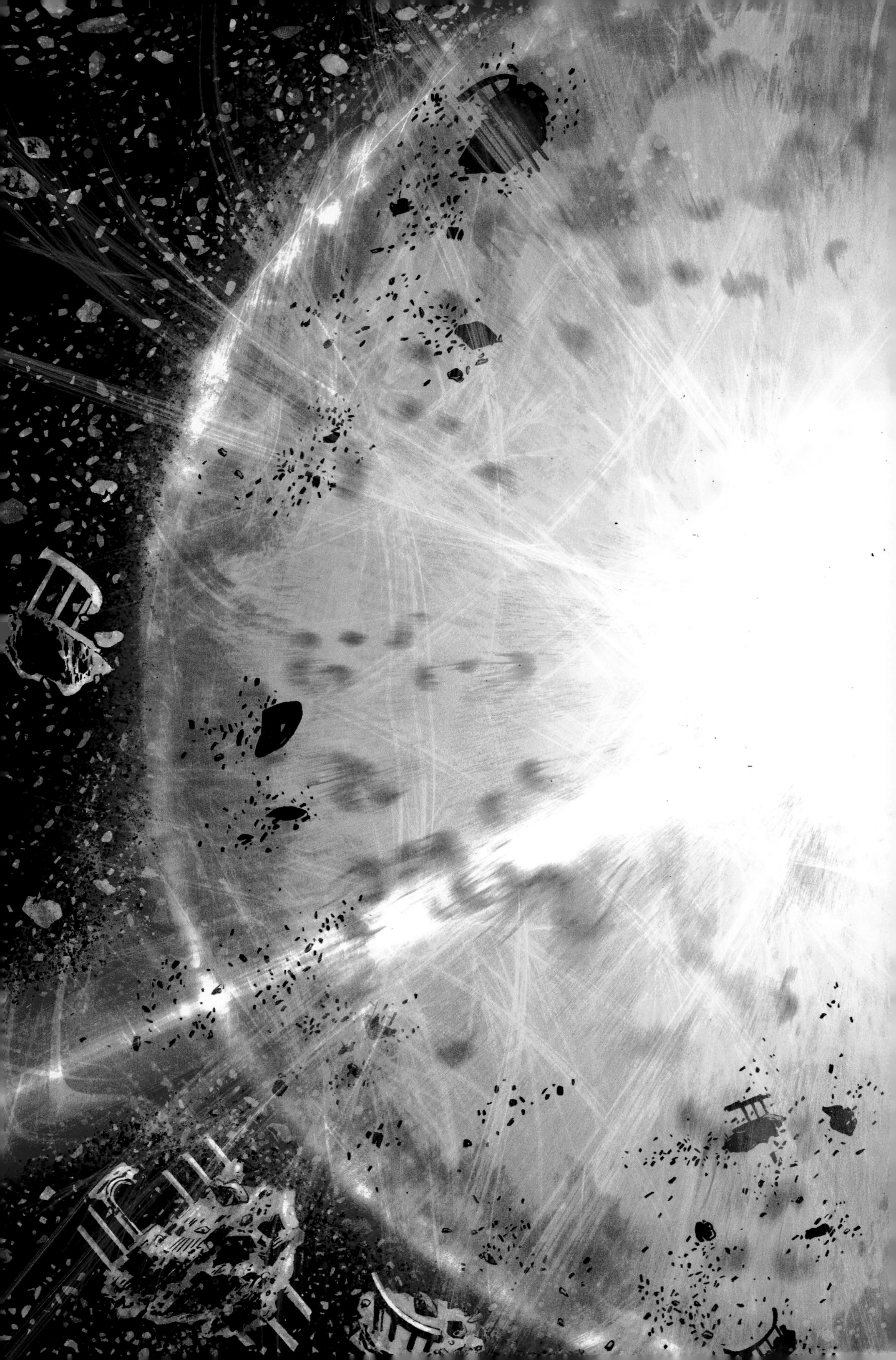

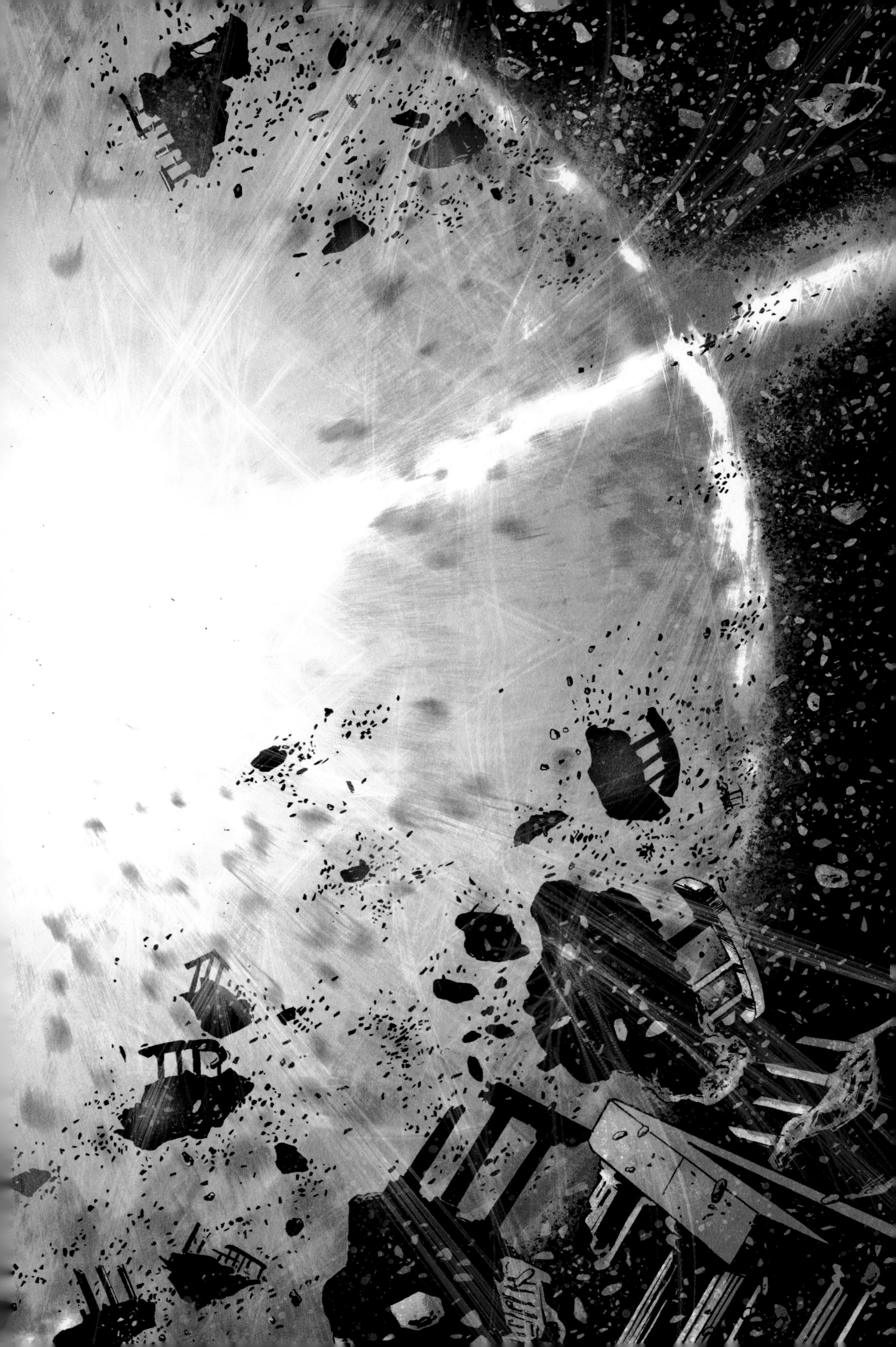

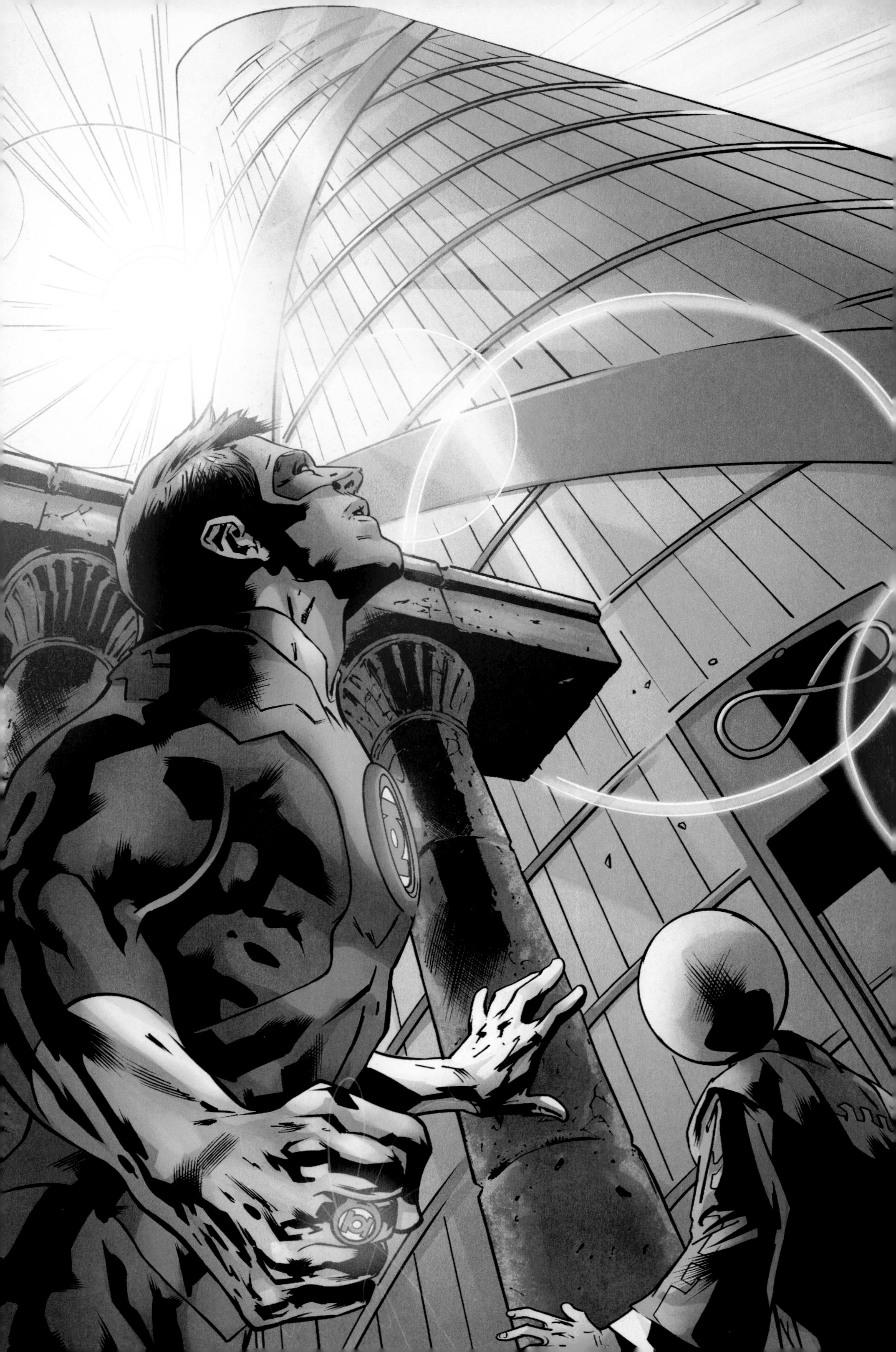

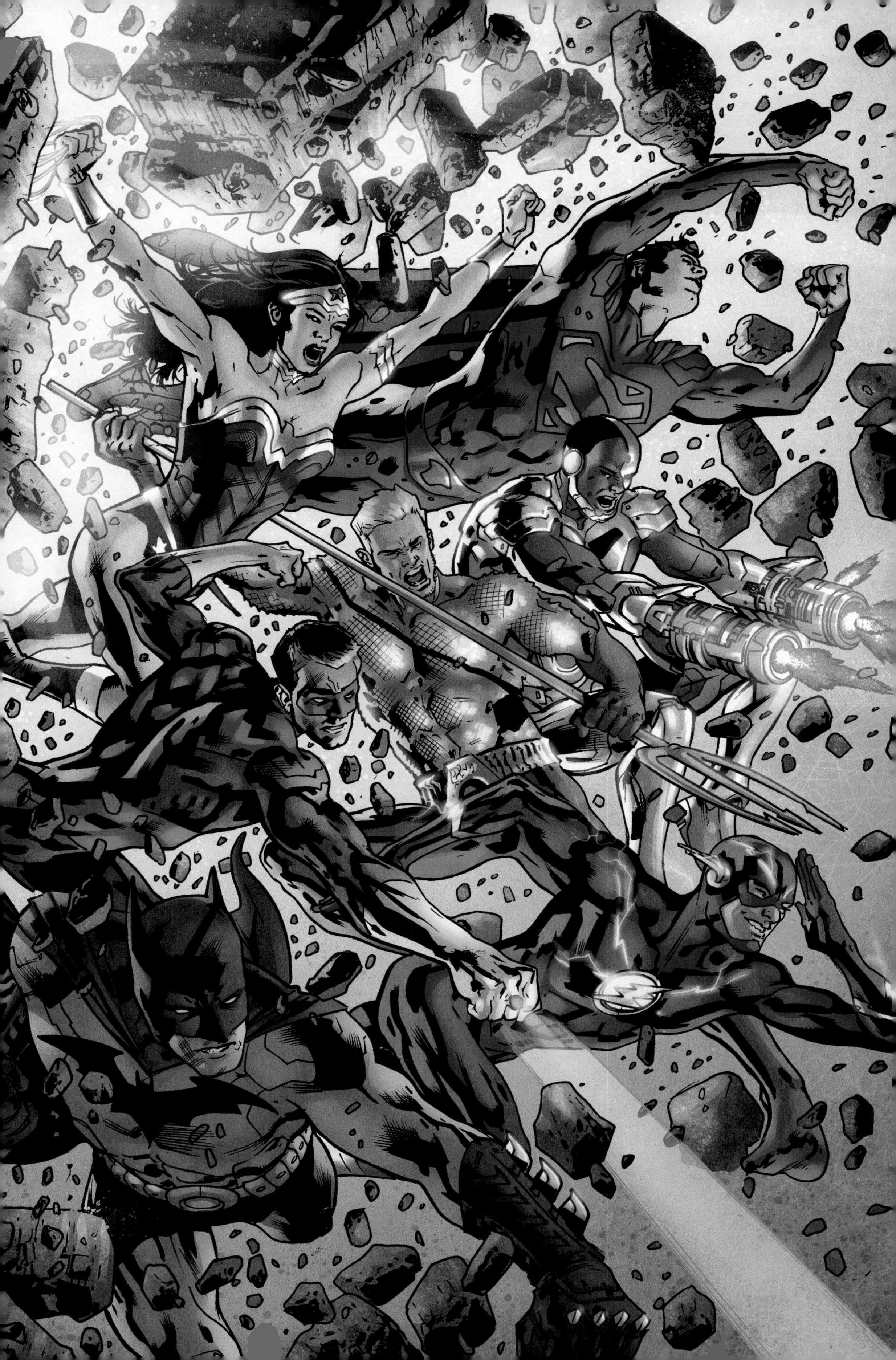

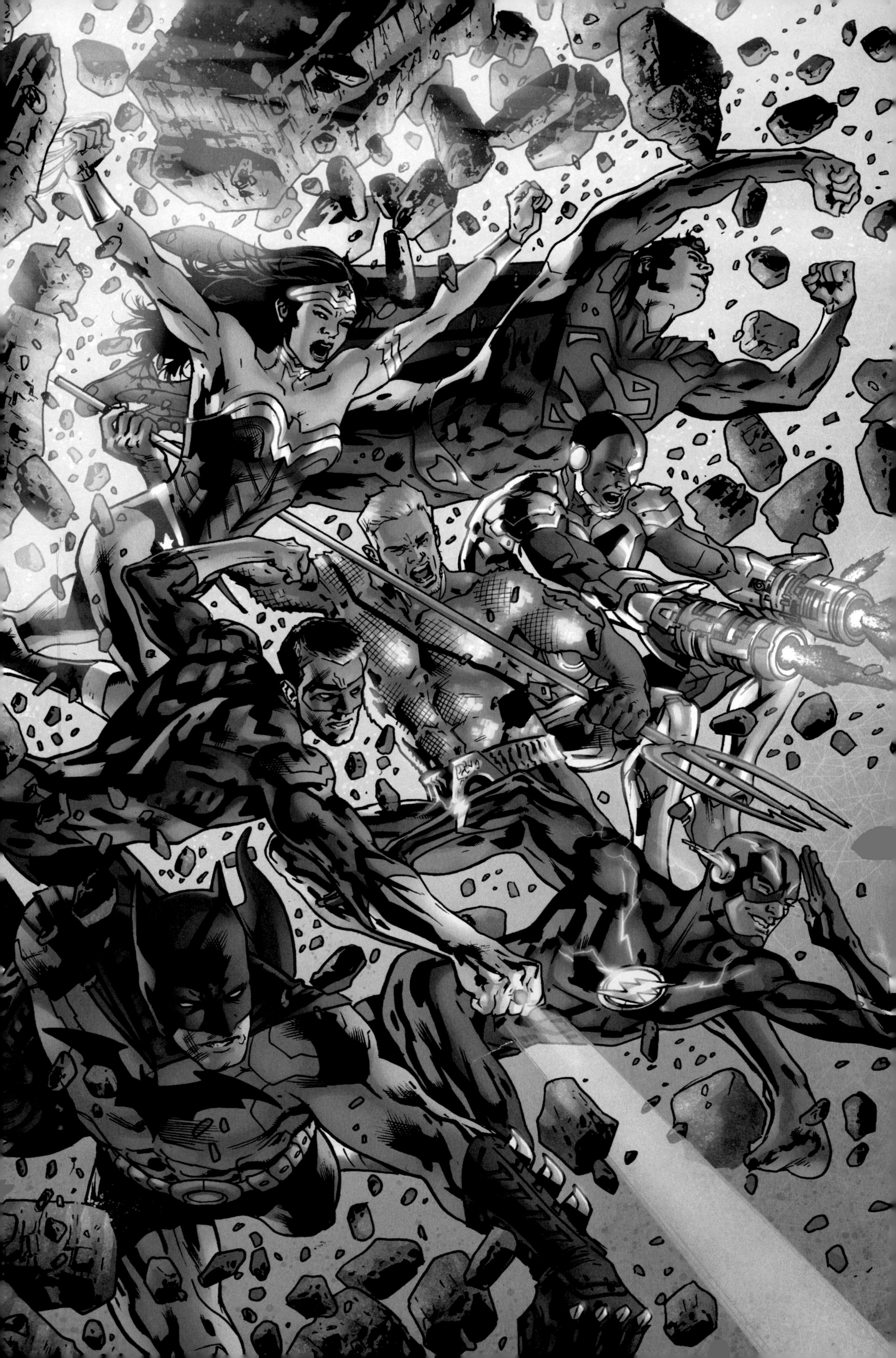

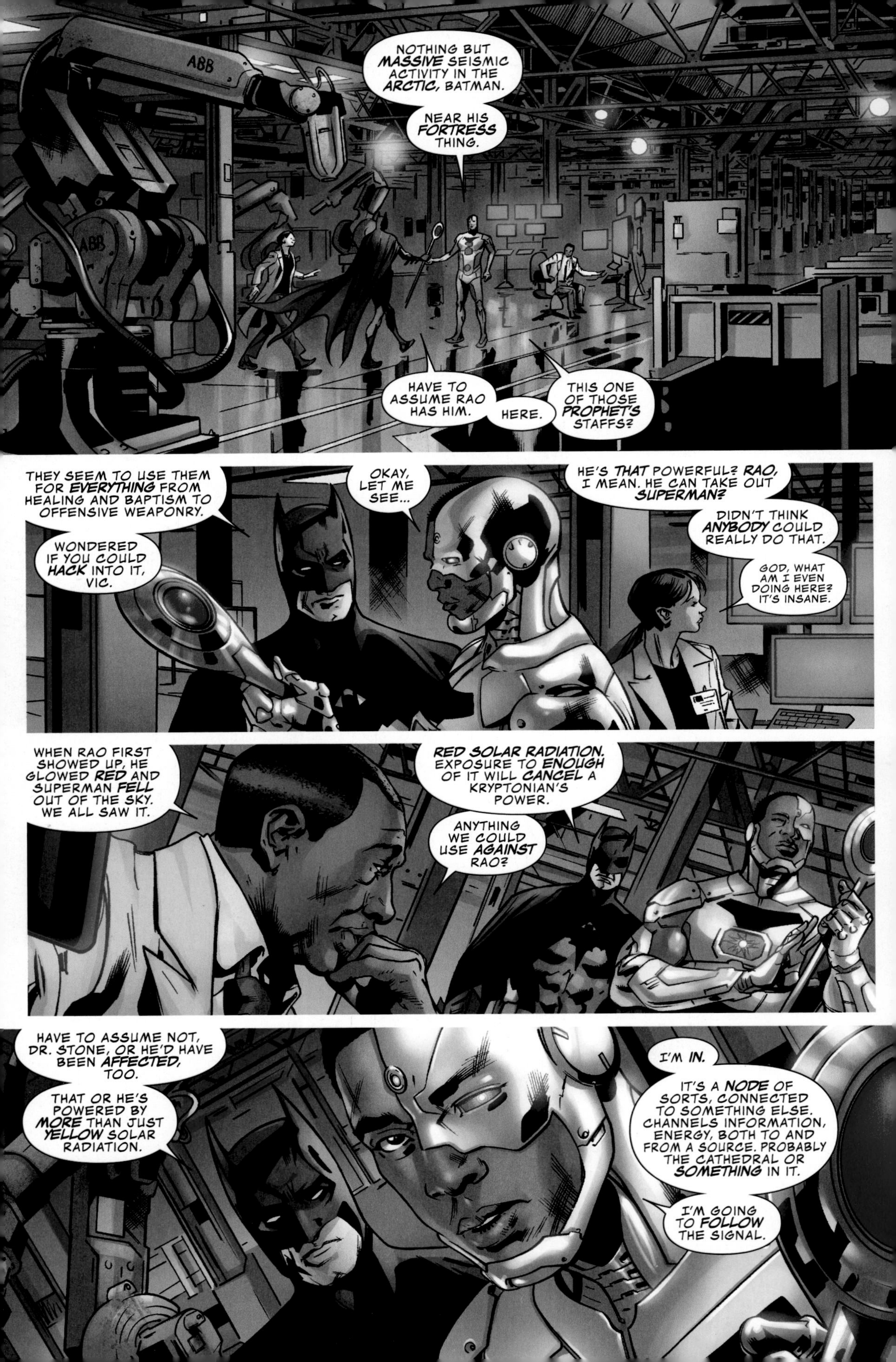
NOTHING BUT MASSIVE SEISMIC ACTIVITY IN THE ARCTIC, BATMAN.
NEAR HIS FORTRESS THING.
HAVE TO ASSUME RAO HAS HIM.
HERE.
THIS ONE OF THOSE PROPHET'S STAFFS?
THEY SEEM TO USE THEM FOR EVERYTHING FROM HEALING AND BAPTISM TO OFFENSIVE WEAPONRY.
WONDERED IF YOU COULD HACK INTO IT, VIC.
OKAY, LET ME SEE...
HE'S THAT POWERFUL? RAO, I MEAN. HE CAN TAKE OUT SUPERMAN?
DIDN'T THINK ANYBODY COULD REALLY DO THAT.
GOD, WHAT AM I EVEN DOING HERE? IT'S INSANE.
WHEN RAO FIRST SHOWED UP, HE GLOWED RED AND SUPERMAN FELL OUT OF THE SKY. WE ALL SAW IT.
RED SOLAR RADIATION. EXPOSURE TO ENOUGH OF IT WILL CANCEL A KRYPTONIAN'S POWER.
ANYTHING WE COULD USE AGAINST RAO?
HAVE TO ASSUME NOT, DR. STONE, OR HE'D HAVE BEEN AFFECTED, TOO.
THAT OR HE'S POWERED BY MORE THAN JUST YELLOW SOLAR RADIATION.
I'M IN.
IT'S A NODE OF SORTS, CONNECTED TO SOMETHING ELSE. CHANNELS INFORMATION, ENERGY, BOTH TO AND FROM A SOURCE. PROBABLY THE CATHEDRAL OR SOMETHING IN IT.
I'M GOING TO FOLLOW THE SIGNAL.

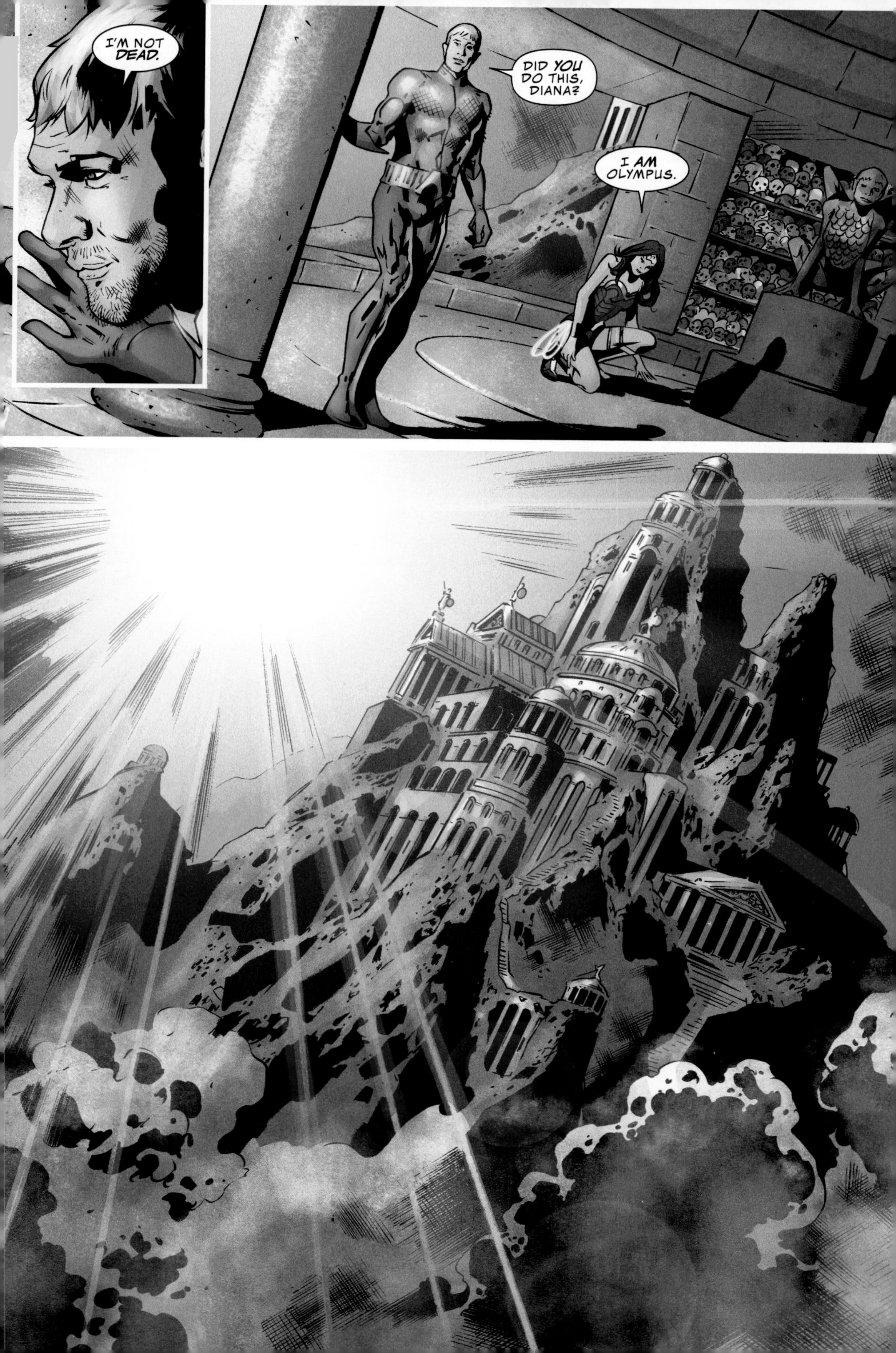
I'M NOT DEAD.
DID YOU DO THIS, DIANA?
I AM OLYMPUS.

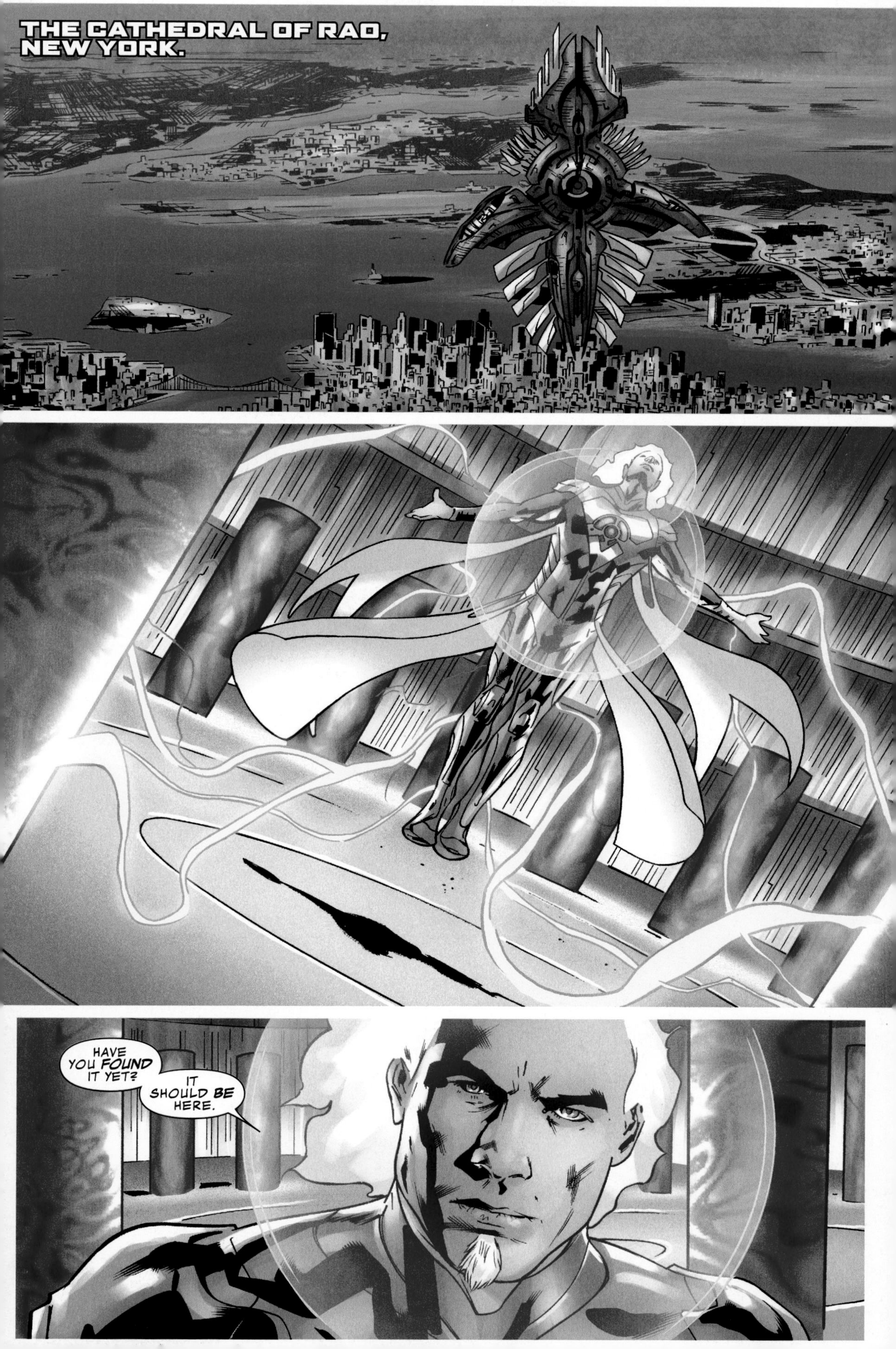
THE CATHEDRAL OF RAO, NEW YORK.
HAVE YOU FOUND IT YET?
IT SHOULD BE HERE.

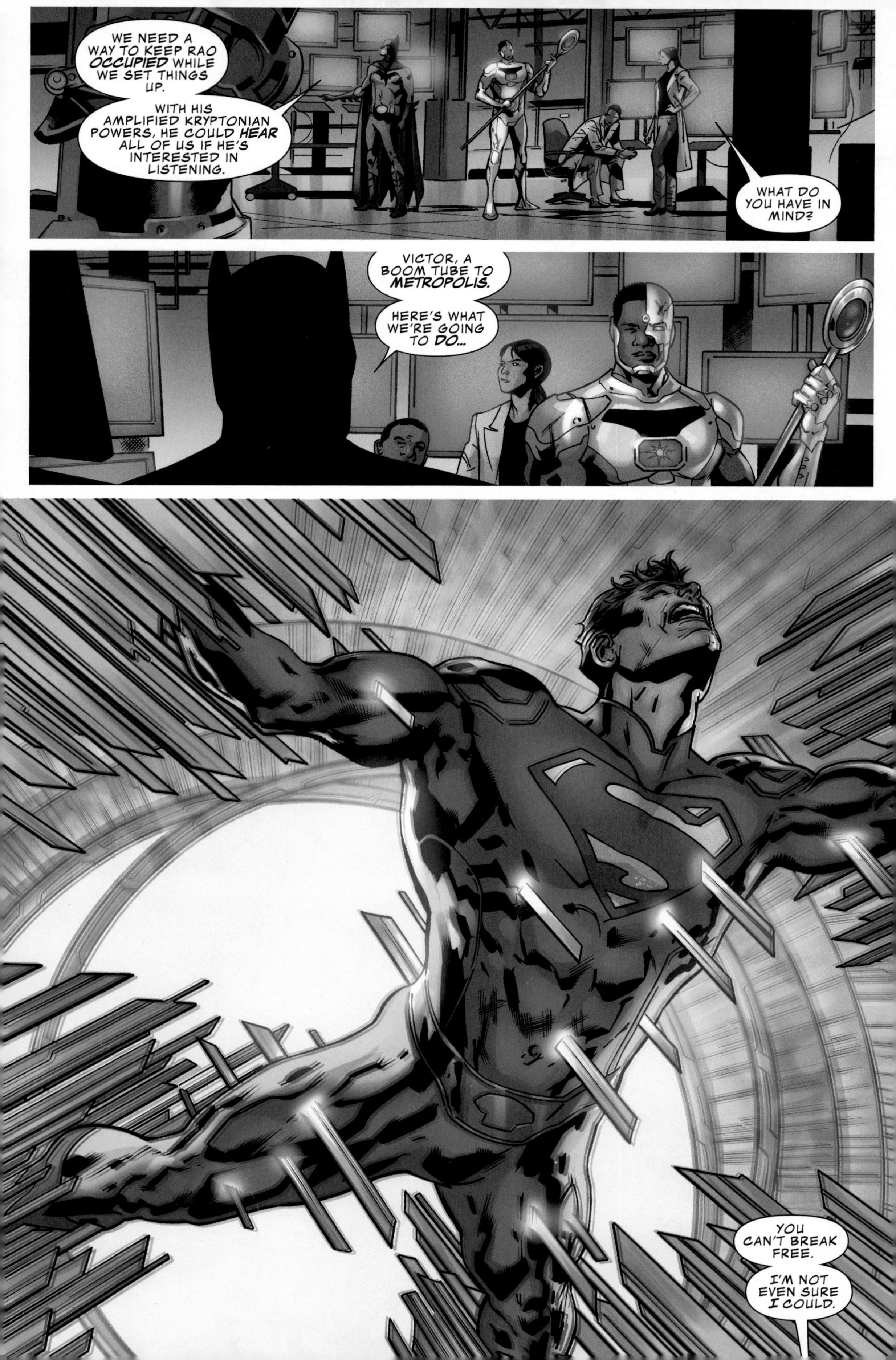
WE NEED A WAY TO KEEP RAO *OCCUPIED* WHILE WE SET THINGS UP.
WITH HIS AMPLIFIED KRYPTONIAN POWERS, HE COULD *HEAR* ALL OF US IF HE'S INTERESTED IN LISTENING.
WHAT DO YOU HAVE IN MIND?
VICTOR, A BOOM TUBE TO *METROPOLIS.*
HERE'S WHAT WE'RE GOING TO *DO*...
YOU CAN'T BREAK FREE.
I'M NOT EVEN SURE *I* COULD.

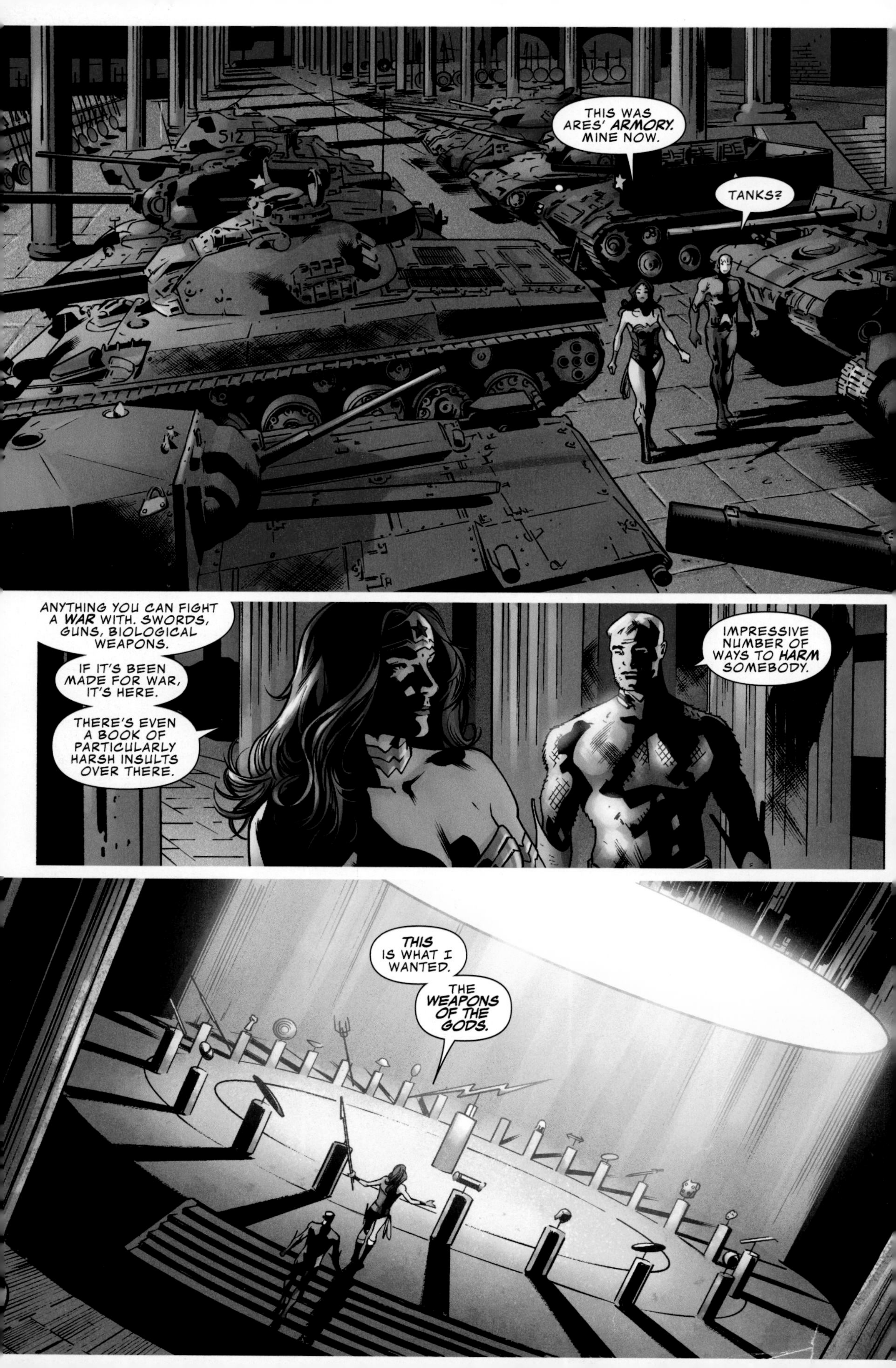
THIS WAS ARES' ARMORY. MINE NOW.
TANKS?
ANYTHING YOU CAN FIGHT A WAR WITH. SWORDS, GUNS, BIOLOGICAL WEAPONS.
IF IT'S BEEN MADE FOR WAR, IT'S HERE.
THERE'S EVEN A BOOK OF PARTICULARLY HARSH INSULTS OVER THERE.
IMPRESSIVE NUMBER OF WAYS TO HARM SOMEBODY.
THIS IS WHAT I WANTED.
THE WEAPONS OF THE GODS.

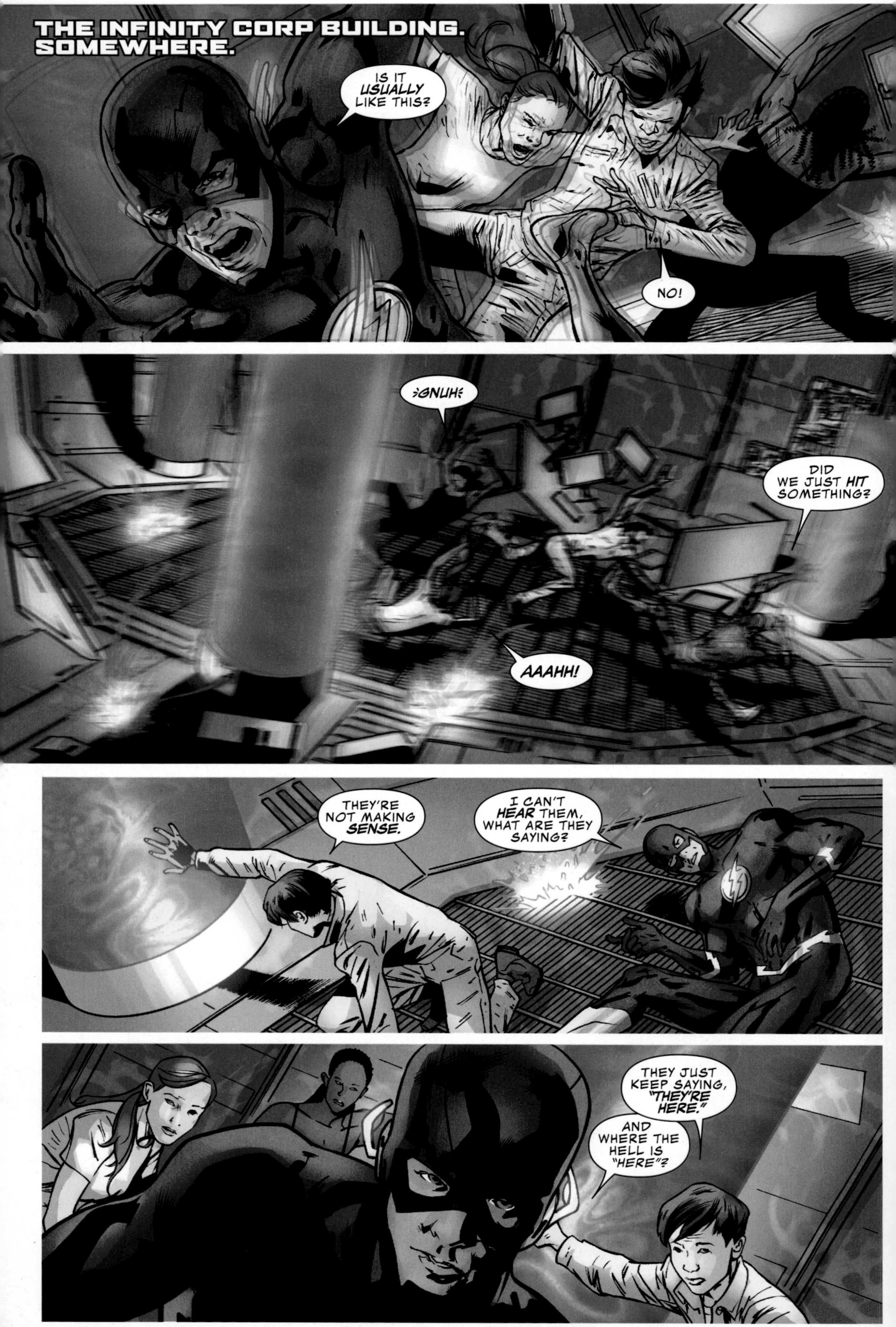
THE INFINITY CORP BUILDING. SOMEWHERE.
IS IT USUALLY LIKE THIS?
NO!
GNUH
DID WE JUST HIT SOMETHING?
AAAHH!
THEY'RE NOT MAKING SENSE.
I CAN'T HEAR THEM, WHAT ARE THEY SAYING?
THEY JUST KEEP SAYING, "THEY'RE HERE."
AND WHERE THE HELL IS "HERE"?

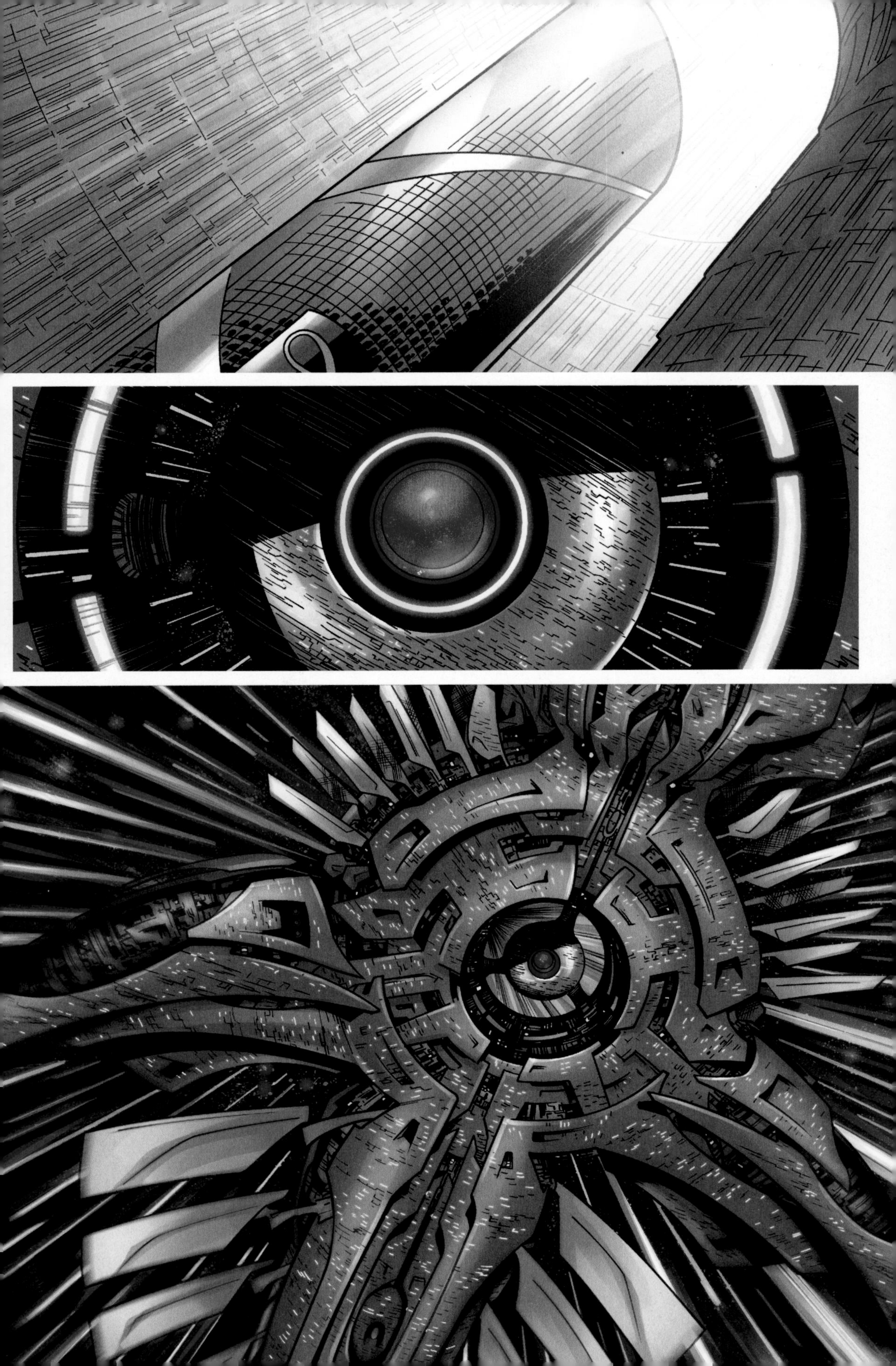

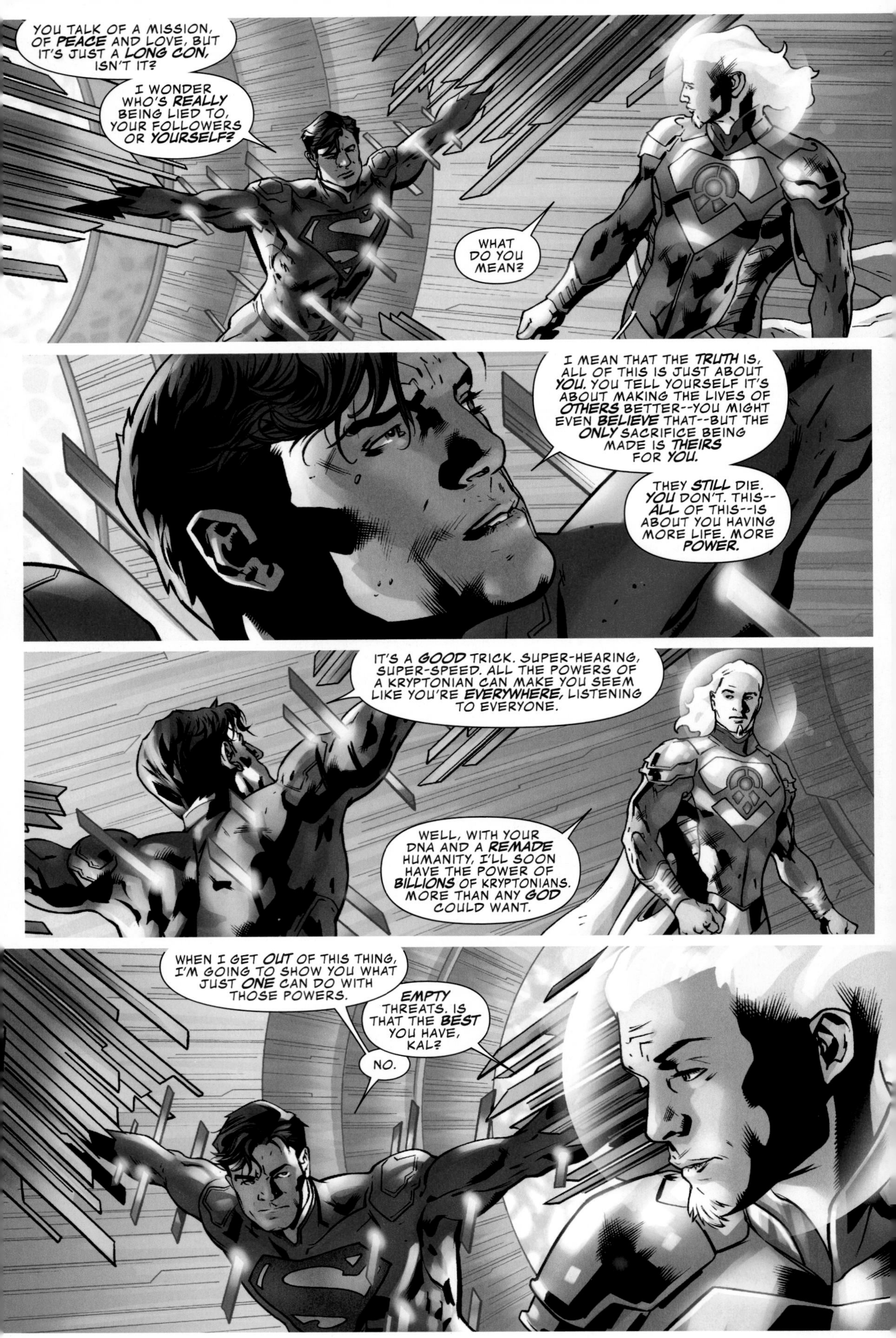
YOU TALK OF A MISSION, OF PEACE AND LOVE, BUT IT'S JUST A LONG CON, ISN'T IT?
I WONDER WHO'S REALLY BEING LIED TO, YOUR FOLLOWERS OR YOURSELF?
WHAT DO YOU MEAN?
I MEAN THAT THE TRUTH IS, ALL OF THIS IS JUST ABOUT YOU. YOU TELL YOURSELF IT'S ABOUT MAKING THE LIVES OF OTHERS BETTER--YOU MIGHT EVEN BELIEVE THAT--BUT THE ONLY SACRIFICE BEING MADE IS THEIRS FOR YOU.
THEY STILL DIE. YOU DON'T. THIS--ALL OF THIS--IS ABOUT YOU HAVING MORE LIFE. MORE POWER.
IT'S A GOOD TRICK. SUPER-HEARING, SUPER-SPEED. ALL THE POWERS OF A KRYPTONIAN CAN MAKE YOU SEEM LIKE YOU'RE EVERYWHERE, LISTENING TO EVERYONE.
WELL, WITH YOUR DNA AND A REMADE HUMANITY, I'LL SOON HAVE THE POWER OF BILLIONS OF KRYPTONIANS. MORE THAN ANY GOD COULD WANT.
WHEN I GET OUT OF THIS THING, I'M GOING TO SHOW YOU WHAT JUST ONE CAN DO WITH THOSE POWERS.
EMPTY THREATS. IS THAT THE BEST YOU HAVE, KAL?
NO.

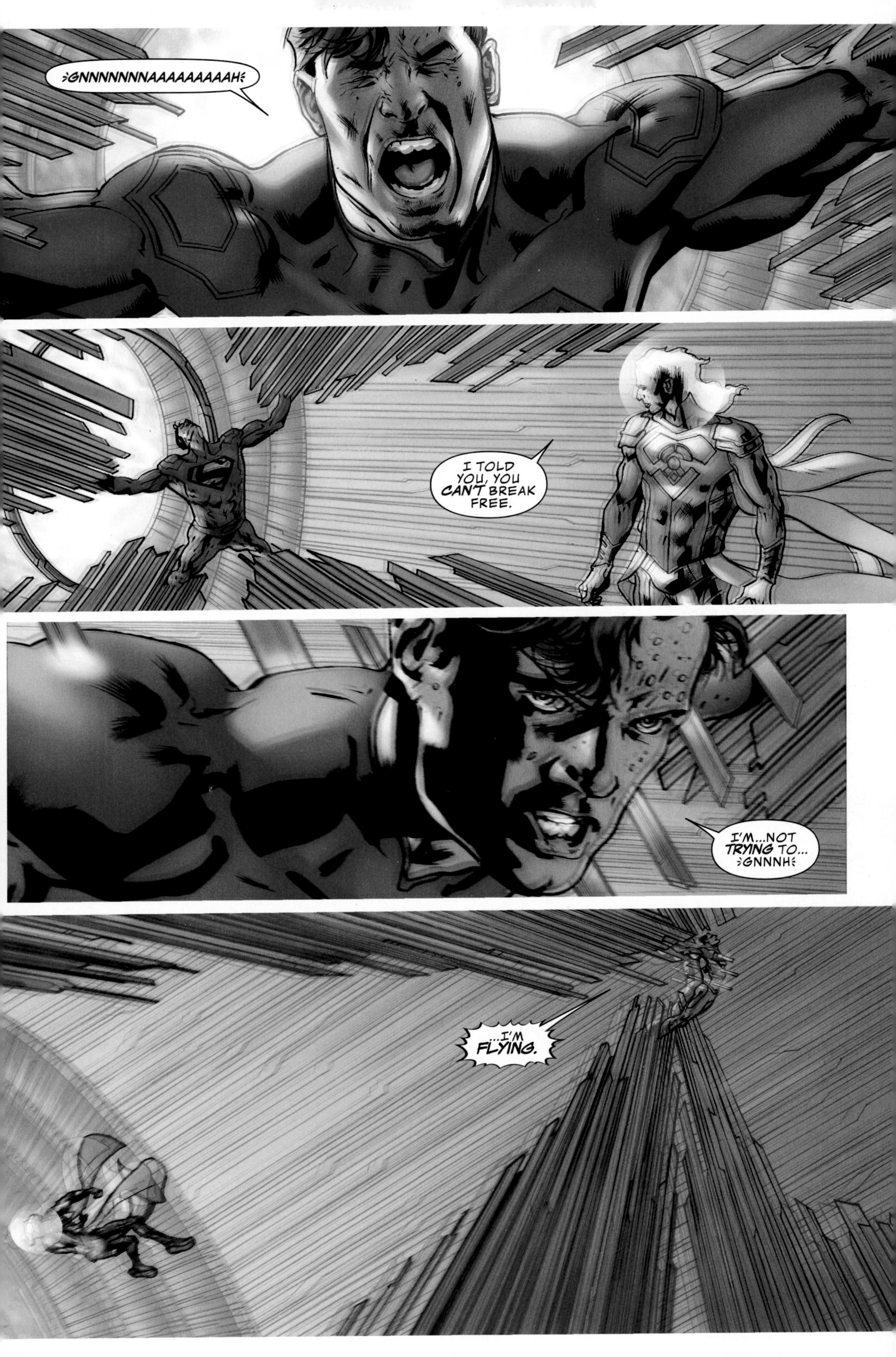
GNNNNNNNAAAAAAAAAH
I TOLD YOU, YOU CAN'T BREAK FREE.
I'M...NOT TRYING TO... GNNNH
...I'M FLYING.

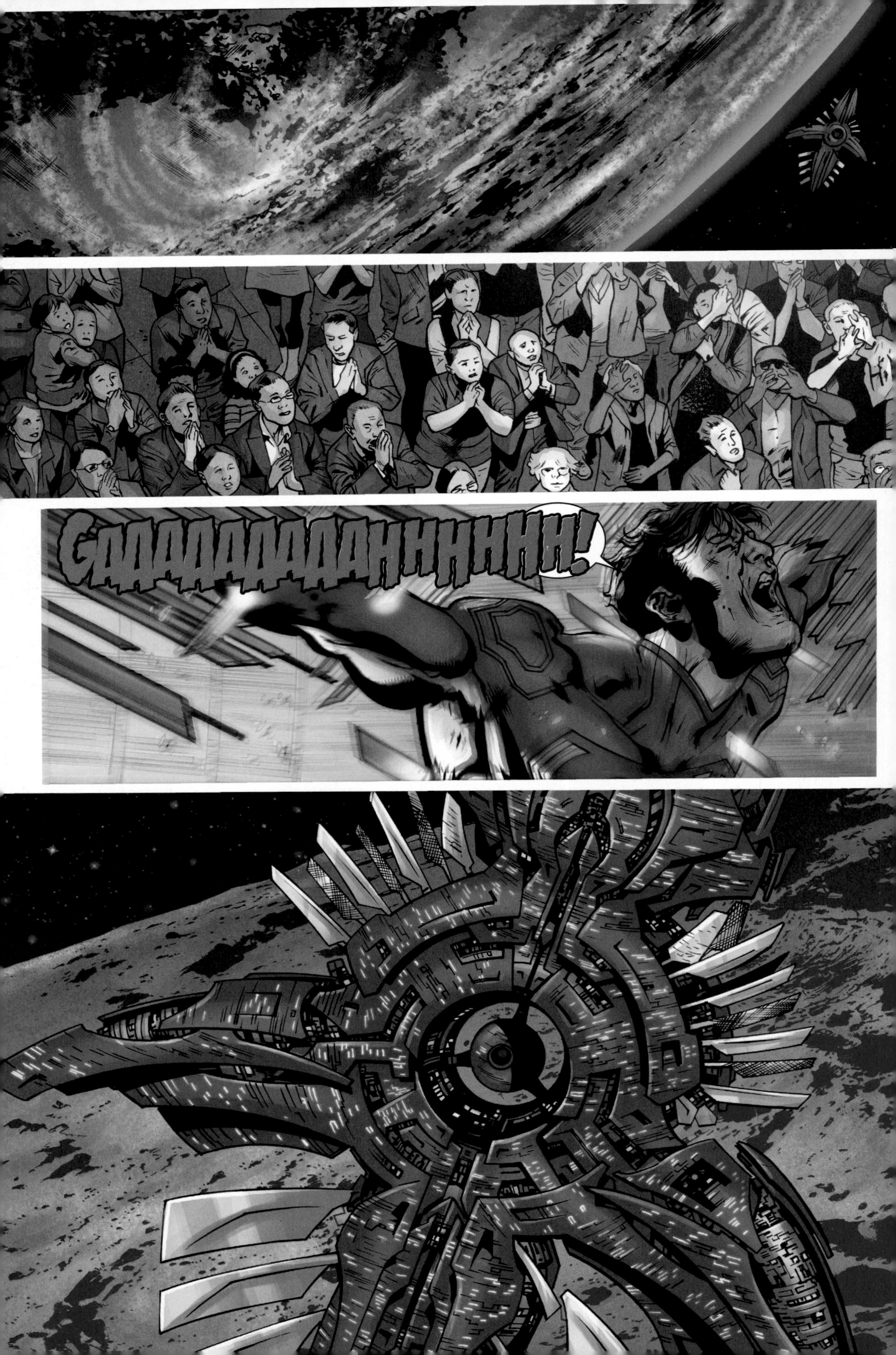
GAAAAAAAAAAHHHHHH!

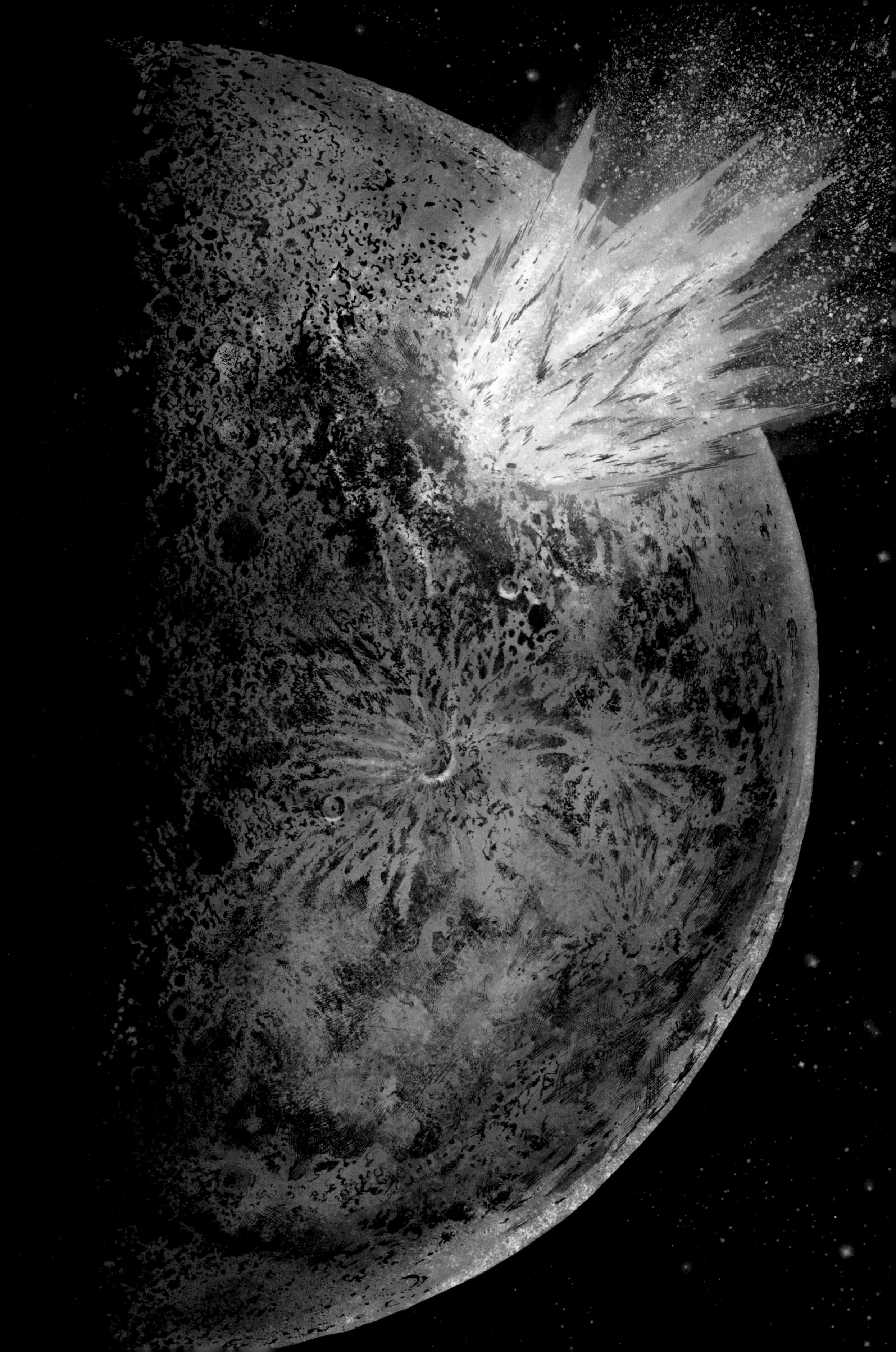

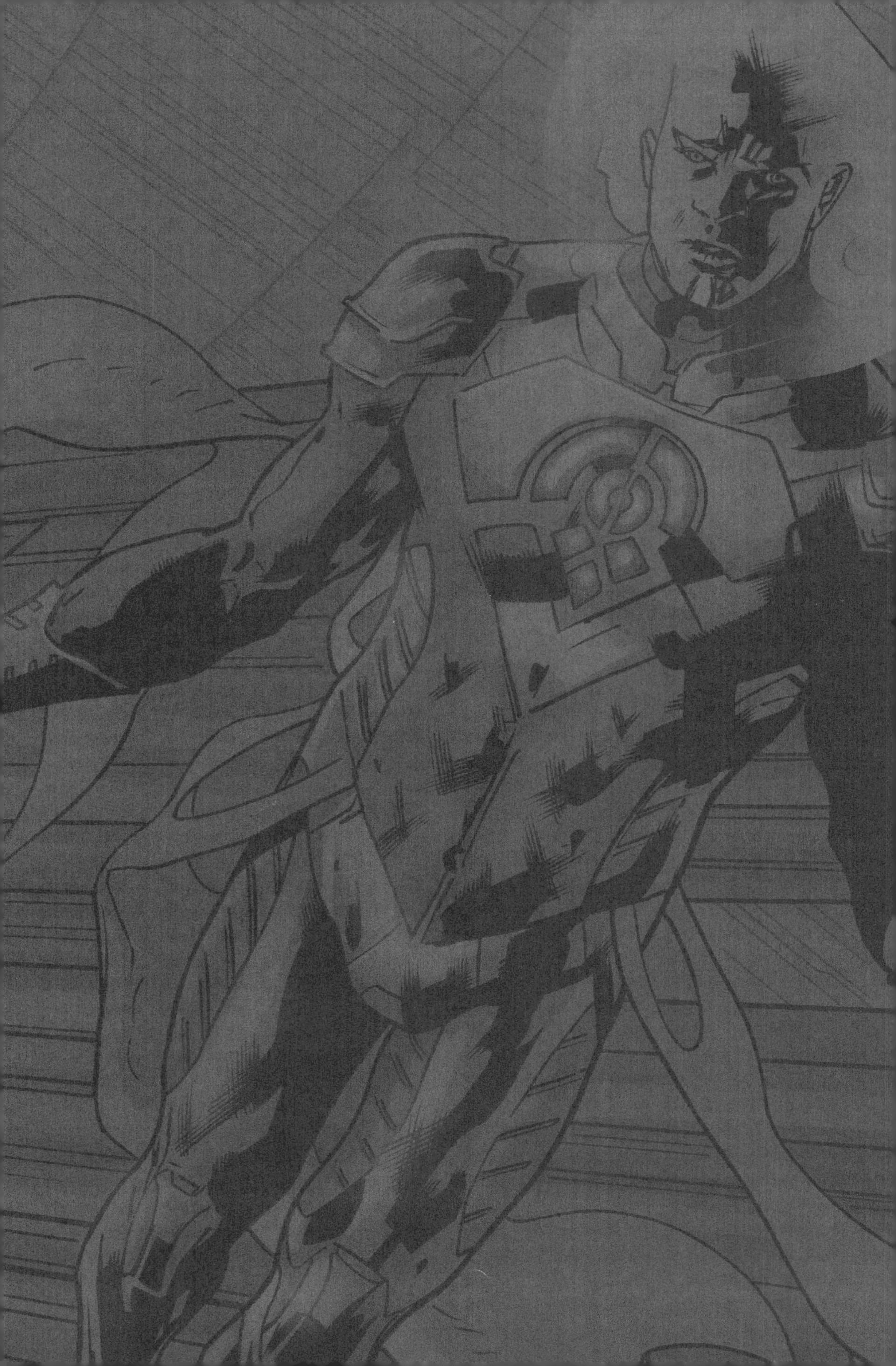

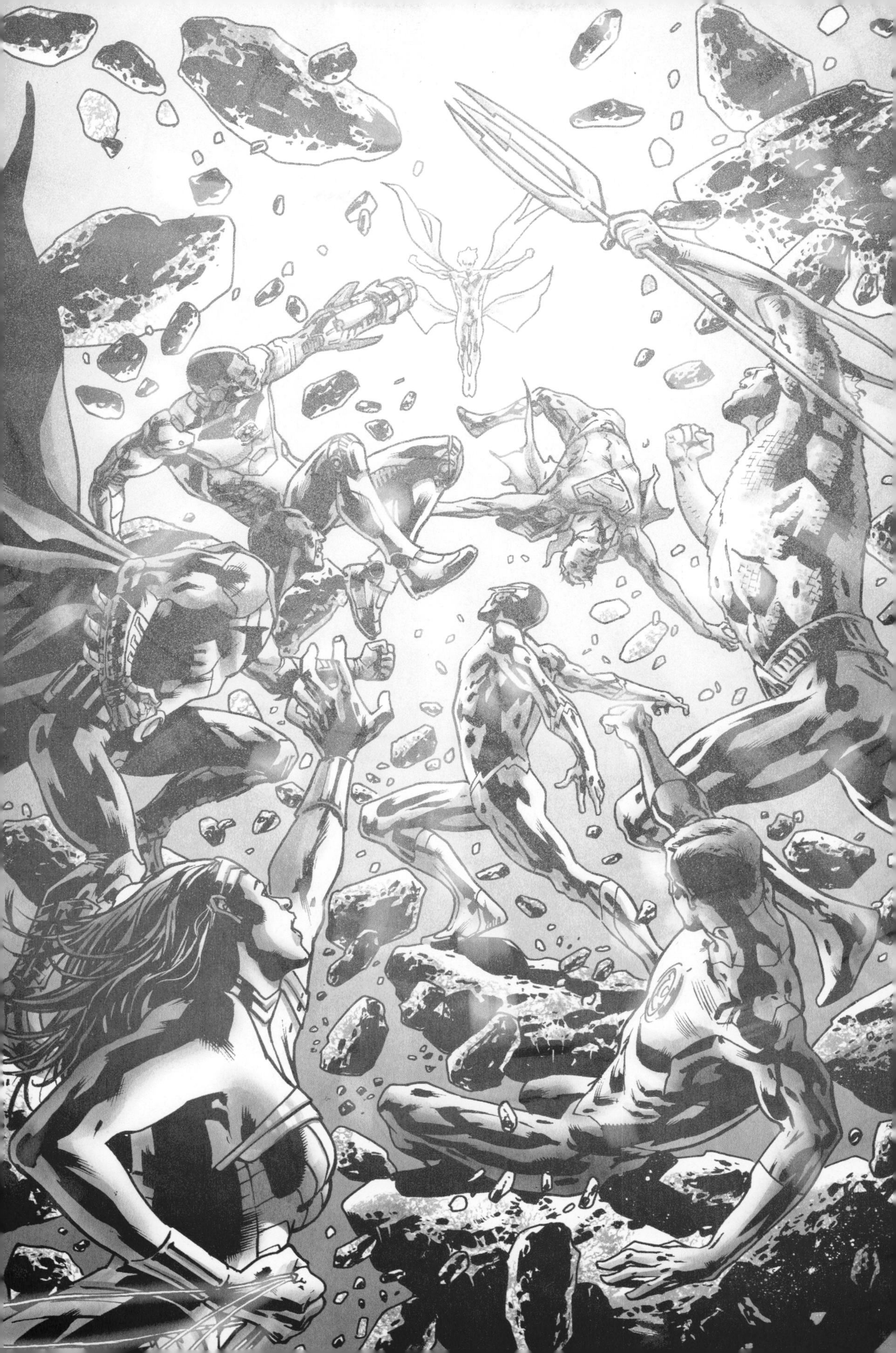

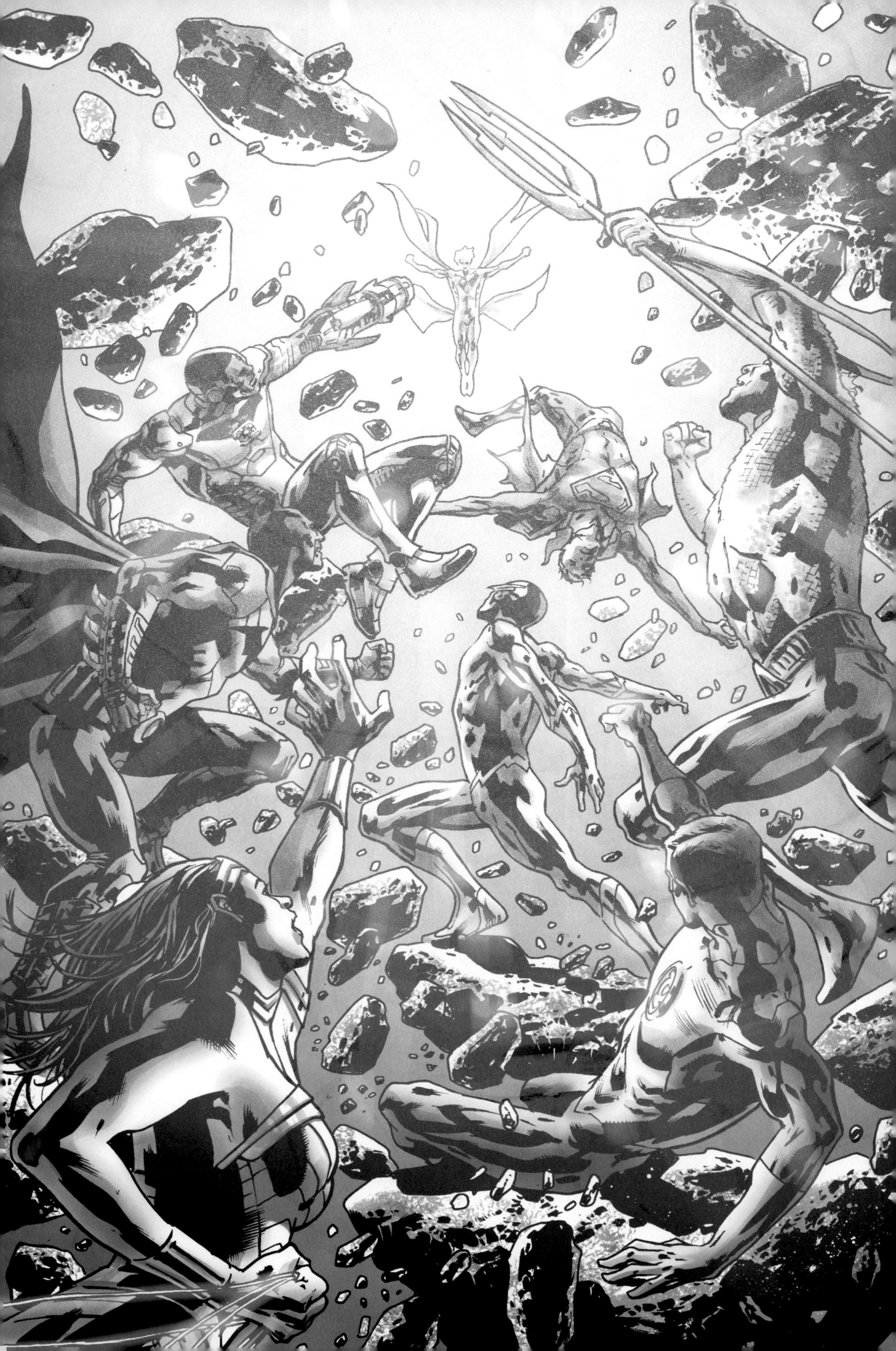

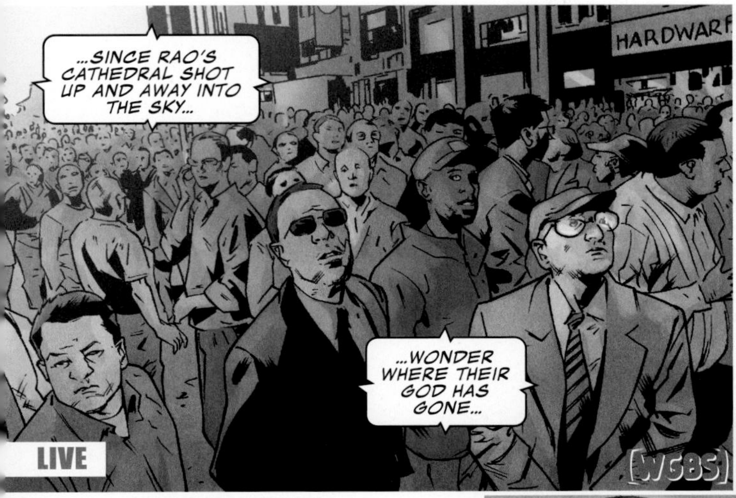
...SINCE RAO'S CATHEDRAL SHOT UP AND AWAY INTO THE SKY...
...WONDER WHERE THEIR GOD HAS GONE...
LIVE

DC COMICS PRESENTS

THE JUSTICE LEAGUE OF AMERICA

POWER AND GLORY PART SEVEN

BY BRYAN HITCH

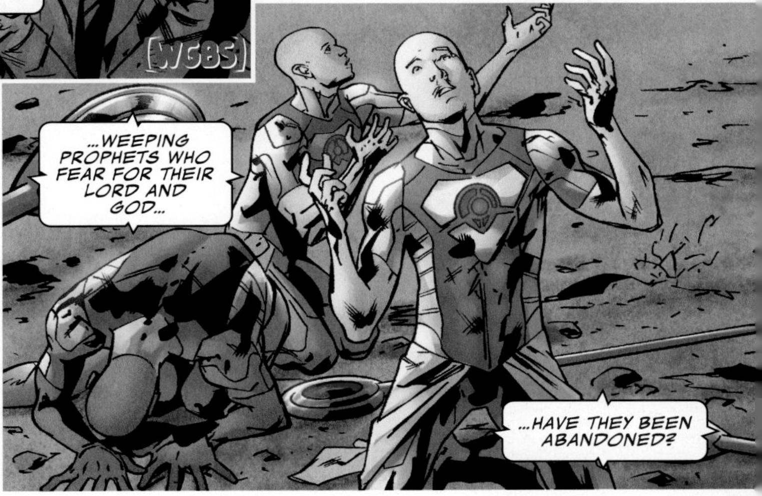
...WEEPING PROPHETS WHO FEAR FOR THEIR LORD AND GOD...
...HAVE THEY BEEN ABANDONED?

INKS BY **DANIEL HENRIQUES**
COLORS BY **ALEX SINCLAIR**
LETTERS BY **CHRIS ELIOPOULOS**
ASSISTS BY **AMEDEO TURTURRO**
EDITS BY **BRIAN CUNNINGHAM**

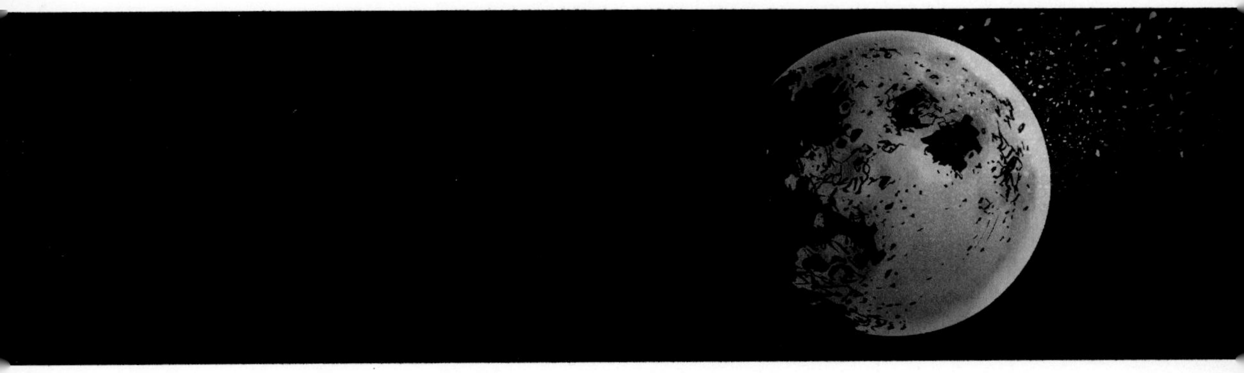

COVER BY **BRYAN HITCH & ALEX SINCLAIR**

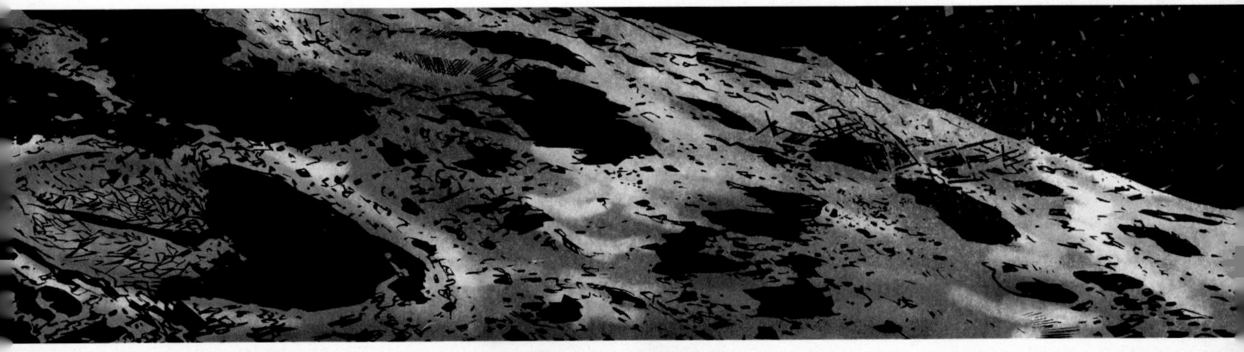

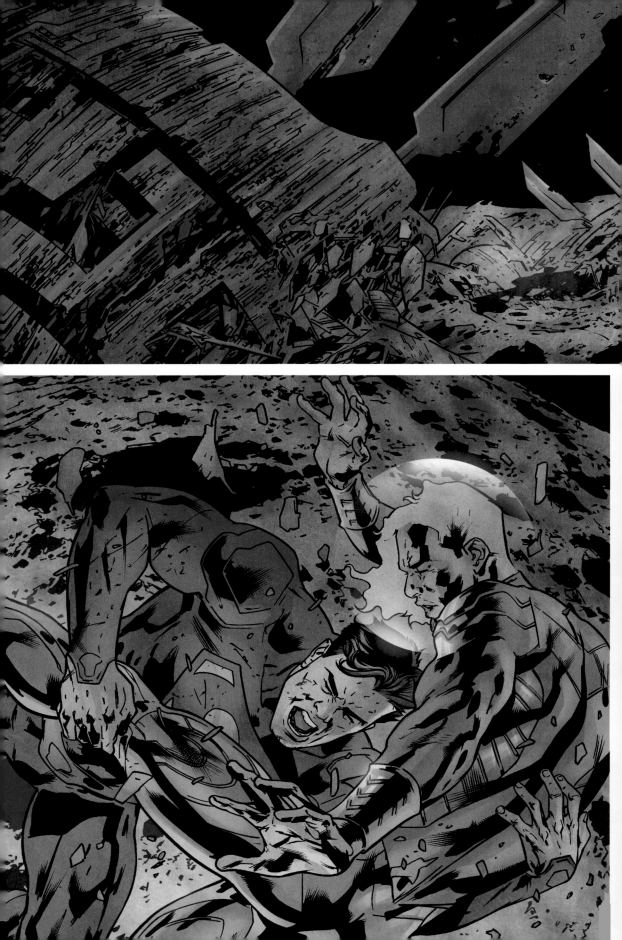

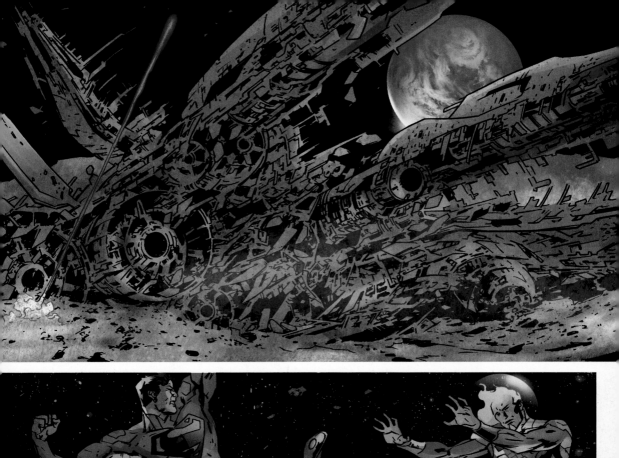

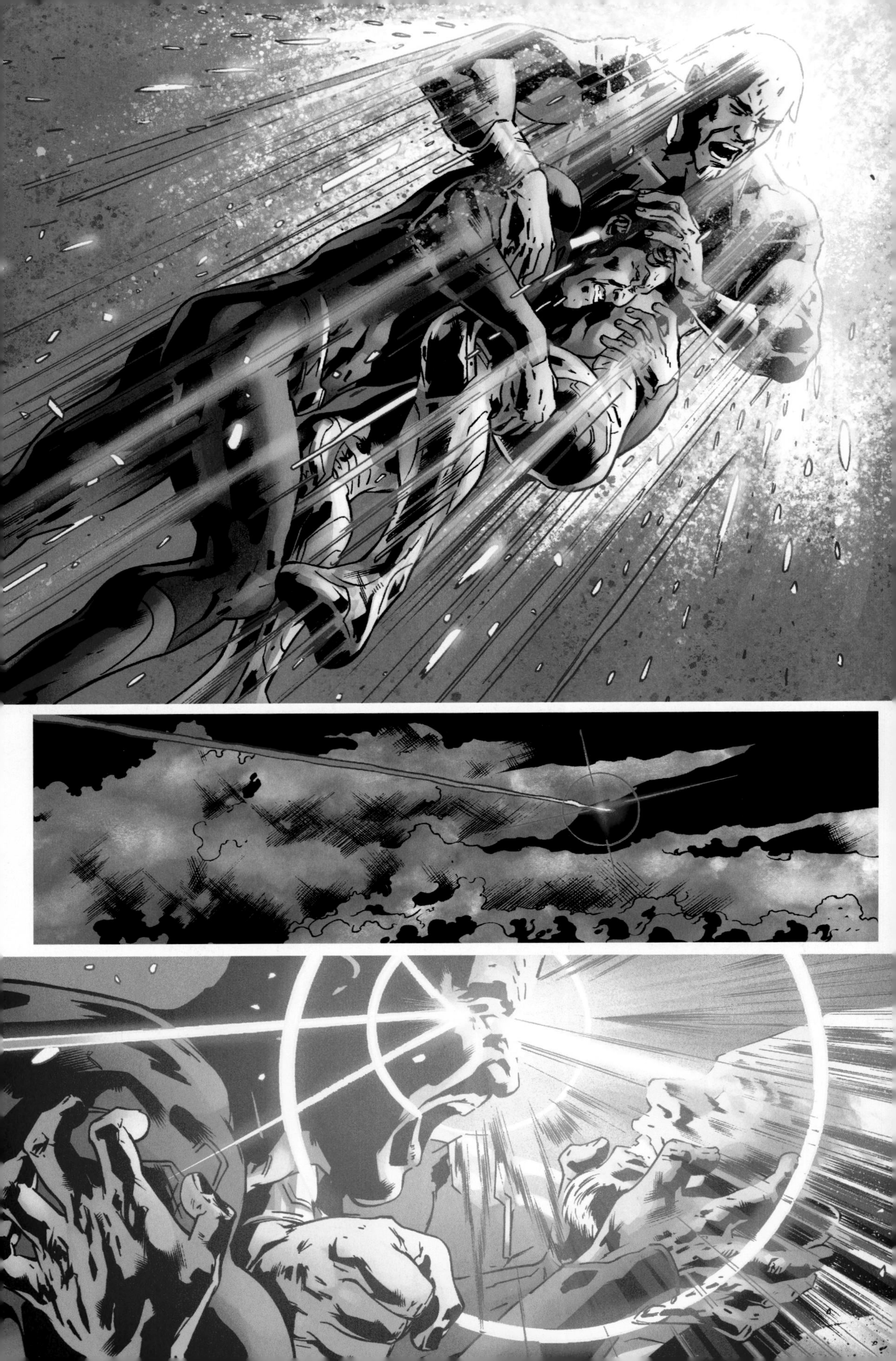

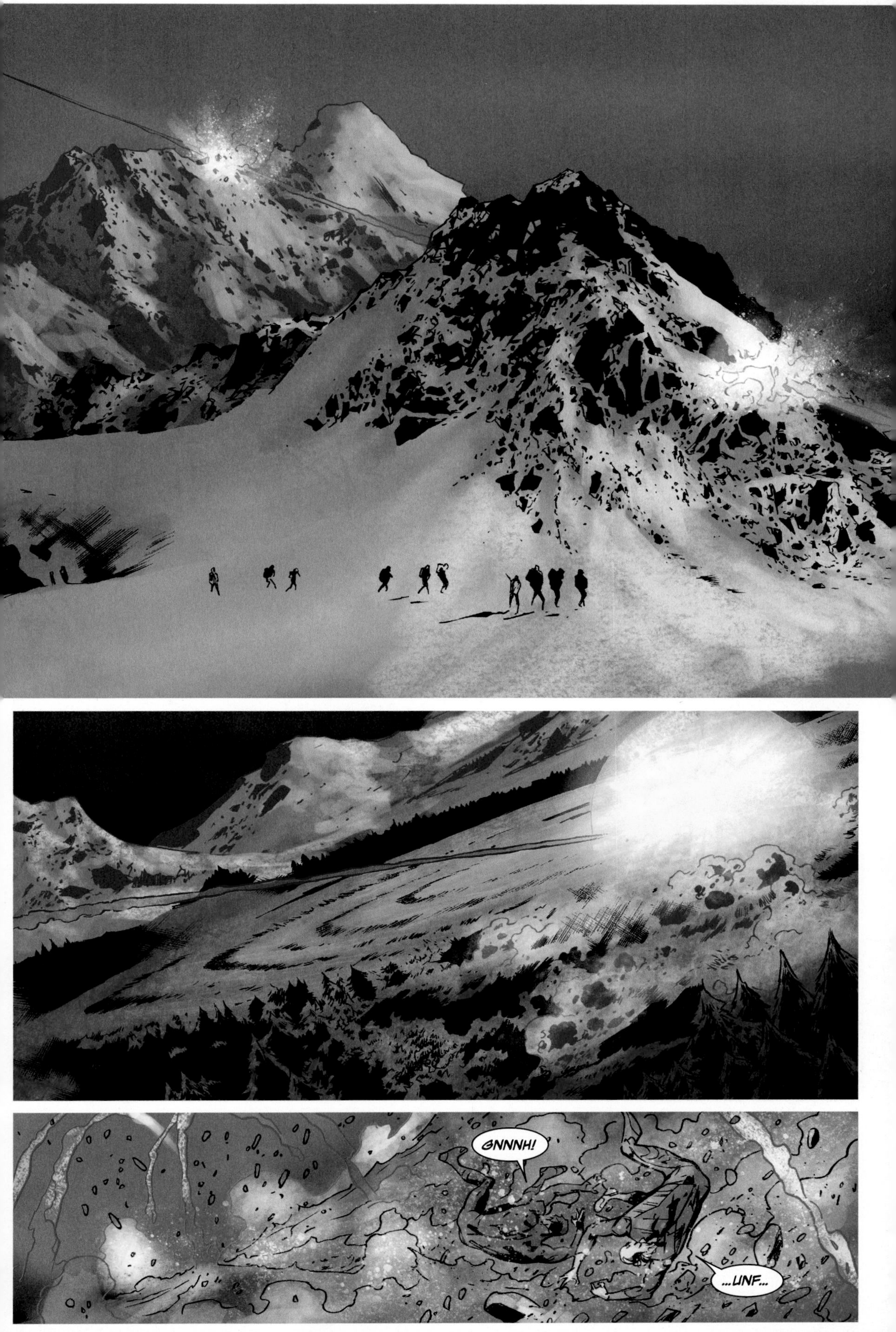
GNNNH!
...UNF...

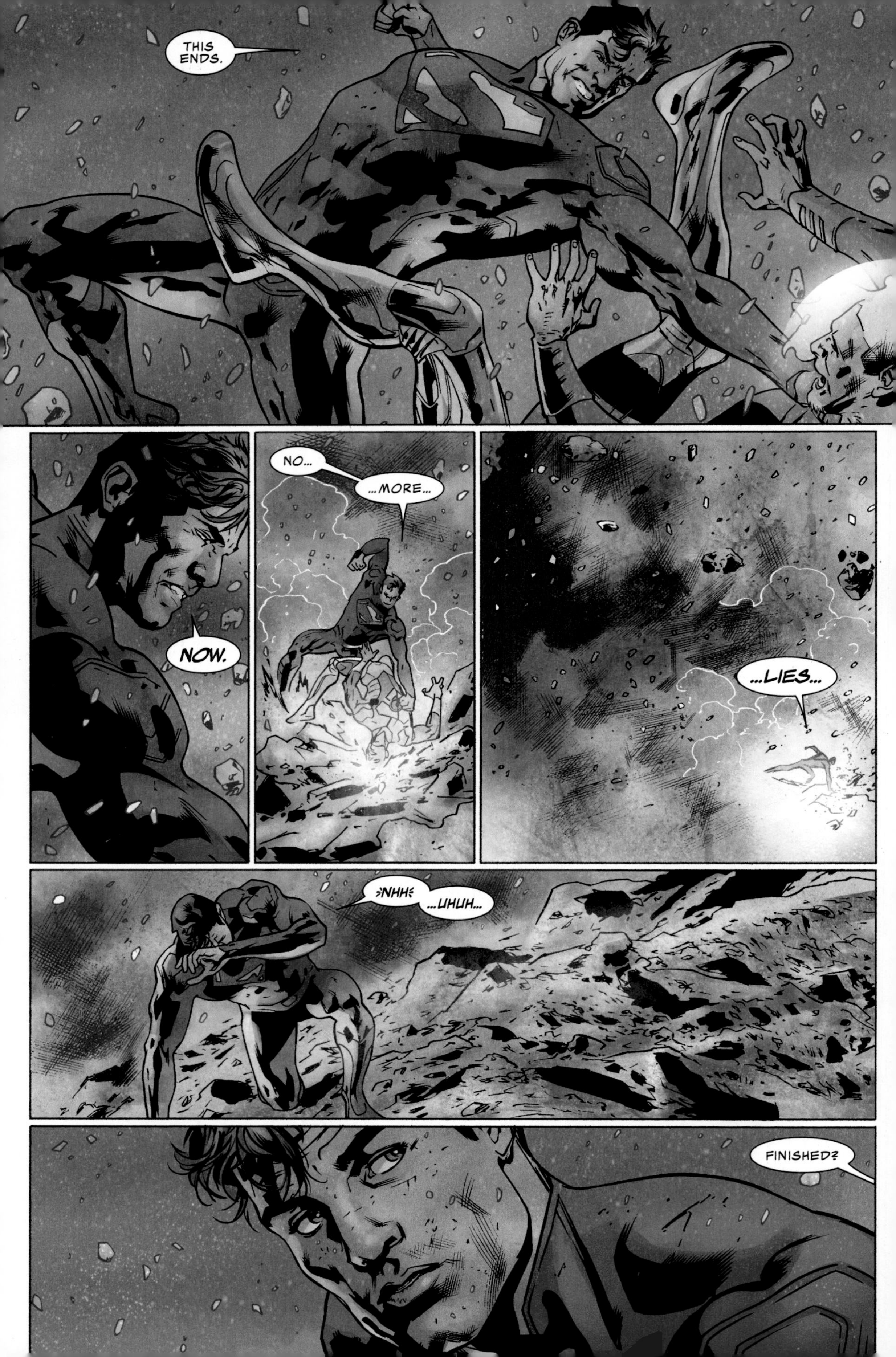
THIS ENDS.
NOW.
NO...
...MORE...
...LIES...
NHH
...UHUH...
FINISHED?

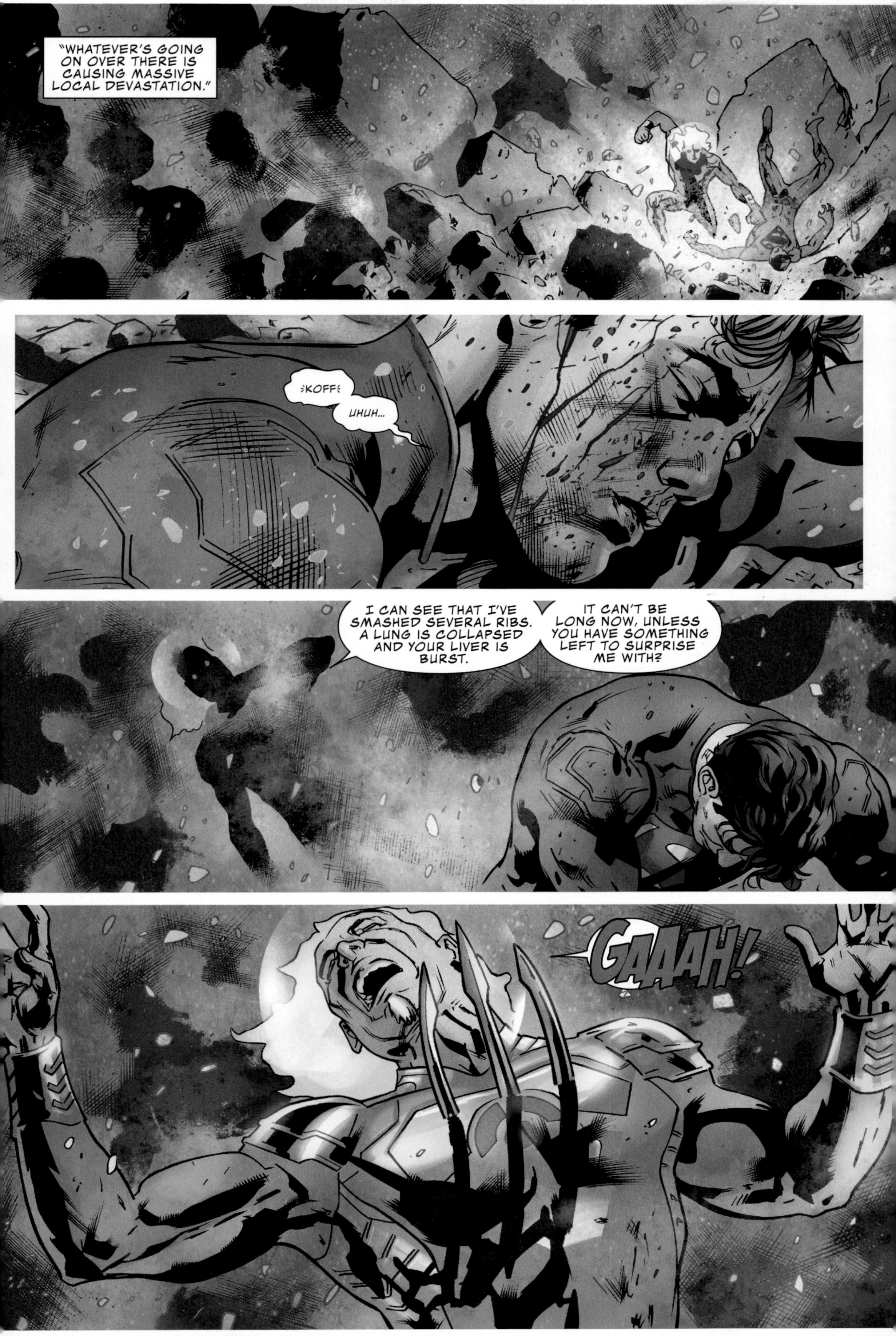
"WHATEVER'S GOING ON OVER THERE IS CAUSING MASSIVE LOCAL DEVASTATION."
KOFF
UHUH...
I CAN SEE THAT I'VE SMASHED SEVERAL RIBS. A LUNG IS COLLAPSED AND YOUR LIVER IS BURST.
IT CAN'T BE LONG NOW, UNLESS YOU HAVE SOMETHING LEFT TO SURPRISE ME WITH?
GAAAH!

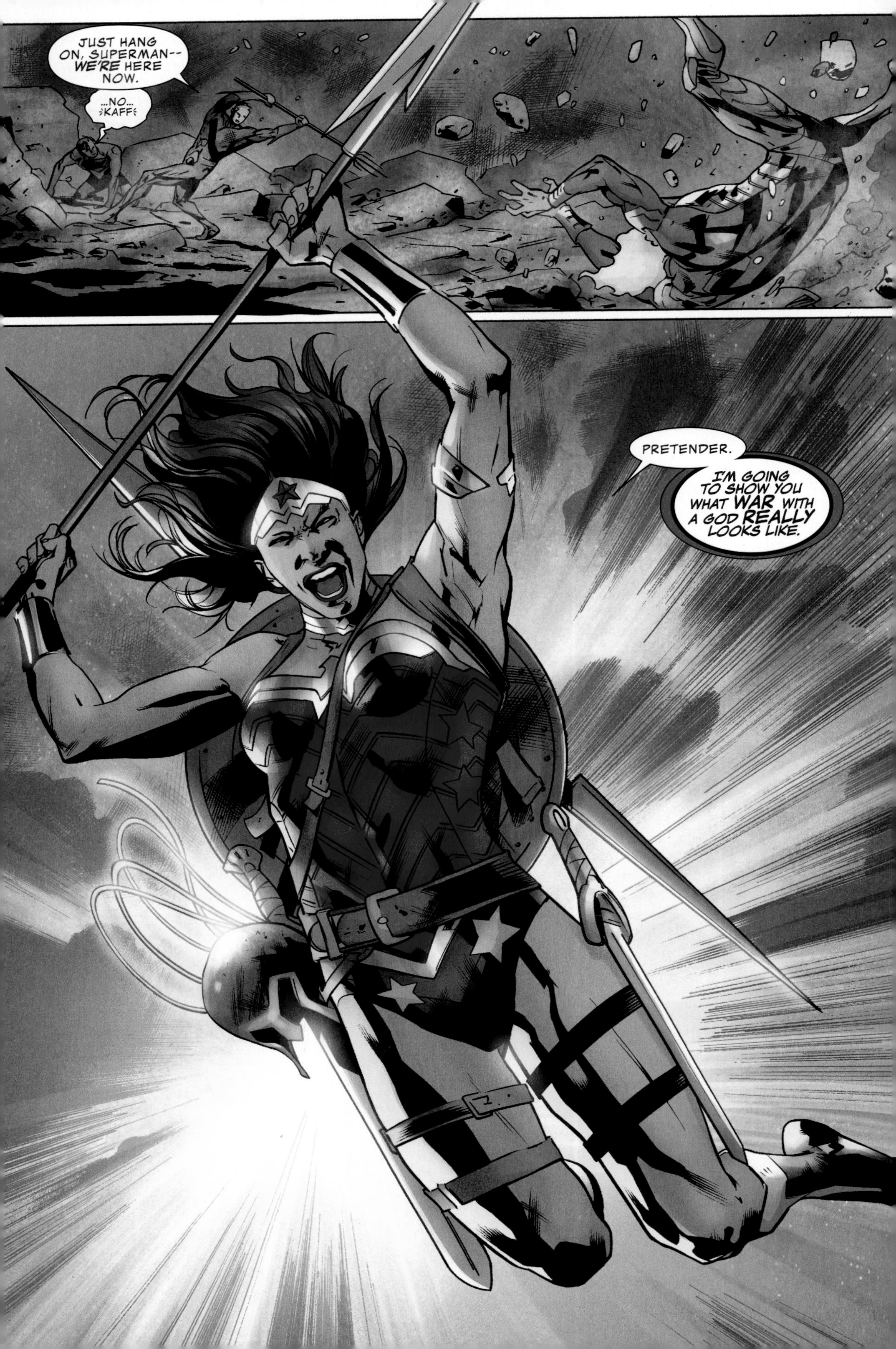
JUST HANG ON, SUPERMAN-- WE'RE HERE NOW.
...NO... KAFF
PRETENDER.
I'M GOING TO SHOW YOU WHAT WAR WITH A GOD REALLY LOOKS LIKE.

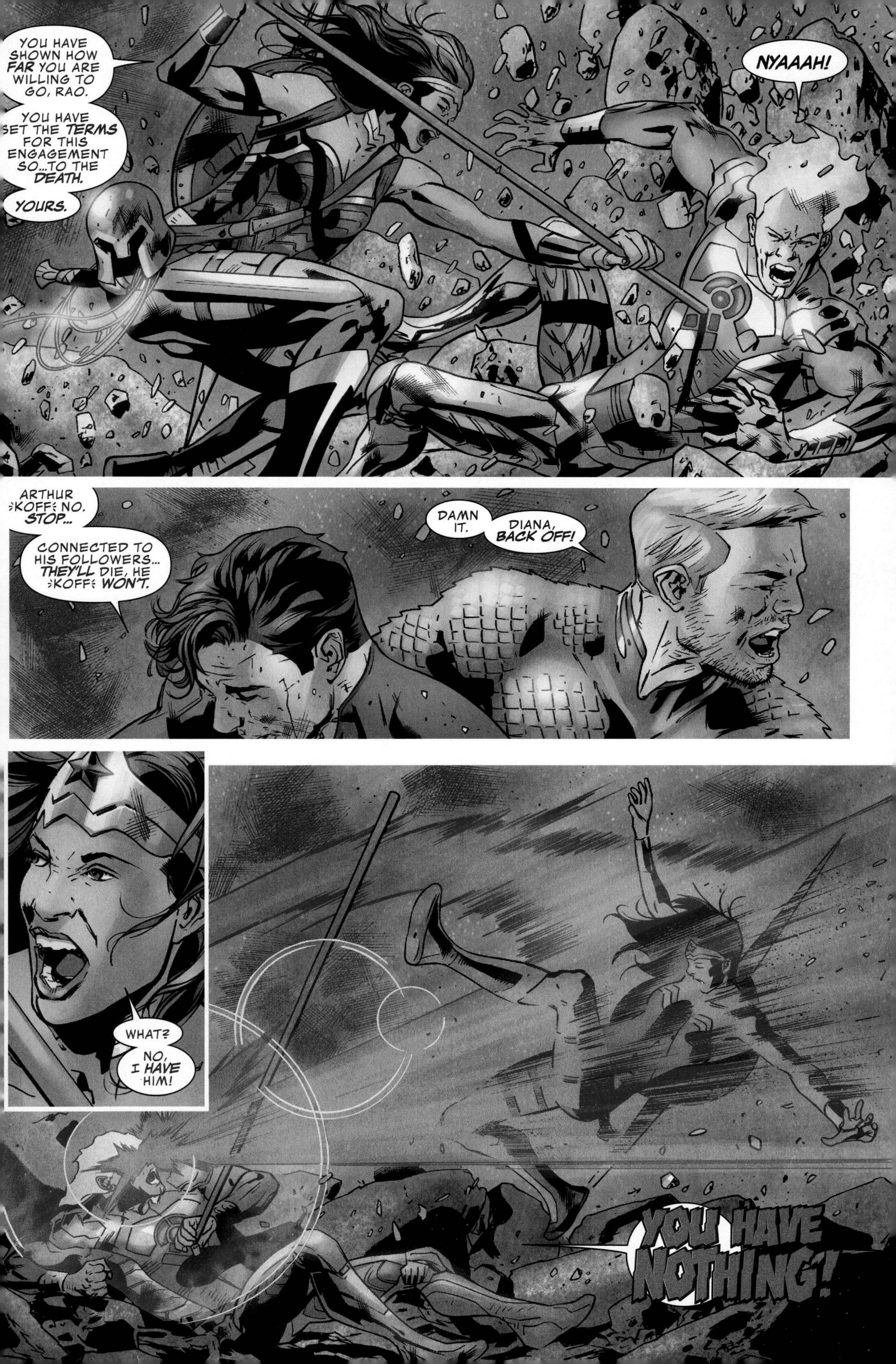
YOU HAVE SHOWN HOW FAR YOU ARE WILLING TO GO, RAO.
YOU HAVE SET THE TERMS FOR THIS ENGAGEMENT SO...TO THE DEATH.
YOURS.
NYAAAH!
ARTHUR *KOFF* NO. STOP...
CONNECTED TO HIS FOLLOWERS... THEY'LL DIE, HE *KOFF* WON'T.
DAMN IT.
DIANA, BACK OFF!
WHAT?
NO, I HAVE HIM!
YOU HAVE NOTHING!

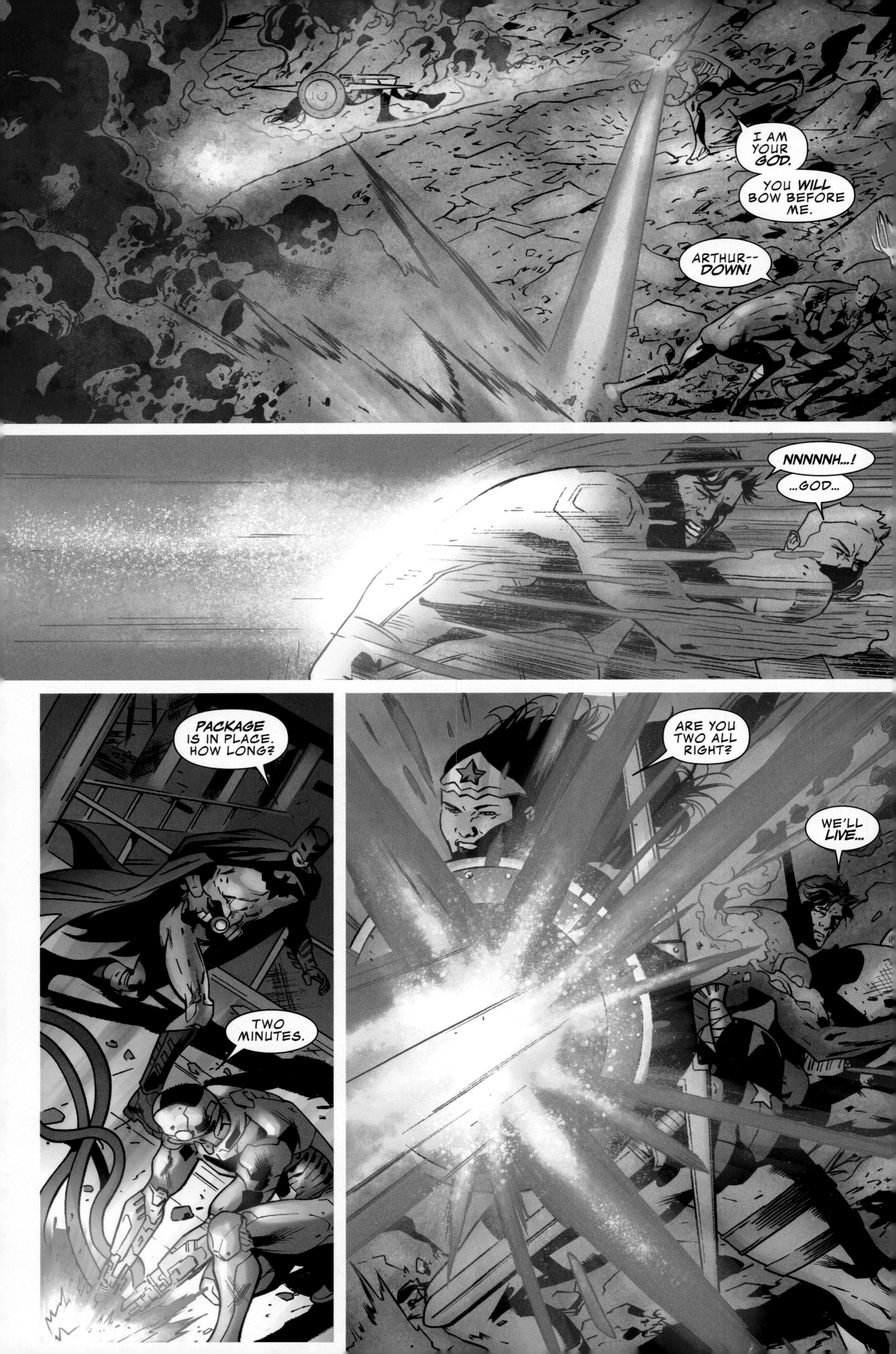
I AM YOUR GOD.
YOU WILL BOW BEFORE ME.
ARTHUR-- DOWN!
NNNNNH...!
...GOD...
PACKAGE IS IN PLACE. HOW LONG?
TWO MINUTES.
ARE YOU TWO ALL RIGHT?
WE'LL LIVE...

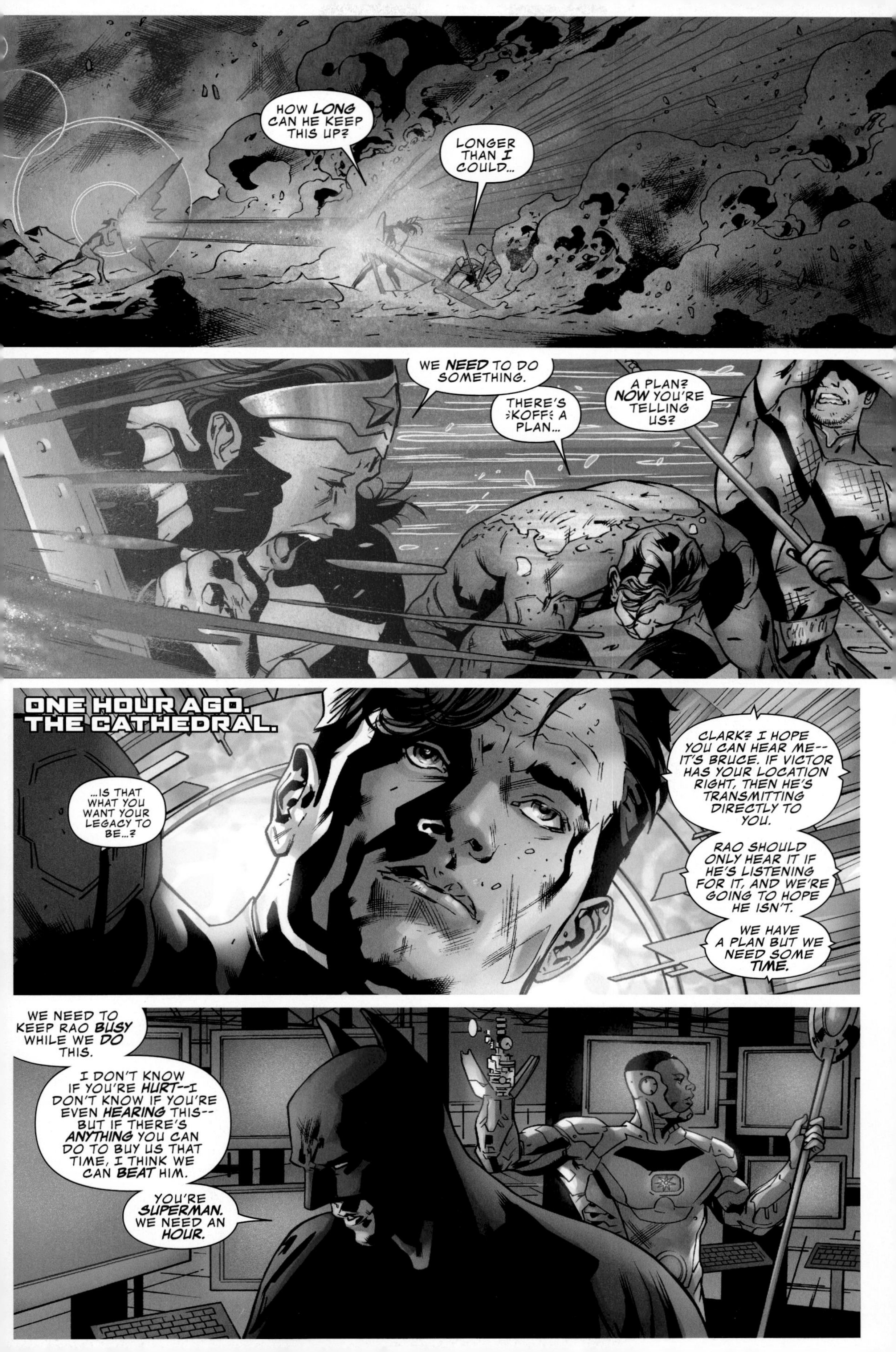
HOW LONG CAN HE KEEP THIS UP?
LONGER THAN I COULD...
WE NEED TO DO SOMETHING.
THERE'S ≷KOFF≶ A PLAN...
A PLAN? NOW YOU'RE TELLING US?
ONE HOUR AGO. THE CATHEDRAL.
...IS THAT WHAT YOU WANT YOUR LEGACY TO BE...?
CLARK? I HOPE YOU CAN HEAR ME-- IT'S BRUCE. IF VICTOR HAS YOUR LOCATION RIGHT, THEN HE'S TRANSMITTING DIRECTLY TO YOU.
RAO SHOULD ONLY HEAR IT IF HE'S LISTENING FOR IT, AND WE'RE GOING TO HOPE HE ISN'T.
WE HAVE A PLAN BUT WE NEED SOME TIME.
WE NEED TO KEEP RAO BUSY WHILE WE DO THIS.
I DON'T KNOW IF YOU'RE HURT--I DON'T KNOW IF YOU'RE EVEN HEARING THIS-- BUT IF THERE'S ANYTHING YOU CAN DO TO BUY US THAT TIME, I THINK WE CAN BEAT HIM.
YOU'RE SUPERMAN. WE NEED AN HOUR.

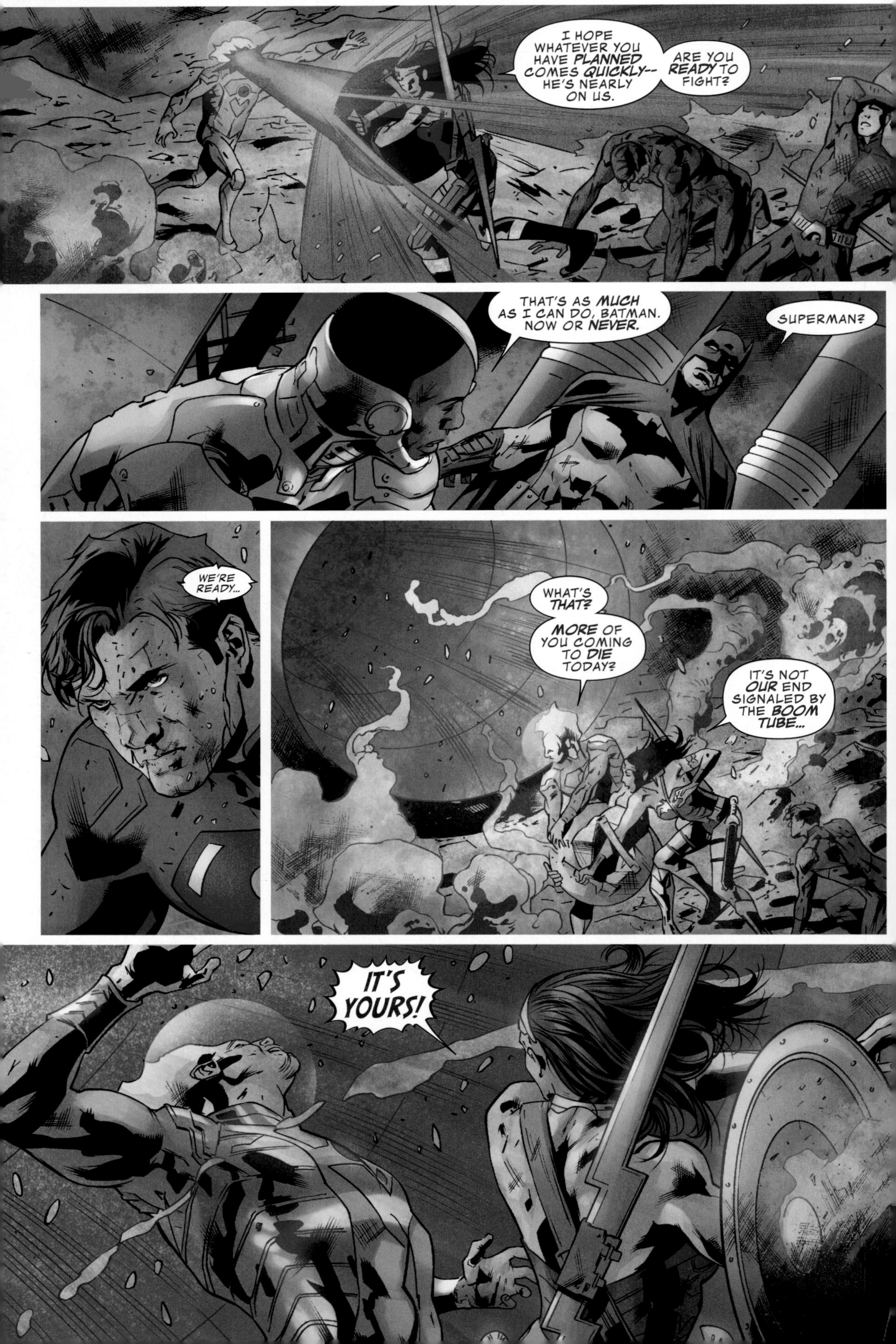

I HOPE WHATEVER YOU HAVE PLANNED COMES QUICKLY-- HE'S NEARLY ON US.
ARE YOU READY TO FIGHT?
THAT'S AS MUCH AS I CAN DO, BATMAN. NOW OR NEVER.
SUPERMAN?
WE'RE READY...
WHAT'S THAT?
MORE OF YOU COMING TO DIE TODAY?
IT'S NOT OUR END SIGNALED BY THE BOOM TUBE...
IT'S YOURS!

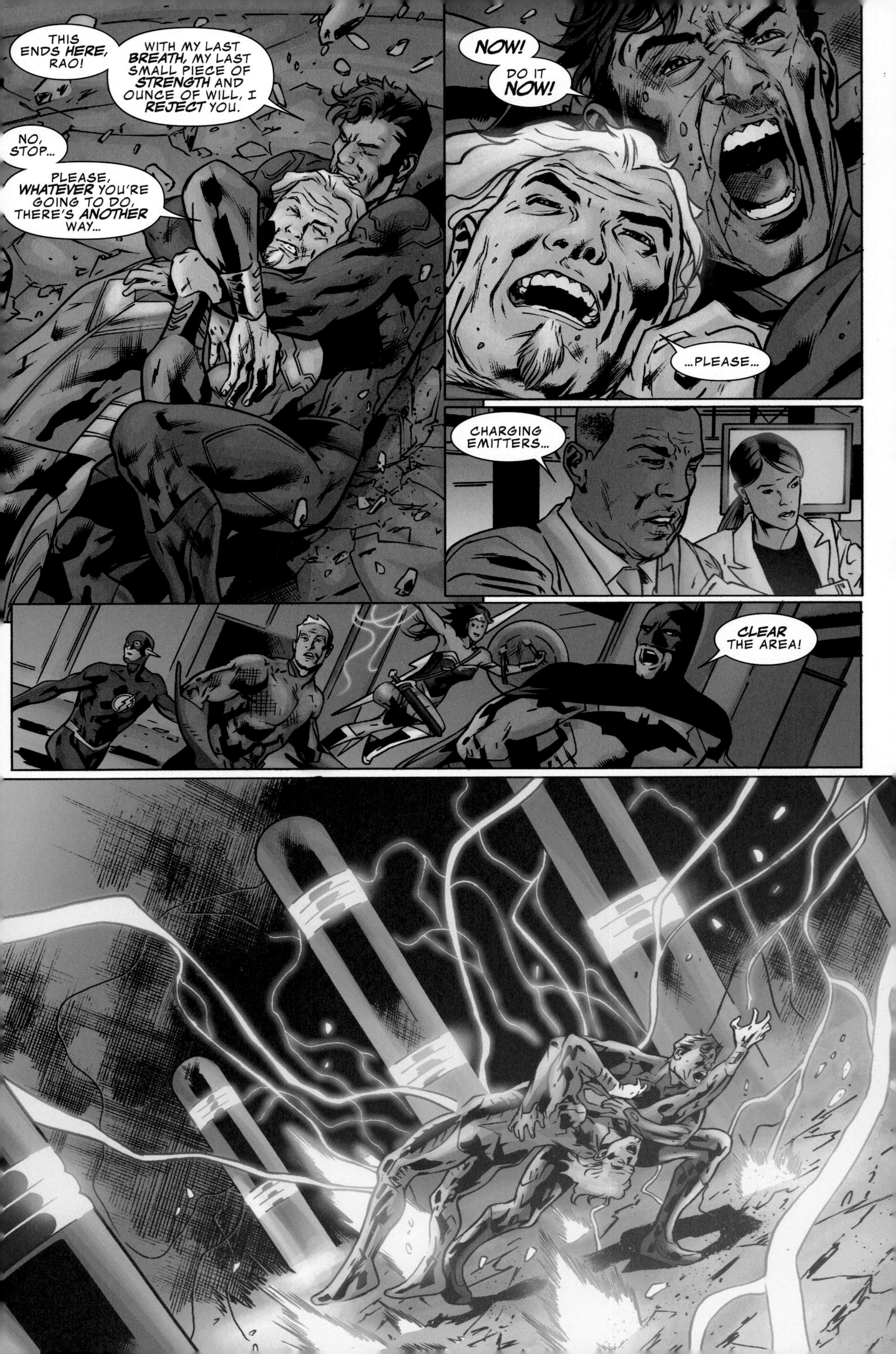
THIS ENDS HERE, RAO!
WITH MY LAST BREATH, MY LAST SMALL PIECE OF STRENGTH AND OUNCE OF WILL, I REJECT YOU.
NO, STOP...
PLEASE, WHATEVER YOU'RE GOING TO DO, THERE'S ANOTHER WAY...
NOW!
DO IT NOW!
...PLEASE...
CHARGING EMITTERS...
CLEAR THE AREA!

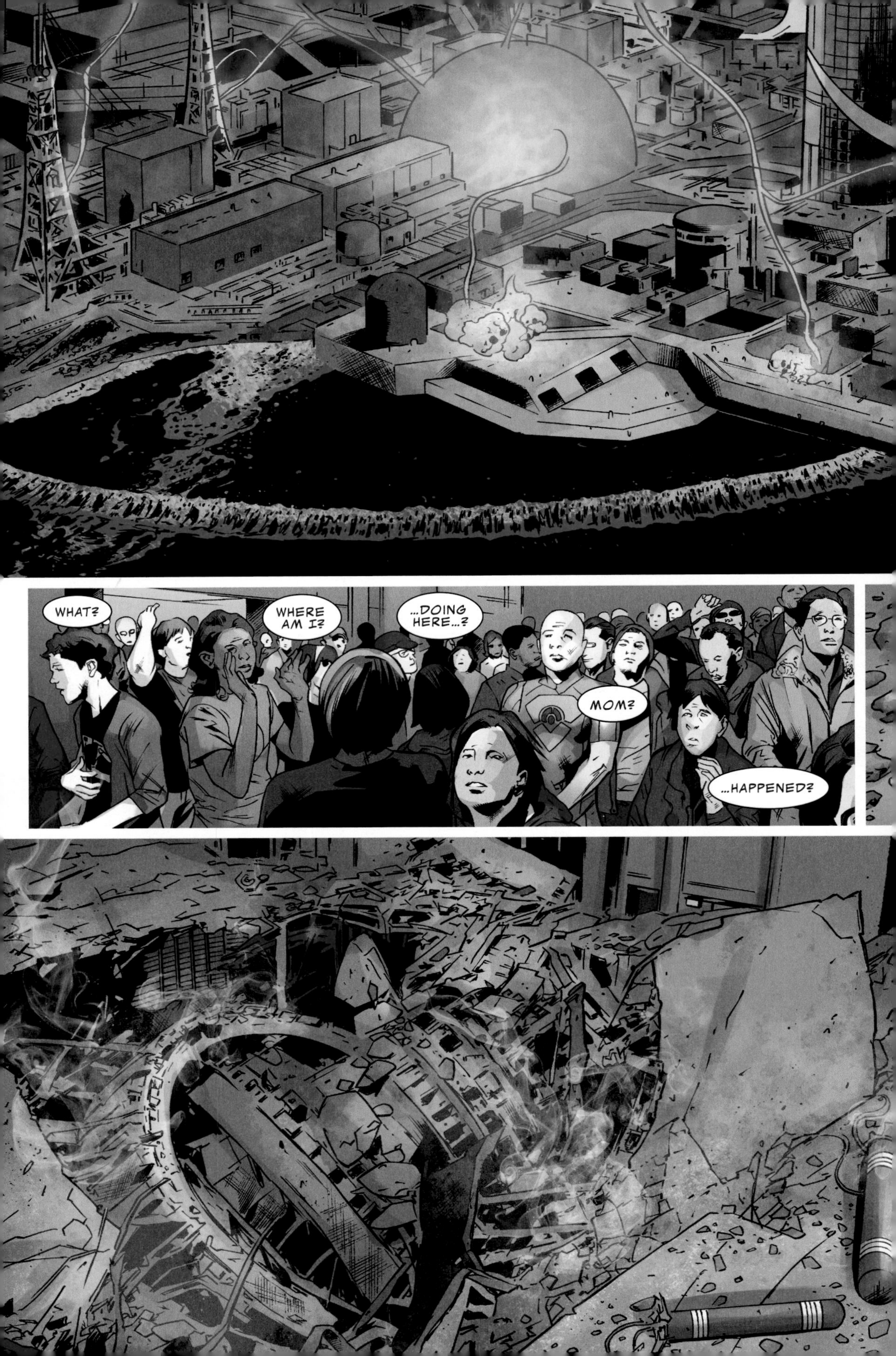
WHAT?
WHERE AM I?
...DOING HERE...?
MOM?
...HAPPENED?

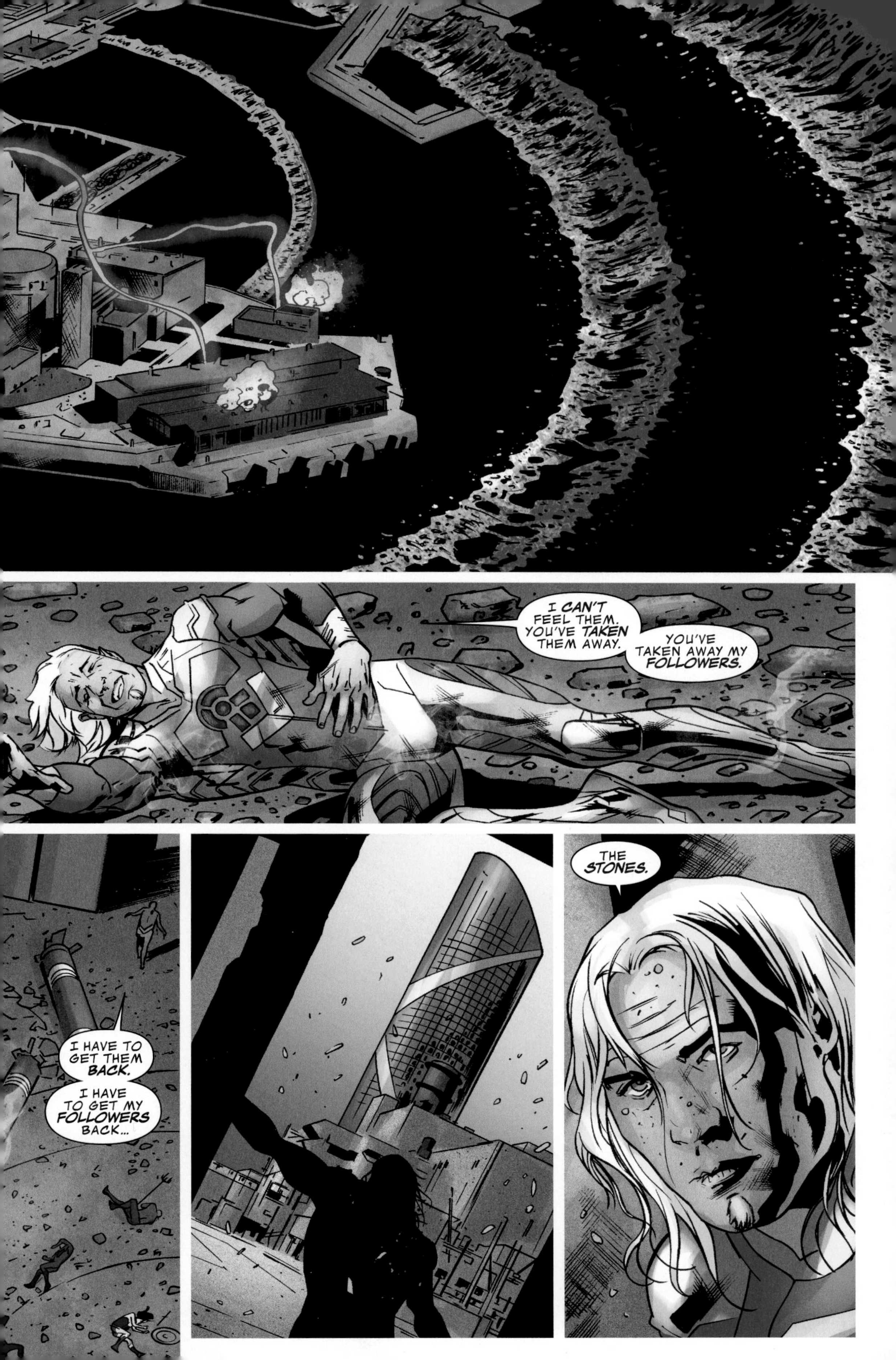
I CAN'T FEEL THEM. YOU'VE TAKEN THEM AWAY.
YOU'VE TAKEN AWAY MY FOLLOWERS.
I HAVE TO GET THEM BACK.
I HAVE TO GET MY FOLLOWERS BACK...
THE STONES.

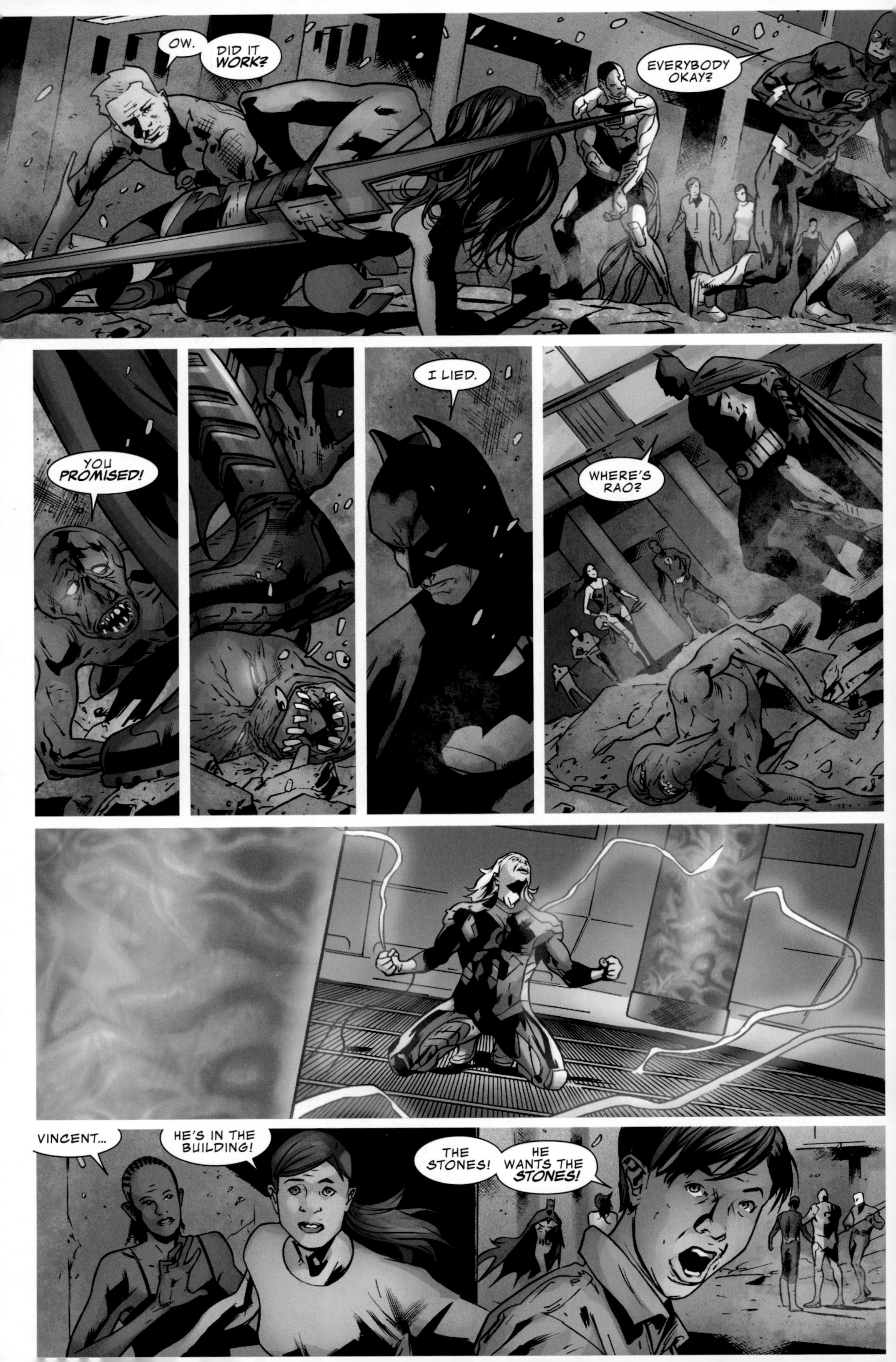
OW.
DID IT WORK?
EVERYBODY OKAY?
YOU PROMISED!
I LIED.
WHERE'S RAO?
VINCENT...
HE'S IN THE BUILDING!
THE STONES!
HE WANTS THE STONES!

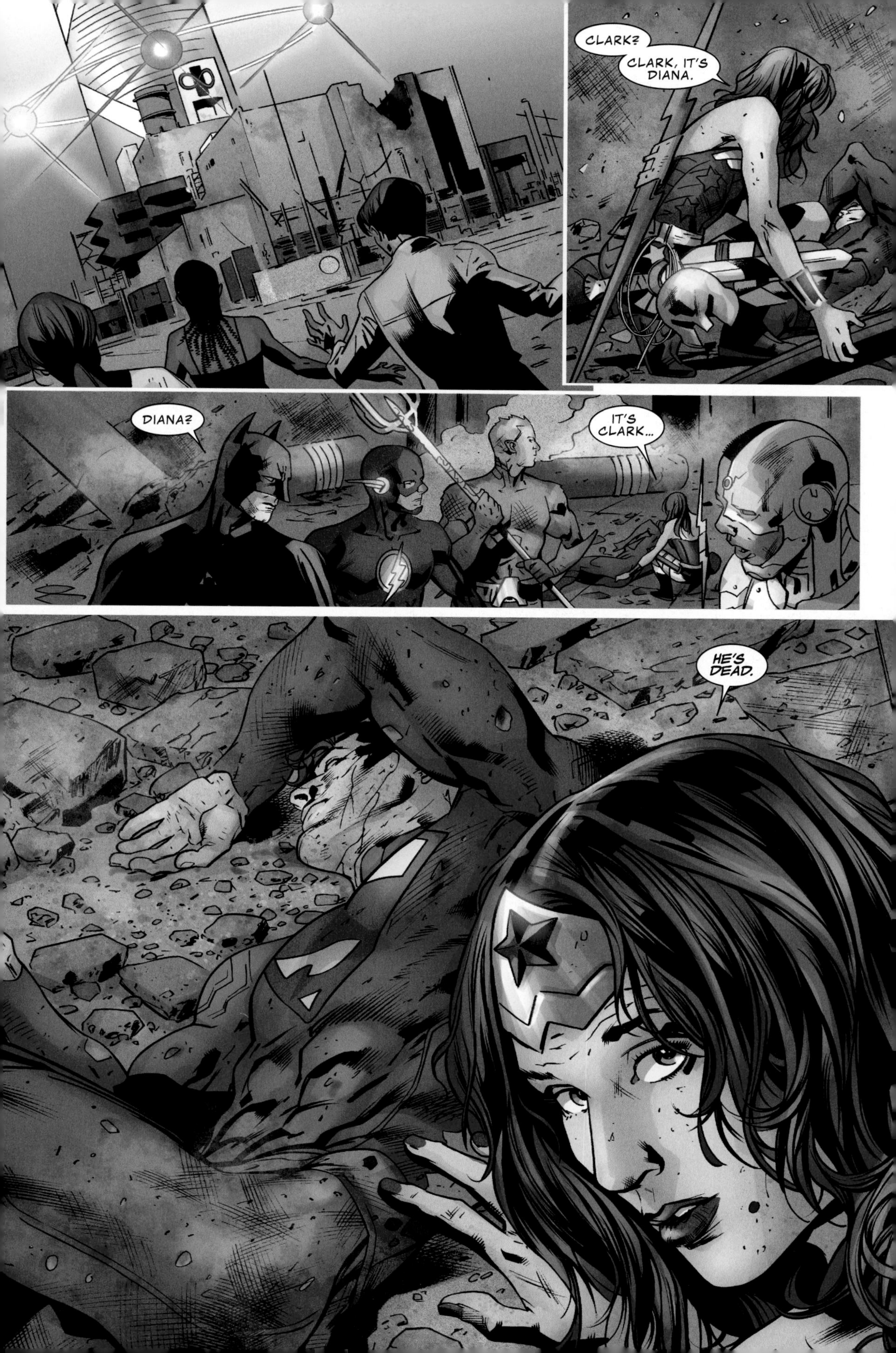
CLARK?
CLARK, IT'S DIANA.
DIANA?
IT'S CLARK...
HE'S DEAD.

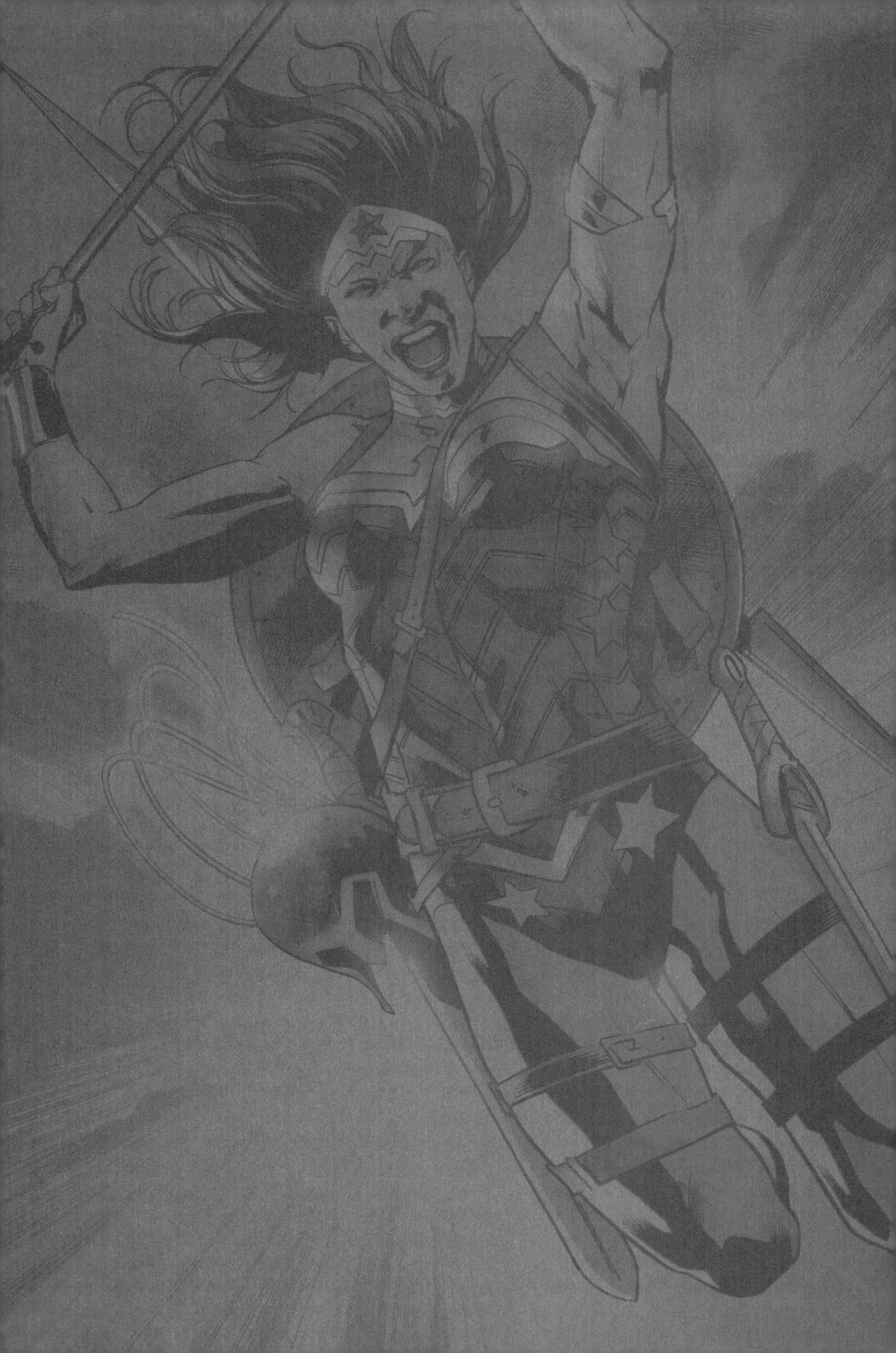

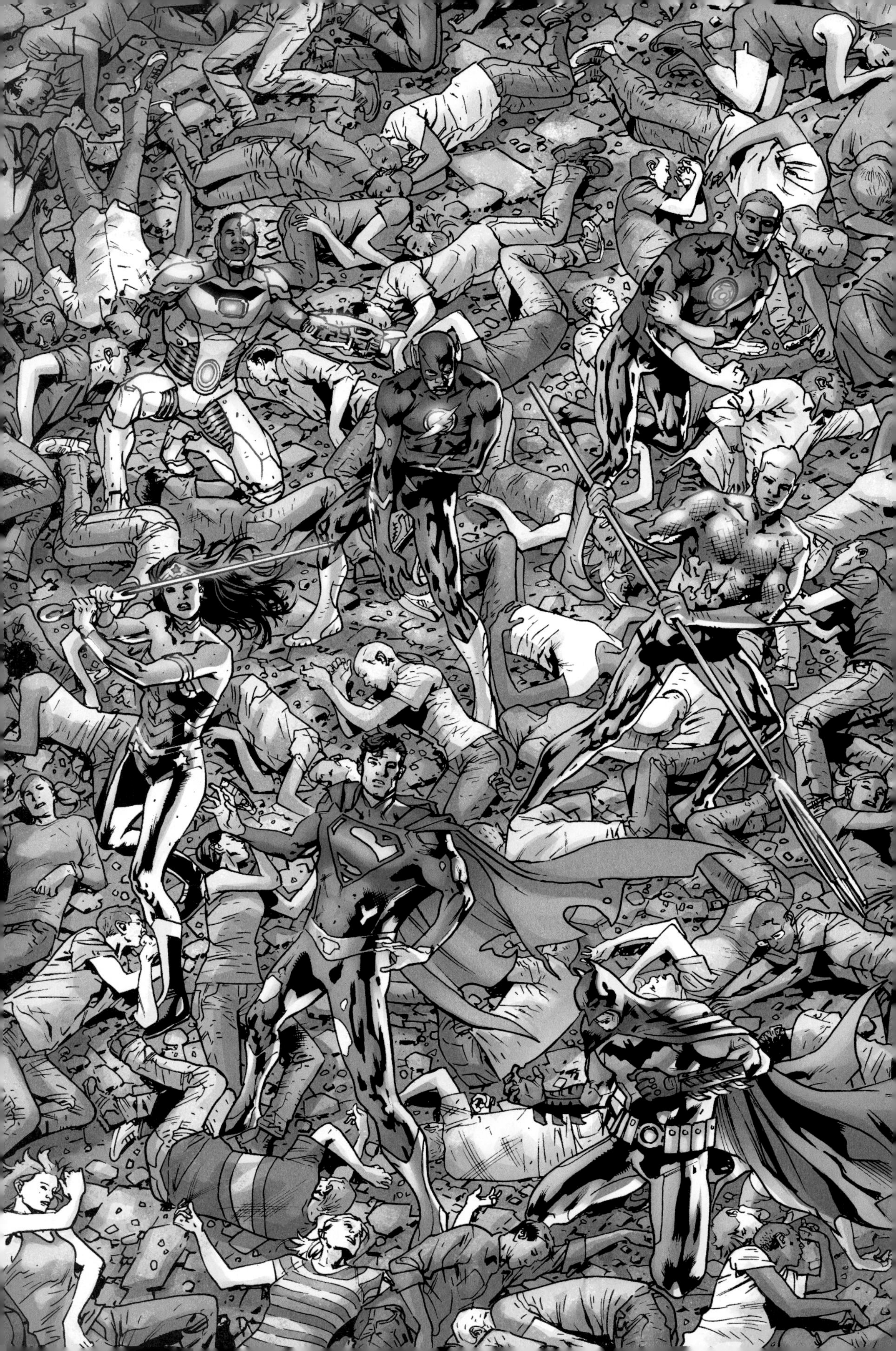

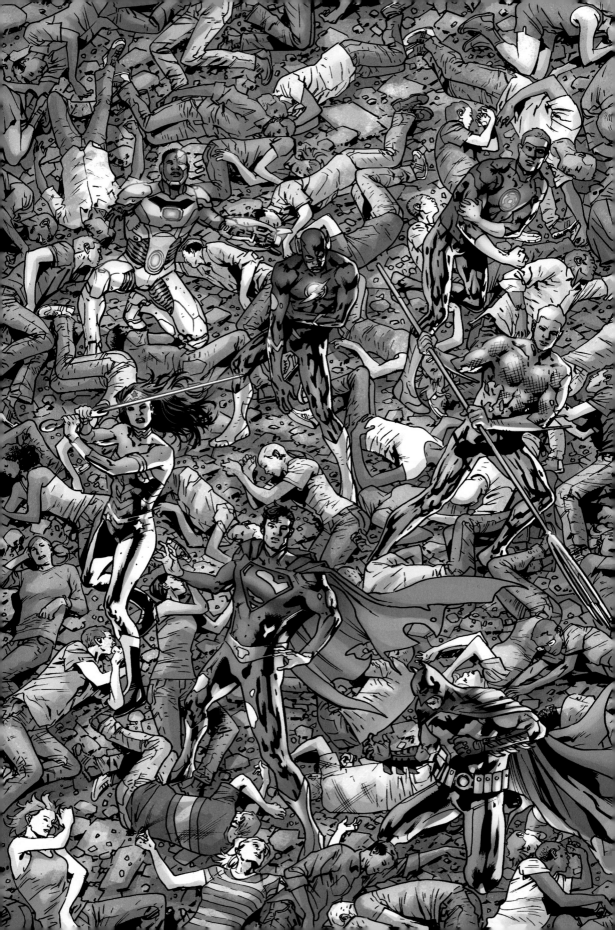

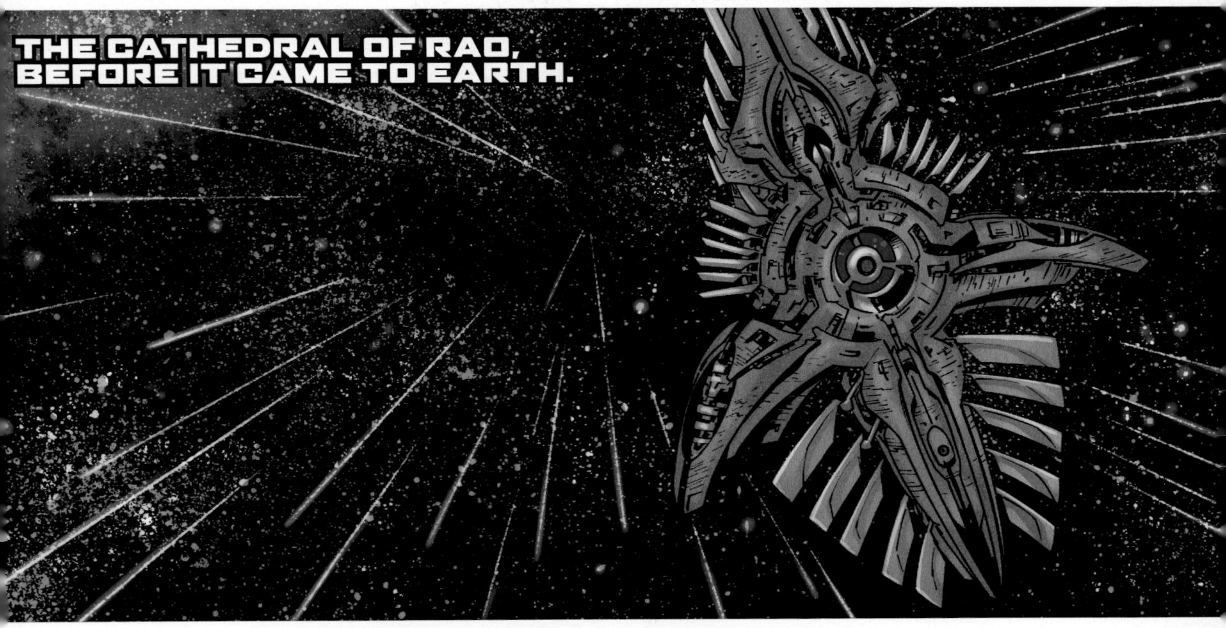
THE CATHEDRAL OF RAO, BEFORE IT CAME TO EARTH.

DC COMICS PRESENTS

THE JUSTICE LEAGUE OF AMERICA POWER AND GLORY

PART EIGHT

BY BRYAN HITCH

DANIEL HENRIQUES INKER
ALEX SINCLAIR COLORIST
CHRIS ELIOPOULOS LETTERER
AMEDEO TURTURRO ASSISTANT EDITOR
BRIAN CUNNINGHAM EDITOR
COVER BY BRYAN HITCH AND ALEX SINCLAIR

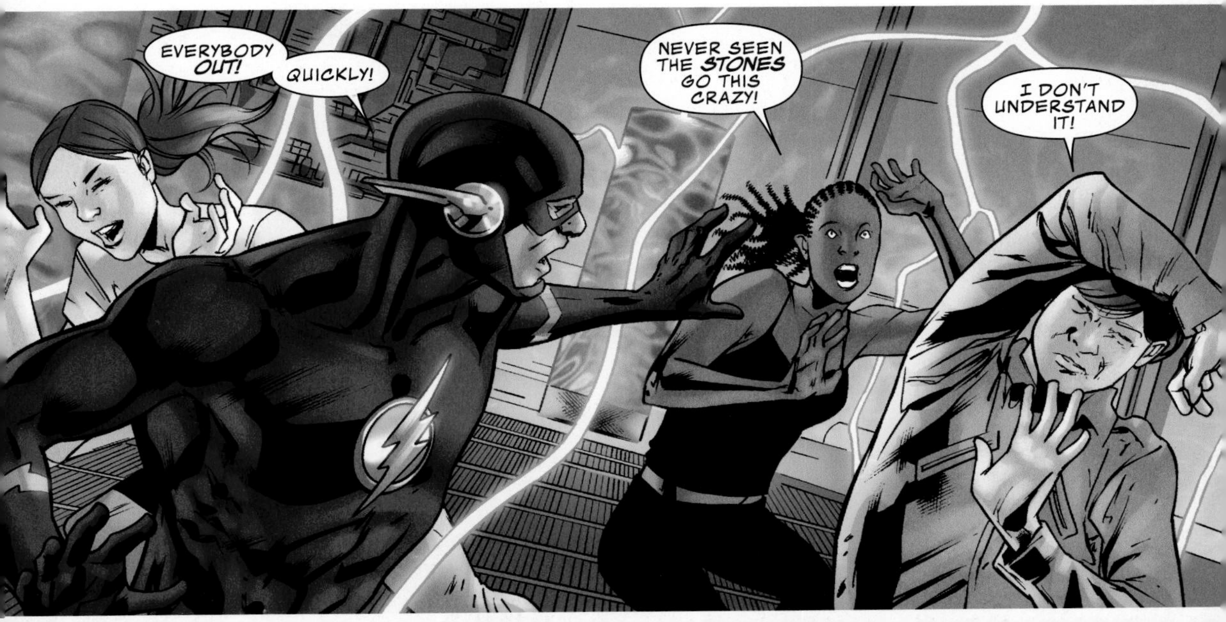
EVERYBODY OUT!
QUICKLY!
NEVER SEEN THE STONES GO THIS CRAZY!
I DON'T UNDERSTAND IT!

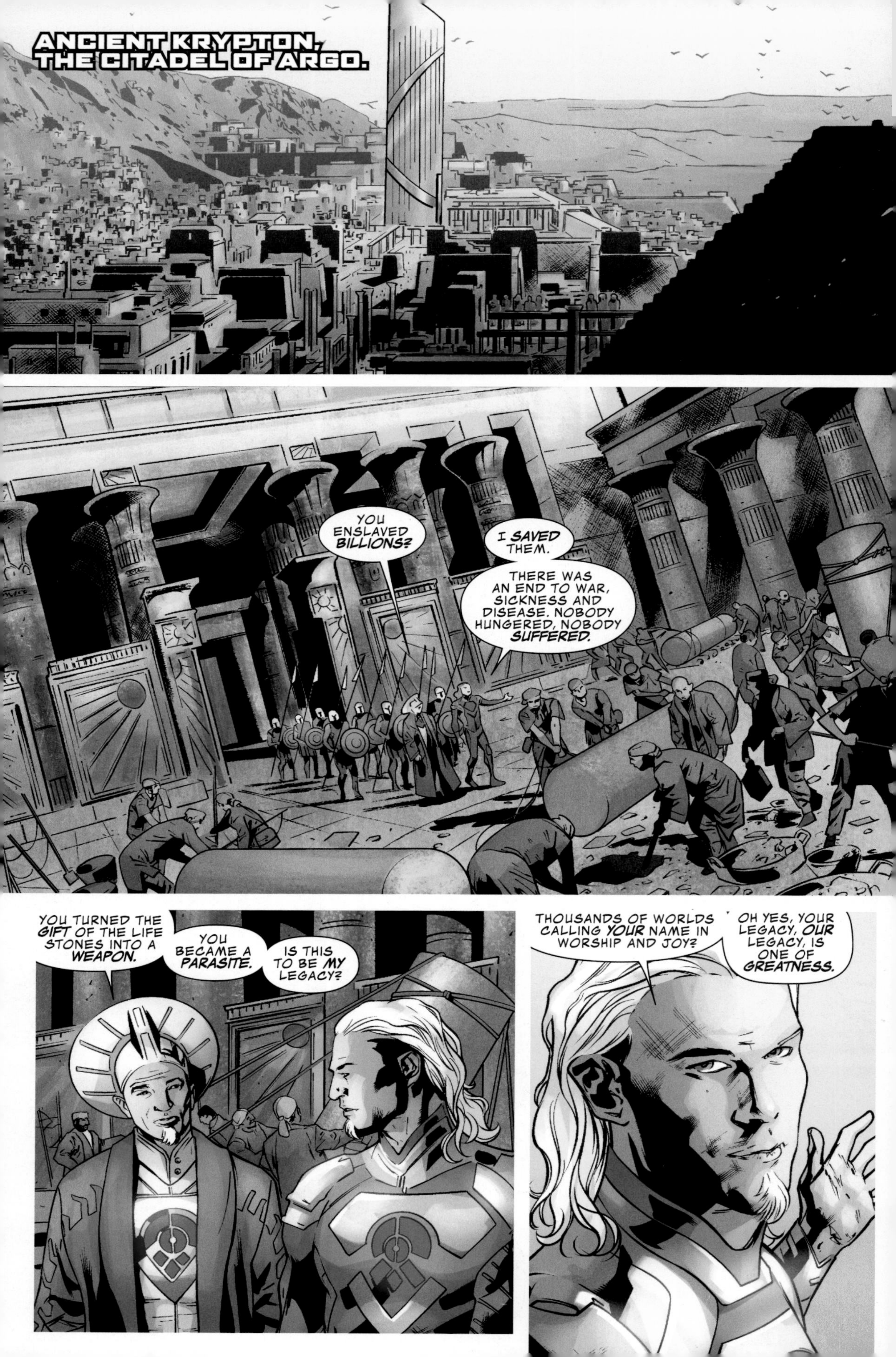

ANCIENT KRYPTON, THE CITADEL OF ARGO.
YOU ENSLAVED BILLIONS?
I SAVED THEM.
THERE WAS AN END TO WAR, SICKNESS AND DISEASE. NOBODY HUNGERED, NOBODY SUFFERED.
YOU TURNED THE GIFT OF THE LIFE STONES INTO A WEAPON.
YOU BECAME A PARASITE.
IS THIS TO BE MY LEGACY?
THOUSANDS OF WORLDS CALLING YOUR NAME IN WORSHIP AND JOY?
OH YES, YOUR LEGACY, OUR LEGACY, IS ONE OF GREATNESS.

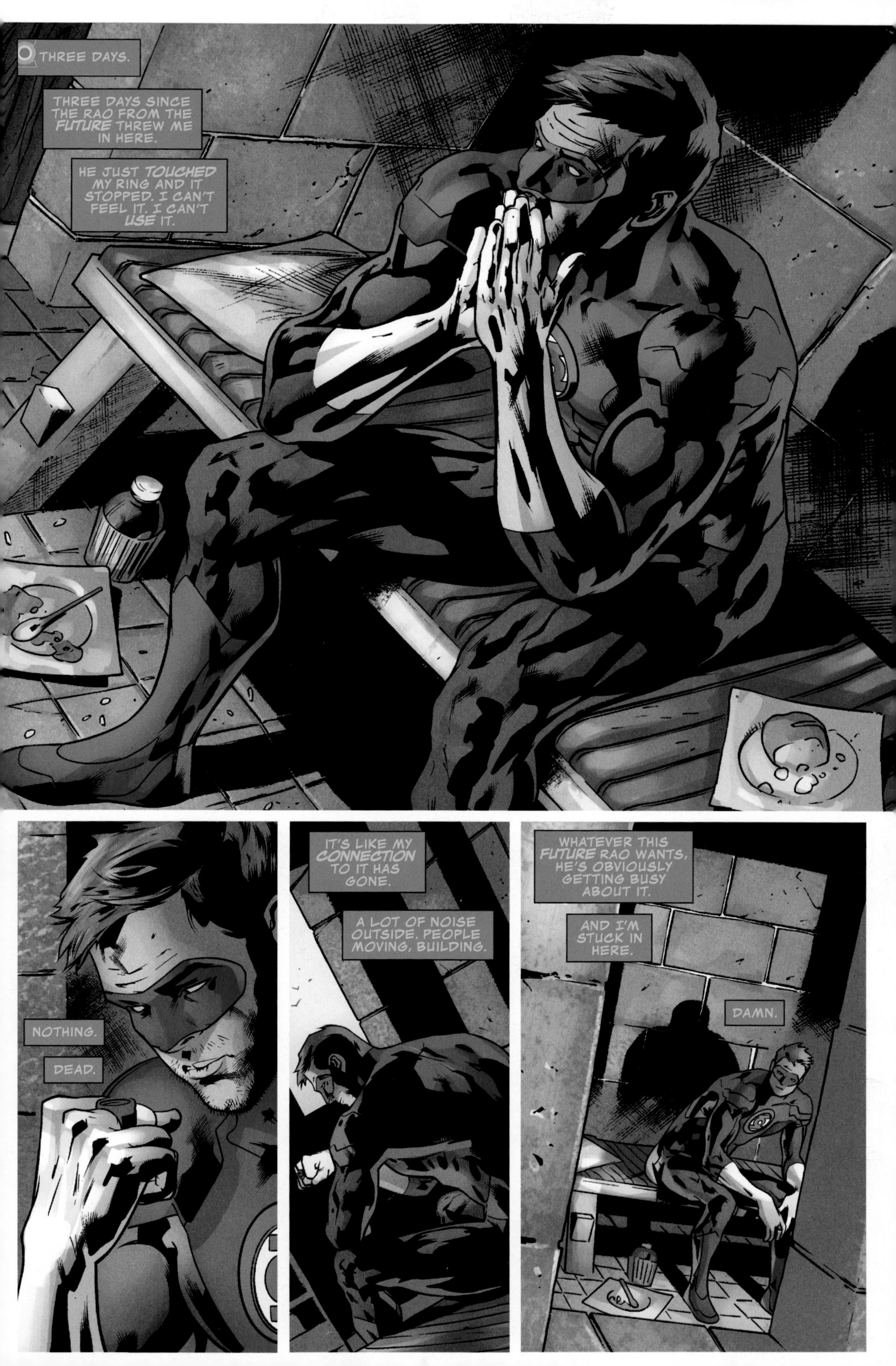
THREE DAYS.
THREE DAYS SINCE THE RAO FROM THE FUTURE THREW ME IN HERE.
HE JUST TOUCHED MY RING AND IT STOPPED. I CAN'T FEEL IT. I CAN'T USE IT.
NOTHING.
DEAD.
IT'S LIKE MY CONNECTION TO IT HAS GONE.
A LOT OF NOISE OUTSIDE. PEOPLE MOVING, BUILDING.
WHATEVER THIS FUTURE RAO WANTS, HE'S OBVIOUSLY GETTING BUSY ABOUT IT.
AND I'M STUCK IN HERE.
DAMN.

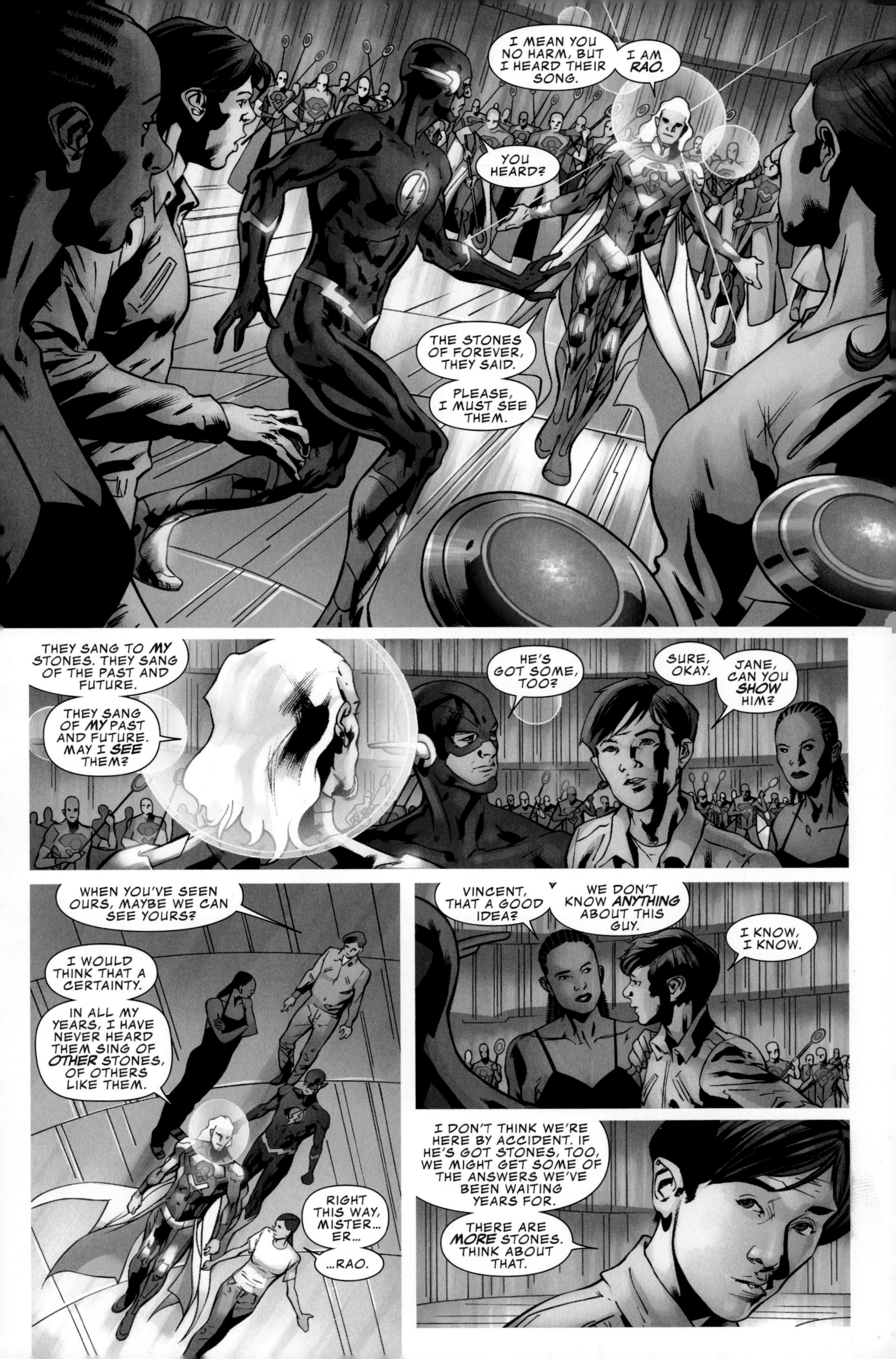
I MEAN YOU NO HARM, BUT I HEARD THEIR SONG.
I AM RAO.
YOU HEARD?
THE STONES OF FOREVER, THEY SAID.
PLEASE, I MUST SEE THEM.
THEY SANG TO MY STONES. THEY SANG OF THE PAST AND FUTURE.
THEY SANG OF MY PAST AND FUTURE. MAY I SEE THEM?
HE'S GOT SOME, TOO?
SURE, OKAY.
JANE, CAN YOU SHOW HIM?
WHEN YOU'VE SEEN OURS, MAYBE WE CAN SEE YOURS?
I WOULD THINK THAT A CERTAINTY.
IN ALL MY YEARS, I HAVE NEVER HEARD THEM SING OF OTHER STONES, OF OTHERS LIKE THEM.
RIGHT THIS WAY, MISTER... ER...
...RAO.
VINCENT, THAT A GOOD IDEA?
WE DON'T KNOW ANYTHING ABOUT THIS GUY.
I KNOW, I KNOW.
I DON'T THINK WE'RE HERE BY ACCIDENT. IF HE'S GOT STONES, TOO, WE MIGHT GET SOME OF THE ANSWERS WE'VE BEEN WAITING YEARS FOR.
THERE ARE MORE STONES. THINK ABOUT THAT.

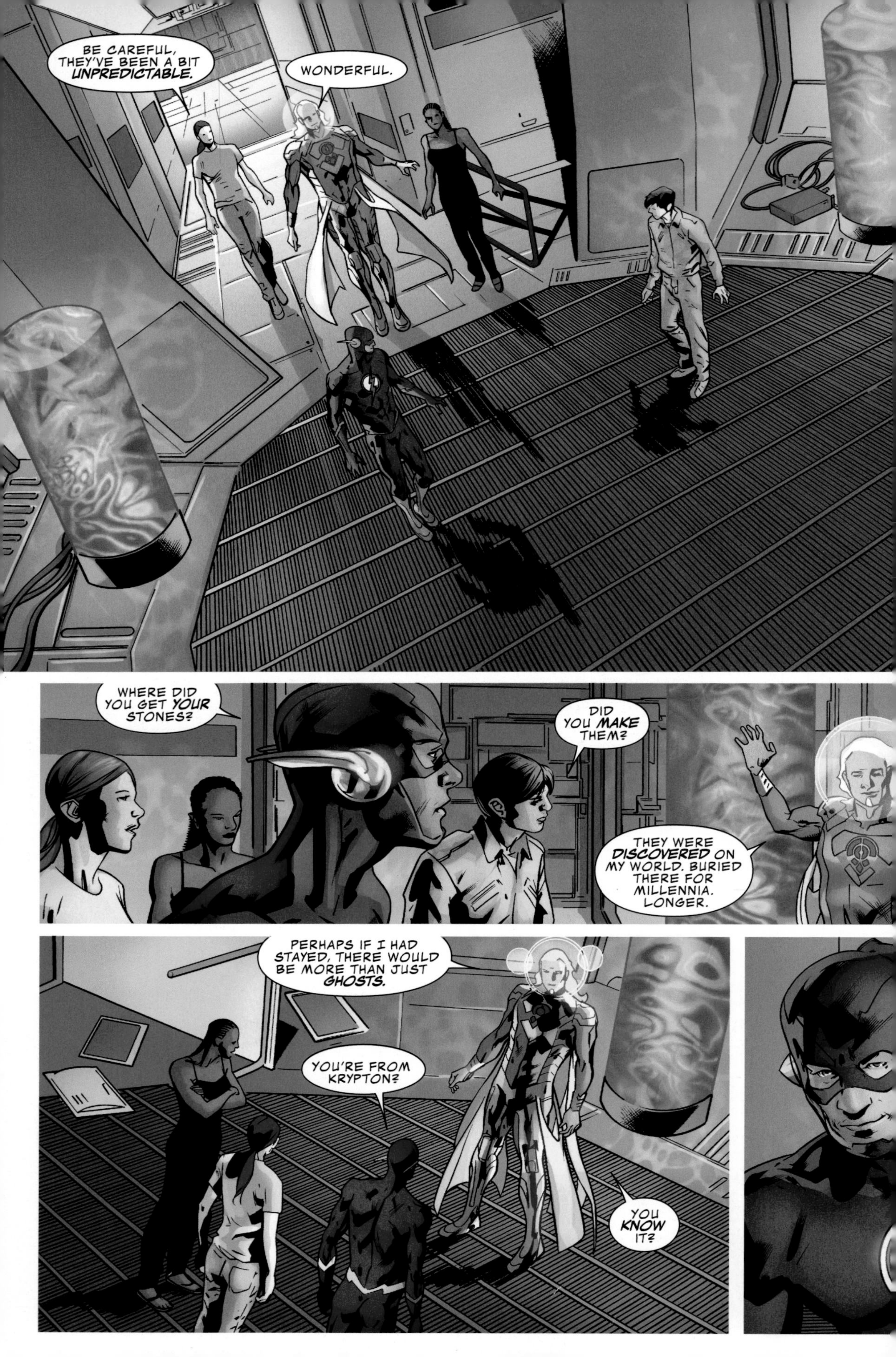
BE CAREFUL, THEY'VE BEEN A BIT UNPREDICTABLE.
WONDERFUL.
WHERE DID YOU GET YOUR STONES?
DID YOU MAKE THEM?
THEY WERE DISCOVERED ON MY WORLD. BURIED THERE FOR MILLENNIA. LONGER.
PERHAPS IF I HAD STAYED, THERE WOULD BE MORE THAN JUST GHOSTS.
YOU'RE FROM KRYPTON?
YOU KNOW IT?

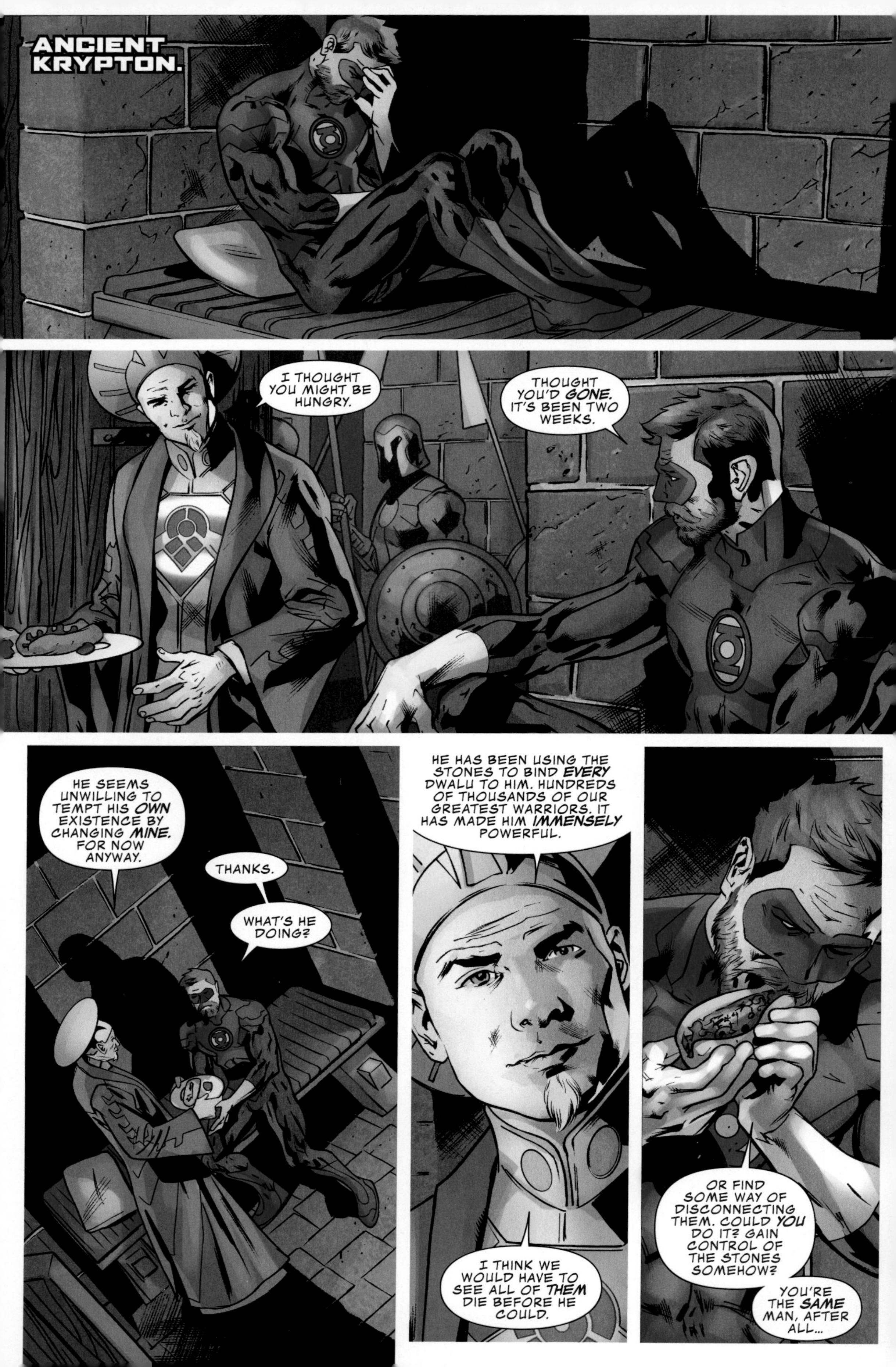
ANCIENT KRYPTON.
I THOUGHT YOU MIGHT BE HUNGRY.
THOUGHT YOU'D GONE. IT'S BEEN TWO WEEKS.
HE SEEMS UNWILLING TO TEMPT HIS OWN EXISTENCE BY CHANGING MINE. FOR NOW ANYWAY.
THANKS.
WHAT'S HE DOING?
HE HAS BEEN USING THE STONES TO BIND EVERY DWALU TO HIM. HUNDREDS OF THOUSANDS OF OUR GREATEST WARRIORS. IT HAS MADE HIM IMMENSELY POWERFUL.
I THINK WE WOULD HAVE TO SEE ALL OF THEM DIE BEFORE HE COULD.
OR FIND SOME WAY OF DISCONNECTING THEM. COULD YOU DO IT? GAIN CONTROL OF THE STONES SOMEHOW?
YOU'RE THE SAME MAN, AFTER ALL...

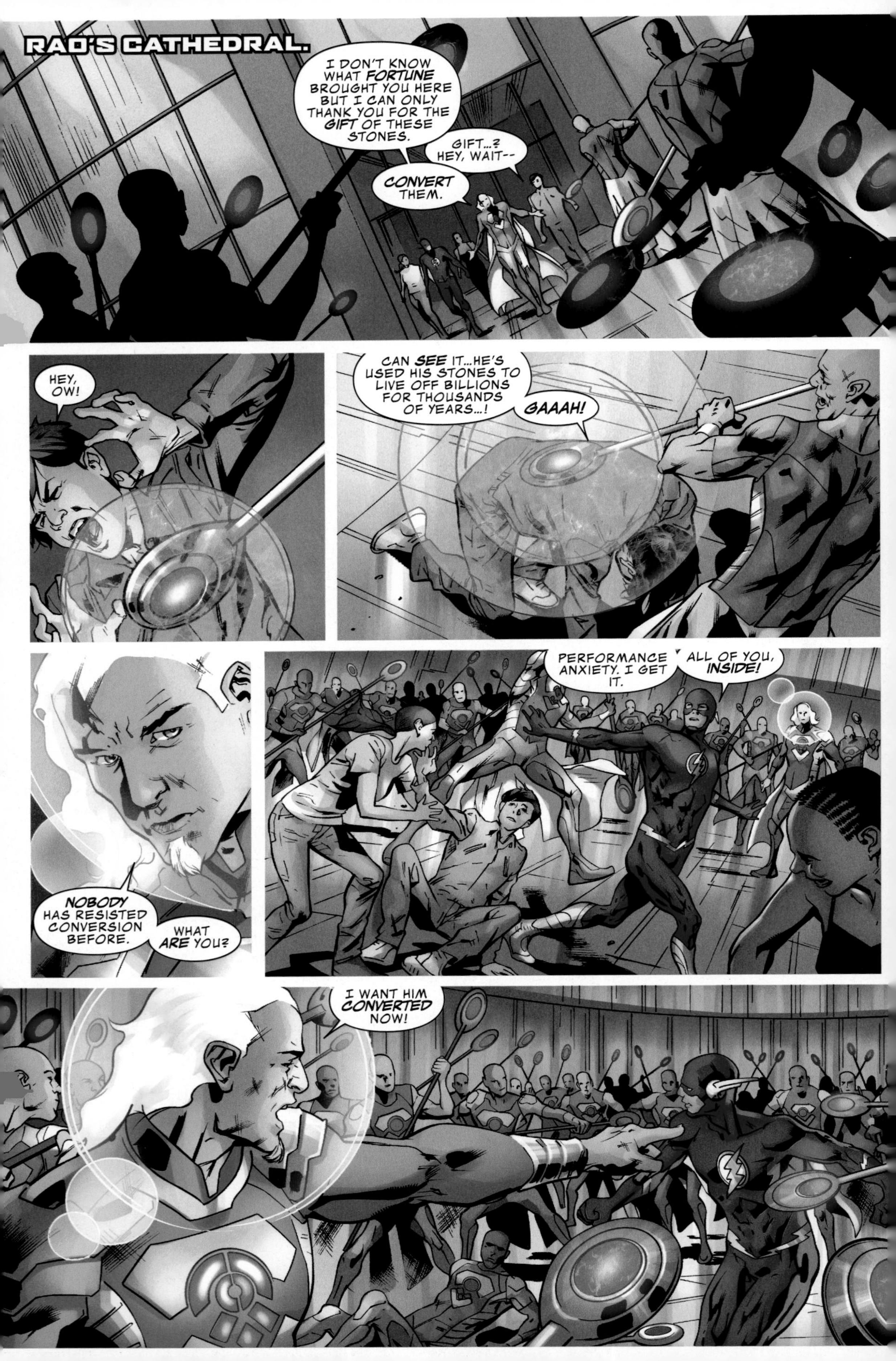
RAD'S CATHEDRAL.
I DON'T KNOW WHAT FORTUNE BROUGHT YOU HERE BUT I CAN ONLY THANK YOU FOR THE GIFT OF THESE STONES.
GIFT...? HEY, WAIT--
CONVERT THEM.
HEY, OW!
CAN SEE IT...HE'S USED HIS STONES TO LIVE OFF BILLIONS FOR THOUSANDS OF YEARS...!
GAAAH!
NOBODY HAS RESISTED CONVERSION BEFORE.
WHAT ARE YOU?
PERFORMANCE ANXIETY. I GET IT.
ALL OF YOU, INSIDE!
I WANT HIM CONVERTED NOW!

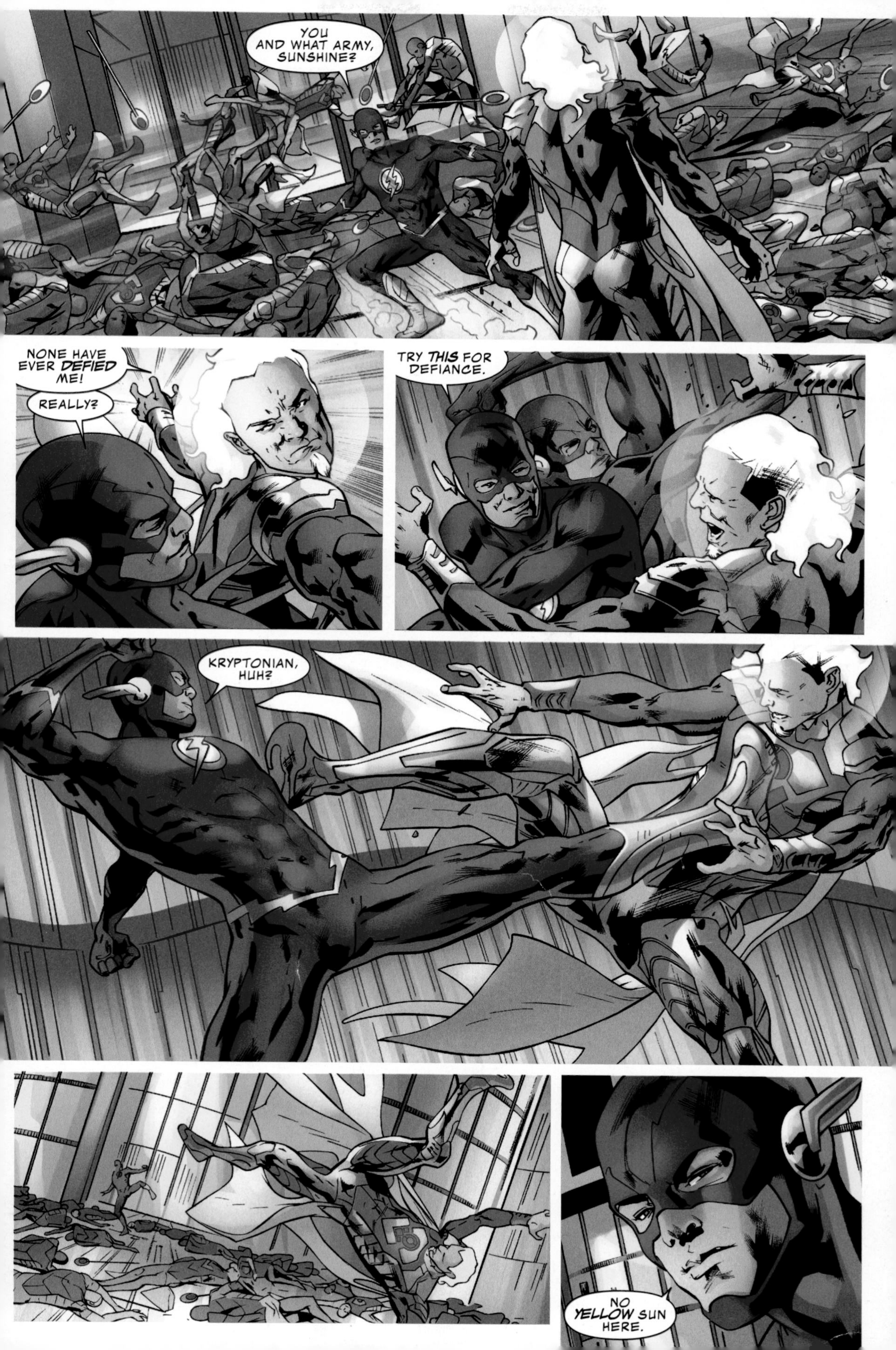
YOU AND WHAT ARMY, SUNSHINE?
NONE HAVE EVER DEFIED ME!
REALLY?
TRY THIS FOR DEFIANCE.
KRYPTONIAN, HUH?
NO YELLOW SUN HERE.

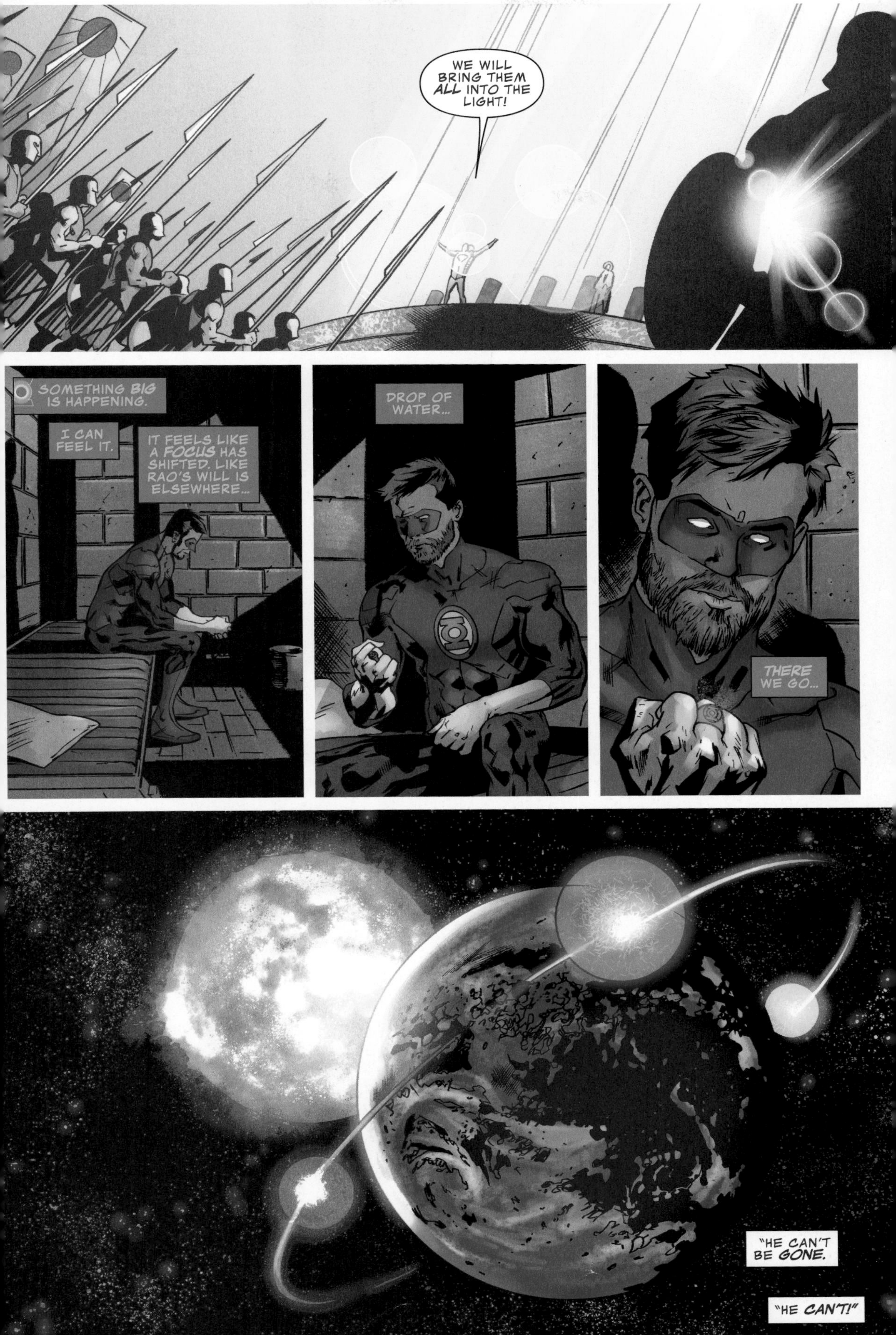

WE WILL BRING THEM ALL INTO THE LIGHT!
SOMETHING BIG IS HAPPENING.
I CAN FEEL IT.
IT FEELS LIKE A FOCUS HAS SHIFTED. LIKE RAO'S WILL IS ELSEWHERE...
DROP OF WATER...
THERE WE GO...
"HE CAN'T BE GONE.
"HE CAN'T!"

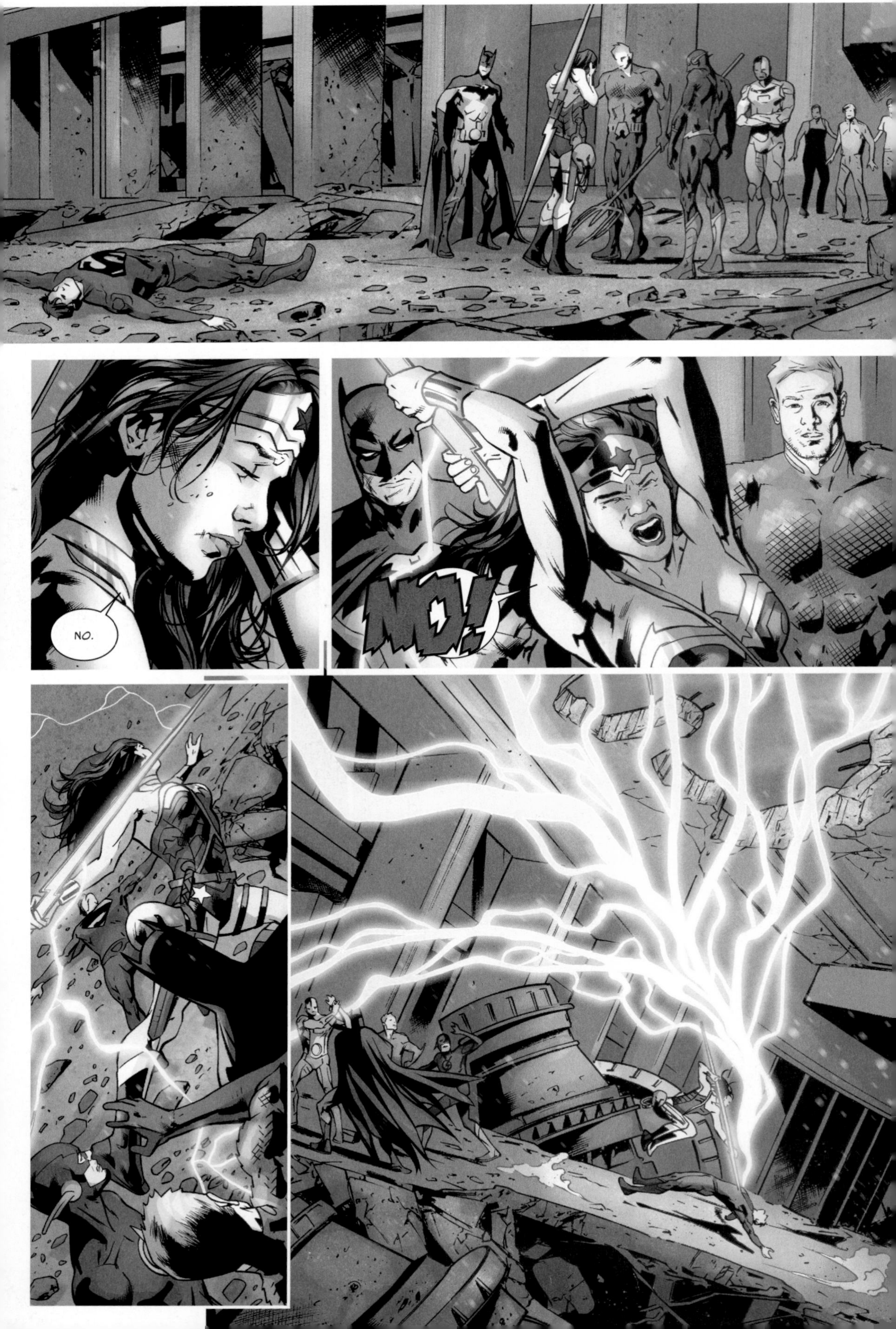
NO.
NO!

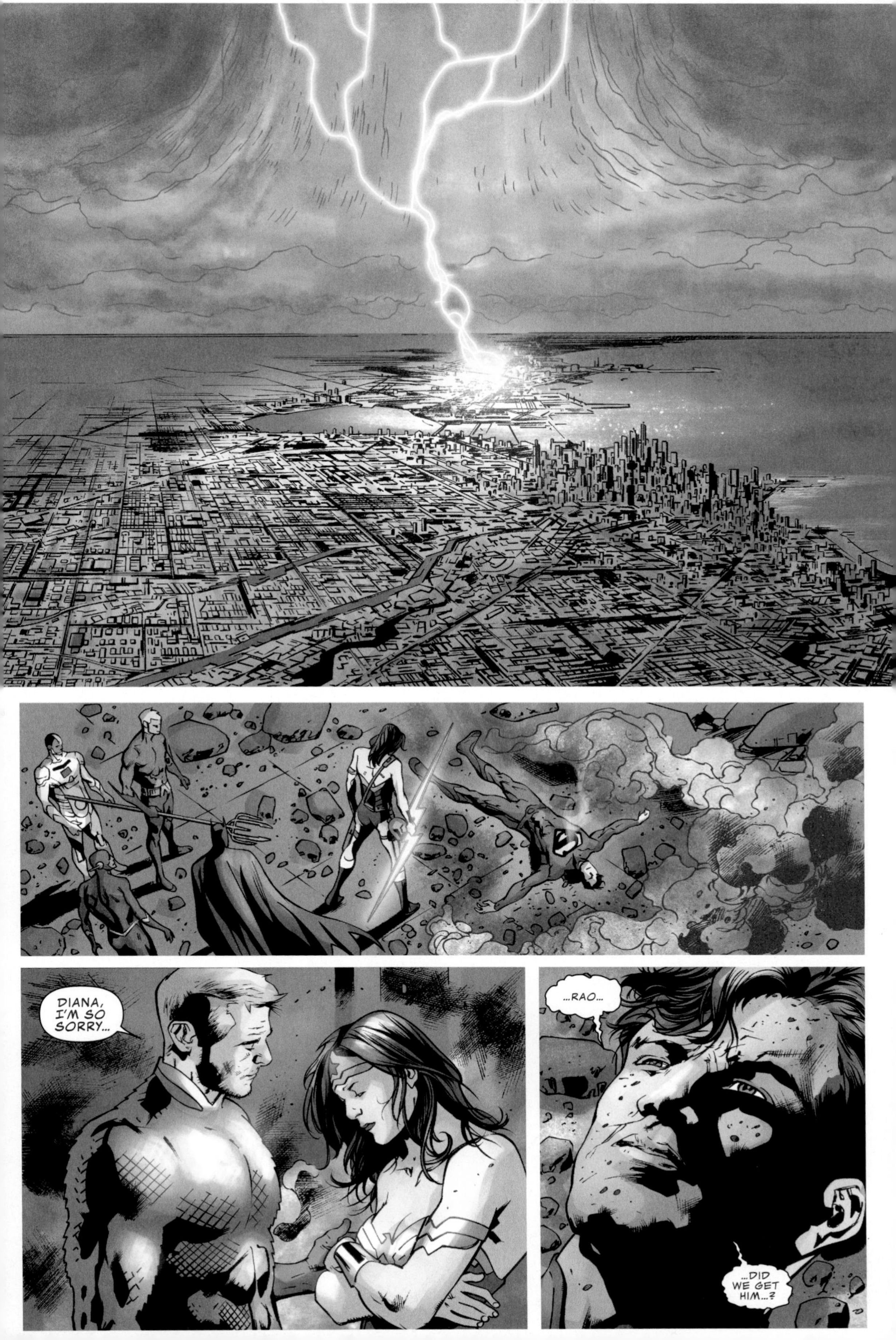
DIANA, I'M SO SORRY...
...RAO...
...DID WE GET HIM...?

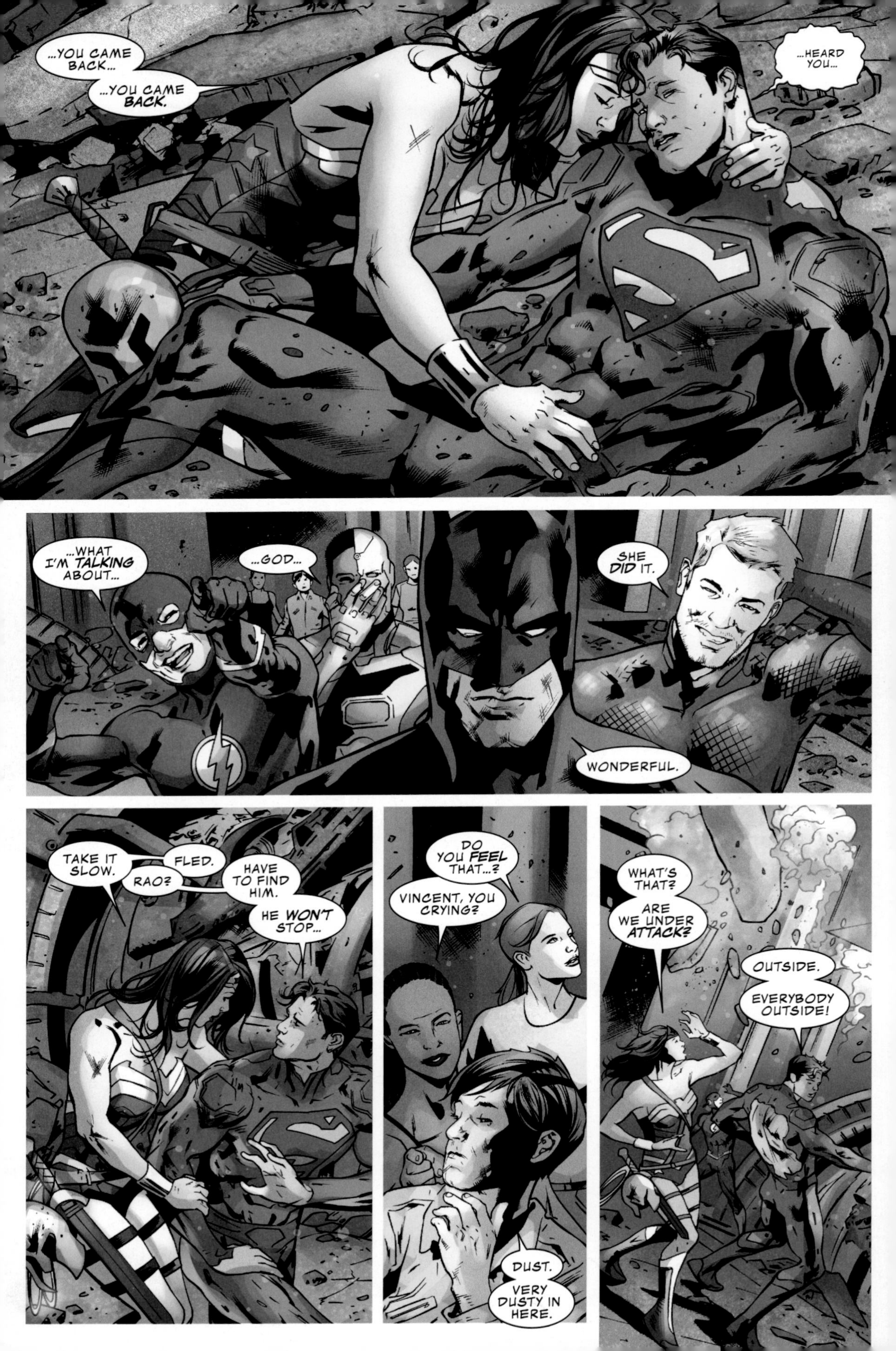
...YOU CAME BACK...
...YOU CAME BACK.
...HEARD YOU...
...WHAT I'M TALKING ABOUT...
...GOD...
SHE DID IT.
WONDERFUL.
TAKE IT SLOW.
FLED.
RAO?
HAVE TO FIND HIM.
HE WON'T STOP...
DO YOU FEEL THAT...?
VINCENT, YOU CRYING?
DUST.
VERY DUSTY IN HERE.
WHAT'S THAT?
ARE WE UNDER ATTACK?
OUTSIDE.
EVERYBODY OUTSIDE!

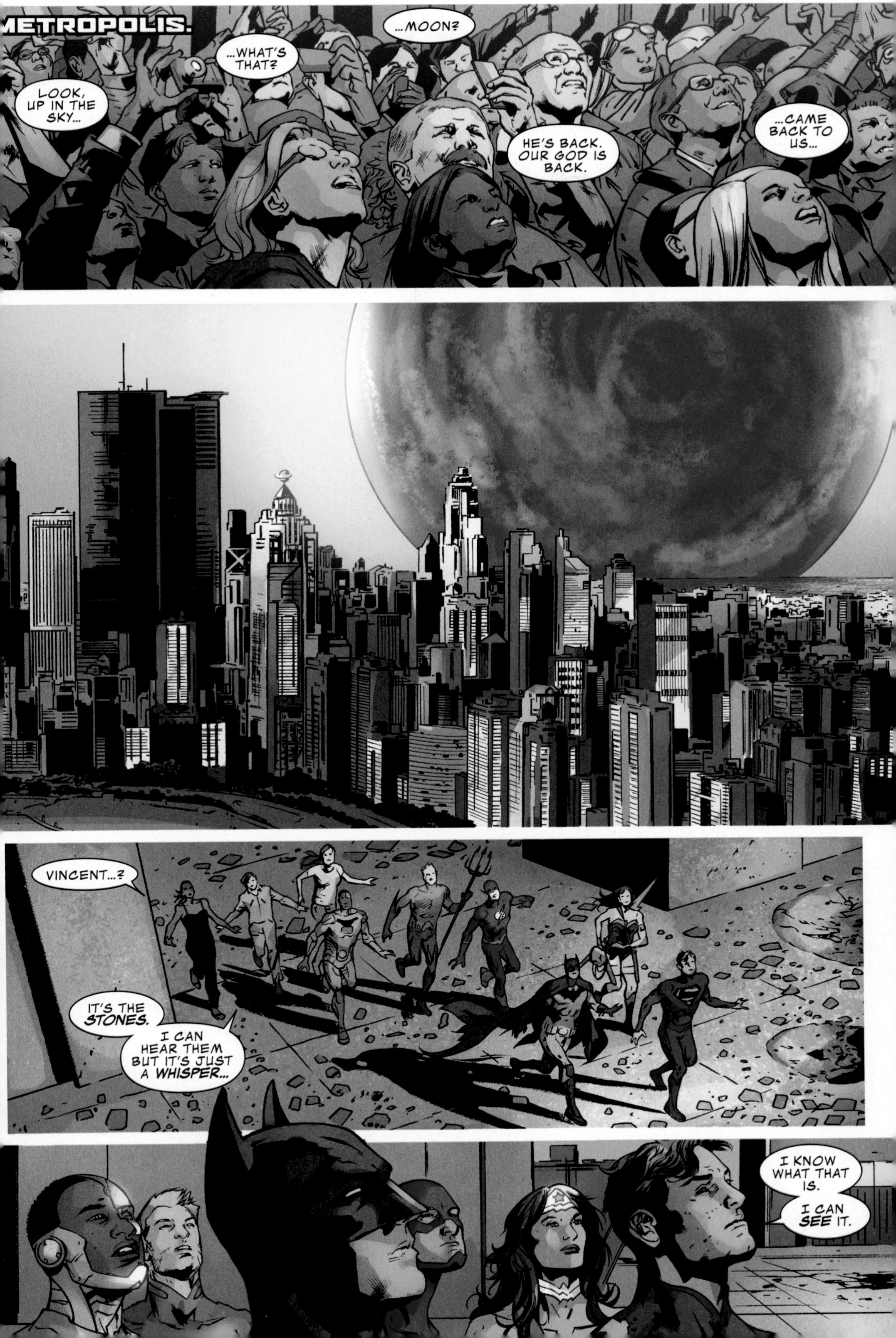
METROPOLIS.
LOOK, UP IN THE SKY...
...WHAT'S THAT?
...MOON?
HE'S BACK. OUR GOD IS BACK.
...CAME BACK TO US...
VINCENT...?
IT'S THE STONES.
I CAN HEAR THEM BUT IT'S JUST A WHISPER...
I KNOW WHAT THAT IS.
I CAN SEE IT.

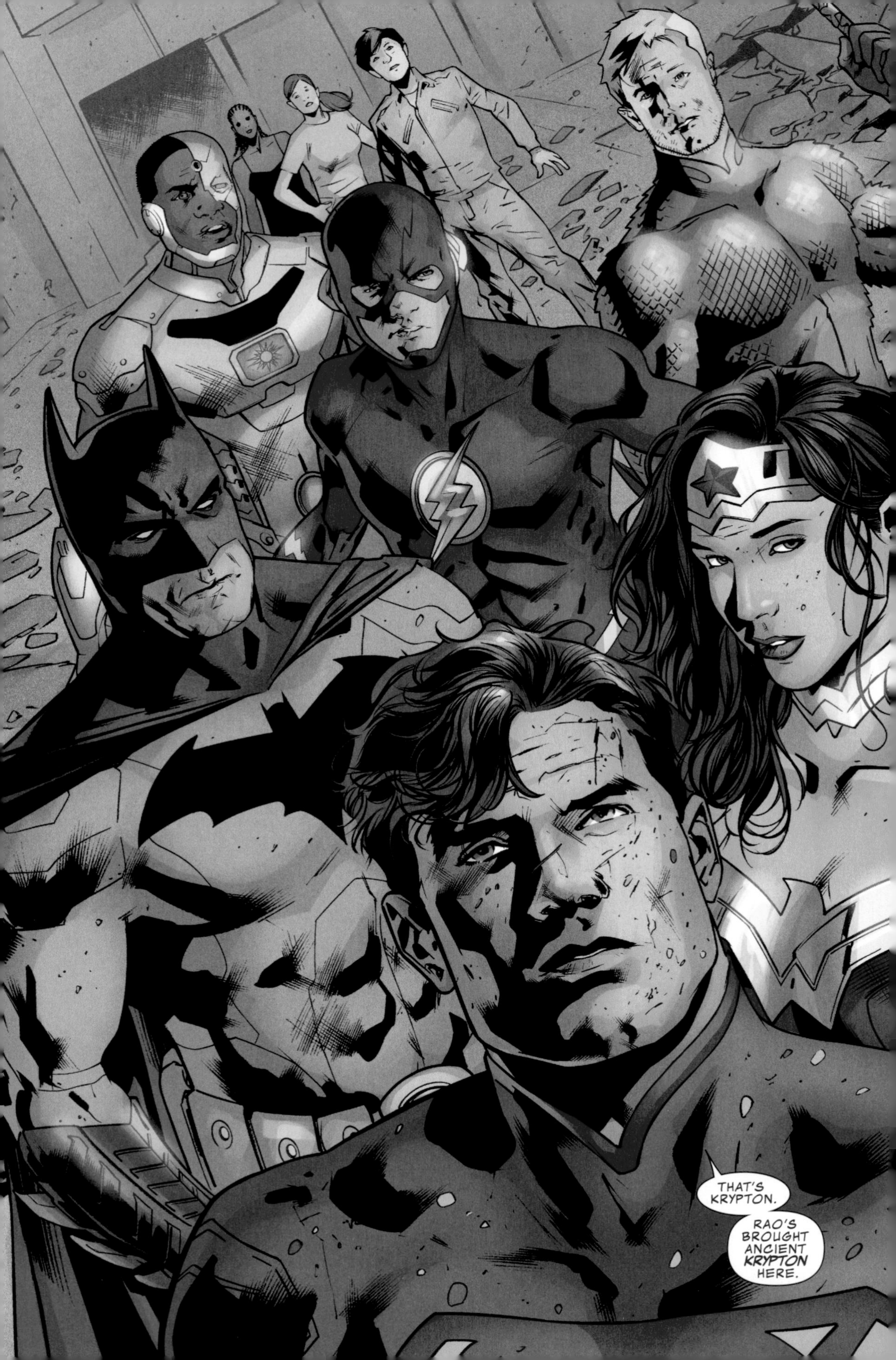
THAT'S KRYPTON.
RAO'S BROUGHT ANCIENT KRYPTON HERE.

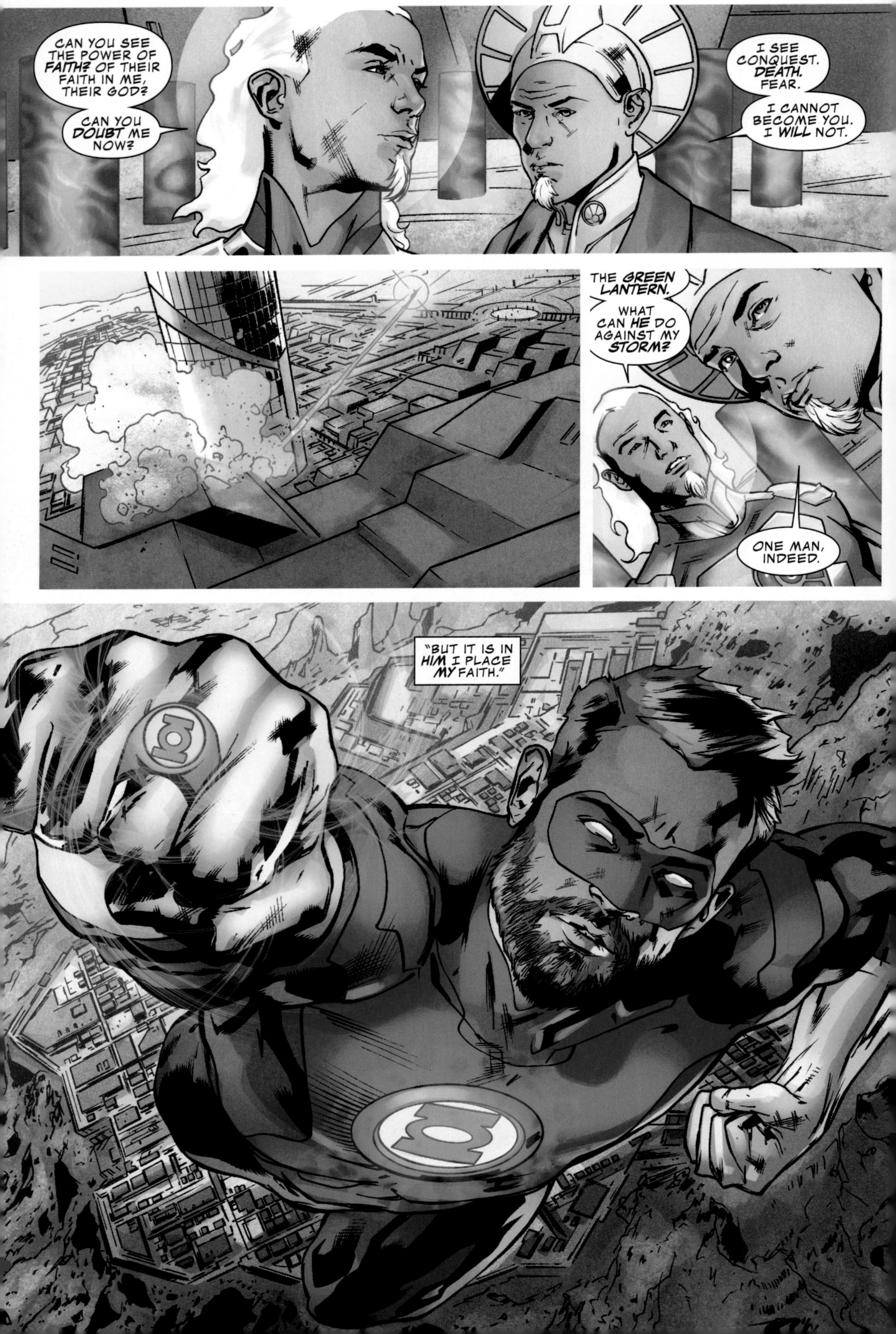
CAN YOU SEE THE POWER OF FAITH? OF THEIR FAITH IN ME, THEIR GOD?
CAN YOU DOUBT ME NOW?
I SEE CONQUEST. DEATH. FEAR.
I CANNOT BECOME YOU. I WILL NOT.
THE GREEN LANTERN.
WHAT CAN HE DO AGAINST MY STORM?
ONE MAN, INDEED.
"BUT IT IS IN HIM I PLACE MY FAITH."

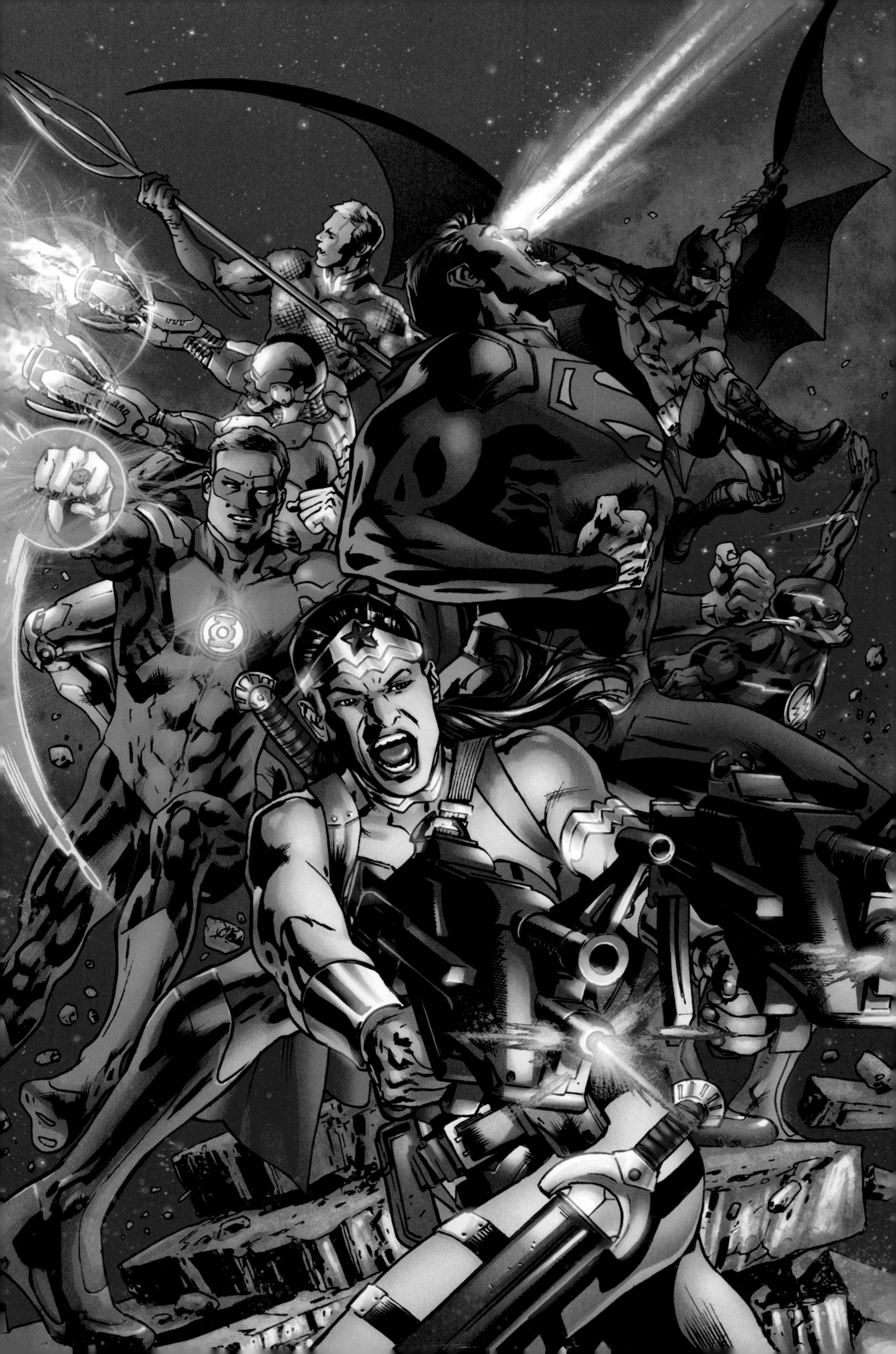

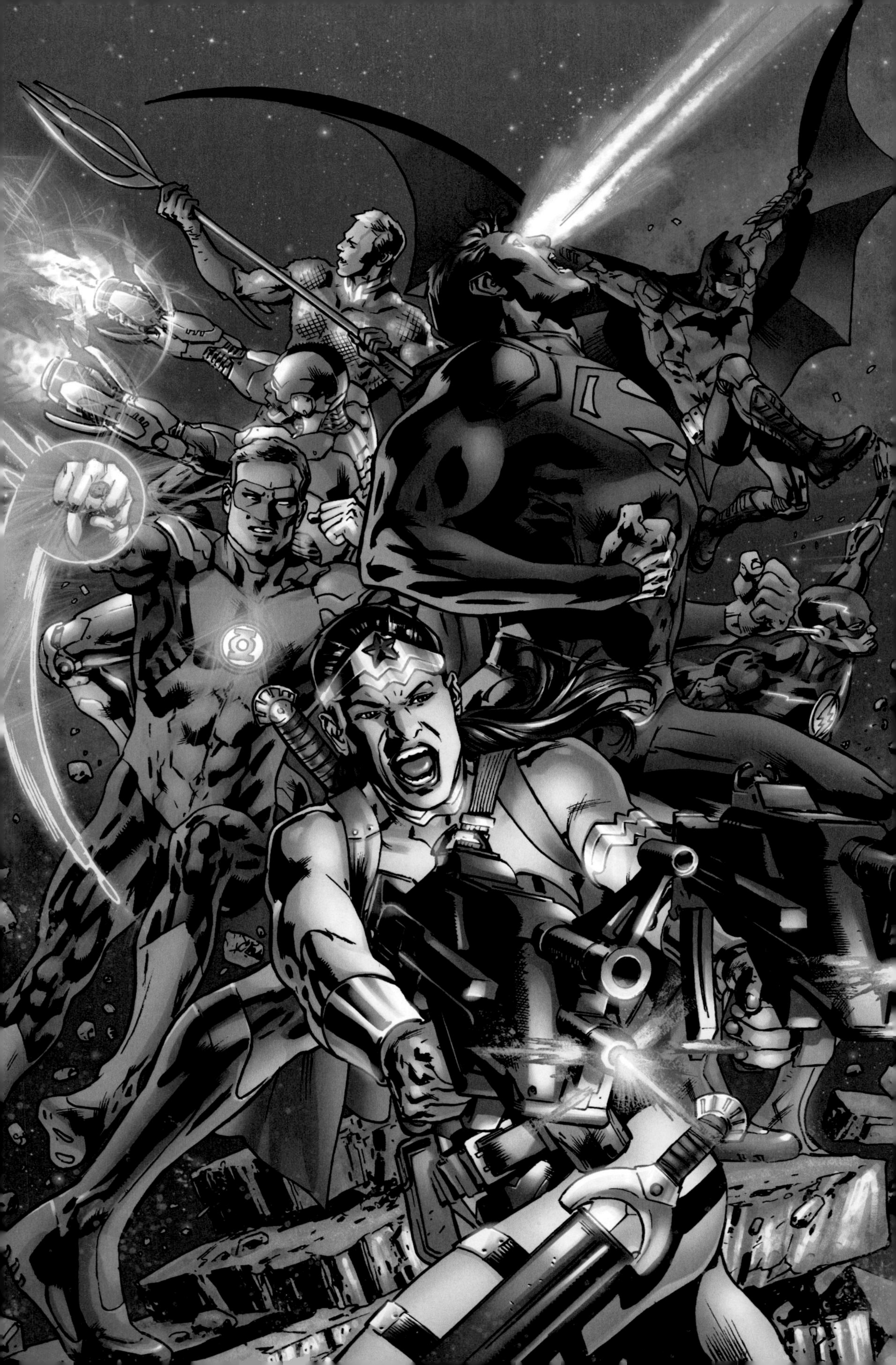

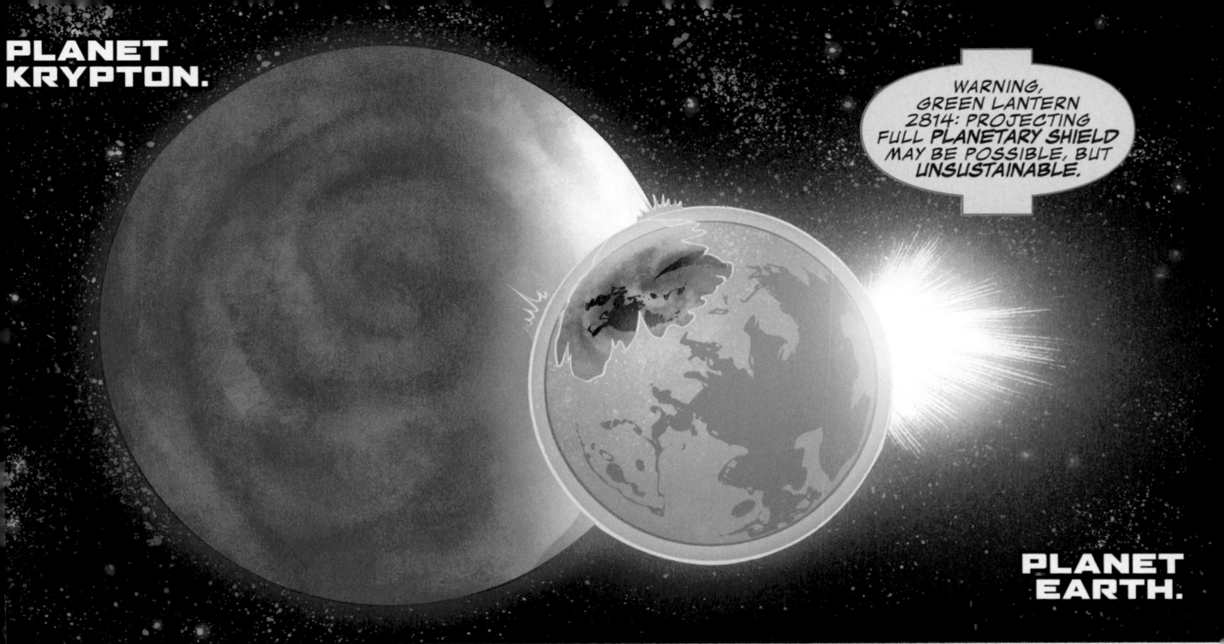
PLANET KRYPTON.
WARNING, GREEN LANTERN 2814: PROJECTING FULL PLANETARY SHIELD MAY BE POSSIBLE, BUT UNSUSTAINABLE.
PLANET EARTH.

DC COMICS PRESENTS

THE JUSTICE LEAGUE OF AMERICA POWER AND GLORY

PART NINE

BRYAN HITCH PLOT
TONY BEDARD SCRIPT
TOM DERENICK PENCILLER
DANIEL HENRIQUES & SCOTT HANNA INKERS
JEREMIAH SKIPPER COLORIST
CLAYTON COWLES LETTERER
AMEDEO TURTURRO & DIEGO LOPEZ ASSISTANT EDITORS
BRIAN CUNNINGHAM EDITOR
COVER BY BRYAN HITCH AND ALEX SINCLAIR

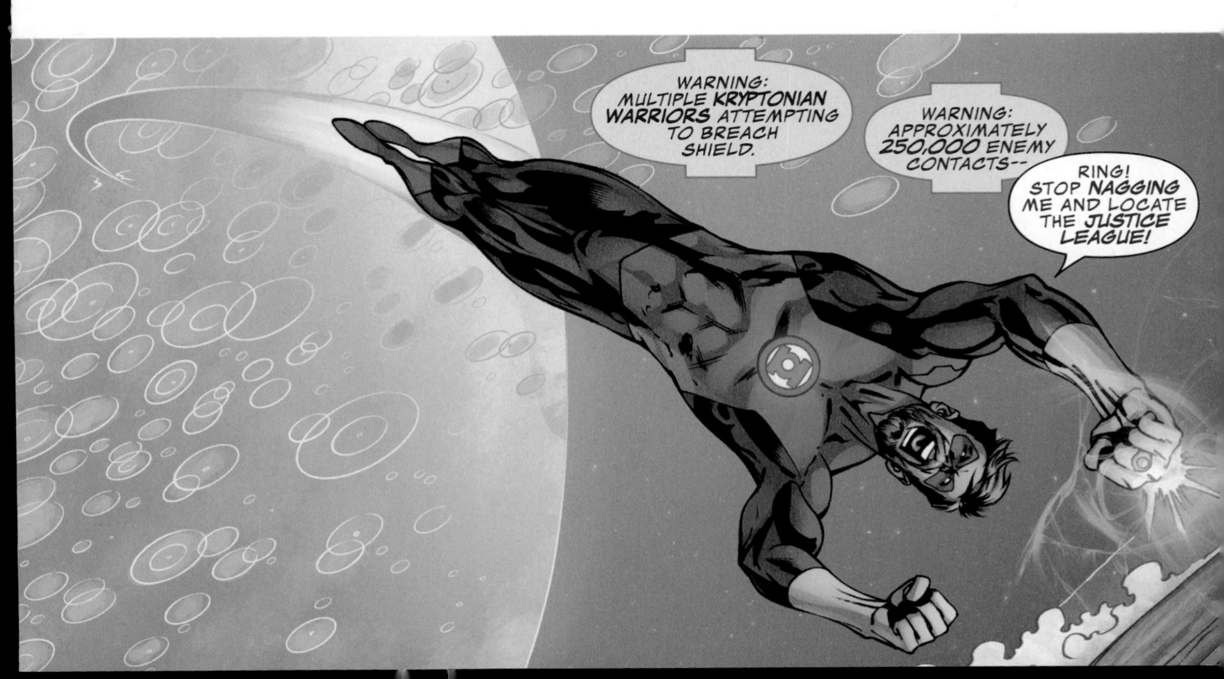
WARNING: MULTIPLE KRYPTONIAN WARRIORS ATTEMPTING TO BREACH SHIELD.
WARNING: APPROXIMATELY 250,000 ENEMY CONTACTS--
RING! STOP NAGGING ME AND LOCATE THE JUSTICE LEAGUE!

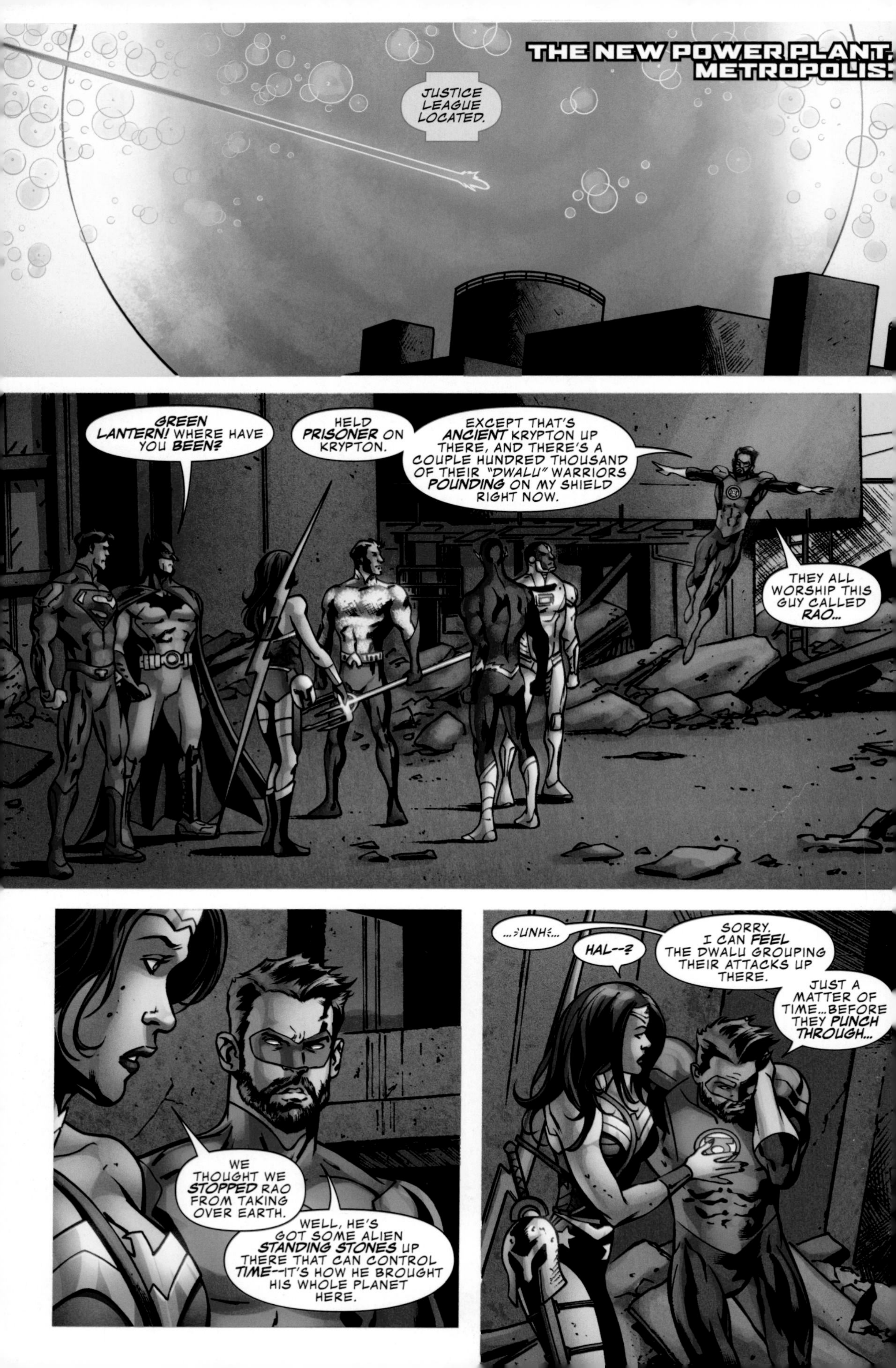
THE NEW POWER PLANT, METROPOLIS:
JUSTICE LEAGUE LOCATED.
GREEN LANTERN! WHERE HAVE YOU BEEN?
HELD PRISONER ON KRYPTON.
EXCEPT THAT'S ANCIENT KRYPTON UP THERE, AND THERE'S A COUPLE HUNDRED THOUSAND OF THEIR "DWALU" WARRIORS POUNDING ON MY SHIELD RIGHT NOW.
THEY ALL WORSHIP THIS GUY CALLED RAO...
WE THOUGHT WE STOPPED RAO FROM TAKING OVER EARTH.
WELL, HE'S GOT SOME ALIEN STANDING STONES UP THERE THAT CAN CONTROL TIME--IT'S HOW HE BROUGHT HIS WHOLE PLANET HERE.
...UNH...
HAL--?
SORRY. I CAN FEEL THE DWALU GROUPING THEIR ATTACKS UP THERE.
JUST A MATTER OF TIME...BEFORE THEY PUNCH THROUGH...

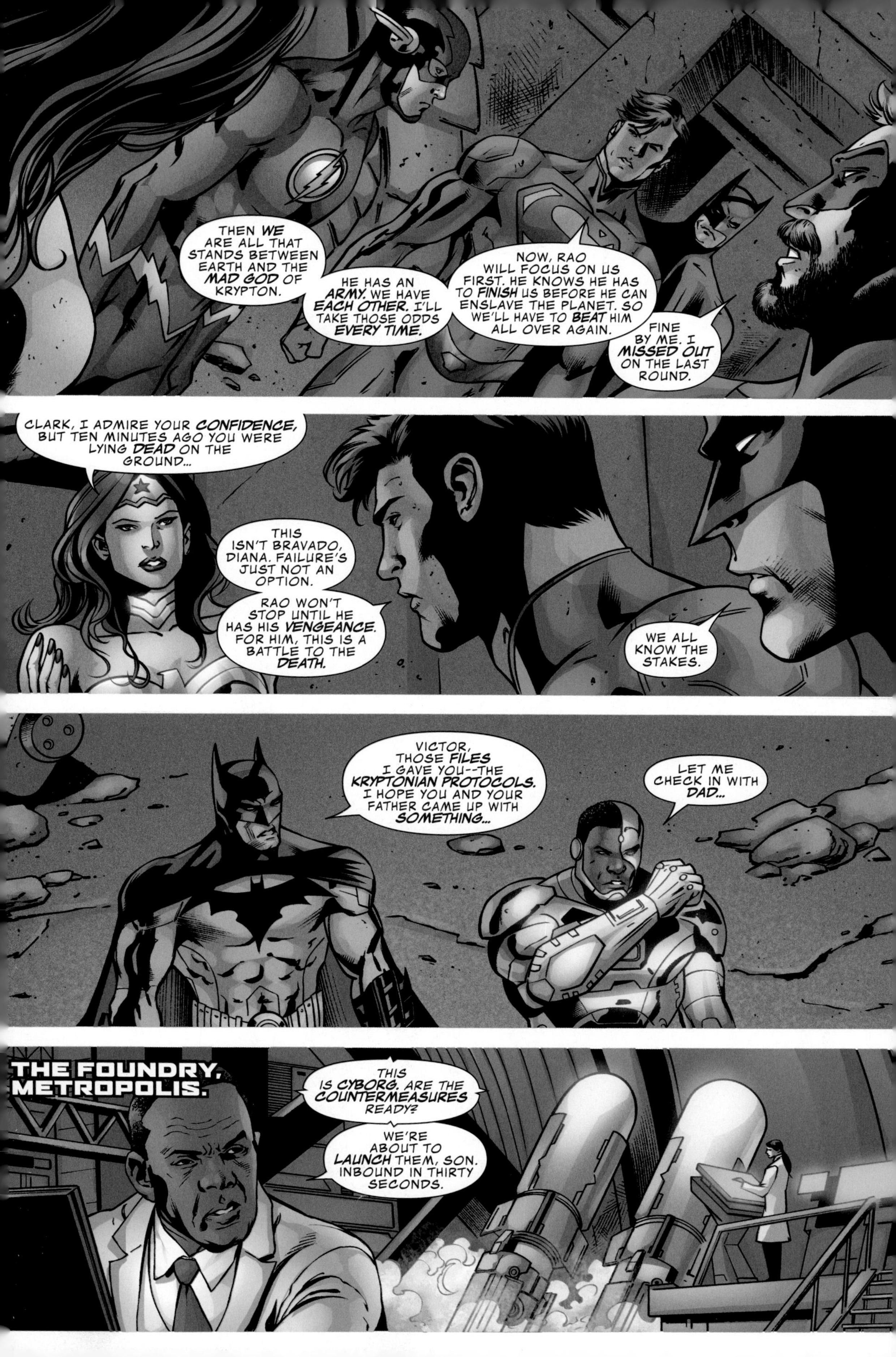
THEN WE ARE ALL THAT STANDS BETWEEN EARTH AND THE MAD GOD OF KRYPTON.
HE HAS AN ARMY. WE HAVE EACH OTHER. I'LL TAKE THOSE ODDS EVERY TIME.
NOW, RAO WILL FOCUS ON US FIRST. HE KNOWS HE HAS TO FINISH US BEFORE HE CAN ENSLAVE THE PLANET. SO WE'LL HAVE TO BEAT HIM ALL OVER AGAIN.
FINE BY ME. I MISSED OUT ON THE LAST ROUND.
CLARK, I ADMIRE YOUR CONFIDENCE, BUT TEN MINUTES AGO YOU WERE LYING DEAD ON THE GROUND...
THIS ISN'T BRAVADO, DIANA. FAILURE'S JUST NOT AN OPTION.
RAO WON'T STOP UNTIL HE HAS HIS VENGEANCE. FOR HIM, THIS IS A BATTLE TO THE DEATH.
WE ALL KNOW THE STAKES.
VICTOR, THOSE FILES I GAVE YOU--THE KRYPTONIAN PROTOCOLS. I HOPE YOU AND YOUR FATHER CAME UP WITH SOMETHING...
LET ME CHECK IN WITH DAD...
THE FOUNDRY, METROPOLIS.
THIS IS CYBORG. ARE THE COUNTERMEASURES READY?
WE'RE ABOUT TO LAUNCH THEM, SON. INBOUND IN THIRTY SECONDS.

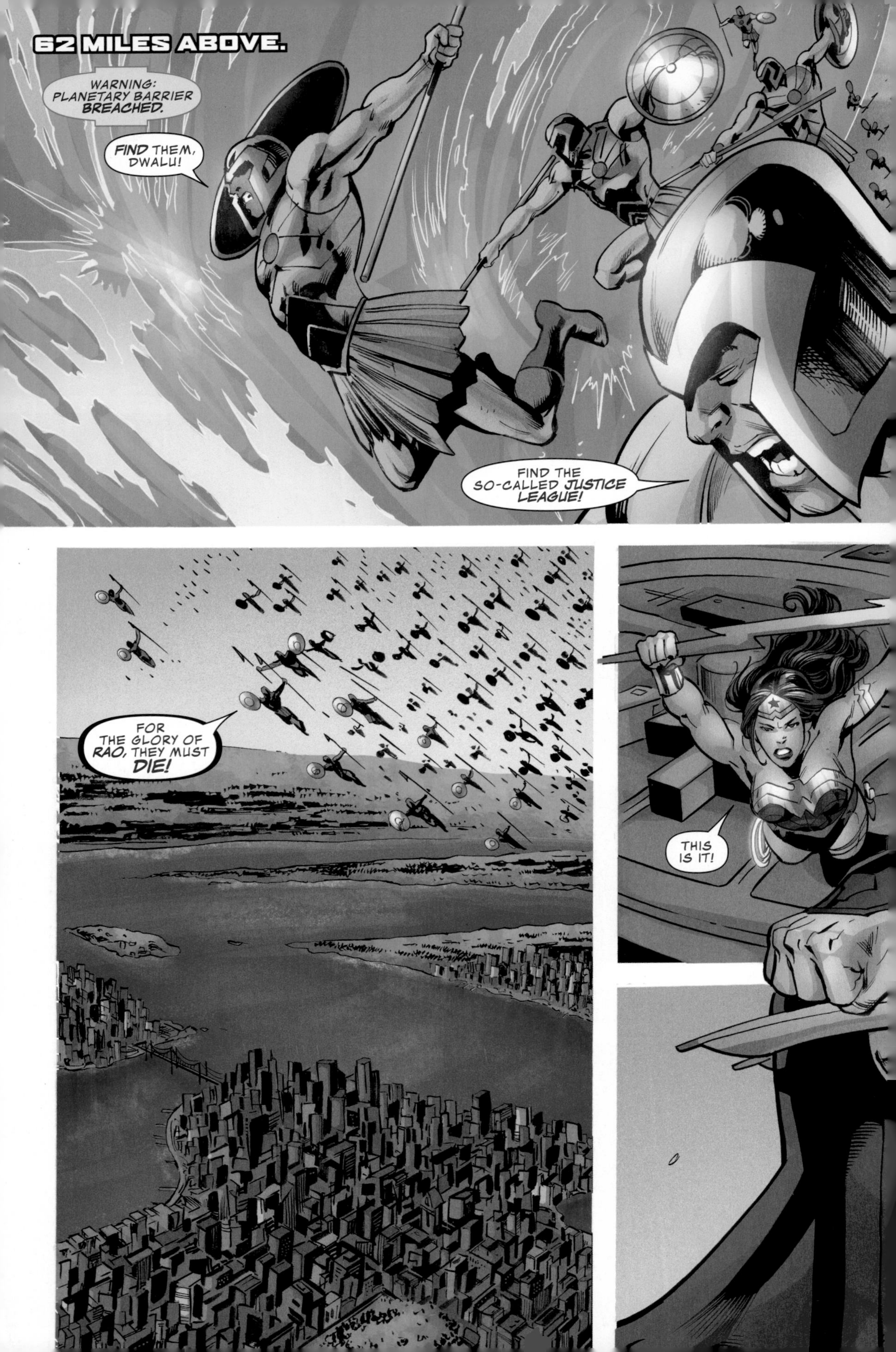

62 MILES ABOVE.
WARNING: PLANETARY BARRIER BREACHED.
FIND THEM, DWALU!
FIND THE SO-CALLED JUSTICE LEAGUE!
FOR THE GLORY OF RAO, THEY MUST DIE!
THIS IS IT!

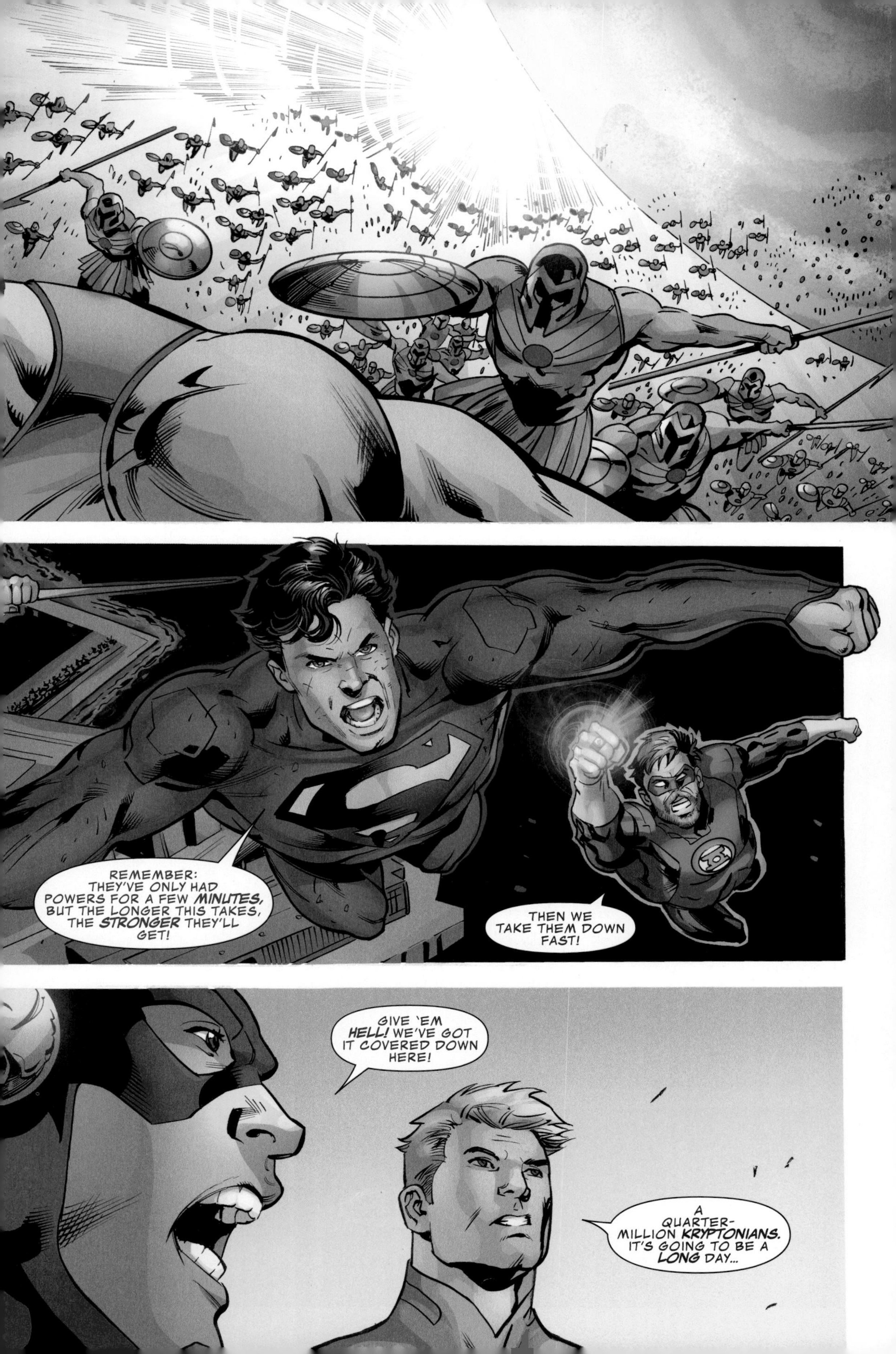
REMEMBER: THEY'VE ONLY HAD POWERS FOR A FEW MINUTES, BUT THE LONGER THIS TAKES, THE STRONGER THEY'LL GET!
THEN WE TAKE THEM DOWN FAST!
GIVE 'EM HELL! WE'VE GOT IT COVERED DOWN HERE!
A QUARTER-MILLION KRYPTONIANS. IT'S GOING TO BE A LONG DAY...

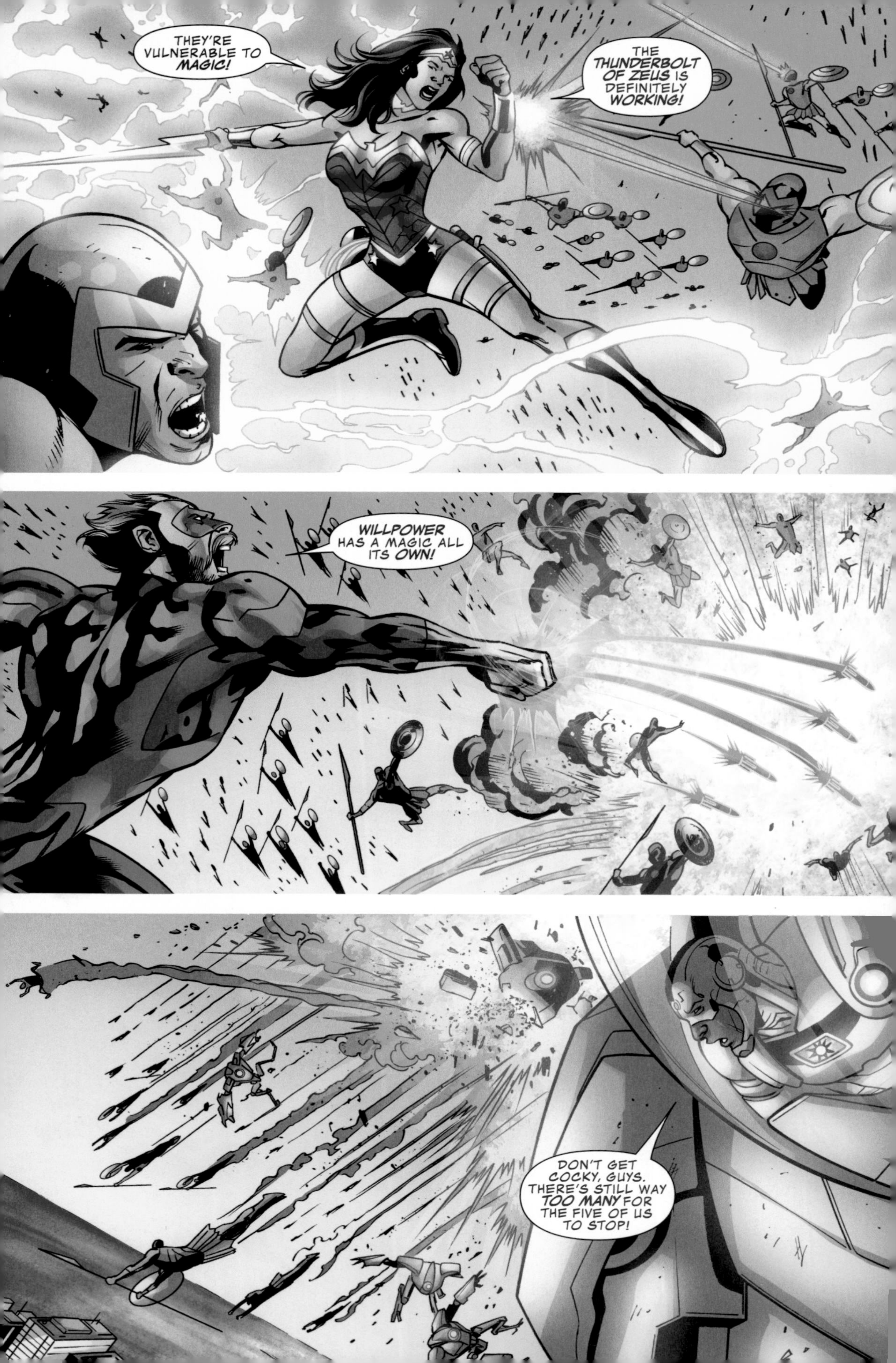
THEY'RE VULNERABLE TO MAGIC!
THE THUNDERBOLT OF ZEUS IS DEFINITELY WORKING!
WILLPOWER HAS A MAGIC ALL ITS OWN!
DON'T GET COCKY, GUYS. THERE'S STILL WAY TOO MANY FOR THE FIVE OF US TO STOP!

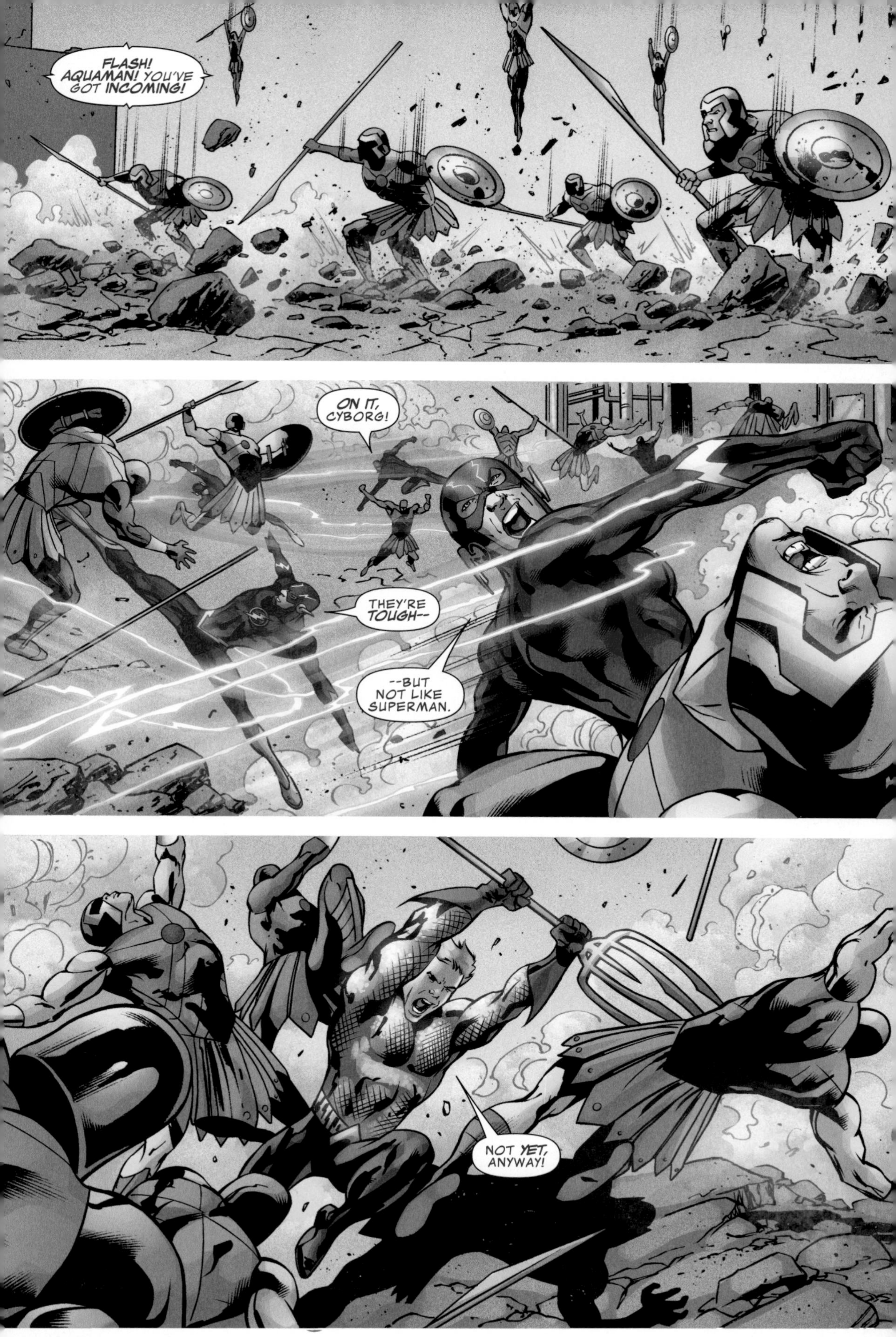
FLASH! AQUAMAN! YOU'VE GOT INCOMING!
ON IT, CYBORG!
THEY'RE TOUGH--
--BUT NOT LIKE SUPERMAN.
NOT YET, ANYWAY!

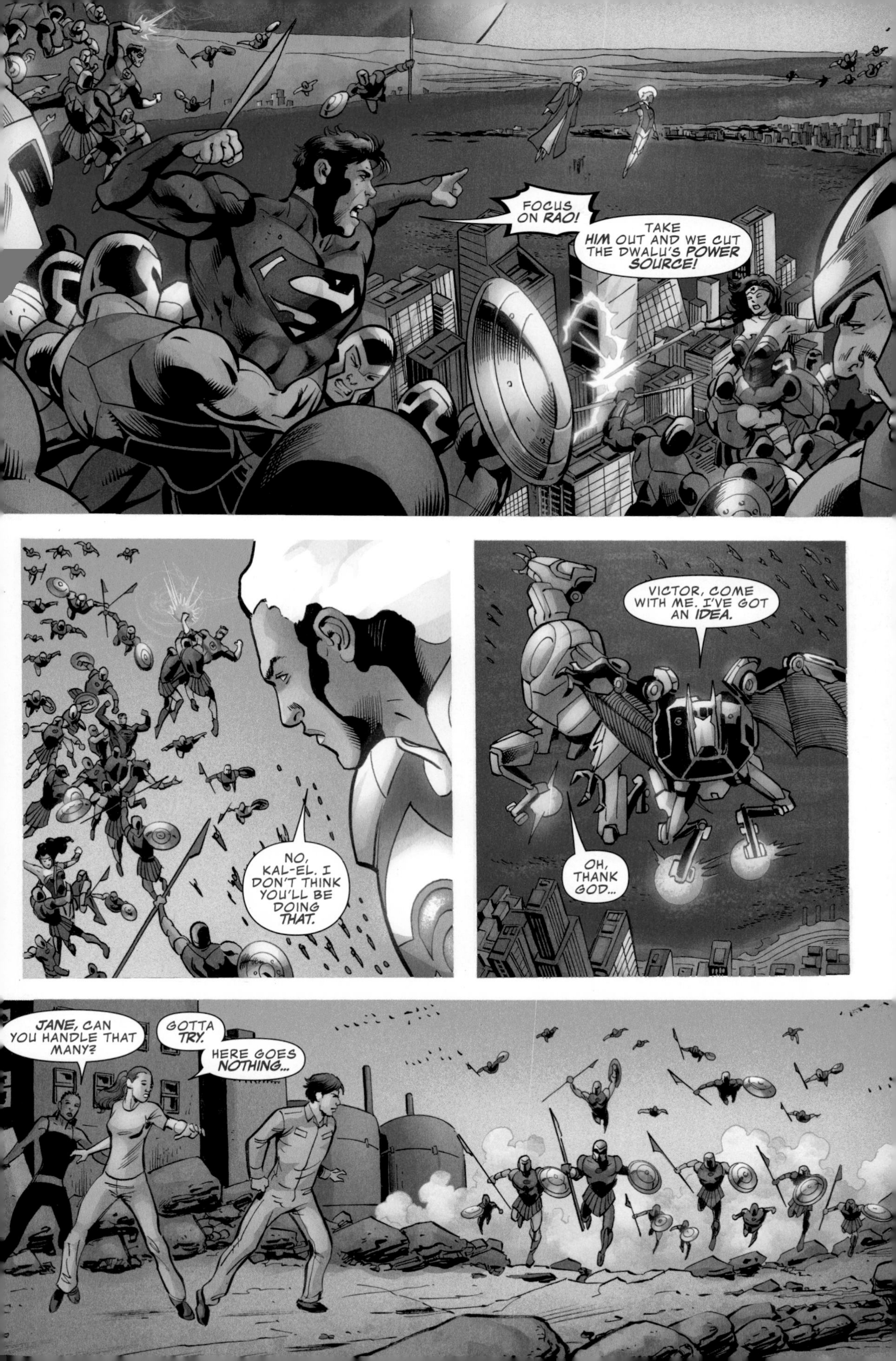
FOCUS ON RAO!
TAKE HIM OUT AND WE CUT THE DWALU'S POWER SOURCE!
NO, KAL-EL. I DON'T THINK YOU'LL BE DOING THAT.
VICTOR, COME WITH ME. I'VE GOT AN IDEA.
OH, THANK GOD...
JANE, CAN YOU HANDLE THAT MANY?
GOTTA TRY.
HERE GOES NOTHING...

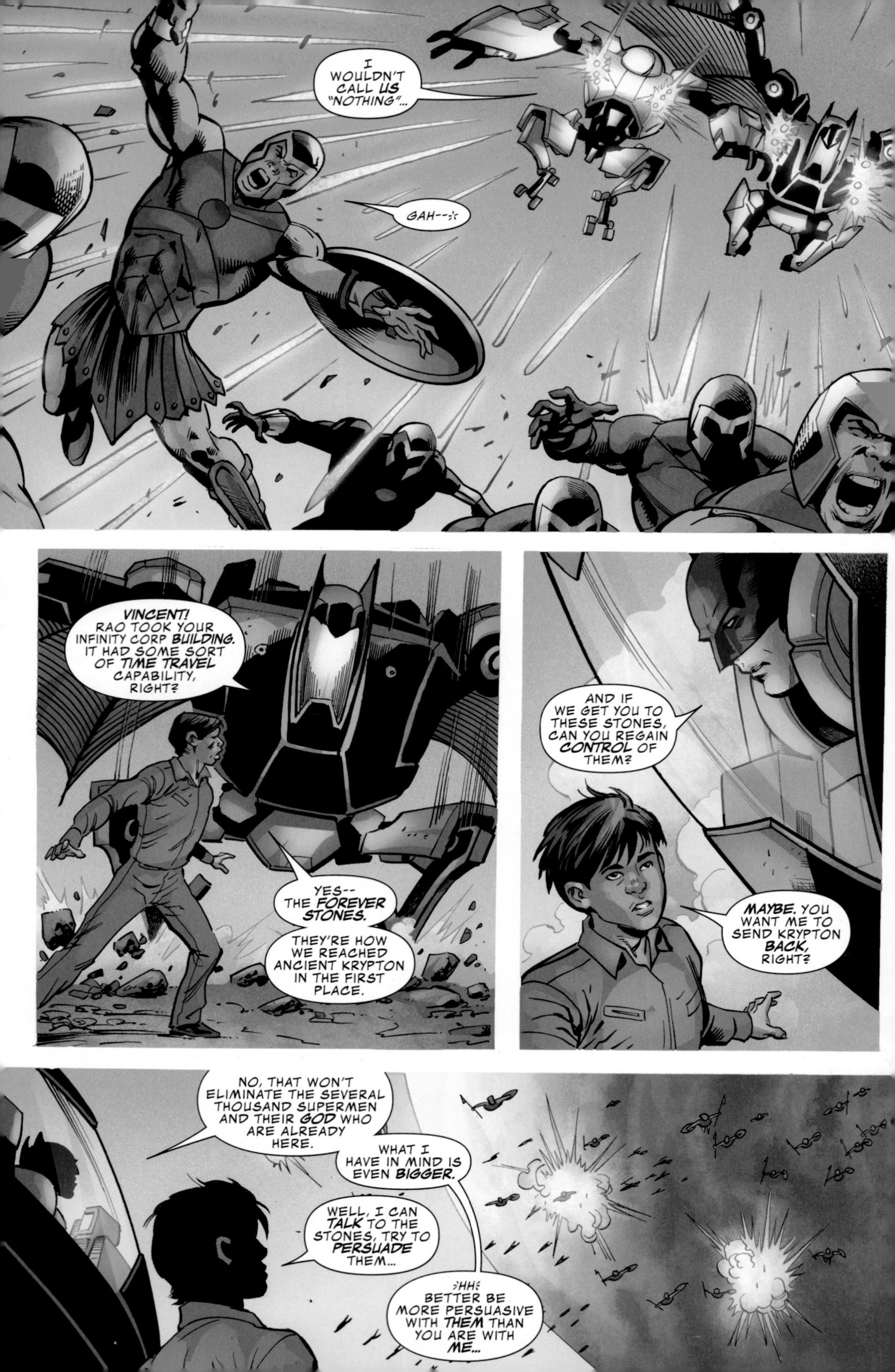
I WOULDN'T CALL US "NOTHING"...
GAH--
VINCENT! RAO TOOK YOUR INFINITY CORP BUILDING. IT HAD SOME SORT OF TIME TRAVEL CAPABILITY, RIGHT?
YES-- THE FOREVER STONES.
THEY'RE HOW WE REACHED ANCIENT KRYPTON IN THE FIRST PLACE.
AND IF WE GET YOU TO THESE STONES, CAN YOU REGAIN CONTROL OF THEM?
MAYBE. YOU WANT ME TO SEND KRYPTON BACK, RIGHT?
NO, THAT WON'T ELIMINATE THE SEVERAL THOUSAND SUPERMEN AND THEIR GOD WHO ARE ALREADY HERE.
WHAT I HAVE IN MIND IS EVEN BIGGER.
WELL, I CAN TALK TO THE STONES, TRY TO PERSUADE THEM...
HH BETTER BE MORE PERSUASIVE WITH THEM THAN YOU ARE WITH ME...

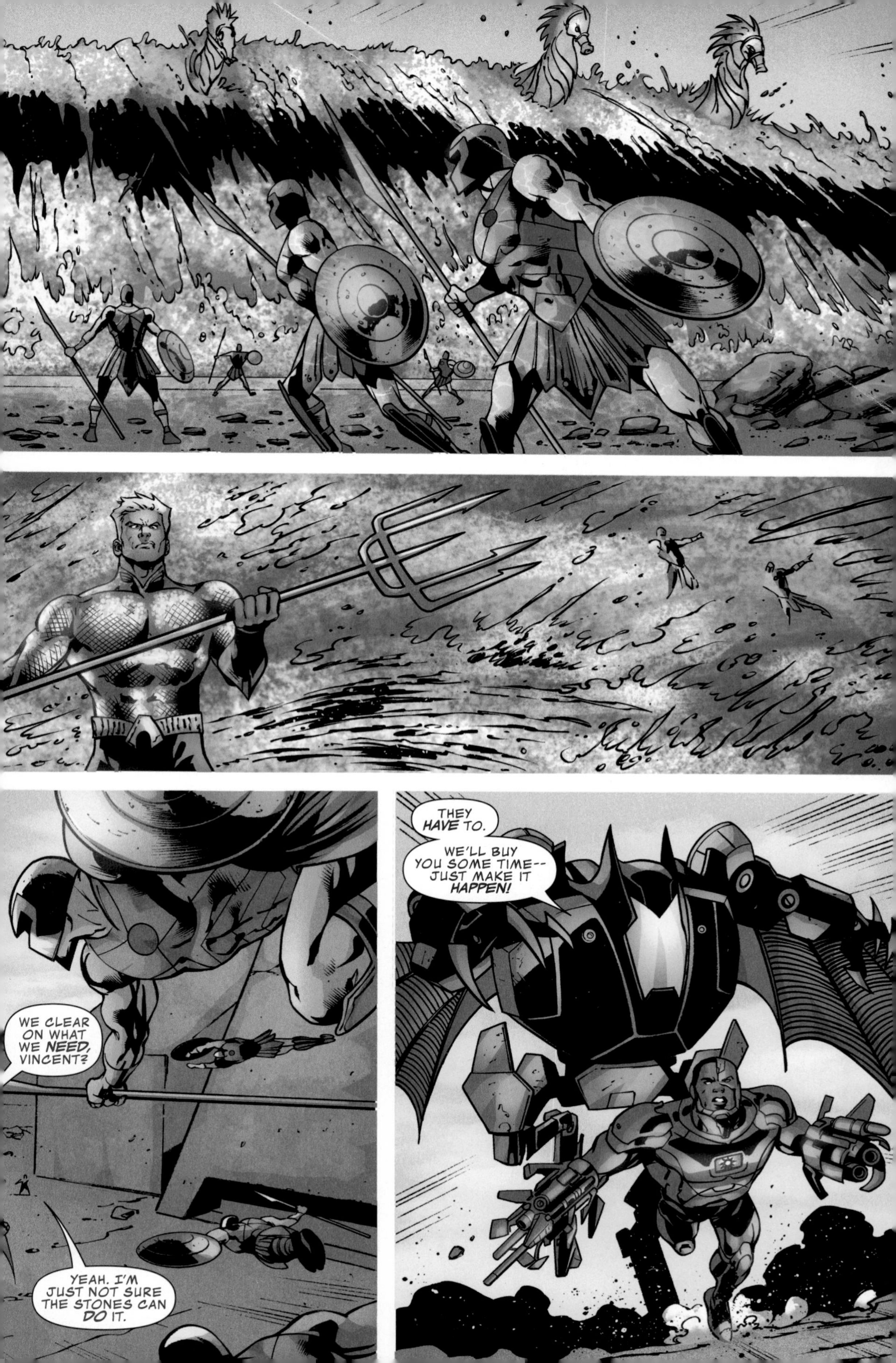
WE CLEAR ON WHAT WE NEED, VINCENT?
YEAH. I'M JUST NOT SURE THE STONES CAN DO IT.
THEY HAVE TO.
WE'LL BUY YOU SOME TIME-- JUST MAKE IT HAPPEN!

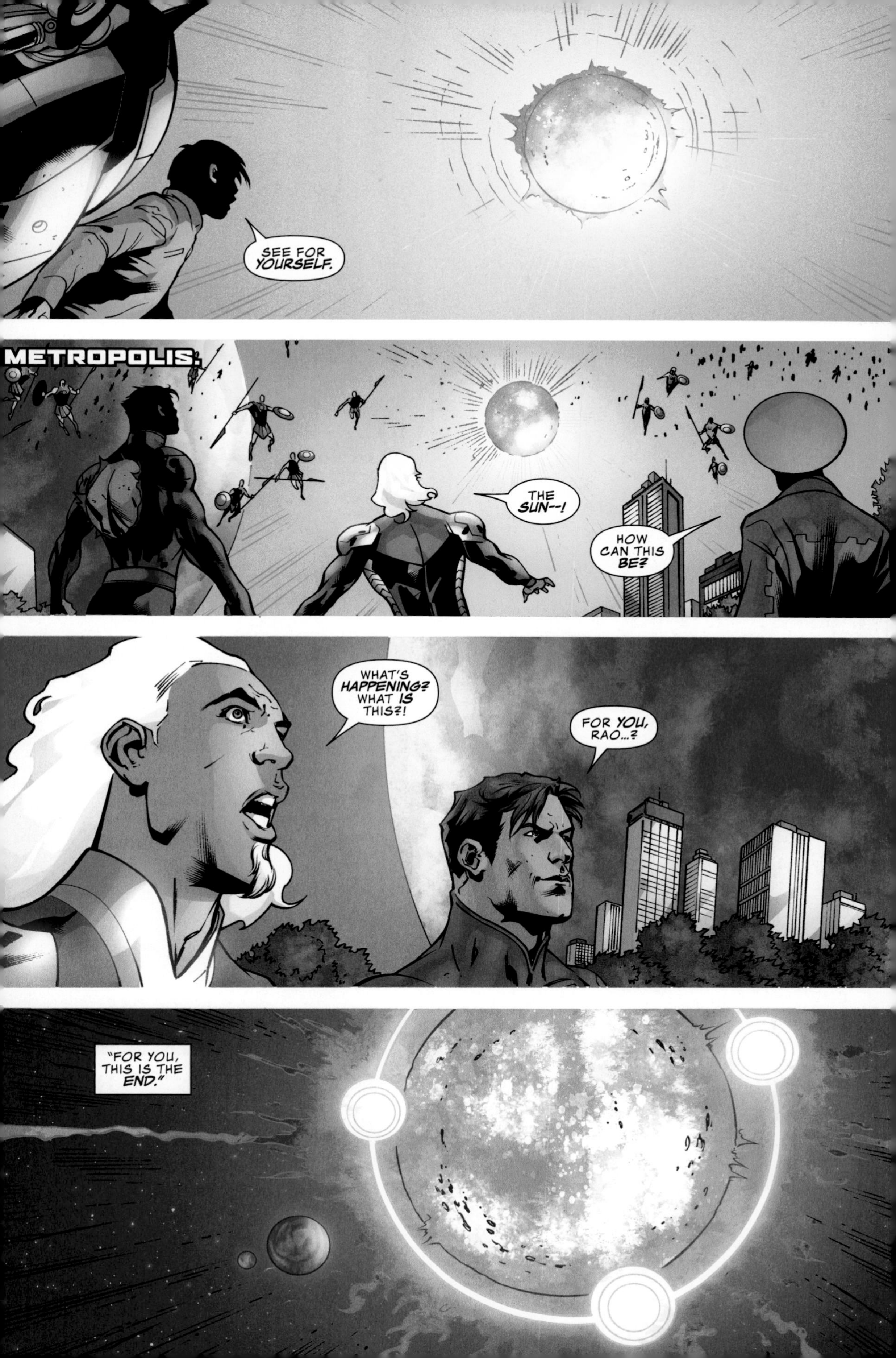
SEE FOR YOURSELF.
METROPOLIS.
THE SUN--!
HOW CAN THIS BE?
WHAT'S HAPPENING? WHAT IS THIS?!
FOR YOU, RAO...?
"FOR YOU, THIS IS THE END."

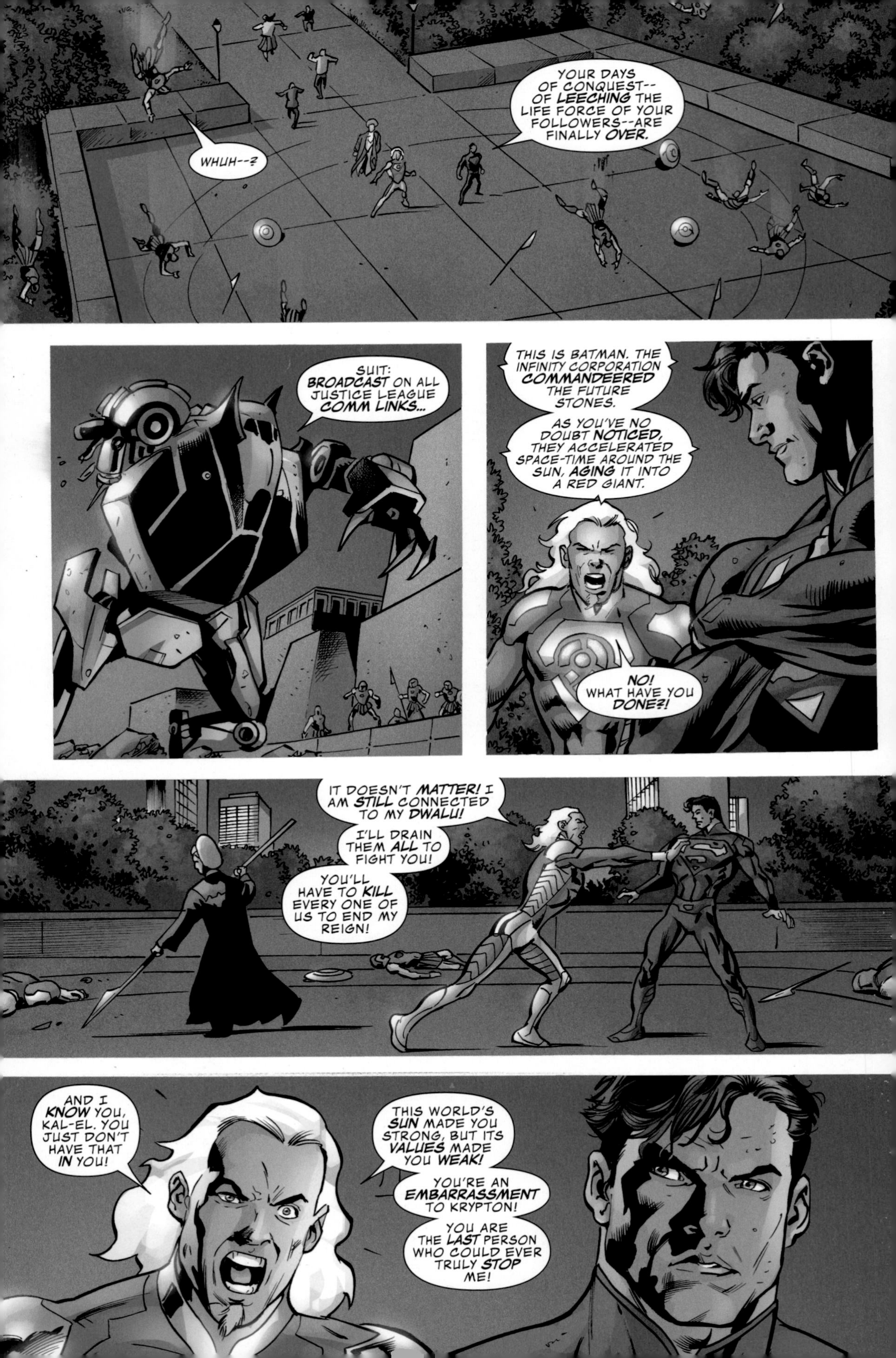
YOUR DAYS OF CONQUEST--OF LEECHING THE LIFE FORCE OF YOUR FOLLOWERS--ARE FINALLY OVER.
WHUH--?
SUIT: BROADCAST ON ALL JUSTICE LEAGUE COMM LINKS...
THIS IS BATMAN. THE INFINITY CORPORATION COMMANDEERED THE FUTURE STONES.
AS YOU'VE NO DOUBT NOTICED, THEY ACCELERATED SPACE-TIME AROUND THE SUN, AGING IT INTO A RED GIANT.
NO! WHAT HAVE YOU DONE?!
IT DOESN'T MATTER! I AM STILL CONNECTED TO MY DWALU!
I'LL DRAIN THEM ALL TO FIGHT YOU!
YOU'LL HAVE TO KILL EVERY ONE OF US TO END MY REIGN!
AND I KNOW YOU, KAL-EL. YOU JUST DON'T HAVE THAT IN YOU!
THIS WORLD'S SUN MADE YOU STRONG, BUT ITS VALUES MADE YOU WEAK!
YOU'RE AN EMBARRASSMENT TO KRYPTON!
YOU ARE THE LAST PERSON WHO COULD EVER TRULY STOP ME!

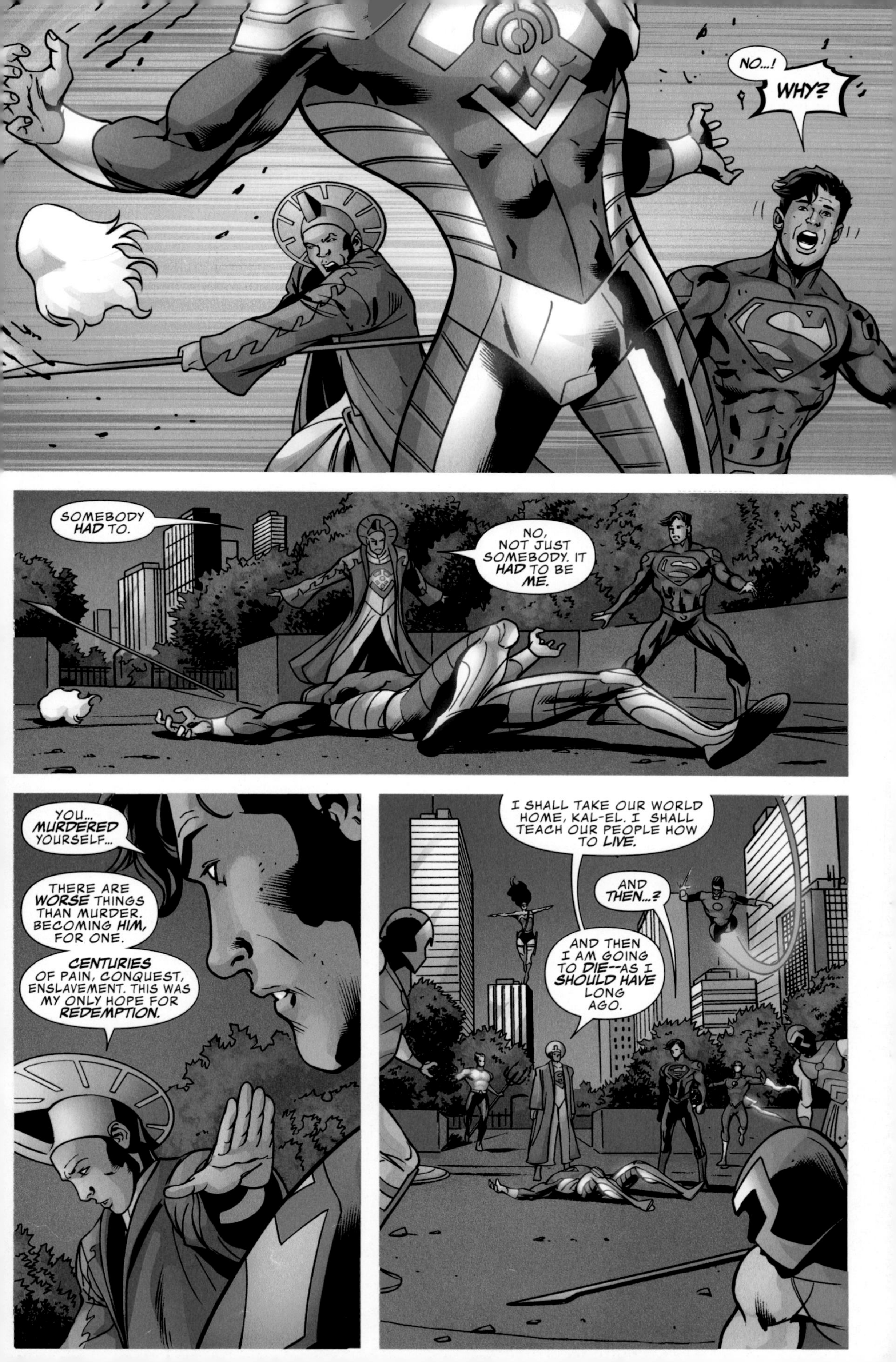
NO...!
WHY?
SOMEBODY HAD TO.
NO, NOT JUST SOMEBODY. IT HAD TO BE ME.
YOU... MURDERED YOURSELF...
THERE ARE WORSE THINGS THAN MURDER. BECOMING HIM, FOR ONE.
CENTURIES OF PAIN, CONQUEST, ENSLAVEMENT. THIS WAS MY ONLY HOPE FOR REDEMPTION.
I SHALL TAKE OUR WORLD HOME, KAL-EL. I SHALL TEACH OUR PEOPLE HOW TO LIVE.
AND THEN...?
AND THEN I AM GOING TO DIE--AS I SHOULD HAVE LONG AGO.

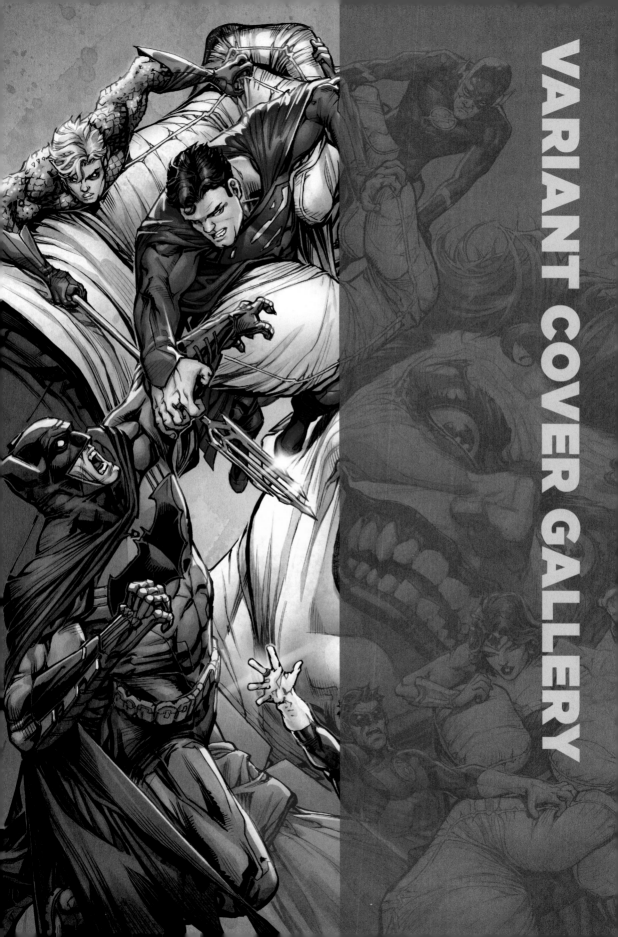

VARIANT COVER GALLERY

JUSTICE LEAGUE OF AMERICA #4
BATMAN VARIANT BY BRYAN HITCH & ALEX SINCLAIR

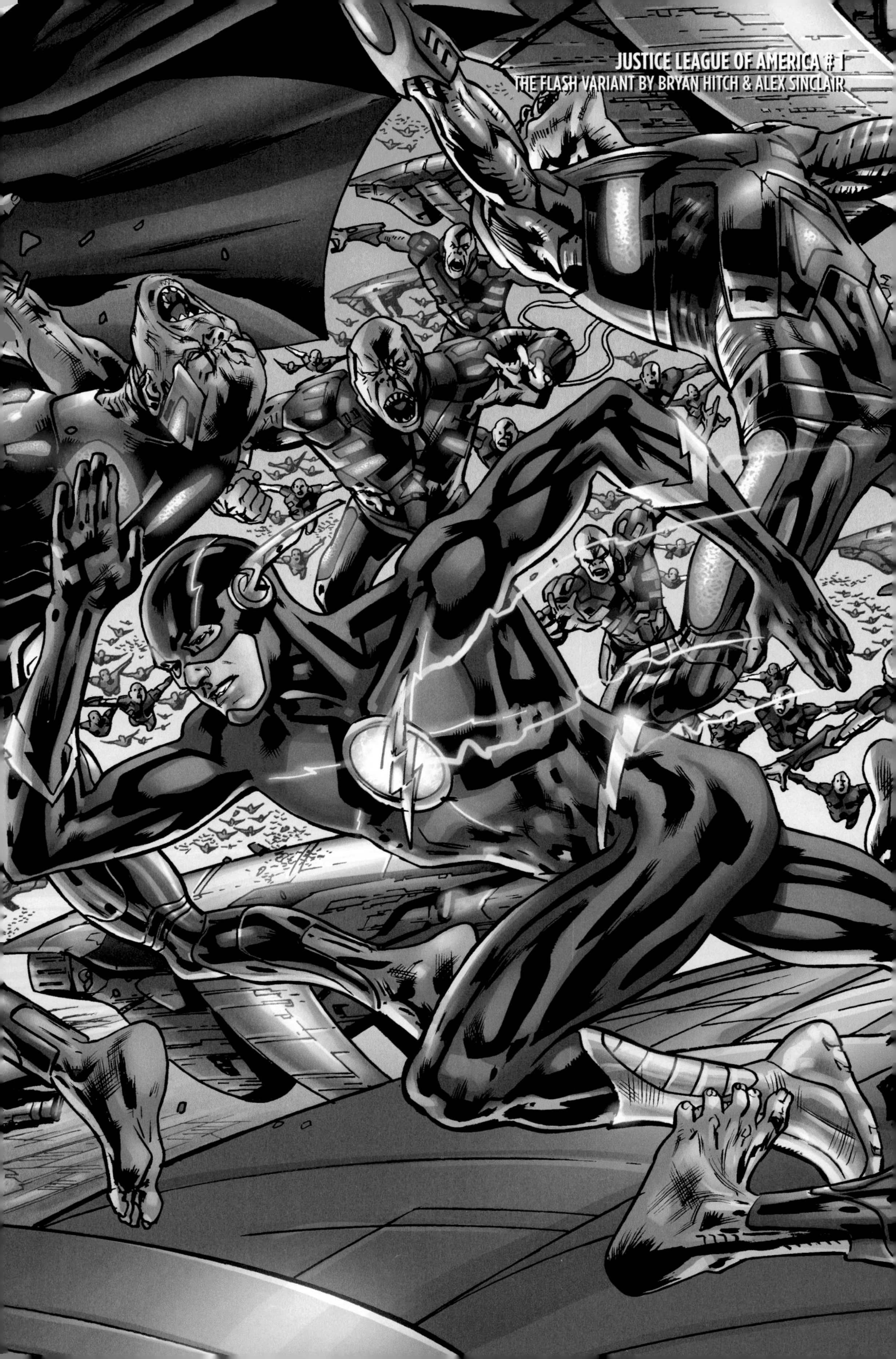

JUSTICE LEAGUE OF AMERICA # 1
THE FLASH VARIANT BY BRYAN HITCH & ALEX SINCLAIR

JUSTICE LEAGUE OF AMERICA # 1
SUPERMAN VARIANT BY BRYAN HITCH & ALEX SINCLAIR

JUSTICE LEAGUE OF AMERICA # 1
GREEN LANTERN VARIANT BY BRYAN HITCH & ALEX SINCLAIR

JUSTICE LEAGUE OF AMERICA #1
WONDER WOMAN VARIANT BY BRYAN HITCH & ALEX SINCLAIR

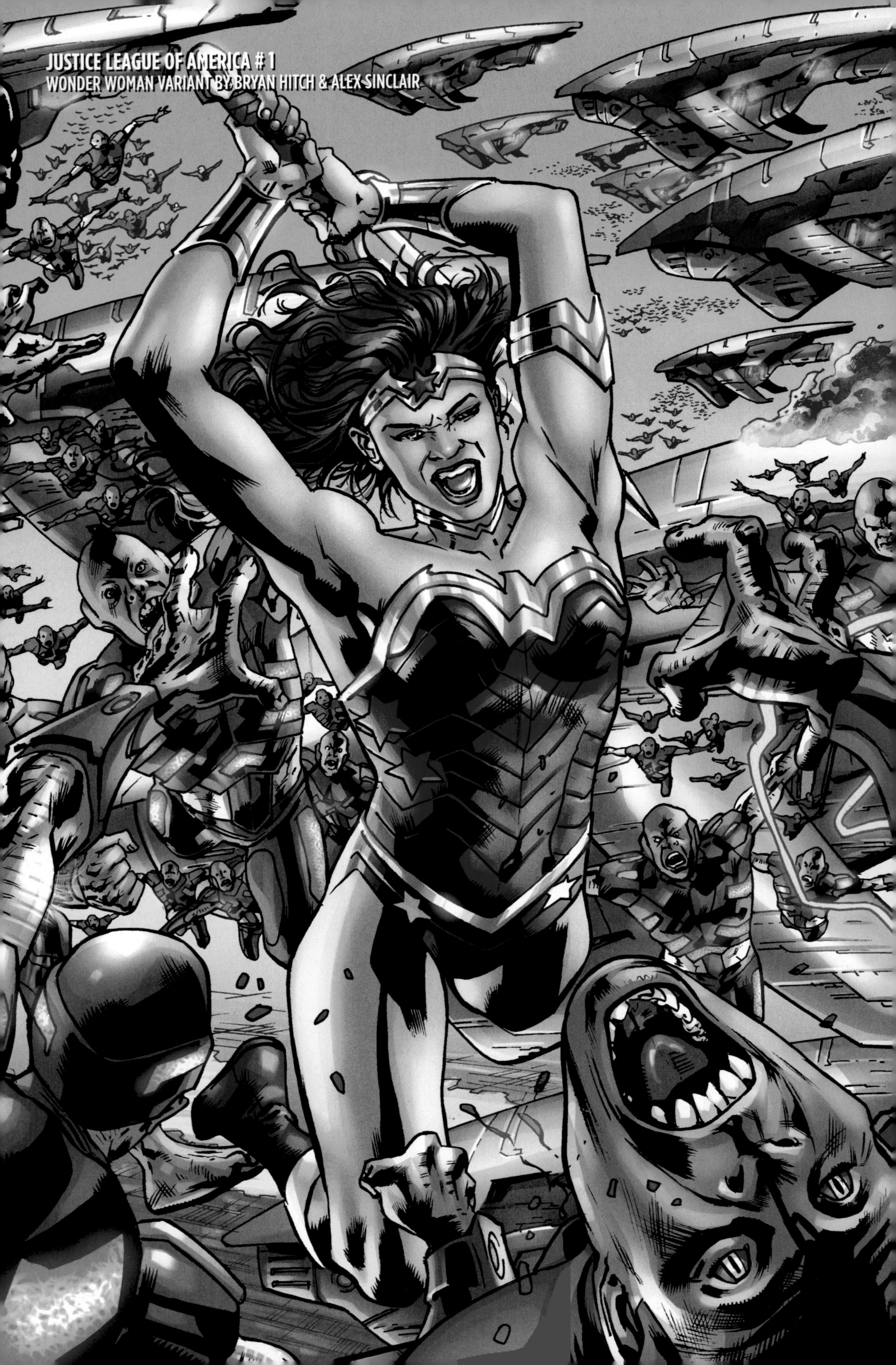

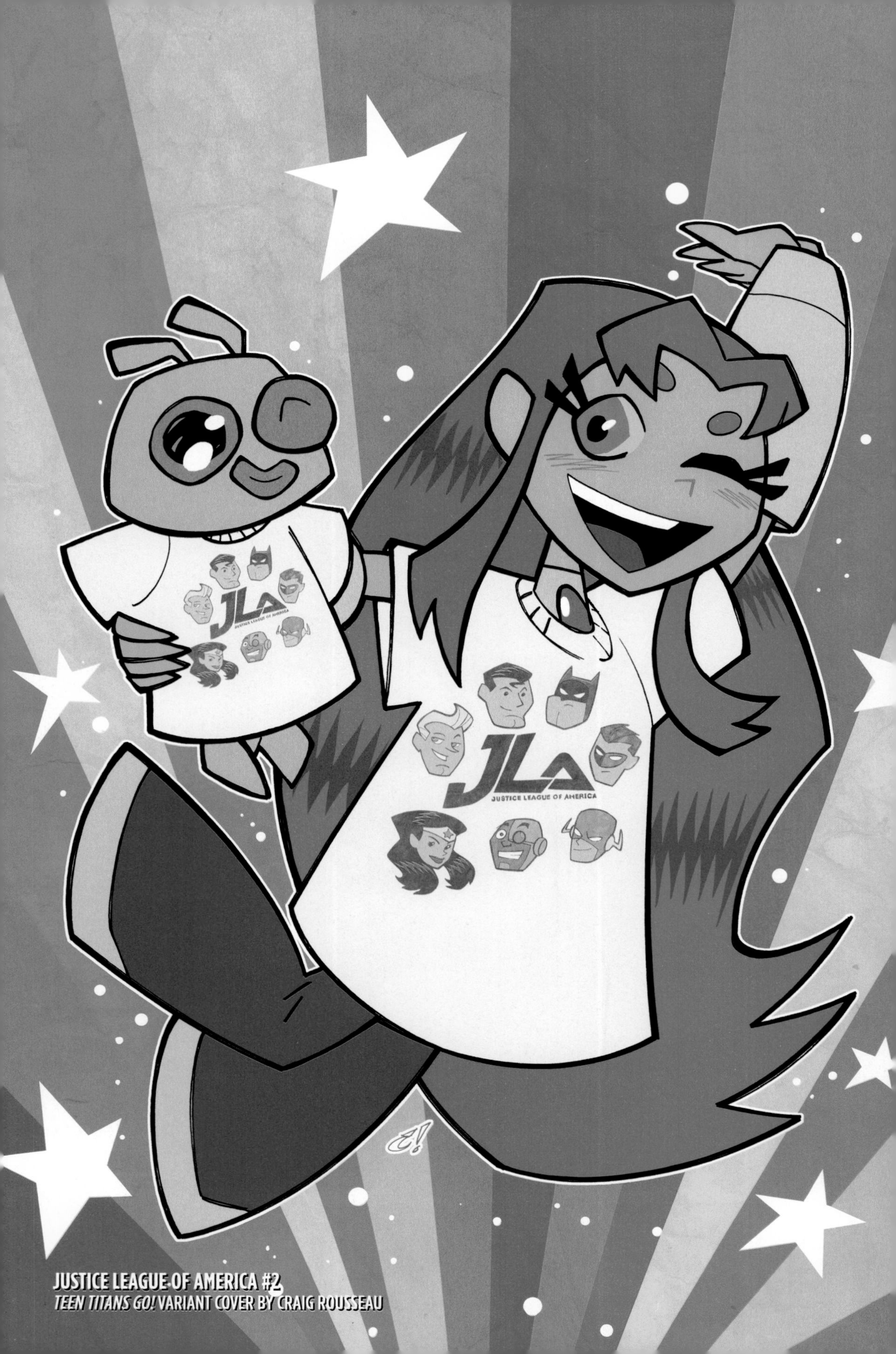
JLA
JUSTICE LEAGUE OF AMERICA
JLA
JUSTICE LEAGUE OF AMERICA

JUSTICE LEAGUE OF AMERICA #2
TEEN TITANS GO! VARIANT COVER BY CRAIG ROUSSEAU

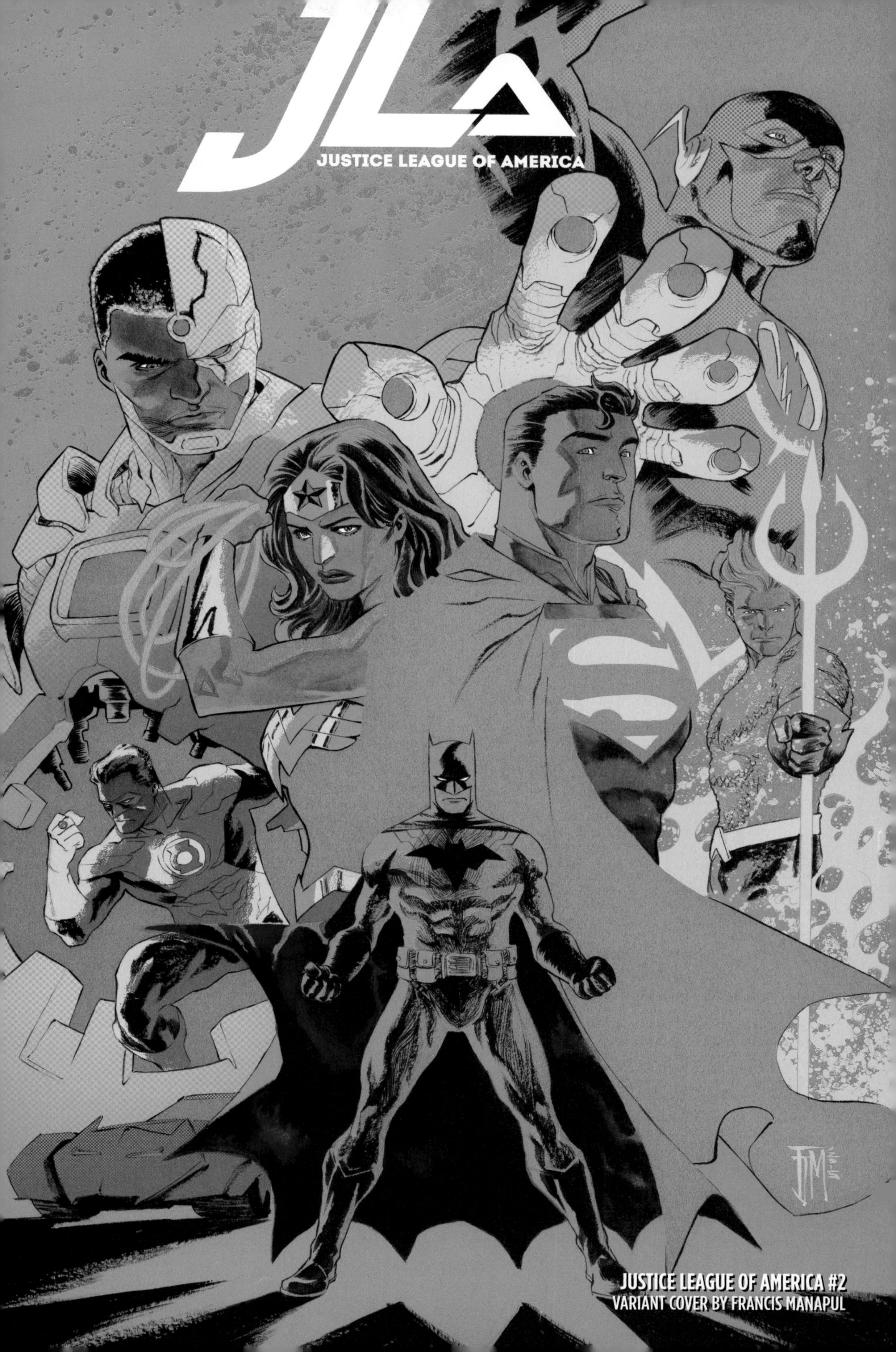
JLA
JUSTICE LEAGUE OF AMERICA

JUSTICE LEAGUE OF AMERICA #2
VARIANT COVER BY FRANCIS MANAPUL

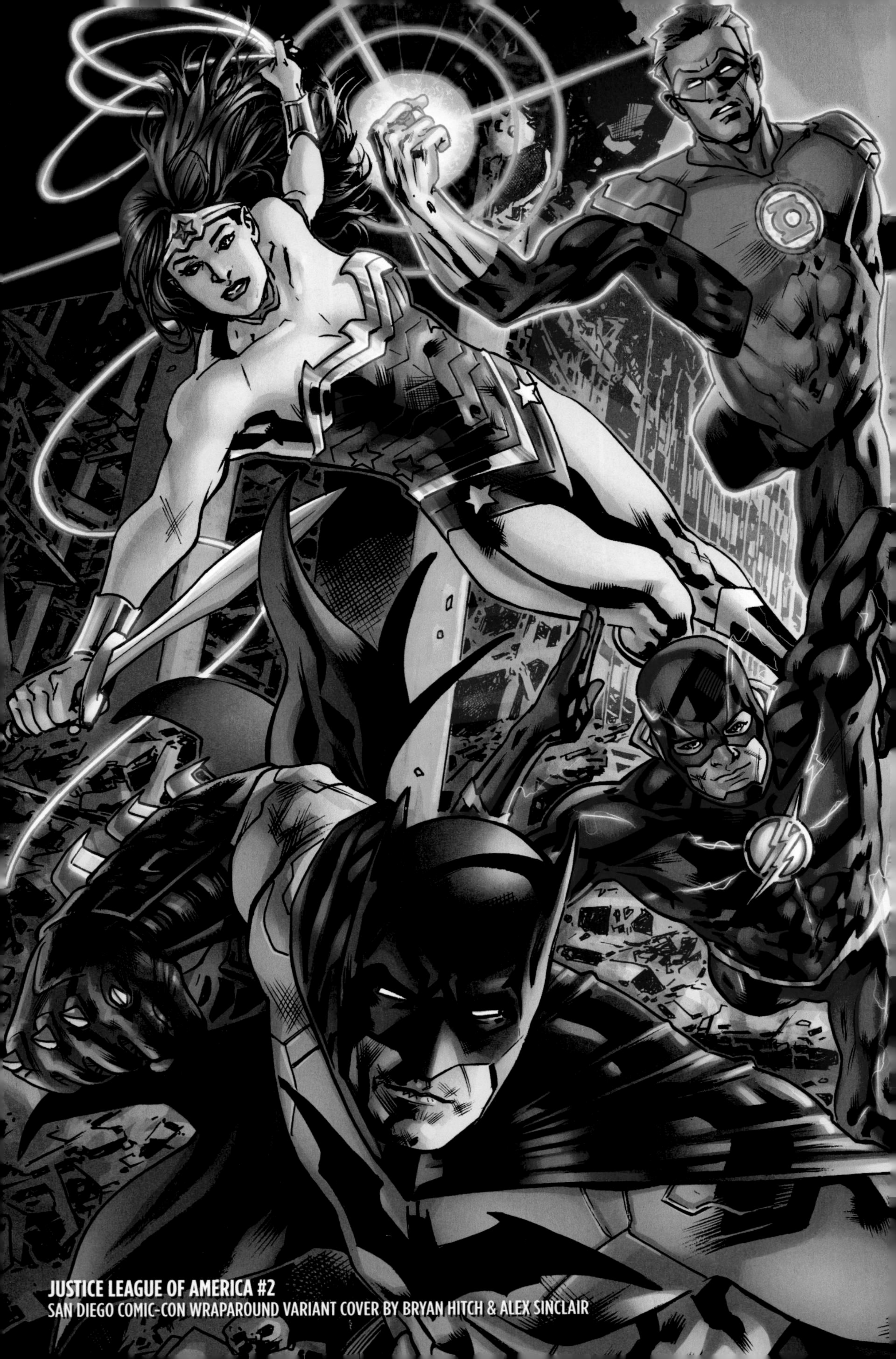

JUSTICE LEAGUE OF AMERICA #2
SAN DIEGO COMIC-CON WRAPAROUND VARIANT COVER BY BRYAN HITCH & ALEX SINCLAIR

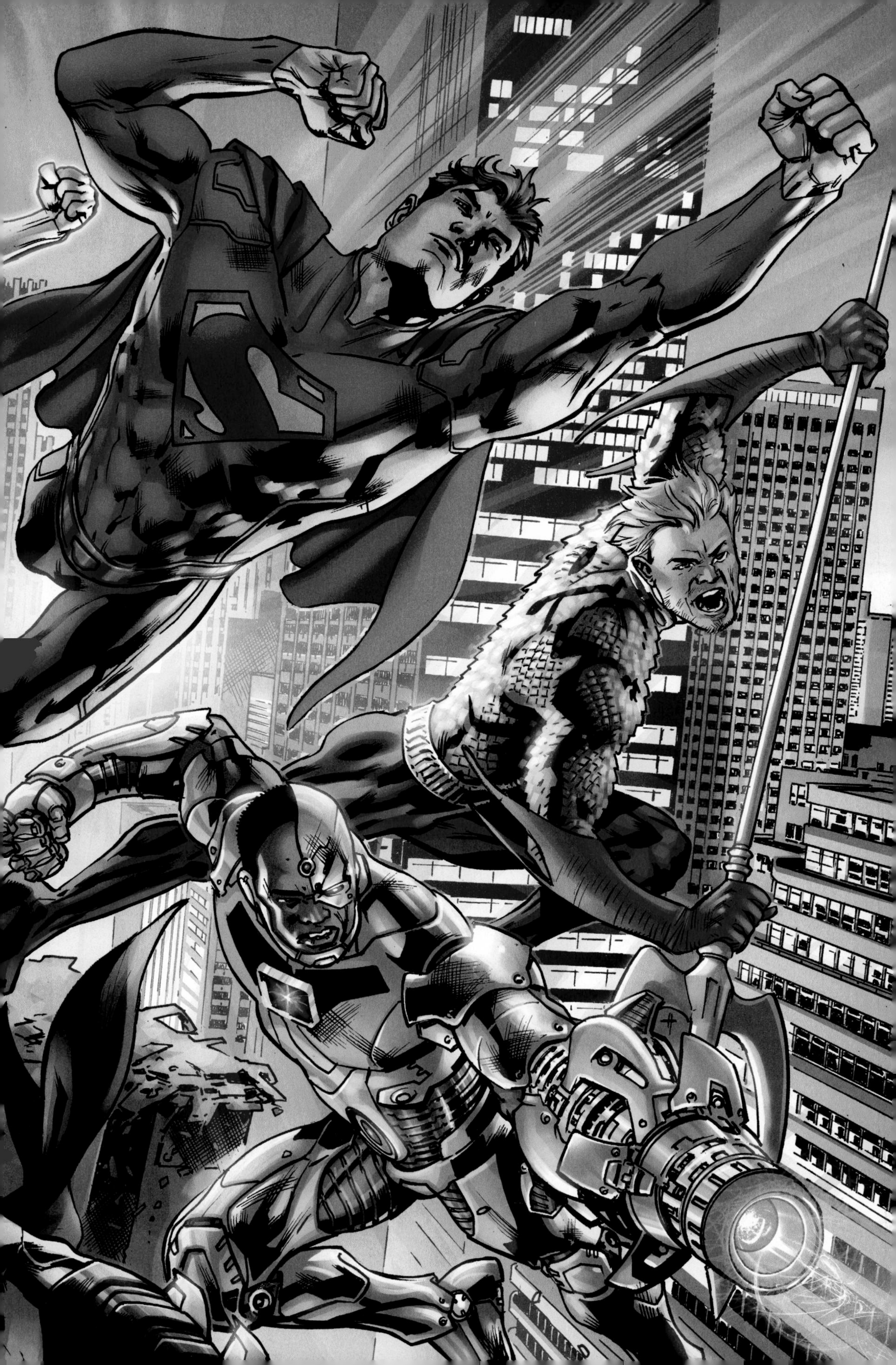

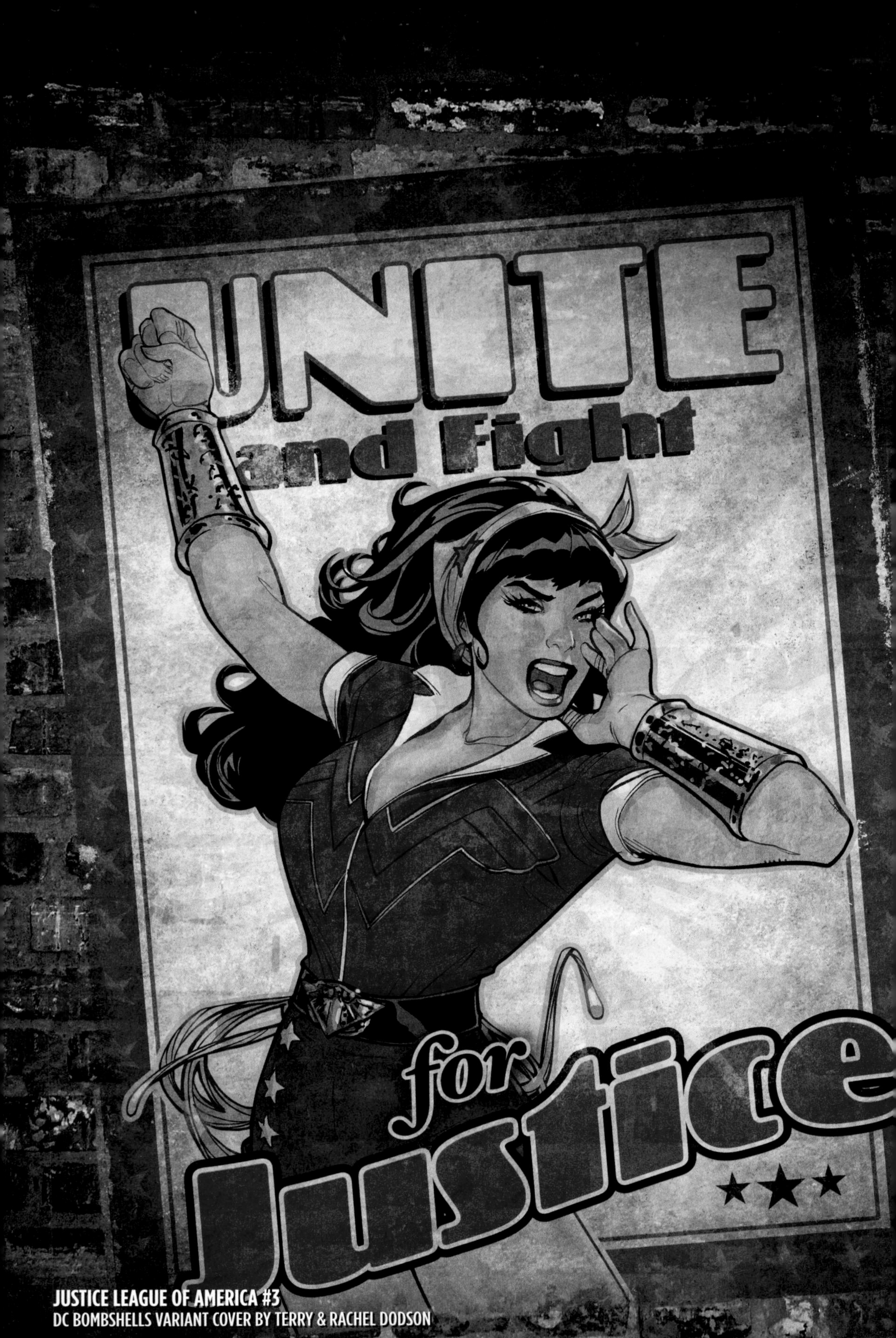
UNITE
and Fight
for
Justice

JUSTICE LEAGUE OF AMERICA #3
DC BOMBSHELLS VARIANT COVER BY TERRY & RACHEL DODSON

JUSTICE LEAGUE OF AMERICA #3
VARIANT COVER BY TRADD MOORE & RICO RENZI

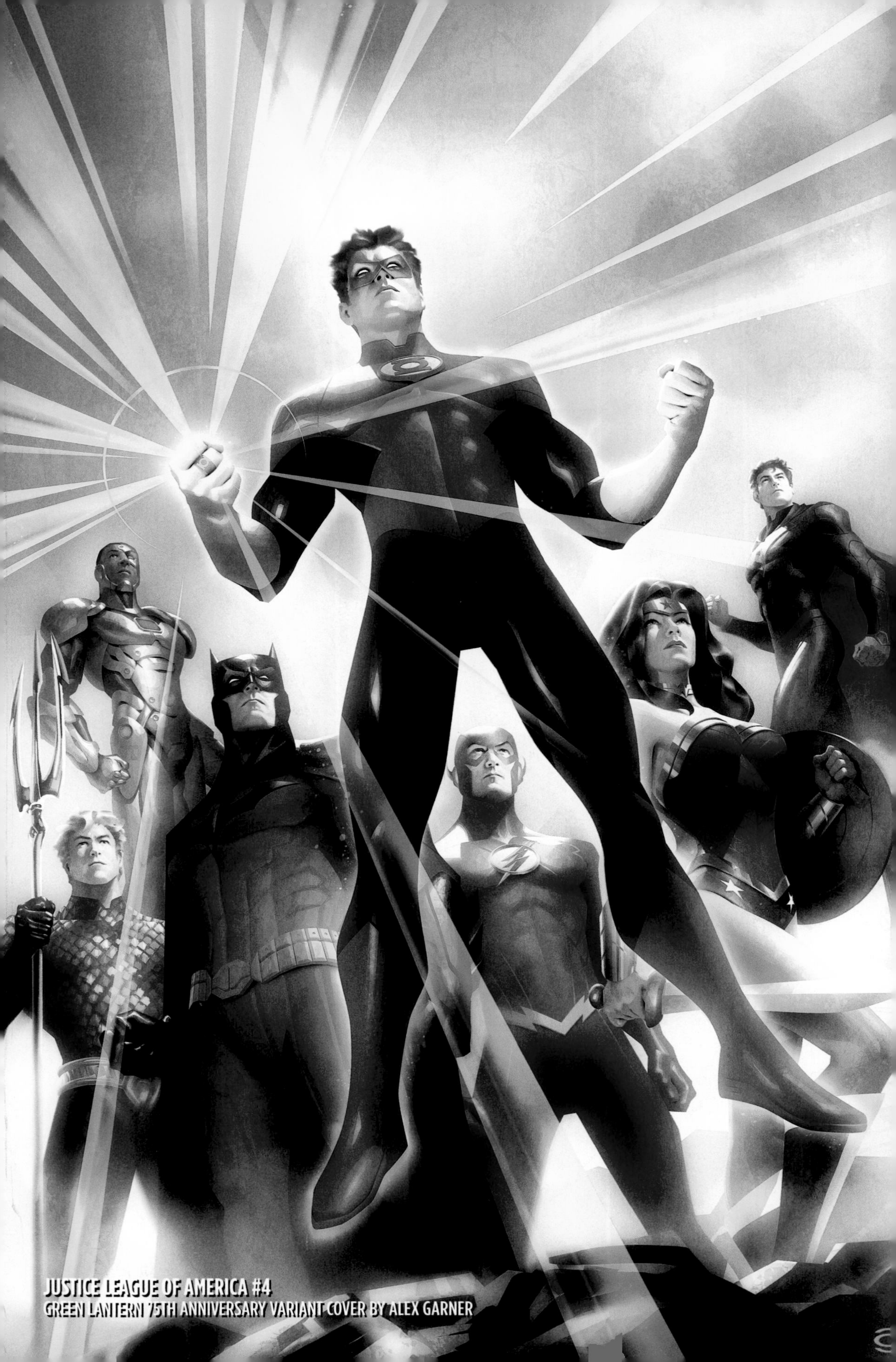

JUSTICE LEAGUE OF AMERICA #4
GREEN LANTERN 75TH ANNIVERSARY VARIANT COVER BY ALEX GARNER

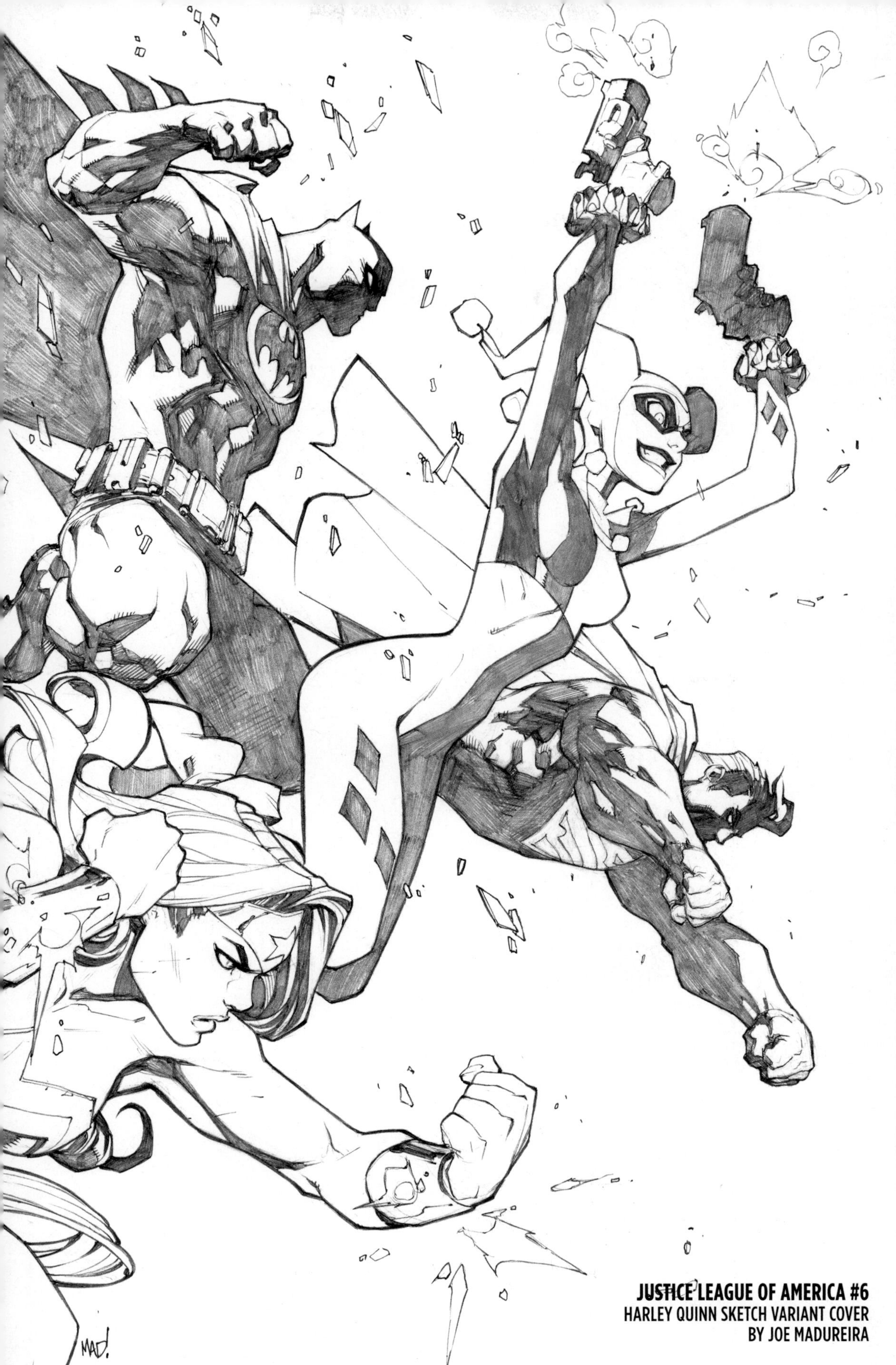

JUSTICE LEAGUE OF AMERICA #6
HARLEY QUINN SKETCH VARIANT COVER
BY JOE MADUREIRA

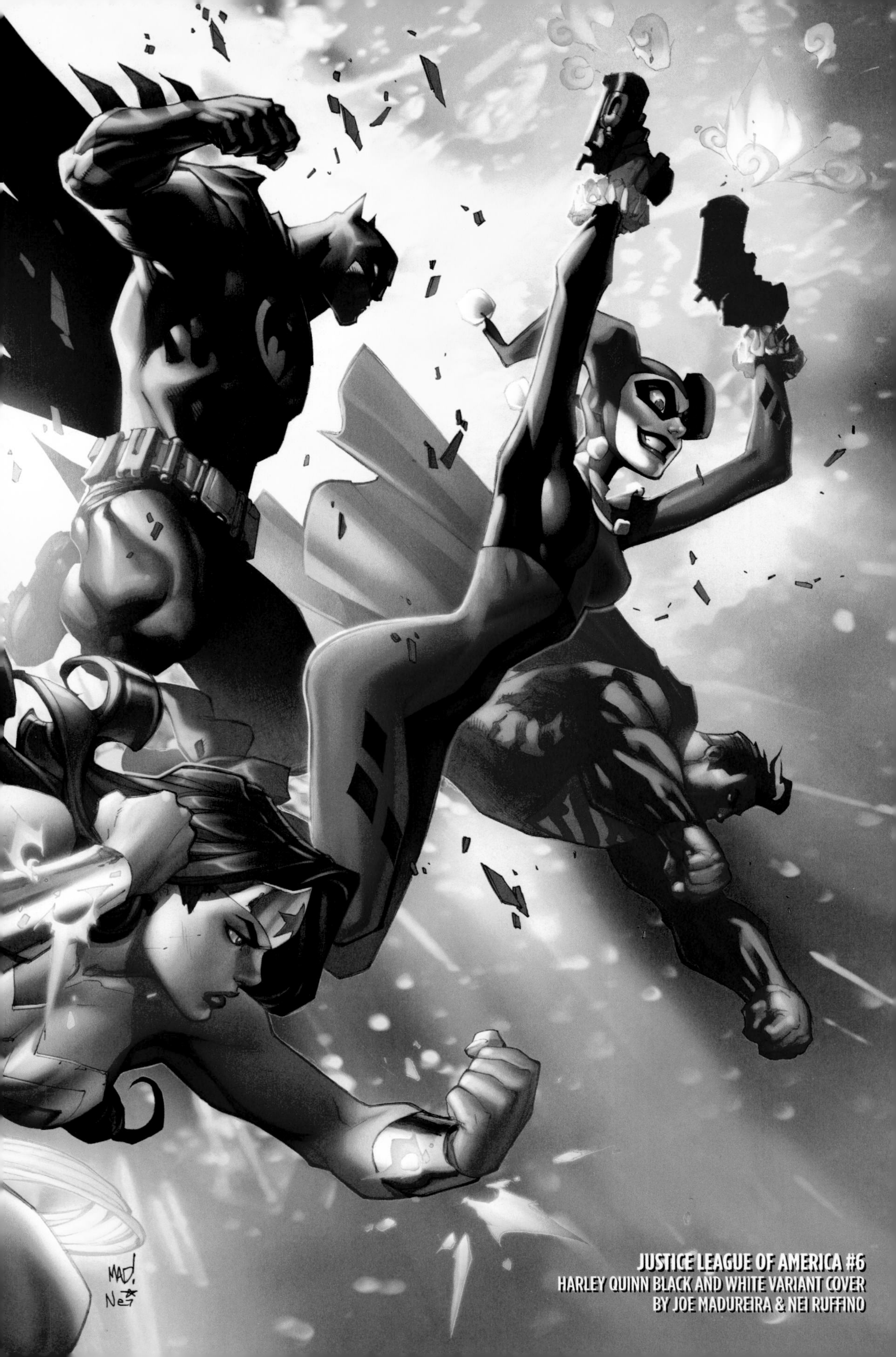

JUSTICE LEAGUE OF AMERICA #6
HARLEY QUINN BLACK AND WHITE VARIANT COVER
BY JOE MADUREIRA & NEI RUFFINO

JUSTICE LEAGUE OF AMERICA #8
VARIANT COVER BY NEAL ADAMS, BILL SIENKIEWICZ & ALEX SINCLAIR

JUSTICE LEAGUE OF AMERICA #9
BATMAN V SUPERMAN VARIANT COVER BY JIM LEE & ALEX SINCLAIR

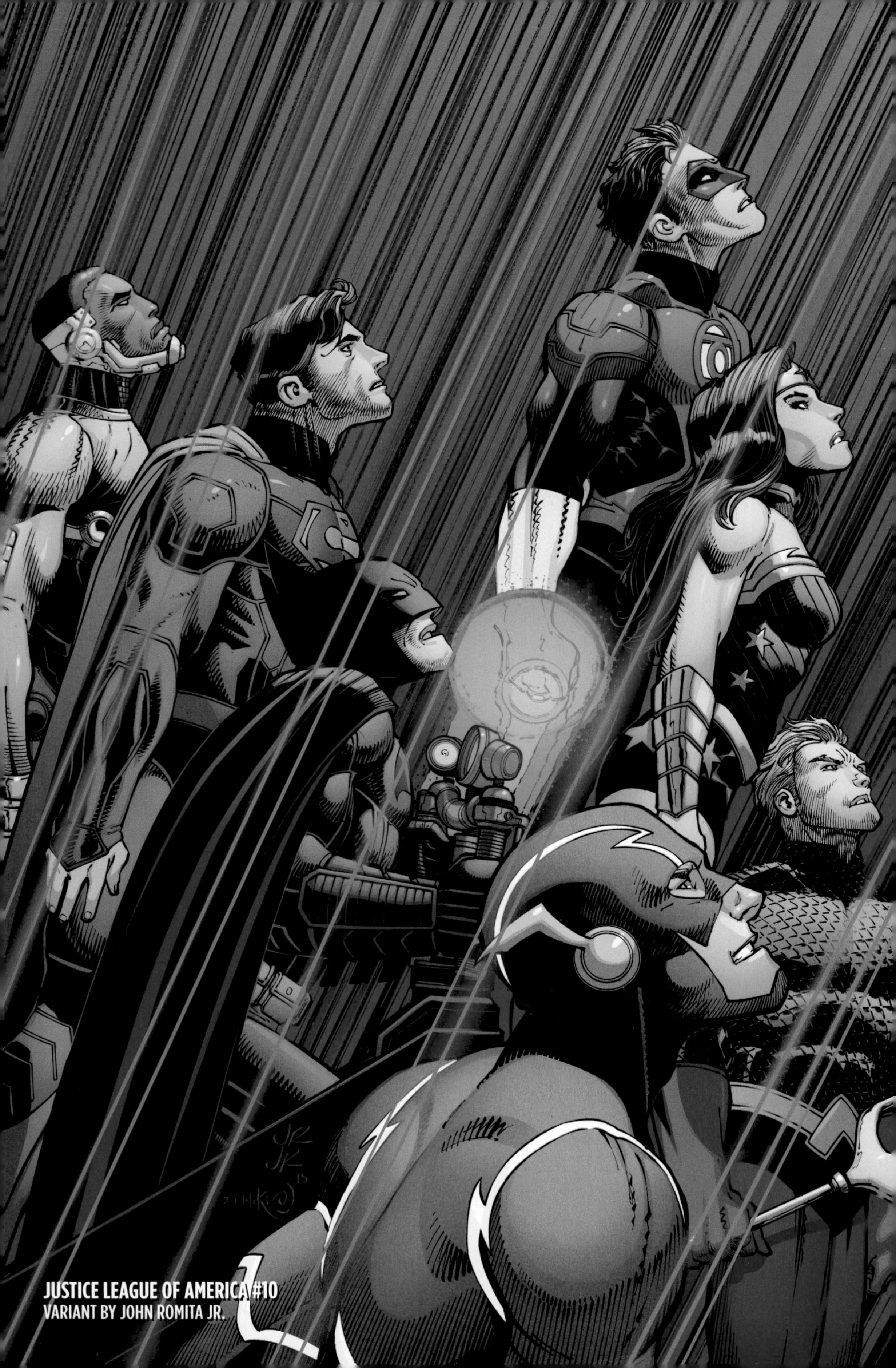

JUSTICE LEAGUE OF AMERICA #10
VARIANT BY JOHN ROMITA JR.

"Some really thrilling artwork that establishes incredible scope and danger."
–IGN

DC UNIVERSE REBIRTH
JUSTICE LEAGUE
VOL. 1: The Extinction Machines
BRYAN HITCH
with TONY S. DANIEL

VOL.1 THE EXTINCTION MACHINES
BRYAN HITCH • TONY S. DANIEL • SANDU FLOREA • TOMEU MOREY

CYBORG VOL. 1:
THE IMITATION OF LIFE

GREEN LANTERNS VOL. 1:
RAGE PLANET

AQUAMAN VOL. 1:
THE DROWNING

"Welcoming to new fans looking to get into superhero comics for the first time and old fans who gave up on the funny-books long ago."
– SCRIPPS HOWARD NEWS SERVICE

JUSTICE LEAGUE

VOL. 1: ORIGIN
GEOFF JOHNS and JIM LEE

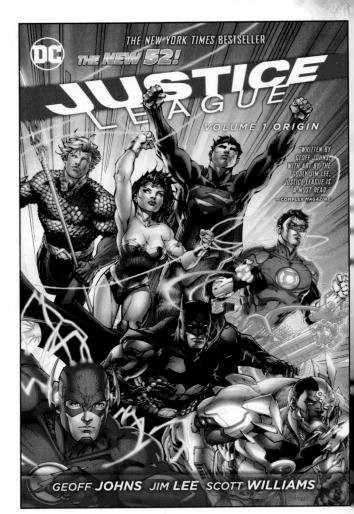

GEOFF *JOHNS* **JIM** *LEE* **SCOTT** *WILLIAMS*

JUSTICE LEAGUE VOL. 2: THE VILLAIN'S JOURNEY

JUSTICE LEAGUE VOL. 3: THRONE OF ATLANTIS

READ THE ENTIRE EPIC!

JUSTICE LEAGUE VOL. 4: THE GRID

JUSTICE LEAGUE VOL. 5: FOREVER HEROES

JUSTICE LEAGUE VOL. 6: INJUSTICE LEAGUE

JUSTICE LEAGUE VOL. 7: DARKSEID WAR PART 1

JUSTICE LEAGUE VOL. 8: DARKSEID WAR PART 2

"The cartoonist Darwyn Cooke is an extraordinary talent...[THE NEW FRONTIER] is an audacious revisionist look at the formation of the Justice League."
– THE NEW YORK TIMES

"Using a classic style, Cooke creates a classic of his own."
– A.V. CLUB/THE ONION

FROM EISNER AWARD WINNER
DARWYN COOKE

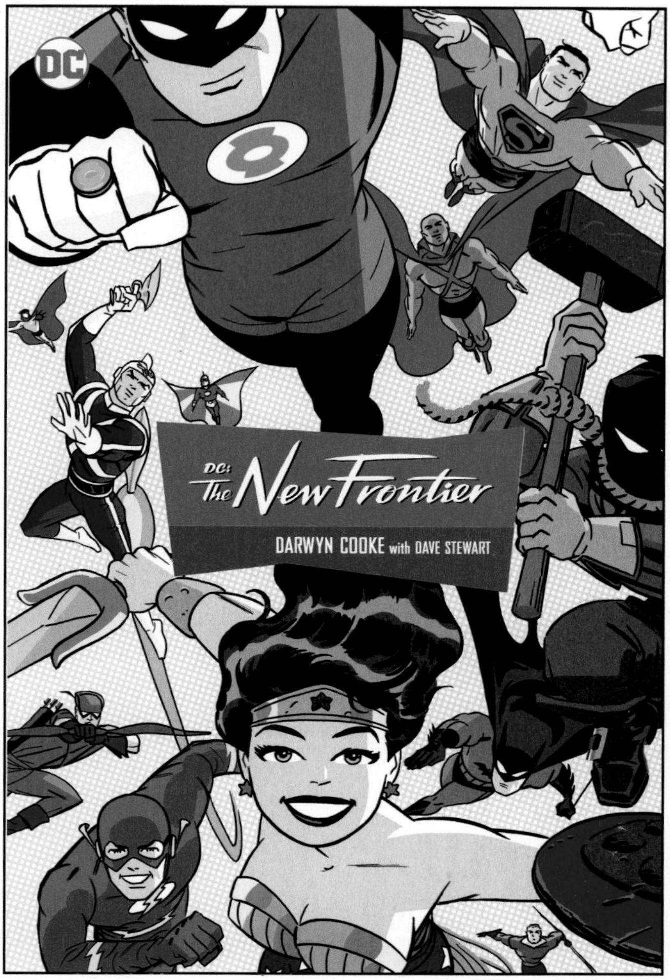
DC
DC: The New Frontier
DARWYN COOKE with DAVE STEWART

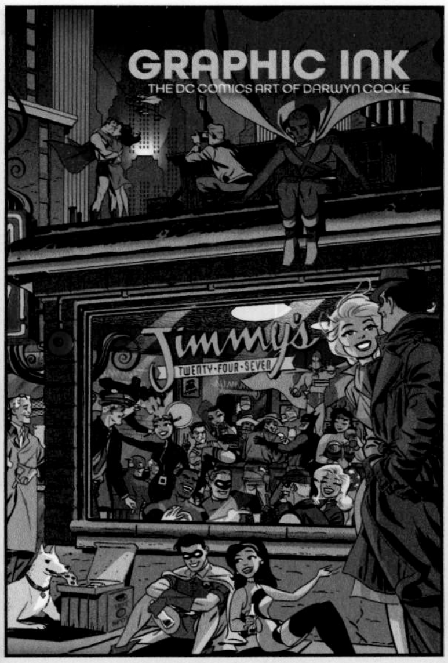
GRAPHIC INK
THE DC COMICS ART OF DARWYN COOKE
Jimmy's
TWENTY-FOUR-SEVEN

GRAPHIC INK: THE DC COMICS ART OF DARWYN COOKE

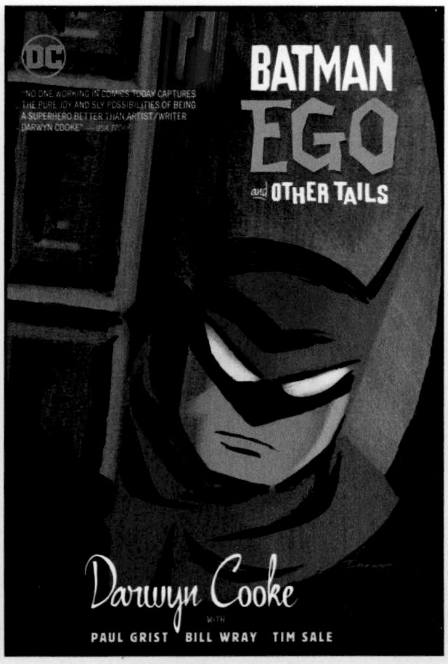
DC
BATMAN
EGO
and OTHER TAILS
Darwyn Cooke
WITH
PAUL GRIST BILL WRAY TIM SALE

BATMAN: EGO AND OTHER TAILS

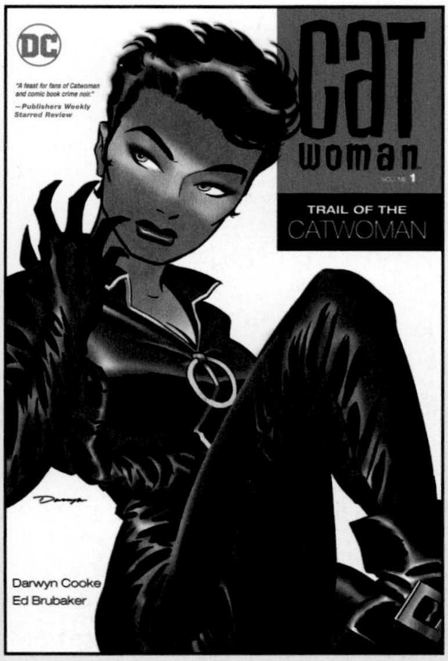
DC
CAT
woman
VOL. 1
TRAIL OF THE
CATWOMAN
Darwyn Cooke
Ed Brubaker

CATWOMAN: TRAIL OF THE CATWOMAN

Get more DC graphic novels wherever comics and books are sold!

MARK WAID
with ALEX ROSS

52 Volume One

THE FLASH BY MARK WAID

SUPERMAN: BIRTHRIGHT